COLORADO POLITICS AND POLICY

*Politics and Governments*
*of the American States*

Founding Editor

Daniel J. Elazar

Published by the University of
Nebraska Press in association
with the Center for the Study of
Federalism at the Robert B.
and Helen S. Meyner Center
for the Study of State and Local
Government, Lafayette College

THOMAS E. CRONIN AND ROBERT D. LOEVY

# Colorado Politics and Policy

## GOVERNING A PURPLE STATE

*For Charlotte Kaye*
*Colorado College 2013*
*Best regards from*

UNIVERSITY OF NEBRASKA PRESS
LINCOLN AND LONDON

*Robert D. Loevy*

Library of Congress Cataloging-in-Publication Data
Cronin, Thomas E.
Colorado politics and policy: governing a purple
state / Thomas E. Cronin and Robert D. Loevy.
p. cm.—(Politics and governments of the
American states)
Includes bibliographical references and index.
Rev. and expanded ed. of: Colorado politics &
government. c1993.
ISBN 978-0-8032-4074-2 (pbk.: alk. paper)
1. Colorado—Politics and government—1951–
I. Loevy, Robert D., 1935– II. Cronin, Thomas E.
Colorado politics & government. III. Title.
JK7816.C77 2012
320.9788—dc23                    2012008246

In loving memory of
Constance Loevy, and to our long,
wonderful friendship with Jerry and Anabel McHugh

# CONTENTS

# TABLES, MAPS, AND FIGURES

FIGURES

# Preface

Colorado has a proud history of being a fiercely independent frontier state. Yet in reality Colorado is largely urbanized. Ninety percent or more of the residents live along the state's two main interstate highways, I-25 and I-70.

Coloradans (it is not Coloradoans) express decidedly negative attitudes toward the U.S. government. The citizen surveys conducted for this book reveal that most Coloradans think the "feds" are too big, too wasteful, and too intrusive. Yet Colorado would be economically devastated if federal installations suddenly left the state and federal contracts and subsidies for a variety of activities and services were ended.

Imagine, for example, a Colorado Springs without the U.S. Army base at Fort Carson, the U.S. Space Command, or the U.S. Air Force Academy. Imagine the Boulder-Golden area without its several national research laboratories. Imagine if Colorado's national forests, parks, and monuments or U.S. Bureau of Land Management lands were privatized.

Coloradans, to be sure, favor a much smaller federal government, but they do not favor the elimination of major U.S. government projects and spending programs in Colorado.

Colorado, in fact, has been uncommonly dependent on the federal government to help manage its mountains and forests, develop its mineral and water resources, build its interstate highways and airports, and provide its human services.

Colorado has a proud history of being fiscally prudent. The state is known for its balanced budgets, low state taxes, and relatively low debt. Most Coloradans are skeptical about government and object to expanding taxing and spending powers. The objections to higher taxes can, however, be overcome when the tax pays for a service that voters like, such as buying open space or furthering historic preservation.

But because of the generally low tax structure, many people believe the state electorate is shirking its responsibility to make critically needed investments for the state's future. Governor John Hickenlooper liked to say that Coloradans have to redefine the role of government to match what the people of the state can afford. In Colorado, this means taxpayer resistance to needed tax increases is a serious brake on state government.

Even incremental policy making in Colorado is a challenge. The state constitution is the third longest in the United States. It deliberately disperses power among different institutions, provides multiple veto opportunities, and sets up various checks and balances. It is much easier in Colorado to defeat new initiatives than to enact them. Divided government has become the new normal. Polarization between and within the two major political parties has grown.

Governmental authority in Colorado is intentionally limited, personal liberty is cherished, private-sector interests are both organized and strong, and political preferences are divided and sometimes shifting. In the surveys for this book, Coloradans said they believe government responds more to "insiders," special interests, and big campaign contributors than to the interests of the average person. Yet on many public policy issues, no single group or political party has a clear or consistent majority.

Over the past generation, Colorado has gradually shifted from being a somewhat "red," meaning Republican, state to becoming a fairly predictable "purple" state in its partisanship leanings. This has been the case both within the state and its electoral patterns, as within the nation. Colorado is often now a battleground or swing state. In statistical terms, Colorado in recent years is right in the middle (ranked 24 or 25) in the nation in its partisanship voting patterns. It does not get more purple than that. We discuss this more in chapter 5.

So who governs Colorado? We are a state without much "old money," with few corporate headquarters, and with less of a defined "establishment" than most states. Can anyone, or any group, lead without political power? Does an increase in governmental authority necessarily mean a diminution of personal liberty?

What will it take to solve the Centennial State's economic problems? What will be required to plan for future growth and to preserve the state's beautiful lands and plentiful resources? What is the proper balance in the financing of economic development, job creation, education, and environmental protection? Can economic development and prudent conservation be done in a harmonious way? How will Colorado handle a doubling of its population over the next fifty to sixty years?

How has a shifting electorate influenced politics in Colorado? And what of the much-debated and now more regularly used citizen-initiative process, where citizens sign petitions to put new laws and state constitutional amendments up for approval by the voters? Has it helped or handicapped public policy making in Colorado? How has this shaped, or reshaped, Colorado's political culture?

Colorado's assets are impressive, yet its challenges are daunting. Inequality is increasing in terms of both social class and geographical location. There is an ever-widening gap between poor counties and rich counties. Colorado's water supplies are overappropriated and understored. The state's highways and road bridges are in rough shape. The state's planning and budget process is unusually complicated and often counterproductive. The list goes on and on.

This book examines how politics and government work in Colorado. It represents an attempt to capture the spirit and distinctive politics that shape parties, elections, and public policy debates.

Our study of Colorado politics was encouraged by the late Professor Daniel Elazar, a respected political scientist at Temple University in Philadelphia. At his invitation, we wrote an earlier book on Colorado politics, published in 1993, which was part of a valuable series on state government in the United States that Elazar edited for the University of Nebraska Press. Each volume in that series examined the specific character of a state's "polity," defined as its political culture, traditions, and practices. Also studied were each state's constitution, governmental institutions, political constituencies, and interest groups.

So much has changed in Colorado politics and government in the past two decades that a new book was needed. For this book, we surveyed and interviewed hundreds of Colorado voters and scores of public officials, political analysts, lobbyists, and state employees. We conducted two statewide public opinion polls that followed up on a survey we did in 1990. In the end, we had to rewrite nearly every part of our earlier work.

We thank those whose writings educated us, and we thank all those who have shared their views about the state and its politics. Please see our acknowledgments and selected bibliography. Views and interpretations in this book are, of course, wholly ours.

# Acknowledgments

We thank hundreds of people who have shared their views with us about Colorado politics, public policies, and government. Sometimes these were brief encounters in cafes or general stores in Holly, San Luis, Salida, Creede, Crestone, Crawford, Durango, Aspen, or Meeker. At other times they were at statewide meetings such as party conventions or the Colorado Water Congress.

But we have also conducted many lengthy interviews with state legislators, lobbyists, judges, the Colorado attorney general, and others. We helped run a several-hour forum with three former Colorado governors. We have gone to state of the state addresses, inaugurations, and sat in on sessions of the Colorado state supreme court and the Colorado Forum.

In addition, we have served on city planning commissions, city charter commissions, county storm-drainage committees, and the 2011 Colorado Reapportionment Commission. We have served as precinct committee members, served on state party executive committees, attended state and national party conventions as elected delegates, and we have managed election campaigns both for candidates and for ballot issues, such as park bonds and building performing arts centers. Both of us have been involved in electoral politics at all levels.

We have traveled extensively around the state, and we have benefited from three statewide public opinion surveys of randomly selected adult Coloradans. These are surveys we designed and raised the funds for.

Among those we especially want to thank are governors Richard Lamm, Roy Romer, Bill Owens, Bill Ritter, and John Hickenlooper; Lieutenant Governor Joe Garcia; Attorney General John Suthers; U.S. senators Floyd Haskell, Gary Hart, Bill Armstrong, Tim Wirth, Ben Nighthorse Campbell, and Michael Bennet; U.S. Court of Appeals Judge Timothy M. Tymkovich; justices Rebecca Love Kourlis, Jean Dubofsky, Luis Rovira, Joseph Quinn, and Greg Hobbs; judges John Gallagher and Rebecca Bromley; state legislators Josh Penry, John Morse, Michael Bird, Chuck Berry, Ralph Cole, Terry Considine, Renny Fagan, Marcy Morrison, Peggy Kerns, Hugh Fowler, Wayne Knox, and Jana Mendez; mayors Federico Pena, Bill Sterling, Linda Shaw, Robert Isaac, and Mary Lou Makepeace; historians Duane Smith, Robert Smith, Patricia Limerick, and Marshall Sprague; newspaper reporters and columnists Bob Ewegen, Fred Brown, Vincent Carroll, Bruce Finley, Tim Hoover, Chuck Green, Charles Roos, Carl Miller, Carl Hilliard, and Ed Quillen; lobbyists and policy advocates Steve Durham, Gail Klapper, Dan Ritchie, Ed Bowditch, Ken Smith, Wade Buchanan, Mark Neuman-Lee, Adam Kretz, Stanley Dempsey, Briggs Gamblin, Pat Ratliff, and Roger Walton; political analysts Floyd Ciruli, Eric Sondermann, Katy Atkinson, Walt Klein, and Bob Drake; political scientists John Straayer and Seth Masket; state public employees Sharon Eubanks, Bob Lackner, Geoff Withers, Susanna Lienhard, Larry Kallenberger, Stewart Bliss, B. J. Thornberry, Eugene Petrone, Jim Westkott, Elizabeth Garner, Bill Porter, Douglas Brown, Todd Saliman, Michael Shea, Craig Welling, Mark Noel, John Stulp, Eddie Hunsinger, Cindy Degroen, John Ziegler, Reeves Brown, Bill Campbell, Jon Sarche, and Katharine Sanguinetti.

We also have been helped by John Andrews, Timothy Egan, Tad Foster, Thad Beyle, Janet Suthers, Jim Carpenter, Alan Salazar, Tom Clark, Bill Hybl, Kyle Hybl, John Weiss, John Hopper, Sean Paige, Armanda Arthur, Larry Deremo, Daniel Johnson, Bill Hochman, Dick Celeste, Walt Hecox, Jack Elder, and Jenn Sides.

Special thanks to Ed Bowditch, Jim Carpenter, Fred Brown, Bob Drake, Gail Klapper, Duane Smith, and John Straayer for their reading of the pre-publication manuscript.

We especially thank Jerry and Anabel McHugh of Denver for their long-term encouragement, friendship, and financial support. We thank our colleagues at Colorado College, and particularly the librarians at Tutt Library, for their help and encouragement.

Research assistants at Colorado College who have helped on this and earlier writings on Colorado politics include John Calhoun, Walter Keller, Michael Shaver, Michael Trevithick, Amy Steinhoff, Alex Truax, Ben Taber, and Joe Jammal.

We are very grateful to copyeditor Lona Dearmont for greatly improving this book. We thank University of Nebraska Press editor Rob Taylor and editorial assistant Courtney Ochsner and all their colleagues for their valuable help.

All the above have helped make this a better, more-informed book, yet we assume responsibility for what is written.

COLORADO POLITICS AND POLICY

# CHAPTER ONE

# The Character and
# Spirit of Colorado

Colorado is big and mountainous and beautiful and has had a history of booms and busts. This nearly perfect rectangle of a state measures 385 miles east to west and about 275 miles north to south (about 104,100 square miles).

Its land area is larger than Portugal or South Korea, twice the size of England, and nearly seven times the size of Switzerland. It is the eighth-largest state in the United States. Colorado is said to be the number-one state in surface land area. If you flattened out all of Colorado's mountains and foothills (which no one is advocating), there would be more land area than either Alaska or Texas (also flattened out).

Colorado is midsized in population in the United States. It ranks twenty-second in population among the fifty states. Still, its over 5.5 million people in recent years make it as populous or more populous than some fifty nations in the United Nations, including Costa Rica, Croatia, Ireland, Latvia, Lithuania, New Zealand, Norway, and Singapore.

And Colorado keeps growing. Colorado has for several years been among the faster-growing states in the nation. State officials predict the state will add up to another 2 to 3 million between 2012 and 2040. It could have a population nearing 10 million by 2050 or 2060.[1]

Colorado's great distance from the two coasts, and even the hundreds of miles between it and Kansas City, Omaha, Dallas, Salt Lake City, and Albuquerque, make it appear even larger and more removed. In many respects the Centennial State, admitted to the Union as the thirty-eighth state in 1876 (the centennial of the Declaration of Independence), is a small, separate nation, isolated in high plains, grasslands, plateaus, and rugged mountain splendor.

Colorado borders seven other states, listed here in order of length of shared border: New Mexico (330 miles), Utah (275), Wyoming (260), Kansas (207), Nebraska (173), Oklahoma (57), and Arizona (just touching Colorado at the "Four Corners" where four states meet at one point).

Colorado is the nation's highest state, with a mean elevation of 6,800 feet above sea level. It ranges from 14,426 feet atop Mount Elbert in the center of the state to 3,317 feet in northeastern Colorado where the Arikaree River flows into northwestern Kansas, almost at the point at which the Colorado, Kansas, and Nebraska borders meet. Colorado has the "highest lowest" point of any state.

This "Switzerland of America" is a magnet for more than about 60 million tourists and visitors each year. Colorado boasts of ten national parks, fourteen national forests and grasslands, more than forty state parks, and twenty-six destination ski areas. More than 40 percent of the state's lands are open to the public for recreational purposes.

The mountains of Colorado provide a scenic splendor that is hard to match anywhere in the world and helps explain the upbeat, optimistic, and positive opinion most Coloradans have toward their state and its rich natural resources.

Colorado boasts some of the most colorful of western names for its small towns. These include Bedrock, Bonanza, Brush, Chimney Rock, Cripple Creek, Deer Trail, Dinosaur, Dove Creek, Elk Springs, Fairplay, Last Chance, Leadville, Powderhorn, Powder Wash, Rifle, Slick Rock, Tincup, Wild Horse, Sawpit, and Yellow Jacket.

Communities and counties along Colorado's southern tier splendidly reflect their rich Spanish heritage with names such as Cortez, Durango, Alamosa, San Luis, Del Norte, Mesita, Antonito, Conejos, La Junta, Costilla, Huerfano, and Archuleta.

What do people think of when they think of Colorado? Coloradans and many who know the state answer with the following: fabulous mountains, sunshine, blue skies, wonderfully dry and fresh air, multiple river headwaters, great skiing, excellent fishing and hunting, outdoor sports, cattle and ranching, mines, ghost towns, alpine lakes surrounded by wild-flowered meadows, Colorado blue spruce trees, billions of conifers and aspen trees, and bighorn sheep grazing on mountain ridges, wild horses in rural Colorado, Rocky Mountain National Park, Pike's Peak, Great Sand Dunes National Park, the Mesa Verde cliff dwellings, the U.S. Air Force Academy, Denver, Aspen, and Vail, the Continental Divide, quarterback John Elway and skier Lindsey Vonn, U.S. secretary of the interior and former U.S. senator Ken Salazar, the late country and pop singer John Denver, Coors beer, and the Denver Broncos football team, the Denver Nuggets in basketball, the Colorado Avalanche ice hockey team, and the Colorado Rockies baseball team.

Colorado is of course far more than the Rocky Mountains or beautiful scenery or any of these above-mentioned places, occupations, or people.

Colorado has become one of America's impressive sports capitals. In addition to having at least eight professional sports teams, Colorado is also home to a growing number of nationally celebrated skiers, snowboarders, runners, and Olympic trainees in a host of sports. The ski resort town of Aspen hosts, among other things, the annual and much-hyped "Winter X" games. Colorado Springs is the hub for the U.S. Olympic Training Center and a number of national and international ice skating and golf competitions. Colorado also hosts the National Western Stock Show that attracts 650,000 or more visitors each year.

Colorado ski resorts attract over 12 million snow skiers annually. A national multistage bicycle road race, the USA Pro-Cycling Challenge, takes place in Colorado. Mountain bikers from around the world come to Bureau of Land Management (BLM) lands near Fruita and Grand Junction to ride through the desert.

Tourism is among Colorado's leading industries. It flourishes in good part because it attracts hikers, hunters, fishing enthusiasts, rafters, skiers, snowboarders, and others who like outdoor sports. It also attracts those who like to relax in one of Colorado's forty hot springs.

Colorado nowadays has a relatively diversified economy. Yet the state is forever trying to avoid the cycles of booms and busts that have dominated its economic and political past. Coloradans are painfully aware of the booms and busts of gold, then silver, then gold again, coal, molybdenum, oil and gas, oil shale, military spending, and real estate speculation.

Colorado's leading industries are tourism, agriculture, energy, aerospace, biosciences, information technology, federal lands, and military installations and national laboratories. Walt Hecox, a professor of economics in the environmental program at Colorado College, defines Colorado as "a natural resources state that will always have the booms and busts associated with natural resources."[2]

What follows is a review of the geographical, political, economic, and social realities that have to be appreciated before one can *comprehend* the character of Colorado. They are not in any strategic order. No one alone can explain the political culture or the political behavior in the Centennial State. Yet collectively they go a long way in helping to understand the views, values, and political culture of those who live, vote, and pay taxes in Colorado.

One last note of introduction. In interviews, several of the leading pollsters, political analysts, and political reporters in the state were asked to reflect on what unifies Colorado. "What brings the citizens of the state together and makes them Coloradans?" After a pause, many interviewees wondered whether there was much, if anything, that unifies the people of the state. Some pointed to the mountains, or a frontier outlook, or a spirit of independence. On the other hand, everyone could list, and did list, a large number of factors or forces that divide the people of Colorado. They include eastern Colorado versus western Colorado, urban versus rural, urban versus suburban, Denver versus the rest of the state, Anglo versus Hispanic, natives versus newcomers, developers versus environmentalists, Republicans versus Democrats, black interests versus white interests, the legislature versus the governor, and on and on.

Much that unifies Colorado, paradoxically, also divides it. Thus Coloradans revere the mountains even as those same mountains create a huge barrier between the highly populated center of the state and the less-populated Western Slope. Everyone wants everyone else's water, yet Coloradans are united in not wanting to let Texans, Californians, Nebraskans, or anyone else get more of Colorado's water than they are legally due. And most Coloradans who live far from Denver view the state's largest city as a mixed blessing at best, yet sports fans from Julesburg to Cortez and from Springfield to Rangely root for the Denver Broncos on Sunday afternoons each autumn, especially when the team has won a few games.

Here are the forces, factors, and realities that have shaped Colorado politics, then and now.

### THE MOUNTAINS CAME FIRST

"Very little in the world can compare to the scenery of Colorado," wrote journalist John Gunther in 1947. "The vistas here stretch the eyes, enlighten the heart, and make the spirit humble."[3] Katherine Lee Bates wrote her poem *America the Beautiful* after she visited the top of Pike's Peak (14,110 feet above sea level):

> O beautiful for spacious skies,
> For amber waves of grain
> For purple mountains majesty
> Above the fruited plain!

The mountains dominate Colorado as they do no other state. A Colorado without mountains is impossible to imagine, although geologists have determined that about 70 million years ago much of Colorado was part of an ocean bed. These mountains are the state's greatest natural asset, and they also have consequences. It snows a lot, both in the mountains and on the prairies at the foot of the mountains. It snows somewhere in the state every month of the year, and perhaps even every day of the year. One of us, for example, was snowed on while hiking on Lost Man Trail near Independence Pass (between Twin Lakes and Aspen) at high noon on a July 15. The other was late to a meeting in Vail because a late June snowstorm closed Vail Pass.

The apex of the Rocky Mountain chain is in Colorado. More than a thousand summits in the state rise above the ten-thousand-foot mark. The most famous of Colorado's peaks are the fifty-four over fourteen thousand feet, known as the Fourteeners. Colorado holds about 80 percent of the Fourteeners in the contiguous forty-eight states of the United States.

The impressive and rugged Rockies are also the great divider of waters, as the Continental Divide winds through the heart of Colorado's mountains. Water flows east and south to the Gulf of Mexico (Atlantic Ocean watershed) or west and south to the Gulf of California (Pacific Ocean watershed), depending on which side of the divide the water falls on at this crest of the continent.

The mountains have always been major obstacles for east–west transportation. This divides the state and makes it hard to fashion a statewide sense of community. The mountains, their daunting passes and unpredictable weather, help explain why Colorado was one of the last states to be settled by Anglo-Americans.

A recent problem in Colorado has been traffic jams on I-70, the interstate highway that cuts through the mountains from the Denver metropolitan area to the nationally known ski areas to the west. On Sunday afternoons and evenings in the winter, the road is jammed with vehicles filled with skiers and snowboarders making their way eastward from the mountains to Denver. Economist Walt Hecox warned: "Colorado will have to fix the I-70 access from Denver to the mountains, otherwise the upscale people who love to ski and recreate in the mountains might begin to leave Denver."[4]

Colorado's borders are unnatural and arbitrary. What really defines Colorado, its signature, are the Rocky Mountains. Ninety-five percent of Colorado's population can see the mountains from their home neighborhood, although perhaps only 5 percent or so of Coloradans really live in them (that is, live in real mountain towns like Crestone, Estes Park, Fairplay, Garfield, Granby, Leadville, Rico, Silverton, Somerset, Tincup, and Victor).

The mountains are the jewels of Colorado, and they justify the sometimes harsh and forbidding winter weather. When Coloradans are asked why they live in the state, the predictable answer is that they love the mountains. Coloradans hike, backpack, fish, ski, cycle, jog, hunt, raft, canoe, windsurf, and in other ways relax and enjoy themselves in and around the mountains, rivers, lakes, canyons, and valleys of their state.

People from the eastern United States came to Colorado to extract gold and silver, and later, scores of other treasures in the mountains. Colorado is a mineral-rich state. It has more than 250 metallic and nonmetallic minerals. At various times it has produced more tin, molybdenum, uranium, granite, sandstone, and basalt than any other state. Experts say Colorado has a potential of 80 billion tons worth of bituminous coal and perhaps as much as 500 billion barrels of oil that could be extracted from oil shale (oil combined with rock). Petroleum and natural gas from drilled wells are a growing part of the economy.

Once-defunct or near-defunct mining villages in the mountains, as notably is the case in Aspen, Crested Butte, and Breckenridge, are now tourist meccas that live off the beauty and recreational assets of the mountains, principally skiing.

The mountains leave a psychological impact on Coloradans. They are rugged and rocky. They test one's independence as well as one's character. Climbers and skiers view them as a challenge. In many ways the mountains inspire Coloradans and at the same time separate them from the rest of the country. In some ways they may confer a superiority complex and encourage a sense of freedom, space, and separateness. John Denver's popular musical hit "Rocky Mountain High" was adopted a few years ago as one of two official state songs. The mountains remain a frontier, a temptation for escapism, and they remind Coloradans in various ways that the rugged individualism and independent spirit once necessary to just ascend and "tame" these mountainous areas are also qualities that need to be celebrated and encouraged today.

The "every man for himself" ethos of the 1850s frontier, exaggerated into legend by historians of the romantic school, is still a part of the character of Colorado. Although many Coloradans do not hunt, fish, ski, or rock climb, the spirit of the Native Americans and the fur trappers and the mountain men and women is still a part of the mountain "mystique" that helps shape the political outlook of contemporary Coloradans.[5]

Colorado, of course, is much more than mountains. The mountain portion of the state comprises less than two-fifths of the state's land. The non-mountainous sections of the state, however, are dwarfed by the mountains and their worldwide reputation.

## WATER POLITICS

The Colorado Rockies contain the source of many rivers, and water has been indispensable to the economic growth and prosperity of Colorado. The availability, diversion, and proper use of water has been a political issue throughout the history of the region.

Both the Eastern Plains and the western plateaus and canyon lands of Colorado are semiarid (semidesert) with low annual rainfall. The state averages 16 to 17 inches of rain. This ranges from about seven inches a year in the San Luis Valley and about eight inches in and around Grand Junction, to over 40 inches each year in the San Juan Mountains. Moreover, what is less understood is that 14 to 15 inches of dry snow (and most snow in Colorado is dry) equates to just one inch of rainwater.

Colorado generates, on average, about 16 million acre-feet of water each year. An acre-foot is enough water to cover one-acre of ground up to one foot deep, or enough water to serve two four-person families for one year. Under various legal compacts, however, nearly two-thirds of Colorado's water must be allowed to flow down rivers to other states.

As the rain and melted snow flow down the Colorado Rockies onto the Eastern Plains and the western deserts, much of the water is dammed and diverted through canals to irrigate farm crops. As much as 80 percent of diverted water in the Rocky Mountain West is used for agricultural purposes. Also, water is stored in a dozen or more mountain reservoirs and then piped into the water supply systems of major cities along the eastern side of the mountains.

These cities, located in a north–south urban corridor at the eastern foot of the Rockies, are called the Front Range because they sit at the foot of the "front range" of the Rocky Mountains. This elongated strip city, or megalopolis, includes Fort Collins, Greeley, Boulder, Denver, Aurora, Colorado Springs, and Pueblo. See Map 1.

Four major river systems begin in Colorado, all four of them with headwaters located high in the Rockies. The Platte River (both its north and south branches) rises in the mountains west of Denver. The North Platte flows northward out of the state toward Laramie, Wyoming, eventually joining the South Platte at North Platte, Nebraska. The South Platte flows northeastward through Denver and off through northeast Colorado (and through James Michener's fictionalized town of Centennial) on into Nebraska, eventually emptying into the Missouri River near Omaha.

The Arkansas River also rises in the mountains west of Denver, descending southeast before turning due east and flowing through the cities

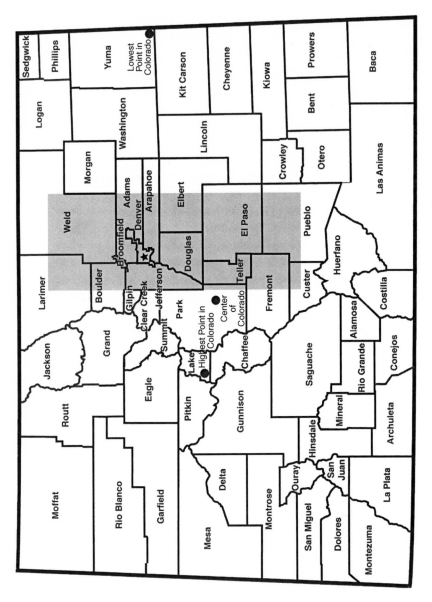

Map 1. Colorado's Predominant Population Center

of Pueblo, La Junta, and Lamar into Kansas. It eventually flows into the Mississippi River in Arkansas.

The Rio Grande rises in the mountains of south-central Colorado. It is the longest river to begin in this state. It flows generally southeast through the San Luis Valley and the city of Alamosa to New Mexico, eventually forming the Texas-Mexico boundary as it empties into the Gulf of Mexico.

The North and South Platte Rivers, the Arkansas River, and the Rio Grande are all on the Eastern Slope of the Continental Divide and eventually flow into the Atlantic Ocean. The Colorado River rises on the Western Slope of the Continental Divide near the resort community of Grand Lake and flows westward across the state into Utah. The Colorado and its many tributaries (the Yampa, Gunnison, San Miguel, Dolores, Animas, and San Juan Rivers) drain the entire Western Slope of Colorado. From Utah the Colorado River flows to Lake Meade and the Hoover Dam in Arizona. It then flows through the Grand Canyon. It eventually marks the Arizona-California boundary before entering Mexico, where it dries up. At one time the Colorado River flowed into the Gulf of California, but it has not done so since about 1998. See Map 2.

An overriding fact of political and economic life in Colorado is that water is scarce. "Whiskey is for drinking," a saying in this region has it, "but water is for fighting over." Another old saw in the West holds that "water runs uphill toward money." Both tell a lot about Colorado politics.

Another reality about water here is that over 80 percent of the state's water exists on the Western Slope of the Rocky Mountains while more than 80 percent of the state's population lives on the Front Range in the eastern part of Colorado.

Farmers on both the Eastern Plains and the Western Slope always want more water, and they have been the beneficiaries of some of the largest U.S. government public works projects—giant dams and diversions—in U.S. history. The U.S. Reclamation Act of 1902 brought cheap water to the farmers, thereby helping to transform Colorado as well as other states in the West.

Farmers received large amounts of water first. Later, developers, manufacturers, and the energy and ski industries also would get water. In the early 1990s the tourist industry began to argue it is in the best long-term interest of the state to leave as much water as possible in the streams, lakes, and rivers that make Colorado so attractive for visitors.

Developers, as well as many economists, say farmers use water inefficiently. Water boards and water providers, such as the Denver Water Board

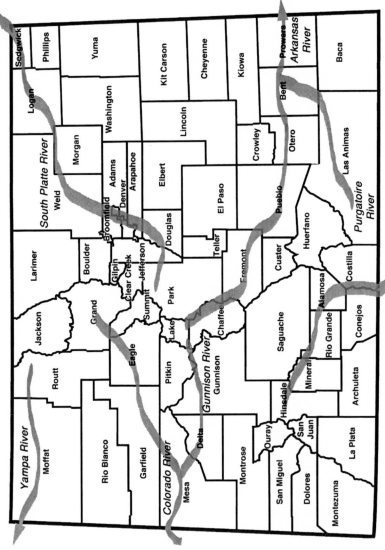

Map 2. Major Rivers in Colorado

and the Colorado Water Congress, lament the recent halt in the building of storage dams and diversion projects and say the state is losing water to which it is entitled because of the lack of adequate structural storage facilities. Environmentalists, not surprisingly, want Coloradans to change their consumption habits and grow low-water maintenance lawns so the state might retain its water in mountain streams and not divert it to water Kentucky bluegrass lawns in Front Range cities.

Coloradans have continually battled Coloradans over water diversion schemes. Denver's populous suburbs and Colorado Springs all have wanted and need water from the high country and Western Slope. But since water is virtually blood in Colorado, western Coloradans resent the financial and legal deals concocted by Front Range cities to "rip them off."

Water management, water court rulings, and water policy choices have been the preserve of a small group of water experts and lawyers. Key questions are: What are the most efficient and proper uses of water? How can the state provide for them? What price should be paid for water? Should water policy decisions be left to a small band of water experts? How can the state regulate the rapidly growing use of water to drill for oil and gas? What new policies and legal frameworks will be needed for population growth, economic development, and drought conditions?[6]

To understand Colorado politics and political leaders, one has to understand the long-standing fights over water rights, the new realities that most of Colorado is chronically in a drought, and that Colorado's water is generally "overappropriated."

### DEVELOPMENT VERSUS ENVIRONMENT

Virtually everyone in Colorado agrees on the importance of a healthy, expanding economy that can provide jobs and reasonable prosperity for everyone who lives in the state. Most Coloradans also want more open-space wilderness areas and want government to enforce existing conservation laws by imposing fines on industries that pollute the air and water or damage the scenery.

But when abstract considerations are brought down to specific problems, the people of Colorado often divide into two groups. One group believes Colorado is obliged to use its resources to provide jobs and expand business opportunities. The other believes that preservation, conservation, and regulations that limit development are both desirable and, in the long run, in the vital economic interest of the state.

This divide was reflected in our 2010 statewide public opinion survey.

Fifty-one percent of Coloradans described themselves as "environmentalists" yet 46 percent did not identify themselves that way.

Many Coloradans want the U.S. government to designate more open-space wilderness areas. Yet "open space" means different things to different people. To conservationists it means a place where backpackers can go to appreciate the spectacular mountains and parks of the state. To Western Slope ranchers it means more regions for grazing cattle or sheep. To the tourism industry it means more regions to promote as fishing, rafting, skiing, or camping sites.

An issue arose in 1990 that illustrates this dialectic. Several people in Colorado Springs and in some of the counties in the western suburbs of Denver thought there should be stronger environmental restrictions placed on firms that quarry rock for cement and building use. A few notably ugly quarry scars had been left, especially near Colorado Springs. The scars were so noticeable that local business leaders complained they were an enduring detriment to attracting tourists and businesses to the area, not to mention the permanent loss of visual beauty to the thousands who regularly had to drive near or past those scars.

A bill was introduced in the Colorado legislature requiring certain modest changes in quarry approval. Immediate opposition came from lobbyists for the Colorado Rock Products Association. Even these modest changes, they said, would increase the costs of home building in Colorado, eliminate jobs, and lead to increased importation of rocks for cement from nearby states, such as Wyoming, that had fewer restrictions on quarry operators. The bill died in a legislative committee.

In 2010 several rafting outfits that raft the Taylor River (and elsewhere) advocated new legislation to establish a "right to float" in Colorado. Property owners on riverbanks, calling themselves the "Creekside Coalition," opposed the legislation. This pitted property owners against the tourist industry. Rafting companies claimed they had been rafting the riverways for decades, even where both banks were private property. This was a classic skirmish of property owners versus outdoor recreationists and tour-guide companies. It also raised the question of whether rivers are private or public property. This 2010 legislation died, but it symbolized an illustrative Colorado policy fight that may eventually have to be resolved in the courts.[7]

Virtually every boom in Colorado's history has had its environmental costs, from the radioactive uranium tailings in the Durango area to the range erosion often caused by shortsighted ranchers. "The rancher is a man who supplants the native grasses with tumbleweed, snakeweed, mud, dust and flies," wrote the late novelist Edward Abbey. "He drives off elk and antelope and shoots eagles, bears and cougars on sight. And then leans back and grins at the TV cameras and talks about how much he loves the American West."[8]

Business and political leaders deny Colorado has to choose between unrestrained economic growth and zealous environmentalism. "Balance economic development with concern for the environment" is what the Colorado Association of Commerce and Industry (CACI) urged. CACI's *Blueprint for Colorado: A Look at the 90s* almost sounded as if there were no environmental crises in Colorado's future: "Besides our people, Colorado's greatest asset is its unique physical environment, which is being protected, maintained, and preserved. A long-range environmental plan, based on scientific data and technical feasibility, has been embraced by all segments of society. . . . Coloradans recognize the link between a healthy environment and a strong economy."[9]

What CACI's *Blueprint* said was valid, up to a point. Many programs, such as a statewide land use commission, are in place, but these programs have been inadequately funded. Environmental programs have been adopted yet sometimes poorly implemented.

Most Coloradans appreciate the link between a healthy environment and a healthy economy. Statewide polls indicate, however, that people divide on how much they are willing to change their lifestyles or pay increased taxes to ensure an improved quality of life. Most Coloradans are opposed to building more dams, but they still want cheap water to keep their lawns and shrubs green. Most Coloradans want clean air, yet they also want to drive their cars whenever and wherever they want.

A clear majority of Coloradans fear that "if Colorado continues to grow as fast as it has over the past few years, the quality of life in the state will be ruined." Yet in 2007, Coloradans by a two-to-one margin backed allowing energy companies to drill on the Western Slope's Roan Plateau "to reduce dependence on oil imports," especially if the revenues from such drilling were used to help fund public higher education. Coloradans, similar to people most places, want it both ways.

These divisions are even more sharply observed in the state legislature as it debates proposed laws on the environment, economic development, and especially oil and gas companies' use of hydraulic fracturing. The legislature has usually been probusiness, pro-jobs, and pro-growth. Groups such as the Denver Metro Chamber of Commerce, the Colorado Association of Commerce and Industry, homebuilders, realtors, and kindred associations typically prevail over the Sierra Club, Colorado Conservation Voters, the Western Colorado Congress, the Colorado Environmental Coalition, and other wilderness, fish habitat, conservation, and preservation-oriented groups.

The major political action committees and the lobbyists with the highest salaries and reputed "clout" are commonly promoters and advocates of economic development, or at least "reasonable economic development." Conservation groups and environmentalist legislators are typically on the defensive at the state capitol.

Colorado, however, is the only state in the nation that has a state lottery whose profits mainly go to protecting open spaces and wildlife habitat and to providing for trails and parks. But, says landscape photographer and ecologist John Fielder, "neither Colorado's biodiversity nor its economy will survive the consequences of prolonging the progression of unfortunate changes that have ravaged the landscape in recent decades." Fielder laments that the extractive industries now pervade "every corner of the state, affecting both public and private lands in ways from which they will never recover."[10]

Sensible laws are obviously needed to provide for balanced growth and ecological sustainability.

### U.S. GOVERNMENT PRESENCE

There has always been a federal government presence in Colorado. The popular yet mythical idea of the rugged, independent frontiersperson conquering the Rocky Mountain West, completely unassisted, is misleading. Expeditions by Zebulon Pike and by Lewis and Clark, the Native American pacification by the U.S. Army, the postal service, railroad land grants, and the Homestead Act, to name just a few examples, suggest that the hand and the help of the federal government were here even as the region was being first settled.

Thirty-seven percent of modern-day Colorado is owned by the U.S. government. Moreover, virtually two-thirds of Colorado west of Denver and the Front Range is designated "federal land." The U.S. government has been in Colorado early and often, and its impact is enormous.

National forests, national parks, Bureau of Land Management holdings, and major military installations are found all over the state. The U.S. Forest Service owns and operates more than 15 million acres here. The U.S. Bureau of Land Management supervises over 8 million acres of surface land. Nearly 780,000 acres in Colorado are National Park Service lands. Over 160,000 acres are run by the Fish and Wildlife Service, and yet another 200,000 acres are U.S. Bureau of Reclamation land.

The Denver metropolitan area has one of the largest concentrations of U.S. government employees outside the Washington DC metro area. There are over one hundred thousand federal employees living and working in Colorado, nearly 50 percent of them in defense-related work.

Denver is the seat of both a federal district court and the U.S. Tenth Circuit Court of Appeals. It is home to a U.S. Mint facility and it houses regional offices of many of the U.S. cabinet-level departments. Colorado also has a large contingent of forest rangers and other Department of Interior and Department of Agriculture officials who work in the national parks, forests, and monuments in the state. The Defense Department has a variety of installations, including the U.S. Air Force Academy, Fort Carson (a major army base), and the U.S. Space Command.

The U.S. government provided major subsidies and concessions to bring the railroads to Colorado. And, as noted, the "feds" have been indispensable to the building of scores of dams, diversion projects, and related reclamation projects. A rash of federal subsidies in various forms also came to the cattlemen, the wheat growers, the sugar beet farmers, and others who made agricultural production one of Colorado's leading industries.

In recent decades, however, Coloradans have often fought with officials of the U.S. government's Environmental Protection Agency (EPA) over what they think are excessive air, water, and chemical regulations. Thus farmers were annoyed when the EPA outlawed or limited the use of weed spray and animal poison in areas where farmers and ranchers viewed these chemicals as essential.

A "sagebrush rebellion" brewed in the early 1980s in Colorado and other western states. Its aim was to force the federal government to turn over large tracts of land to the states. Self-determination and freeing up land for development were the twin goals of the movement. In Colorado, the sagebrush rebellion was strongly backed by energy and cattle interests, and their motto was "resources have been put on earth for men to develop."

In the spring of 1981 a bill was passed in the Colorado legislature calling for the U.S. government to turn over 15 million acres of national forest and 8 million acres of BLM land to the state by 1983. The bill's supporters argued that "lands held by the federal government are a burden on the state of Colorado" and that "the state could administer them better than the absentee federal 'landlord.'"[11]

The bill was vetoed by then Colorado governor Richard Lamm, and urban and suburban legislators helped sustain the veto. But the sagebrush rebellion symbolized discontent about the way the U.S. government dominates much of the Centennial State.

Coloradans are in a long-term awkward embrace with the U.S. government. The state and its businesses and universities want all the federal grants, subsidies, and assistance possible, yet they do not want, or like, federal standards and controls. Colorado and the U.S. government need each other, and the question is always one of finding a balance, fine-tuning the relationship, and tactfully negotiating compromises on a whole range of public policy questions.

## THE MULTIPLE STATES OF COLORADO

Colorado was born of multiple parents. Native Americans, Spaniards, French, Mexicans, and Anglo-Americans all made contributions. Colorado remains today a more diverse state than most. Geographical, ethnic, and social divisions abound.

It did not take long after the Anglo-Americans arrived for Denver to be founded and to dominate territorial and, later, state politics. Denver soon became the financial, political, and cultural capital of the state, as it still is.

One consequence of Denver's concentration of population and economic importance is that the rest of the state is at least a little disaffected and sometimes jealous of Denver's multiple powers and influence. Such a relationship lends itself to a "we versus they" alienation. Western Slope residents (people living west of the Continental Divide) especially believe they are neglected by "the powers that be" over in the big city of Denver.

Rural residents also often have an anti-Denver attitude. Some folks down in Holly used some crude language as they gave one of us an earful of what they thought of the people, especially the politicians, in Denver. The cities of Colorado Springs, Pueblo, Fort Collins, and more recently Lakewood and Aurora have viewed Denver as a rival, sometimes as a bitter rival when it came to patronage, state projects, federal projects, water, and other highly valued commodities. For example, all these communities have economic development councils that compete with Denver to recruit new businesses and expand tourism.

Socially and politically, a north–south division also exists in Colorado. Northern Coloradans, probably unwittingly yet nonetheless overtly, look down on Pueblo and many of the southern tier counties of the state. Pueblo and other southern counties are poorer and contain a sizeable Latino population. On more than one occasion, some whiners have suggested that all concerned would be happier if the southern counties were detached from Colorado and merged with New Mexico.[12]

In recent decades, the development of resort communities in Aspen,

Vail, and Steamboat Springs has lured wealthy newcomers who have little or no identification with, nor much interest in, the rest of Colorado. Residents there often function as if they lived in foreign enclaves divorced from the central issues and policy debates of the state.

## THE SIX REGIONS OF COLORADO

Based on geography and patterns of human settlement, Colorado can be divided into six distinct regions. They are the Eastern Plains, the Front Range, Denver Metro, the Eastern Foothills, Southern Colorado, and the Western Slope. See Map 3.

The *Eastern Plains* comprise nearly 40 percent of the land in the state and consist mainly of high rolling prairies. This is farm and ranch country, an area resembling popular images of western Kansas more than Colorado. Irrigated-farm communities developed in eastern Colorado to feed the massive gold rush migration. These communities grew up mainly along floodplains of the Arkansas and South Platte Rivers.

Large cattle ranches also developed in these areas. The Homestead Act of 1862 brought a large number of farmers and would-be farmers to this region. Farming was (and is) always precarious on the Eastern Plains, subject to drought, prairie fires, grasshoppers, hailstorms, and tornados. Author Tim Egan's 2006 National Book Award–winning *The Worst Hard Time* vividly captures the great Dust Bowl era in Colorado's southeastern communities.

Diverted water, a major underground water supply (the Ogallala aquifer), and various soil conservation efforts have allowed increased production per acre in this area. But automation and farm foreclosures have had the same effect in eastern Colorado as they have everywhere. There has been a decline in population and a decline in political clout. Less than 4 percent of the people of the state live on the Eastern Plains.

The *Front Range* (which includes Denver Metro) consists of a string of cities from Fort Collins and Greeley, not far from the Wyoming border, to the major cities of Colorado Springs and Pueblo south of Denver. About 82 percent of the state population reside along the Front Range. The Denver Metropolitan area sits right in the middle of and is considered part of the Front Range.

Some farming goes on in this region, but its altitude of between forty-five hundred and seven thousand feet makes farming unrewarding. Manufacturing, military installations, space and technology research and development, tourism, and higher education are the main sources for jobs

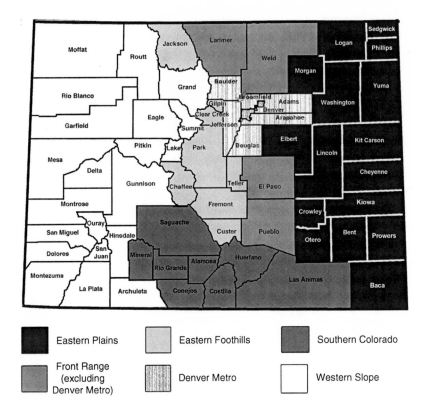

Map 3. The Six Geographical Regions of Colorado

and economic stability. Most of these cities along the Front Range grew dramatically in the post–World War II years. Fort Collins and Colorado Springs were among the fastest-growing communities in the nation in recent decades.

*Denver Metro* is the city of Denver plus the suburban counties of Jefferson, Adams, Arapahoe, Boulder, Broomfield, and Douglas. It is, and since 1858 always has been, the center of the state's population. Over 60 percent of the people of the state live in this greater Denver area. Colorado's wealth is there. Most of its major universities and businesses are located there

Of course, many of the greatest policy problems are also located in Denver Metro, such as air pollution, water pollution, hazardous waste, crime, homelessness, and transportation problems.

Denver Metro and the rest of the Front Range will continue to dominate Colorado in terms of population. The Colorado Department of Natural Resources estimates that most of the 3 million people who will move into Colorado between 2012 and 2040 will settle around Denver and in the rest of the Front Range. That means 85 to 90 percent of all future population growth in Colorado is likely to occur in this relatively small, already crowded geographical area of the state.[13]

The *Eastern Foothills* is a group of counties that run from north to south and sit between the Front Range to the east and the Continental Divide to the west. These counties are blessed with mountain views and gorgeous canyons. They are sometimes referred to as the Central Mountains. Because of their proximity to the Front Range, the Eastern Foothills have long been filled with the vacation homes of people who live and work on the Front Range.

Some of these counties, particularly Gilpin, Clear Creek, Park, and Teller Counties, are experiencing exurban-style population growth because they are relatively handy to Denver and Colorado Springs.

*Southern Colorado* comprises the central portion of Colorado located immediately above the New Mexico border. In the heart of Southern Colorado is the San Luis Valley, one of the largest and visually most spectacular valleys in America. A significant Spanish-speaking population still resides in or near this valley and around the old mining districts of Trinidad and Walsenburg.

The political history of Southern Colorado is a tale of property and water rights battles, poverty, and disgruntlement with being ignored by the political leaders in Denver. There has been a certain amount of cultural assimilation among Hispanics, Native Americans, and Anglo-Americans. Population in this region is declining. Poorly financed county and city governments struggle to make a go of it in this sparsely populated area (5 or 6 percent of the state's population at best).

Then there is the *Western Slope*, the area from the Continental Divide to the Utah border, stretching from New Mexico on the south all the way north to the Wyoming border. This westernmost section of Colorado contains about 10 percent of the state's population, a third or more of the land, and, as noted, more than 80 percent of the state's water. This region contains vast mineral deposits and has experienced more than its share of the boom and bust cycle, most recently in the 1980s oil shale boom and bust in the Grand Junction and Rifle regions. Energy companies are busily extracting resources in this region as we write. Most of the celebrated destination ski resorts are also on the Western Slope.

There is a distinct Western Slope attitude, and it is partly one of feeling exploited by Front Range water boards, developers, and the state's political leadership. Historians Duane Vandenbusche and Duane Smith call the Western Slope "a land alone" in their excellent study of this region.[14]

Tourism, mining, and agriculture provide the employment for this part of the state. But few important political leaders come from the Western Slope, and this leaves residents there with an enduring sense of being unrepresented and even unheard.

Because there is no widely accepted agreement on the subject, we present here our breakdown of which counties are in the six major regions of Colorado:

- Eastern Plains—Logan, Sedgwick, Phillips, Morgan, Washington, Yuma, Elbert, Lincoln, Kit Carson, Cheyenne, Crowley, Kiowa, Otero, Bent, Prowers, and Baca Counties.

- Denver Metro—Denver, Boulder, Broomfield, Jefferson, Adams, Arapahoe, and Douglas Counties.

- Front Range—Denver Metro counties plus Larimer, Weld, El Paso, and Pueblo Counties.

- Southern Colorado—Las Animas, Huerfano, Costilla, Conejos, Alamosa, Rio Grande, Mineral, and Saguache Counties.

- Eastern Foothills—Gilpin, Clear Creek, Park, Lake, Teller, Fremont, Chaffee, and Custer Counties (and maybe Jackson County).

- Western Slope—Moffat, Routt, Rio Blanco, Garfield, Eagle, Grand, Summit, Mesa, Pitkin, Montrose, Delta, Gunnison, San Miguel, Ouray, San Juan, Hinsdale, Dolores, Montezuma, La Plata, and Archuleta Counties (and maybe Jackson County).

In short, Colorado can be divided into six regions. And even these regions are not homogeneous. Aspen, for example, has little in common with Leadville. Rifle has little in common with Vail. Meeker has little in common with Steamboat Springs. Colorado Springs and Pueblo differ sharply. And Douglas and Adams Counties are contrasting suburban Denver communities. Note, too, that some political analysts contend that Pueblo is more Southern Colorado than Front Range, and that Jackson County belongs in the Western Slope cluster. Such debates cannot be completely settled nor need be.

State leaders are forever challenged by the task of building morale and community across the state for new initiatives. And since the state legislature is a product of these diverse sections of the state, it often falls as a burden on governors to try to provide unifying statewide leadership. It is a role in which most governors try hard yet often fail.

### A CONSERVATIVE STATE

Colorado "is conservative politically, economically, financially." So wrote John Gunther at the midpoint of the twentieth century. "I do not mean reactionary. Just conservative, with the kind of conservativeness that does not budge an inch for anybody or anything unless pinched or pushed."[15] This characterization is mostly true in the twenty-first century. Colorado is a probusiness, promilitary, pro-work, pro-gun, antigovernment, and antitax state. Still, Colorado has become in recent years a more "purple" than "red" state.

The only governors who have lasted in office and accomplished much have been those who built strong ties with the business community. One of the few exceptions was Gov. Stephen McNichols, who introduced a number of reform measures to Colorado in the late 1950s. However, he "retired" rather unceremoniously in 1962 (after six years in office) for having raised taxes and for being too much of a programmatic progressive.

In Colorado most elected officials are conservatives or at least fiscal moderates, and as one writer told us, "there is virtually no left left." Democratic governor Richard Lamm (1975–87) and Democratic governor Roy Romer (1987–99) were moderates, as was Republican governor Bill Owens (1999–2007). Romer and Democratic governor John Hickenlooper were viewed as "chamber of commerce Democrats" on most matters of business and growth. There is a long tradition of conservative Democrats holding statewide office. Governor and U.S. senator Edwin "Big Ed" Johnson especially typified this tradition from the 1930s to the mid-1950s.

There is an old saying in American politics that the only extreme that regularly wins is the extreme middle. Well, in Colorado the middle has traditionally been slightly right of center. Normally, a moderately conservative Republican will win statewide elections, although that pattern began to change a bit after 2000 when more moderate Democrats began winning statewide offices. It remains to be seen whether the Democratic victories in Colorado in 2004 through 2010 were temporary interruptions in Republican rule or represented a change in the state's partisan politics.

Only three times in the nearly sixty years from 1952 to 2008 did Colorado vote Democratic for president. Democrat Lyndon Johnson gained Colorado's electoral votes for president in 1964, as did Democrat Bill Clinton in 1992 and Democrat Barack Obama in 2008.

"The safe party in Colorado state elections for most people here," said pollster Paul Talmey, "is the Republican Party."[16] That is to say, Republicans are more predictably conservative and are the least likely to rock the boat, raise taxes, or introduce real change.

In 2004 the Democrats surprised most Colorado political pundits by winning majorities in both houses of the state legislature. The Democrats preserved those majorities in the subsequent 2006 and 2008 general elections. In light of those legislative victories, coupled with the Democrats winning the governorship in 2006 and again in 2010, political analysts now aptly refer to Colorado as a "purple" rather than a "red" state.

However, Republicans scored some victories of their own in 2010. They succeeded in winning control of the state House of Representatives (by one representative) and took two of Colorado's U.S. House of Representatives seats away from the Democrats.

*Denver Post* columnist Bob Ewegen once wrote that "the differences within the parties in Colorado are greater than between the parties," and this is still often accurate.[17] There are Libertarians as well as "Tea Party" activists loosely affiliated with the Republicans and at least a few national Democrats and Jesse Jackson–style liberals within the ranks of the Democrats.

Yet there are a number of conservative Democrats who are just as moderate, centrist, or even conservative as many Republicans in and out of public office in Colorado. Pueblo and Adams Counties are noted for having sizeable numbers of conservative Democrats, folks who are probably as conservative on many policy issues as many Fort Collins, Boulder, or Evergreen Republicans (Evergreen is an upscale mountain suburb west of Denver).

Colorado's conservatism is well illustrated by the voting patterns in the state legislature, which tend to indicate caution about new social and spending programs and opposition to tax increases. The frequency of antitax citizen initiatives is yet another indication of the state's conservative attitude.

Our statewide polls of Coloradans indicate that more than 40 percent of adult Coloradans consistently, over the past two decades, view themselves as "conservative." In contrast, less than 25 percent identify themselves as "liberal." A remaining 30 percent or so respond that they are "middle-of-the-road" in their political outlook.

According to our ranking, Colorado was one of the most evenly balanced (in terms of Democrats vs. Republicans) of the fifty states in statewide elections (president, governor, U.S. senator) from 1992 to 2010.[18] It was one more piece of information that suggested that, in 2000 and beyond, Colorado was losing its "generally Republican" reputation.

Over the years, governor after governor failed to win much support for major high-cost investments in the state's infrastructure such as prisons, highways, state parks, or higher education. Yes, occasional victories were won, but only after everyone was pinched or pushed.

Colorado politics is also marked by a streak of independence. There is a widespread "leave me alone" attitude among Coloradans. It is partly a "you do what you want to do but I'll do what I want to do" disposition. A "Make My Day" law, passed and signed into law in 1985, made it legal in Colorado to shoot and kill threatening intruders in one's home.

It is probably true that pre-1960s Coloradans were even more antigovernment and antitax than is currently the case. Old-timers often dwell on the "frontier ethos" of the Centennial State's past and the accompanying images of rugged individualism and a do-it-yourself society. These legends are probably more mythical and idealized than accurate, as historians like Professor Patricia Limerick of the University of Colorado at Boulder have pointed out.[19]

Perceptions and attitudes often are different from—and exaggerations of—reality. The immigration of some 2 million new residents in the past two generations has transformed Colorado into a more moderate state. Even newcomers, however, relatively quickly take on some of the dominant political values. These include skepticism toward establishments of all kinds, especially elected and party leadership establishments.

One trait of Coloradans that carries over to politics is their love of the outdoors. The mountains are the state's signature icon, and this love of the outdoors is doubtless somehow correlated with a love of freedom and a spirit of independence.

It is hard to quantify this commitment to the outdoor world, yet we know that more than 1.25 million Colorado residents have either a fishing or a hunting license or both. Our 2010 poll shows that 80 percent of Coloradans believe owning a gun is a basic American right. Nearly all the pollsters and political analysts interviewed agreed that this great love of the outdoors characterizes the political mood in Colorado.

Political consultant Walt Klein saw Coloradans as having "a streak of independence." You do not have to live in Colorado very long, he argues, before you feel it. Klein believes the independent nature of Colorado voters explains why there is so much ticket splitting in the state. He concluded: "People in Colorado like their state, like their situations far more than in other states, and there is optimism and upbeat good feeling about living in the region."[20]

National polls have indicated that Colorado has one of the happiest state populations in the nation. Our 2010 statewide survey confirmed this with a whopping 97 percent saying they were generally a happy person.

Yet, as we discuss in chapter 2, Coloradans can be happy personally but antigovernment and politically pessimistic at the same time. Paradoxically, too, while Coloradans are among the happiest in the United States, the state has for several years consistently ranked in the top ten states for suicide. Nearly one thousand Coloradans commit suicide each year.

Why is this? Experts say geographical isolation can exacerbate depression. *Denver Post* reporter Kevin Simpson speculated: "A rugged frontier mentality promotes self-reliance but also discourages seeking mental-health assistance." Simpson added: "Shrinking mental-health resources, particularly in rural areas, often complicate treatment. And in a state where many residents hail from somewhere else, family-support systems can be stretched thin."[21]

Colorado also has one of the highest proportions of registered independent or unaffiliated voters. Parties are weak in Colorado, and a large number of people who move into the state seem to prefer to wait and watch politics for a while before affiliating with one or the other major political parties.

Coloradans are independent in other ways too. They occasionally throw judges out of office in judicial-retention elections under the Missouri Plan for selecting and electing judicial officials. And though voters turned down an initiative to limit judicial terms, citizens still tell pollsters they favor term limits for judges in Colorado.

Parties mean a lot in the state legislature, and they still count when people have to vote for candidates they do not know. Nearly 70 percent of registered voters do have a preference, and even many of the so-called independents lean regularly to the Republicans or the Democrats in their partisan preferences. Party orientation, however, declines as a crucial factor in statewide and presidential elections when issues and character qualities are enlarged by television ads, debates, news, and media coverage.

Colorado has a populist tradition as well. In 1892 miners together with farmers and pro-silver forces helped elect Populist Party candidates to Congress and to the statehouse. The Populist Party candidate for U.S. president also won Colorado's electoral votes that year.

A progressive movement, although different in its bases of support and its goals from the Populist Party of the 1890s, also developed in Colorado.

Progressive candidates received support from those who believed the existing two political parties (Republicans and Democrats) failed to respond to new and necessitous conditions.[22]

Later efforts, such as the anti-Olympics campaign of 1972, the legislature's sagebrush rebellion legislation in the 1980s, and tax-limitation and term-limitation campaigns in the 1990s, were illustrative of populist or semipopulist outbursts.

The 1990 campaign for governor opened with a debate before the Colorado Municipal League in which both the incumbent Democrat and the challenging Republican claimed to be the true populist.

"I'm probably the most populist governor in the past fifty years in this state," said Democrat Roy Romer. John Andrews, his Republican opponent, replied: "I'm a small *d* Jeffersonian democrat. I trust the people. I'm a decentralizer. I'm a reformer, and I'm an outsider to the political and government establishments. I'm a citizen candidate."

Andrews suggested his stands on issues made him, not Romer, the real populist. "You'll find out, as this campaign proceeds, who really trusts the people," said Andrews. He pointed out that on taxes, voucher systems for school choice, and abortion, he would in effect let the people decide.[23]

Populist Romer defeated populist Andrews in the election.

Populist Ross Perot was more successful in his presidential bids in 1992 and 1996 in Colorado than in most other states. And the populist Tea Party movement in 2010 was louder and more active in Colorado than in most states.

### SOME INSTANCES OF INTOLERANCE

There also has been racial intolerance in Colorado's political heritage. It was noticeable, of course, in the treatment of Native Americans. Federal treaties supposed to be "forever" typically lasted four or five years. In addition to broken treaties, pioneer Anglo-Americans in Colorado sometimes treated the Native Americans unfairly and denied them the most basic of human rights.

Anglo settlers, especially in the early 1860s, saw their wagon trains and stagecoaches attacked and fellow pioneers kidnapped or murdered. This fueled the fever for revenge. One of the legendary revenge retaliations was the 1864 encounter at Sand Creek, Colorado, often called the "Sand Creek Massacre." We discuss this in more detail in chapter 10.

"Nativism," at least as it can be used in the context of Colorado history, has an ironic twist to it. Nativism generally refers to a policy of favoring native inhabitants as opposed to aliens or immigrants. Nativism can also refer to intolerance or prejudice toward foreigners or those without original or indigenous roots.

In the case of Colorado, of course, the Native Americans were resident in or traveling through the area long before the Anglo-Americans arrived. It was the miners and farmers from New England, the Midwest, Texas, and elsewhere who were the newcomers. But many Anglo-Americans quickly assumed an attitude of superiority. In the shortest time imaginable, they began to practice exclusion, discrimination, and ill-treatment of anyone unlike themselves.

There is a contemporary version of nativism in Colorado. It takes the form of disdain for the large numbers of people who have been moving into Colorado since the end of World War II. This form of nativism is in part directed at illegal aliens. Interestingly, people who move to Colorado are personally welcome and are treated like everyone else. The dislike is directed not at individuals but at the effect on the state of *so many* newcomers.

Among some groups in Colorado, rapid population growth is blamed for causing open fields to turn into housing developments and shopping centers, quiet suburban roads into automobile-jammed highways, and the beautiful mountains of Colorado to be speckled with too many vacation homes and crowded resort communities.

It is curious that a state so relatively sophisticated in several other ways was discriminatory in its treatment of Native Americans and, to a lesser degree, Mexican Americans. James A. Michener perhaps overstated but caught the flavor of the problem in *Centennial*, his best-selling historical novel about Colorado: "For more than half a century this condition prevailed. No church, no crusading newspaper, no band of women sought to correct this basic evil, and across Colorado, Anglo children who once had been raised to believe that Indians were not humans were now raised to think that Mexicans were even less so."[24]

No matter that this form of discrimination also thrived in neighboring states. It happened in Colorado, and this is a reality in the state's past. Over the years there also have been unfortunate periods of discrimination against a number of outcast groups, including miners, Catholics, Chinese, and Japanese.

A strong state chapter of the American Protective Association emerged in the 1890s. "Behind the patriotism and morality which the organization preached, there were few who misunderstood its anti-Catholic message."[25] It urged its members to vote Catholics out of office, and it called for boycotts of Catholic-owned businesses. It gained considerable influence in the Republican Party, and it had some support within the Democratic Party as well.

Corporate treatment of miners, most famously in Ludlow, Colorado, may be more a case of exploitation rather than outright discrimination. Yet a number of books have documented widespread mistreatment in what is called one of the deadliest labor struggles in American history.[26]

Another episode of discrimination in Colorado was the partial takeover of the state government in 1924 by the Ku Klux Klan. The Republicans nominated and elected a Klansman, Clarence J. Morley, as governor. Klansmen also took control of the state House of Representatives. Several other Klan-backed candidates were elected to major positions, including Democrat Ben Stapleton as mayor of Denver. Later in his political career, Stapleton repudiated the Klan.

This was a somewhat milder or at least different Ku Klux Klan, however, from the infamous one in the South for intimidating and lynching African Americans. The version of the Klan that swept the nation in the early 1920s and gained a serious foothold in Colorado was more of a patriotic law-and-order organization that primarily used the ballot box rather than physical threats to try to achieve its goals. But sadly, even Colorado's Klan preached a shameless hatred for a variety of minority groups.

The Colorado Ku Klux Klan in the 1920s was opposed to "moral laxity," "suggestive" new dances, and "titillating" movies. One of its major goals was to unite Protestants in an effort to advance Christian fundamentalism and stop the teaching of evolution in public schools. Note that this happened many years prior to Focus on the Family campaigning for its Christian fundamentalist goals from Colorado Springs. Rather than African Americans, who were a very small part of Colorado's population at the time, the 1920s Klan in Colorado was primarily opposed to Catholics, Jews, and immigrants.

Once in office, the Klan members tried to repeal civil rights laws and strengthen enforcement of laws prohibiting alcoholic beverages. They urged measures such as a ban on marriages between whites and Asians, and they tried to require Catholic children to go to public schools rather than Catholic schools. The Klan governor even called for outlawing sacramental wine in Colorado, a guileful attempt to undermine Catholic mass.

Fortunately, Democrats in the Colorado Senate allied with supportive Republicans opposed to the Ku Klux Klan. Thus, an anti-Klan majority in the Colorado Senate voted down most of the discriminatory legislation presented by the Klan. The anti-Catholic, anti-Jewish, anti-immigrant agenda of the Ku Klux Klan was never achieved in Colorado.[27]

The Centennial State was by no means alone in having Klan activity. In the 1920s the Klan was powerful in California and much of the Midwest.

Along with Indiana and Oregon, however, Colorado was said to be among the strongest Klan centers outside the South.[28]

It is also a part of Colorado's history that there were at least sixty-eight hangings without the benefit of a courtroom trial, for such things as cattle rustling and claim jumping of mines.

By the early 1990s a small lingering Colorado Klan had refined its message with slogans such as: "Equal rights for all; special privileges for nobody." The *New York Times* and other national news media interviewed a Klansman from Aurora, Colorado. He was Shawn Slater, who led the group that disrupted the Martin Luther King Jr. Day celebration in Denver in 1992.

Slater said he was not a white supremacist and that he had many black friends. Yet he had been arrested a few years earlier for wearing Nazi emblems. He called his organization "white Christian" and said, "There's no way a Jew could get in." He proudly talked of his pilgrimage to Tennessee to help celebrate the 125th anniversary of the founding of the Ku Klux Klan.

On his telephone answering machine, the *New York Times* reported, Slater recorded a message saying he wanted to run for governor of Colorado someday, asked callers to leave a message, then cheerfully added: "Have a nice day for white America."[29]

At one point in Colorado there was an attempt to exclude outsiders for economic reasons. In 1936 Gov. Ed Johnson "closed" Colorado's southern border with New Mexico to prevent migrant farm laborers and other "unwanted" individuals from entering the state. Members of the National Guard were sent to the border crossing to repel "aliens, indigents, and invaders."

Governor Johnson argued that Mexican beet workers were depriving Coloradans of jobs. "Jobs in this state are for our citizens," he said. "Barricades went up; trains, busses, cars, and trucks were stopped and occupants questioned." A headline in the *Durango Herald-Democrat* proclaimed: "Governor Calls Out National Guard to Halt Influx of Undesirables into Colorado."[30]

Dozens of non-Coloradans were turned away over a ten-day period. Eventually, this unconstitutional "foreign policy" was rescinded and the border with New Mexico reopened. Still, it was another manifestation of how some people in Colorado felt about "outsiders."

In more recent years, fear of "outsiders" has taken the form of anti-immigration and the "send-the-illegal-aliens-home" type of politics. U.S. representative and 2010 gubernatorial candidate Tom Tancredo of Colorado was the most visible and vociferous voice in this movement.

"Coloradans are basically pragmatic," said former governor Richard Lamm. "They are sometimes conservative, sometimes populist. They find neither party always to their satisfaction, and they cross over and switch parties a lot at election time."

Then how do things ever get done? Lamm's answer: "Good people have to put coalitions together across party lines and try to bring about progress, and this does happen."[31]

### INDIVIDUALISTIC AND MORALISTIC

Political scientists use the term "political culture" to refer to a set of widely shared beliefs, values, and norms concerning the relationship of citizens to government and to one another. Americans and Coloradans, for example, have always been united by their commitment to liberty and more or less united by their commitment to equal rights and equality of opportunity. Another shared belief is that the government should exist to serve the people rather than the other way around.

Daniel J. Elazar, a student of state politics and federalism, suggested several years ago that there are three dominant types of political culture or subcultures in the United States. They are the moralistic, the individualistic, and the traditionalistic.[32] Each of these three cultures first developed on the East Coast and then spread westward as pioneer settlers moved to the Midwest and then to the Mountain West.

The moralistic culture first developed in colonial New England. Mainly because of the influence of the Puritan religion, New Englanders came to view politics and government as existing to promote the public good. They believed it was the job of government to improve society and to build a "commonwealth" in which government would work to better social and economic conditions in the society.

The moralistic political culture came to Colorado as New Englanders spread westward across Ohio and Michigan to Illinois and Iowa and then came up the South Platte River into northeast Colorado and the Denver area. Moralistic political culture was probably best represented in Colorado history in the founding of the "colony towns," such as Greeley and Colorado Springs. These towns were specifically founded to be ideal places to live. They were to be communities with extensive parks and excellent schools and other public facilities that would provide what is now known as "a high quality of life."

Sharply contrasting with the moralistic political culture is the individualistic political culture. The individualistic political culture developed in the Middle Atlantic states, particularly New Jersey, Pennsylvania, Delaware, and Maryland.

Free of the moralistic and reformist influences of the Puritan church, the individualistic political culture emphasized the idea that governments should do only those things individuals cannot do for themselves. Thus, government should have no lofty goals or purposes, the individualist culture holds, and should simply create a "marketplace," rather than a "commonwealth," in which individuals are free to compete fairly with one another as they go about leading their individual lives.

An individualistic political culture spread westward to Colorado from the Mid-Atlantic states through southern Ohio and Illinois, thence across Missouri and Kansas and up the Arkansas River into southeastern and central Colorado.

The individualistic political culture was particularly strong among the gold and silver miners who came during the gold and silver rushes that occurred throughout the state's history. With their willingness to move frequently and to take great risks in hopes of finding a fortune, the gold and silver miners were naturally inclined to the individualistic political culture. Cattlemen, and the nomadic cowboys who worked for them, also represented the individualistic philosophy in early Colorado.

The third type of political culture, the traditionalistic, is present yet relatively weak in Colorado. It came into the state two ways. One way was with the Spanish settlers, who came up the Rio Grande from New Mexico. The other way was that of former southerners, who came up the Arkansas River.

The Spanish settlers who came from Mexico and New Mexico brought with them the political and social conventions of Spain. The Spanish tradition emphasized preservation of the status quo, particularly the idea that the dominant role in society and government should be played by a limited number of socially prominent families with large landed estates. Elements of this Spanish tradition can still be found in Southern Colorado, yet it plays a relatively modest part in the state's overall political life.

The traditionalistic political culture of the American South was also brought into Colorado by a number of immigrants who came up the Arkansas River valley, some of them from Missouri. Similar to Spanish attitudes, the traditionalistic political culture of the southern United States emphasized opposition to rapid change and reliance on well-established groups to govern the society.

The notion of political cultures provides a means of analyzing various patterns of political behavior in Colorado. One of the major enduring divisions in Colorado politics is between the individualistic, or semilibertarian, and the moralistic, or semicommunitarian, political culture.

Individualists in Colorado are noted for their strong embrace of economic freedom and their strong opposition to taxes and big government. The moralists in Colorado generally try to make Colorado a better place, at least selectively, by using government as a means toward these ends. Thus moralists are communitarians who want better public schools and are willing to pay more taxes to get them.

Moralists also back reforms of the political process, such as open-meeting laws and campaign-finance reform. Where individualists fear and oppose government intrusions, moralists at least occasionally are willing to view governmental programs in a more affirmative light.

Republicans in the state legislature more or less typify the individualistic culture. Many of the governors in the past three generations, especially Steve McNichols, Richard Lamm, Roy Romer, Bill Ritter, and John Hickenlooper, more often than not acted as agents of a moralistic political culture.

In broad, general terms the Republican Party can be viewed as embodying the individualistic culture whereas the Democratic Party is more illustrative of the moralistic or communitarian culture. Of course there are various cross-cultural political figures in the state, and they are of special interest because of their balancing and perhaps integrating activities.

Neither the individualistic nor the moralistic political culture has succeeded in completely dominating Colorado politics. Moralism and individualism appear locked in a continuing struggle in the state, one side winning on certain issues and the other winning on yet different issues.

### A DISPERSED LEADERSHIP STRUCTURE

No one individual, leader, party, interest group, or lobbyist rules Colorado. On the contrary, the state's public policy agenda is shaped by a multiplicity of competing interests. As pollster Paul Talmey put it: "There is no one in the state who can say let's do X and it gets done. A few people can veto things."[33] Or as former Governor Lamm put it: "There is no epicenter" in Colorado politics.

It is not that there are no leaders in Colorado. Rather it is just that no one leader in or out of government has great amounts of authority or influence over public policy matters. Colorado's governorship has certain powers, such as the veto and the item veto, and considerable influence in appointing state and local judges, yet Colorado's governor is only one of several political players when it comes to shaping the state's budget.

The legislature often takes the lead on budget matters, yet few legislators are noted for shaping overall state policy in more than one or two areas, usually the policy areas reflected by their committee assignments.

Interest groups and lobbyists are influential in Colorado. Yet according to one study, they are not as influential or powerful as in many states.[34] Unlike the Anaconda Copper Company's once strong influence in Montana, or gambling and hotel interests in Nevada, or farming interests in Kansas and Nebraska, Colorado's economy is diversified. Mining and agricultural interests may have once dominated Colorado political decision making, but today tourism, manufacturing, high tech, aerospace companies, water interests, clean energy supporters, environmental groups, teachers, and a host of other interests have matched if not eclipsed their influence.

In years past, noted lobbyists such as Dave Rice of the Colorado Cattlemen's Association, Ray Kimball of the Colorado Association of Commerce and Industry, John A. Schwartz of the Colorado Fuel and Iron Company, and a handful of lobbyists for AMAX (a major mining concern) were viewed as decidedly influential on matters of state legislation. Nowadays, Colorado Concern, comprised of a few dozen of the state's leading business executives, is regularly recognized as a behind-the-scenes agenda setter.

Yet in recent legislative sessions, more than six hundred individuals are registered lobbyists, and no one or two or even a dozen persons or groups could be singled out as a dominant change maker.

Some interest groups are important because they represent significant numbers of people. Thus the Colorado Education Association represents large numbers of teachers, and various public employee organizations represent state and local government workers.

As elsewhere, money in the form of campaign contributions buys access and usually a careful hearing, if not votes. Most legislators say they listen carefully to the information that friendly lobbyists provide them, yet few will admit to being strongly influenced by lobbying pressure.

Among the groups that regularly donate to a large number of legislative campaigns are the Colorado Association of Realtors, the Colorado Education Association, Colorado AFL-CIO, Colorado Home Builders Association, Coors Brewing Company, Colorado Association of Commerce and Industry, Colorado Rock Products Association, Colorado Trial Lawyers Association, Colorado Contractors Association, and various transportation, communication, insurance, energy, agricultural, financial, and medical associations. It is not uncommon for key legislators to receive substantial campaign contributions, even those having relatively safe seats. In "battleground" districts, however, the total amounts of money spent can be as high as several million dollars.

Cities and counties and their elected officials are also an important voice in state public policy matters. Groups such as the Colorado Municipal League, Colorado Counties, Inc., and the Colorado District Attorneys' Council are often cited by state legislators and their aides as "major players" in the way legislation gets written. The Colorado Bar Association and the Colorado Water Congress are also, on occasion, influential.

Various citizen and "good government" associations have grown in strength in recent years. Although they are not viewed as "powerful" at the statehouse, they are nonetheless a presence there in raising consciousness about certain issues, demanding hearings and rallying public support in initiative elections.

Groups such as the League of Women Voters, Sierra Club, Common Cause, Colorado Conservation Voters, and the progressive-leaning Colorado Fiscal Policy Institute and the Bell Policy Center, all decidedly rooted in the moralistic political culture, serve as watchdogs for their constituencies. The Colorado Fiscal Policy Institute, for example, has as its motto: "Justice and Economic Security for *All* Coloradans." Such groups try to act as a counterweight to the more dominant financial and business interest groups in Colorado.

Plainly, certain interests are more powerful than others. Well-known businessmen and lawyers in or near Denver who successfully solicit large campaign contributions for candidates for governor or competitive state legislative seats get a more careful hearing than does a concerned yet average citizen from Conejos, Crawford, Cortez, or Craig. So, too, building contractors and cattlemen obviously are better represented in the state legislature than are the homeless and handicapped.

Further, those who can afford the service will hire on retainer certain of the experienced statehouse lobbyists, such as Steve Durham, Steve Balcerovich, Larry Hudson, Ruben Valdez, Jim Cole, Adam Eichberg, Will Coyne, Ruth Aponte, Gayle Berry, Mary Kay Hogan, Becky Brooks, Mike Beasley, Virginia Morrison Love, Loren Furman, David Foster, and Ed Bowditch. Or they can hire senior partners in the top "Seventeenth Street" law firms to prepare bills and lobby for their interests. People who can hire lobbyists and lawyers are in a better position to influence the legislature than those who just write letters. But legislators and statewide elected officials do read their mail and e-mail, and many of them hold local town meetings around the state.

Complicating matters further is that for a long while, prior to 1999, one party, the Republicans, controlled the state legislature, and the other party, the Democrats, controlled the governor's office. The state's congressional delegation also has been split in recent years, the Republicans dominating at one time and the Democrats at another. Similarly party registration in recent decades has been pretty evenly divided in three ways with a third or more registered as Republicans, nearly a third registered as Democrats, and yet another third registered as unaffiliated or independent. This pattern, with minor shifts, held steady from 1990 through at least 2013.

Critics might justifiably call it a "nobody's-in-charge" system. In reality Colorado has a system of multiple vetoes and a system that forces alliance-building and the forging of coalitions across party, ideological, and regional lines. In a state that has distinctive regional barriers and competing political cultures, leadership in Colorado is dispersed and decentralized.

On occasion, however, a strong governor with a lot of help from leading legislators, interest groups, local officials, and supportive media can bring about innovations and achieve desired breakthroughs.

Sometimes it is the business leaders in and around Denver that lead the way as they, along with the governor, the mayor of Denver, and countless elected and other officials, push for and help achieve such things as a new convention center in Denver, a major new international airport for Denver (DIA), or the T-REX transportation initiative. At other times important water projects have resulted from similar alliances. Also, improvements in air and water quality have been realized only when broad coalitions have been formed to promote these goals.

Citizens in Colorado are represented by elected officials, by political parties, by interest and lobbying groups, by citizen activist organizations, and through democratic elections. Colorado politics are characterized by a partisan legislature, by constitutionally modest yet entrepreneurial governors, and by an open and porous policy process. Probusiness and other "inside" lobbyists have a say in how laws get written and budgets are allocated, but "citizen power" can also be a force in Colorado politics. On matters such as conservation, official English, funding for K–12 public education, term limits for elected officials, lottery funding for open space purchases, and antitax measures (to mention just a few), the voice of the people through the initiative process has been influential.

In sum, political and policy leadership in Colorado is fragmented or simply diverse, depending on one's perspective. For those who prefer neat, well-organized, predictable statewide leadership, it often looks pretty fragmented. On the other hand, leadership in Colorado can also be described as reasonably diverse, and thus democratically reflective of the state and its multiple organized interests and representative institutions.

## CONCLUSIONS

Colorado may have an image as a rural state with much of its population living on ranches or farms or in small mountain communities. In fact, however, Colorado is one of the most urban states in the United States, with at least 82 percent of its residents living in metropolitan Denver and a group of nearby Front Range cities. And, strikingly, about 90 percent of Coloradans live nearby either I-25 or I-70 (the north–south and east–west interstate highways that cross the state). Colorado is a probusiness state, and yet it is home to few corporate headquarters.

Colorado is a many-splendored as well as a many-splintered state. The state is decidedly remote from most of the major centers of commerce in the nation, and it is also a decentralized and diverse state. Its diversity reflects a citizenry of varied backgrounds and political views.

The state's enormous number of assets, such as its optimistic people, its remarkable beauty, and its wealth of minerals and tourism opportunities, outweigh the state's liabilities. Colorado's problems are viewed by most of its citizens as challenges, as solvable, or even as opportunities, and not as paralyzing burdens. Unifying leadership may be hard to come by and hard to exercise in Colorado, yet somehow, from time to time, it emerges.

# CHAPTER TWO

# Coloradans and
# Their Political Beliefs

Who are the people of Colorado? What are their political interests and beliefs? This chapter examines what demographics and poll data tell us about Coloradans. We also call upon scores of interviews we have had with political activists, media people, and state political leaders.

Surveys and poll results are merely a snapshot of what citizens are thinking at a particular point in time. Times vary, and so do citizens' views about politics and politicians. Thus, in economic downturns, people are understandably more negative about political leaders. Also, when Republicans hold office, Republicans are more favorable to their officeholders and the political offices they hold. Democrats similarly give much higher favorable rankings when their folks are in office.

Specific percentage distributions vary in different polls at different times. It is the *patterns* that are of interest. We have found Coloradans to be rather consistent in their political outlook and in attitudes on issues such as taxes, guns, and the citizens' right to put initiated laws and constitutional amendments on the ballot. Coloradans, as we will discuss, have also been rather consistently conservative and anti–federal government over the past generation. On certain other issues, such as whether they approve or disapprove of a certain governor or whether on not they consider themselves "environmentalists," we find some changes.

We have conducted three statewide random-sample surveys of adult Coloradans. These were taken in 1990, 2006, and 2010. The polls were conducted by Talmey-Drake Research and Strategy, Inc. In the 2010 poll, we devoted extra effort to include people who primarily or exclusively use cell phones. There are, it turns out, few differences between those with cell phones and traditional telephone landline users.

When possible we have used other surveys made available to us by the media, pollster Floyd Ciruli, the Denver Metro Chamber of Commerce, the Gallup Poll, and the Hewlett Foundation. When possible, we compare Colorado findings with similar national surveys.

### MOST ADULTS BORN ELSEWHERE

One of the major demographic realities in Colorado in the twenty-first century is that nearly seven of every ten adult Coloradans were born elsewhere. Colorado is sixth in the nation for state residents claiming some other state as their birthplace. The list of outsiders includes current governor John Hickenlooper, current lieutenant governor Joe Garcia, and current U.S. senators Mark Udall and Michael Bennet. Colorado thus in many ways is and has been a state of "immigrants."

There were nearly one hundred thousand "Coloradans" when the state began in 1876. By World War II, Colorado's population had grown to over 1 million people. In 2013 we were at the 5.3 million mark, and the state could nearly double in size to 10 million or so by 2060.

Where do Coloradans come from? They come from virtually all corners of the United States. Most are either from nearby states or from heavily populated states such as California. More come from the West, Midwest. and South than from the Northeast. Texas, California, Arizona, and Florida alone account for about a third of Colorado's incoming new residents. Illinois also sends a large number. Some of the neighboring states to Colorado, such as Wyoming, Oklahoma, Kansas, and Nebraska, also export a reasonable share of residents to the Centennial State.

U.S. census data also track the out-migration from Colorado. Not surprisingly, the Sun Belt states of California, Texas, Arizona, and Florida lead the list of where Coloradans go when they leave. New Mexico and the state of Washington are next in line for exiting Coloradans. Overall, census data suggest Coloradans stay in the West as opposed to migrating to the Midwest or East.

Colorado has a relatively young population. Young adults, often risk-taking, college-educated, and outdoor-loving adults, come in search of both jobs and the great wilderness and skiing attractions the state so amply provides. Colorado's challenging winters help explain why older Americans probably do not relocate in large numbers to the state. Doubtless, too, these same factors explain why some older Coloradans move to the southern or southwestern United States after retirement.

Colorado has not been considered a major retirement location. The high elevation is hardly an inducement for people concerned about heart troubles, and a majority of people over age seventy have such concerns.

Until recently, the population over age sixty-five has been less than 10 percent of the state total. This is gradually changing. About 11 percent of Coloradans are now sixty-five years old or older, and this is expected to increase to perhaps 18 percent in 2030. Many of the baby boomers who came to Colorado in the 1970s and 1980s are deciding to make Colorado their primary home when they retire.[1]

### EDUCATION AND ETHNICITY

Colorado in recent years has had one of the highest percentages of residents with a college degree, often second or third after Massachusetts. Yet, according to one observer, "half of them earned their degrees in other states, meaning that the good taxpayers of Michigan, Massachusetts, Indiana and Ohio paid for that education, after which the recipient took it to Colorado."[2]

One reason Colorado usually bounces back from its cyclical economic downturns is this reservoir of well-educated younger workers. Colorado's investment in higher education, however, has been decidedly below that of most other states. Indeed, it is one of the Colorado paradoxes that Colorado ranks at the top of the states with residents with college degrees and near the bottom for its state government investment in public higher education.[3]

Colorado's racial and ethnic makeup is predominantly white and European, although the state's minority populations continue to grow. Minorities will comprise about 30 percent of the state's population in 2020 and at least 33 percent in 2035. Hispanics and Asian Americans are the fastest-growing ethnic populations. The largest numbers of Colorado's blacks, Hispanics, and Asian Americans are concentrated in or near Denver.

As of 2012, non-Hispanic whites comprised about 72 percent of Colorado's population, Hispanics at least 20 percent, blacks slightly more than 4 percent, Asians slightly less than 3 percent, and others, including Native Americans and people of mixed races, about 3.5 percent. Colorado is ranked sixth in the nation in numbers of Hispanics and about twenty-eighth in numbers of blacks. See Table 1.

The nation's population, in contrast, is considerably more diverse than Colorado's population. Thus, as noted, Colorado will be about 30 percent minority in 2020, but the United States will be about 40 percent minority. As of this writing, Hawaii, New Mexico, California, and Texas, as well as the District of Columbia, already have minority populations exceeding 50 percent.

Table 1. Recent and Future Demographic Trends

|  | 2000 | 2015 | 2030 |
|---|---|---|---|
| White, non-Hispanic | 75.4% | 71.7% | 68.9% |
| Hispanic origin | 17.1 | 20.2 | 22.7 |
| Black, non-Hispanic | 3.9 | 4.2 | 4.4 |
| Asian/Pacific Islander | 2.6 | 2.8 | 2.9 |
| American Indian | 1.0 | 1.0 | 1.1 |

*Source:* Colorado State Demographer Elizabeth Garner/Colorado Department of Local Affairs.

Women comprise nearly half the workforce. Minorities comprise about 20 percent or more of the workforce. Colorado's minorities earn higher incomes than their counterparts in most parts of the country, yet there is still a wide margin between minority and white, non-Hispanic earning power in the state.

Most Coloradans of all races and ethnic groups believe race relations have improved yet need to be improved further. Significant numbers of blacks still report feeling discriminated against by the police, in housing, in getting a job, and in job promotion. Everyone agrees that schools need to do a better job of teaching minorities, and that everyone should try much harder to be fair.

Sixty percent of those surveyed in our 2010 poll of adult Coloradans agreed with the statement "If minorities are not receiving fair treatment when it comes to jobs or housing, it is the responsibility of government to step in and make sure they are treated fairly." While this is not the same as saying one would pay more taxes to help ensure and enforce fairness, it does suggest a general affirmation of social justice ideals.

Hispanics, in part because of concentrated populations and in part because of strongly developed roots in Colorado's history, have enjoyed reasonable representation in the state legislature. Hispanics have served in major leadership posts in the state Senate and House of Representatives.

Federico Pena, a Texas-born Hispanic, served two terms as mayor of Denver. Lionel Rivera, a Hispanic who is philosophically a conservative and a Republican, was elected to two terms as mayor of Colorado Springs. Denver and Colorado Springs are Colorado's two most-populous cities.

Ken Salazar, a Hispanic from Manassa, a small town in Southern Colorado (and also the home of legendary world-champion prizefighter Jack Dempsey), was elected Colorado attorney general, then U.S. senator from Colorado, and then in 2009 became secretary of the interior for U.S. president Barack Obama. John Salazar, Ken's older brother, served as the

U.S. representative for Colorado's third congressional district from 2005 to 2011.

George Brown, a black who was a former state legislator, was elected lieutenant governor of Colorado in 1974. Another African American, Joe Rogers, served as lieutenant governor from 1999 to 2003. Denver's first black mayor was Wellington Webb, who was elected in 1991 and served three four-year terms. Michael Hancock, also African American, was elected mayor of Denver in 2011.

Although Colorado is only 4 percent African American, in 2009 two blacks served in the top leadership posts in the Colorado state legislature. Peter Groff of Denver was president of the Colorado Senate. Terrance Carroll, also of Denver, was speaker of the House of Representatives. Joe Garcia, a Hispanic American, was elected with John Hickenlooper to serve as lieutenant governor.

Coloradans have thus elected minorities to high political office, even though blacks and Hispanics are still a minority of the voters.

### OTHER CHARACTERISTICS OF COLORADANS

The typical Coloradan is 35.5 years old, lives in the Denver suburbs, is employed, and owns a home. Median household income in Colorado has fluctuated between $55,000 and $61,000 in recent years.

Homeownership declined during the Recession of 2008–10, as did home values. There were some exceptions. Thus, as of this writing, the median price for a single-family home in Aspen, at around $6 million, was the highest in any city in the country. Indeed, the lowest-priced single-family home on the Aspen market was listed for $599,000 (and that was located in a trailer park!).

At the other extreme, nearly fifteen thousand or so homeless people are estimated to be living in the state. Many are homeless for short periods. Colorado's homeless population is proportionally less than a number of states along America's two coasts, yet large enough to make Colorado one of the top ten states for homelessness.

About 28 percent of Colorado households are occupied by a single person, and this rises to about 40 percent in Denver. Analysts explain this as partly the result of people living longer, people getting married later, and divorce and lifestyle factors.

Another twenty-five thousand Coloradans live in state or local correctional facilities. At least eight thousand Coloradans hold elective office of some kind, ranging from U.S. senator to library board member. Around

240,000 work for local governments, including a large number of public school teachers.

Estimates of how many people work for the state government vary from around fifty thousand to over ninety thousand. Estimates are inexact because at least half of state employees work in the public college and university systems, and many of these are part-timers such as student workers, teaching assistants, and adjunct instructors. In addition, some state employment is seasonal, such as state park employees. Others are partly paid by the state and partly paid by U.S. government programs.

Coloradans ski, hunt, fish, and enjoy the outdoors more than most Americans. Colorado is first in the nation in the proportion of citizens who subscribe to outdoor recreation magazines. According to the U.S. Fish and Wildlife Service, Colorado in recent years has led all states in revenue from hunting license sales.

One national study concluded that the Denver area "has nearly three times as many skiers than the national average." Denver area residents also have much higher than average participation as hikers, cyclists, runners, backpackers, and campers.

Colorado median annual household income is about $58,000, having declined from nearly $60,000 before the Recession of 2008–10. That figure was about average in the nation. Coloradan males live on average more than seventy-five years, and women more than eighty years, putting the state among the nation's top ten in terms of longevity. Violent crime occurs less frequently in Colorado than elsewhere. However, no lack of lawyers exists. As of a few years ago, there was one lawyer for every 284 Coloradans.

## COLORADANS VIEW STATE GOVERNMENT

Most Coloradans, 56 percent according to our random sample in 2010, say their state government is inefficient and wasteful of taxpayer dollars. Only 36 percent said state government is "run pretty well and efficient."

Seventy percent say Colorado state government does "a poor or only fair job of keeping taxes down." Seventy-six percent are displeased with the state's ability to get things done. We also asked Coloradans whether they would favor privatizing or "outsourcing" a lot of state operations. Here is the statement we shared with them: "The taxpayers could save money, and a lot of things would get done more efficiently, if more of the functions of state government were turned over to private companies." Coloradans were split on this: 42 percent agreeing, 10 percent neutral or ambivalent, and 43 percent disagreeing.

## GOING IN THE RIGHT/WRONG DIRECTION?

Over the past generation, we and the Talmey-Drake polling organization have asked Coloradans about every five years how things were going in the state. The data in Table 2 speak for themselves. Solid majorities believed Colorado was generally going in the right direction until the 9/11 terrorist attacks on the World Trade Center in New York. Then the Recession of 2008–10 hit. As a result of those two shocks, public opinion on the direction Colorado was going practically reversed from "right direction" to "wrong direction." See Table 2.

We and the Talmey-Drake polling company also asked the question "Has the quality of life in Colorado gotten better, worse, or stayed the same?"

Coloradans in our 2010 survey responded as follows: "better," 9 percent; "stayed the same," 45 percent; and "worse," 44 percent. This response of "worse" was at least a 15 percent increase over similar poll responses in 1990 and 2006.

We also asked Coloradans to evaluate Gov. Bill Ritter, the legislature, and the courts. Coloradans in 2010 were noticeably more critical of their governor and state legislature than over the past generation. Indeed, Governor Ritter and the then Democratic-controlled state legislature earned higher disapproval than approval ratings.

Governors Richard Lamm, Roy Romer and Bill Owens averaged somewhere north of 60 percent approval during their governorships that together spanned thirty-two years.

Bill Ritter won a landslide victory in 2006 with a winning margin of about 16 percent. He enjoyed solid approval in his first year but began to slide in 2008. His popular approval ratings sank in 2009. By April 2010, 45 percent in our survey disapproved of his performance while only 40 percent (mostly Democrats) gave him positive ratings. Yet even among Democrats, Ritter won only two-thirds approval, with a surprising 32 percent either disapproving, not sure, or had no opinion about his leadership performance.

Ritter decided in early 2010 not to seek a second term as Colorado governor. He might have pulled an upset, but the betting as election year 2010 began was that Ritter might join governors John Vanderhoof (1974) and Steve McNichols (1962) as a defeated incumbent, a relatively uncommon event in modern Colorado politics.

Discontent with the Colorado state legislature also was pronounced. Earlier polls in the 1990s, for example, indicated nearly two-to-one ap-

Table 2. Is Colorado Going in Right/Wrong Direction?

QUESTION: "And what about things in Colorado? Would you say things in Colorado are generally going in the right direction, or do you feel things have pretty much gotten off on the wrong track in the past few years?"

|  | September 1990 | May 1995 | June 2000 | June 2006 | April 2010 |
|---|---|---|---|---|---|
| Right track | 59% | 56% | 60% | 51% | 39% |
| No opinion | 11 | 10 | 12 | 15 | 11 |
| Wrong track | 30 | 34 | 28 | 34 | 50 |

*Source:* Colorado College Citizens Polls, 1990, 2000, 2010, and Talmey-Drake Polls, 1995, 2006 (*N* = 614, 601, 600, 613, 603, respectively).

proval of the legislature. An August 2007 survey conducted of registered voters on behalf of the Denver Metro Chamber of Commerce, however, indicated the legislature was held in less esteem than it had been earlier. The poll found 41 percent approval and 36 percent disapproval. Our survey in 2010 found even greater disapproval.

Surely some of this disapproval for both the governor and the legislature can be attributed to the recession that started in mid-2008. But various other surveys we analyzed clearly indicated that citizen disapproval of the governor and the legislature had begun rising in late 2007, even before the major impact of the recession hit the Colorado populace.

The low approval ratings may be a reflection on Governor Ritter's legislative leadership skills or narrow political background. It also reflected the tough economic times. It may also have something to do with Coloradans liking "divided government," when one branch is controlled by one party and the other is controlled by the opposition party. This is difficult to prove, yet Ritter was the first Democrat in over a generation to have a unified rather than a divided government.

Coloradans are more approving of state courts. They are obviously less knowledgeable about the judiciary. Still, the courts won two-to-one voter approval in both our 2006 and 2010 surveys. See Figure 1.

In 2006 Coloradans solidly defeated a ballot initiative proposal to limit the terms of judges and justices to ten years. But our 2010 poll indicates that Colorado voters still like the notion of term limits, which were voted in for state executive and legislative officials in the early 1990s. Two-thirds (66 percent) in our 2010 survey said they would limit the number of years a judge may serve to twelve years.

Conservatives and Republicans favor term limits more strongly than do Democrats and liberals, which is also the case elsewhere around the

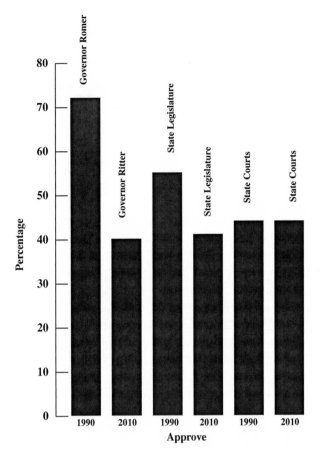

Figure 1. Coloradans' Assessments of Branches of State Government

QUESTION: "Do you approve or disapprove of the job the branches of state government are doing?"

*Source*: Colorado College Citizens Polls, 1990, 2010 (*N* = 614, 603).

country. Doubtless this also reflects the fact the Colorado Supreme Court in these years had a five-to-two Democratic membership and had angered many conservatives, on more than a few occasions, with what conservatives believed to be liberal rulings.

What about the lieutenant governor? The general public is largely unaware of a lieutenant governor's performance. Still, we asked: "Agree or Disagree—the office of lieutenant governor is a waste of money and should

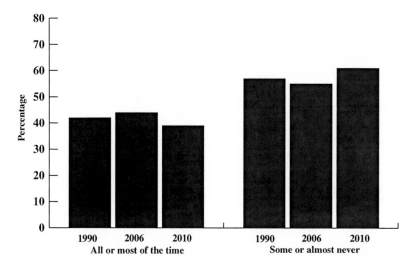

Figure 2. Trust in State Government

QUESTION: "Generally speaking, would you say you can trust our state government to do what is right all the time, most of the time, only some of the time, or almost never?"

*Source*: Colorado College Citizens Polls, 1990, 2006, 2010 (*N* = 614, 613, 603).

be abolished." A slight plurality agreed: 33 percent said yes, 32 percent disagreed, and the rest were either neutral or gave no opinion.

## TRUST IN STATE GOVERNMENT

Overall, at least in 2010, most Coloradans were not confident their state government was doing what was right for the citizens. There was a pervasive skepticism and even a cynicism toward state leaders and state politics. See Figure 2.

Let us look at those who have the least trust in Colorado's state government and the legislature and Governor Ritter. Those who were least satisfied with the state and its officials, not surprisingly, say they were bored or turned off by politics and politicians. Those who say officials don't care what people "like me" think also said they don't trust their government to do what is right.

Lower-income Coloradans and older people also have less trust in government. But at least in 2010, the most consistently distrustful of state government respondents were conservative in political outlook and Republicans, Libertarians, and "Tea Party" supporters. Close to 80 percent of conservative Republicans and their allies told us they do not trust Colorado's state government to do what they—conservatives—believe is right.

Note, however, that this snapshot poll was taken at an unusual moment when the governor, both chambers of the state legislature, and Colorado's Supreme Court were all "controlled" by Democrats, as were the White House and the U.S. Congress.

Thus, much of this conservative distrust may well be rational judgment in so far as those in presumed power positions were not the people they voted for. Their party and ideological outlook had lost—at least for the time being. Just a few years earlier, Republicans and conservatives had indicated much higher levels of trust in a Republican governor, Bill Owens, and in their Republican president, George W. Bush. Partisanship is obviously a powerful filtering lens through which a majority of Coloradans frame how they evaluate public officials and whether they trust governments to act in their interests.

### ATTITUDES TOWARD THE U.S. GOVERNMENT

If Coloradans were harsh in their political attitudes toward state officials and state government, they were downright hostile toward the more removed and "more taxing" national government. As noted, a majority of Coloradans think their state government is inefficient or worse, but they still prefer state government over the U.S. government. One citizen in rural Crawford (on the Western Slope) told us: "The local and state governments aren't all that bad, but I don't like the government in Washington—they really know how to waste money."[4]

Data in Figure 3 suggest six times as many Coloradans believe local governments are more efficient in their use of tax dollars than is the federal government.

"The closer government is to the people, the more we trust it," wrote *Denver Post* editor Dan Haley. "Coloradans, it seems, are pretty comfortable with their hometown leaders and their local governments." Haley explained: "In small towns, and even in cities the size of Denver, a small pebble tossed by a citizen into political waters can make waves. But the government in Washington DC is too far removed from the people."[5]

Six out of ten Coloradans in both our 2006 and 2010 surveys said things in Washington "have pretty seriously gotten off on the wrong track in the past few years." Similar national polls found people around the country had almost identical disappointment in the federal government.[6]

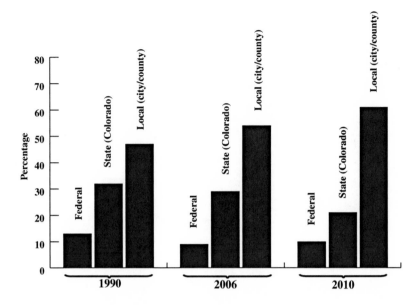

Figure 3. Efficiency of Levels of Government

QUESTION: "Which of the levels of government—federal, state, or local—do you think is most effective?"

*Source*: Colorado College Citizens Polls, 1990, 2006, 2010 (*N* = 614, 613, 603).

Trust or confidence in the U.S. government, both by Coloradans and other Americans, fell to a new low in 2010. Back in the late 1950s and early 1960s, nearly 70 percent of Americans believed that leaders in Washington would do the right thing, namely act on behalf of the public or national interest. Nowadays, less than 30 percent of the public has that kind of confidence in the national government. Similarly, Coloradans are even more distrustful of the "feds" than in the past.

A majority of Coloradans think the federal government has become too powerful and too intrusive in their everyday lives. Those conducting our poll read three statements, listed in Figure 4, to those being interviewed. The statements were randomized so as not to bias the results.

Conservatives and Republicans, not surprisingly, were by far the most hostile to the role of the federal government. Liberals and environmentalists held a decidedly more affirmative view of the role and responsibilities of the federal government.

Part of what is now being called the "new populism" is that people around the country are not just angry at big banks, big corporations, and

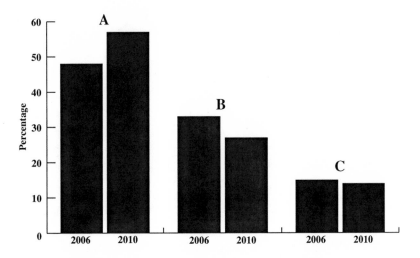

Figure 4. Coloradans on the Role of the U.S. Government

QUESTION: "I will read you three statements, and after I read each, please tell me which of the three comes closest to your view about government today."

A. "The federal government today has become too powerful and too intrusive in the everyday life of Americans."

B. "The power of the federal government today is just about right given today's situation and needs."

C. "Given the world we live in today, the federal government should exert even more power to protect our citizens and promote the well-being of all segments of society."

*Source*: Colorado College Citizens Polls, 2006, 2010 (*N* = 613, 603).

Wall Street. They regularly express displeasure with the federal government, its deficits, and its huge role in American life. Average citizens may not trust big business, but they also do not trust Washington to stand up for them either.

"In other words," writes political analyst Matt Bai, "voters perceive both business and government as part of an interdependent system, and it is hard for them to separate out the culpability of either."[7]

ON POLITICS AND POLITICIANS

Coloradans, like most people elsewhere in the United States, are not fond of politicians. They understand we need politicians from the political parties to make compromises and conduct the public business.

Table 3. Populist Initiatives—Right and Left

---

*Conservative initiatives*

---

TABOR tax and spending limits

Term limits for state officials

No special rights for gays and lesbians (Amendment 2 in 1992)

6% limit on annual increase in state expenditures

---

*Progressive initiatives*

---

Guaranteed funds for K–12 education (Amendment 23)

Transparency in the state legislature (GAVEL Amendment)

Legalization of medical marijuana

High-stakes 24-hour gambling in three historic mining camps, with tax income devoted to
    historic preservation and community colleges

Lottery funds mainly devoted to open space and recreation

Strict limits on lobbyists' gifts to state legislators

Requirements for wind power in generating electricity

Strict limits on campaign contributions for state officials

Yet 64 percent of Coloradans said they were "generally bored or turned off by most politicians." Those who are most turned off by politics and politicians say they do not follow the news regularly, they are more likely to be unaffiliated, and they tend to live outside the Denver metropolitan area.

Elected officials campaign for office saying they will listen a lot and be representative as well as work hard on behalf of all their constituents. But that's not what most Coloradans believe is the case. Sixty-one percent of those polled said they do not believe most politicians care about "what people like me think." More than 70 percent of Coloradans complain that Colorado state officials do not do a good job of representing them. And this percentage has steadily increased over twenty years.

Most people believe taxes are too high (despite Colorado's comparatively low tax burden), that government is too inefficient, and that there should be term limits on all public officials. Term limits already exist for the governor and state legislators. Our polls indicate, as noted earlier, majority support for limiting state judges to something like a twelve-year term.

Colorado is well known for its use of citizen initiatives. These come from both the right and the left. See Table 3.

Most elected political leaders, along with many business leaders, would make it harder for Colorado citizens to place ballot initiatives on election-year ballots. Several governors, state legislators, and business officials complain that too many complicated and overly restrictive citizen initiatives have been approved in recent years. They would prefer that lawmaking be left to lawmakers. Many political leaders argue that Colorado's frequent use of the initiative weakens representative government. Establishment leaders want a "representative democracy," not a "direct democracy," and do not want "ballot-box budgeting."

Lawmaking, they say, should mainly be left for the regular legislative process, where thoughtful hearings can take place, all points of view can be considered, and reasonable compromises can be artfully worked out. This is not, however, how the average citizen views it. Public opinion surveys for the Denver Metro Chamber of Commerce regularly show two-thirds to even three-quarters of registered voters are supportive of the current Colorado initiative system that allows the people to petition for a statewide vote on changes in the state constitution.

Coloradans in our polls worry that there are sometimes "too many" initiatives on their ballots, but a majority actually respond that there are not enough or there are about the right number of initiatives put before the voters.

Many conservative and progressive populists insist that Colorado's initiative process is still a much-needed safety valve for addressing policy controversies on which the state legislature either cannot or will not act. And both liberals and conservatives, libertarians and communitarians, can point to a number of victories they have achieved over the past couple of generations because of the initiative process.

Less than a third of Coloradans favor making it more difficult to place initiatives and referendums on the Colorado ballot. See Figure 5.

Conservatives and unaffiliated voters are more strongly in favor of keeping the initiative process as it is. In contrast, those who would make it harder to qualify initiatives on the ballot tend to be Democrats with a liberal political outlook. This may be explained in part because these individuals understand that the Taxpayers' Bill of Rights (TABOR) initiative and some of its kindred constitutional amendments have forced a slower rate of growth in the government programs than they would prefer or even forced cutbacks of a number of state government services that they, liberal Democrats, support.

Another reason Coloradans are "turned off" or disappointed in politics is that they perceive that wealthy people or rich "special interests" exercise an undue influence through campaign contributions or lobbying efforts. One longtime Republican county leader in Mineral County told us that, after years of watching Colorado politicians, he was afraid to say it, "but most of

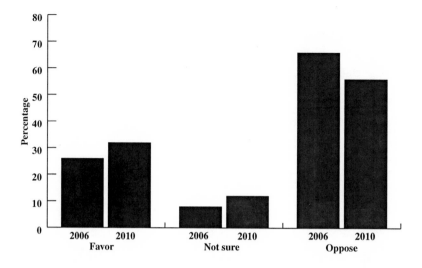

Figure 5. Making Referendums and Initiatives More Difficult

QUESTION: "Suppose there were a proposed amendment to the Colorado Constitution that would make it more difficult to place initiatives and referendums on Colorado's ballots, by increasing the number of signatures required to place a citizen initiative on the ballot. If the election were held today, would you vote in favor of, or against, a proposal to make it more difficult for citizens to place initiatives and referendums on the ballot on Colorado?"

*Source*: Colorado College Citizens Polls, June 2006, April 2010 (*N* = 613, 603).

them are bought and paid for."[8] Poll respondents in both parties concurred with his sentiment. A remarkably small percentage of Coloradans seem to think elected officials decide on behalf of people like themselves. See Figure 6 for the survey results and trends on this issue since 1990.

Yet another reason people are disappointed with politics and politicians is the increasing frequency of negative ads. Former Colorado U.S. senator Tim Wirth said all the negativity was one of the reasons he retired from politics. "Negative campaigns work. That is why there are so many of them and so few politicians running on their records or on the issues." He said he knew in 1992 he would have to deal with all that, "but in tearing down my opponent" he knew that he would be diminishing himself and that he risked becoming a person whom he could not respect.[9]

Colorado pollster Paul Talmey once suggested there may be at least a

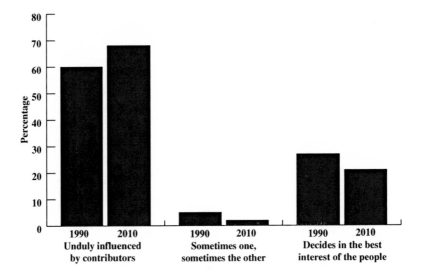

Figure 6. Do Big Campaign Contributors Run State Government?

QUESTION: "Speaking of elections, some people are saying that the way political campaigns for public office in Colorado are financed today has given too much political influence in the state capitol to big contributors. Others say that state government has not been particularly influenced by big campaign contributions and that it generally makes decisions in what it thinks is for the best interest of the people of Colorado. What do you think? Is our state government unduly influenced by big campaign contributions, or does it generally try to decide things in the best interest of the people of the state?"

*Source*: Colorado College Citizens Polls, September 1990, April 2010 (*N* = 614, 603).

touch of political paranoia among Coloradans. "Political paranoia has been stereotypically associated with the right, and while there is no shortage of right-wing paranoids in Colorado," wrote Talmey, "Coloradans who consider themselves politically liberal are actually more likely to accept the notion of a secretive cabal running the country than are those with a conservative bent."[10]

But Talmey wrote those words soon after the Ronald Reagan era. Today, well into the twenty-first century, those who consider themselves "very conservative" are more likely than liberals to fear that powerful elite interests may be making a lot of key political and policy decisions. That we asked this question in the Obama era and not in the Reagan era explains some of this.

In any event, two-thirds (65 percent) agree with this statement: "Even though you almost never hear much about them, there are a few really powerful people in the country who pretty much make all the important decisions about how the country is run."

This notion of people feeling that they, and even their elected representatives, are losing control of their lives and that the American Dream may not be as available as it once was to most people is backed up by other sentiments of powerlessness and pessimism. Thus, as earlier noted, a plurality (47 percent) of Coloradans told us that they believe our best years as a nation are behind us. Only 43 percent said, more hopefully, that our best years are still ahead of us. This is a marked change from just a few years ago. Some of the antigovernment fervor of Tea Party activists similarly indicates disaffection with government, politics, and politicians.

In sum, Coloradans are skeptics when it comes to politics and politicians and political parties. Coloradans are split three ways in party registration—one-third Republicans, one-third Democrats, and one-third unaffiliated voters. Nearly 35 percent of Coloradans identify themselves as Republicans compared to a much smaller 25 percent nationwide. Still, it is the ticket-splitters and independents who really count here.

### THE COLORADO POLITICAL LANDSCAPE

Coloradans are somewhat more conservative in political outlook than are U.S. citizens, yet not as conservative as the citizens in most of our even more conservative neighboring states.

In our 2010 survey, 46 percent identified themselves as conservatives in political outlook. About 31 percent call themselves "middle-of-the-roaders." Only 22 percent said they are somewhat or very liberal. Conservatives hold more than a two-to-one margin over liberals. Further, just 7 percent of Coloradans say they are "very liberal" while 16 percent described themselves as "very conservative."

National surveys in 2010 and 2012 found almost 40 percent calling themselves conservative, 37 percent calling themselves moderates, and around 21 percent calling themselves liberal. Thus Coloradans are somewhat more conservative than folks around the country. This conservatism shapes not only Colorado politics but also the political culture of both the Republican and Democratic parties. It doubtless pulls the Republican Party to the right

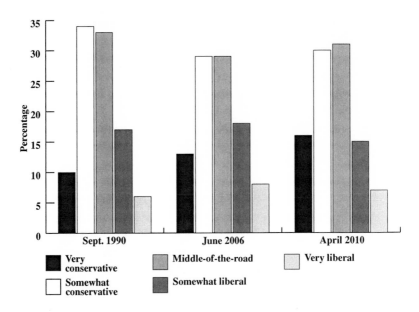

Figure 7. Conservative, Middle-of-the-Road, or Liberal?

QUESTION: "In terms of political outlook, do you normally think of yourself as very conservative, somewhat conservative, middle-of-the-road, somewhat liberal, or very liberal?"

*Source*: Colorado Citizens Polls, 1990, 2006, 2010 (*N* = 603–614). Note that this question was asked of a random sample of citizens, not just registered voters.

and often pulls Democrats, out of necessity, more toward the middle than otherwise might be the case. See Figure 7.

As a result of these findings, which have held pretty steady over the past generation, we concur with election analysts and campaign strategists who often offer the following political profile of likely voters in Colorado elections. Note there are variations over time as one party or ideology enjoys a small resurgence and the other falters. But for the past few decades and probably into the next decade, this is what a typical statewide candidate faced or will face. See Table 4.

As Table 4 lays out, Colorado candidates regularly find a hard core of close to 20 percent staunch "principled conservatives." They vote in high numbers and they consistently prefer Republicans.

The opposite camp of staunchly consistent "principled liberals" is smaller in number, perhaps about 11 percent on a regular basis. And these

Table 4. Colorado's Political Landscape

---

**Principled conservatives** (approximately 16%–18%): Fox News conservatives, Sarah Palin supporters, Mike Rosen (KOA) listeners, Doug Bruce conservative populists, many Tea Party and Ron Paul libertarians, along with Focus on the Family values champions (almost never vote for a Democrat)

**Pragmatic conservatives** (approximately 24%–27%): Many business leaders, many *Wall Street Journal* subscribers, some social conservatives, some fiscal conservatives who are moderates on social issues, some conservatives who occasionally split their vote but generally vote Republican

**Pragmatic centrists–moderates** (approximately 26%–29%): Swing voters, ticket splitters, often do not follow politics closely, often late to decide how they will vote (or even if they will vote), most likely to be swayed by political commercials, hard-hitting negative advertisements, by candidate personality, and by endorsements

**Pragmatic liberals** (approximately 15%–17%): CNN liberals, often National Public Radio listeners, *New York Times* subscribers, fiscal moderates, environmentalists, liberals on social issues

**Principled liberals** (approximately 10%–11%): Paul Krugman, Rachel Maddow MSNBC liberals, view government as a problem solver and not as a problem, strong environmentalists, pro–health care (rarely if ever vote for a Republican)

---

*Note*: These are general estimates made by the authors based on poll data as well as discussions with candidates and political analysts. Each election is shaped not only by party identification and ideological outlook but also by candidate personality and style, by how well financed and managed a campaign is, and by new and sometimes disruptive state and national policy issues. This Colorado Political Landscape is, however, what statewide candidates generally faced in the early years of the twenty-first century.

two groups have little in common with respect to political and ideological views.

These two groups, based on similar national surveys and analysis, have probably become more doctrinaire and ideological in their practical views over the past several decades. Our data suggest this but do not allow us to confirm this.

In between these extremes are three groups that plainly hold the balance of political power in Colorado. Pragmatic conservatives might include nearly 25 percent. Pragmatic liberals are somewhat smaller, in the 16 to 17 percent range. Independents, or centrist moderates, make up the middle. Their numbers vary from election to election, yet they often consist of approximately a quarter of the Colorado electorate. Their numbers decline in lower profile or "more boring" elections.

These moderate independents are the golden treasure trove for political strategists and campaign managers. They sometimes include people who say they are Republicans yet who are socially moderate or believe strongly in investing in education and infrastructure. They can also include Democrats who dislike taxes and wasteful government programs. They are also, as we indicate in Table 4, typically more influenced by a candidate's character, personality, and style than are hard-core liberals and conservatives.

The well-respected Pew Research Center in Washington DC conducted a similar national survey in early 2011, several months after our 2010 Colorado College Citizens Poll. They found similar results, although they were polling a national population somewhat more liberal than Colorado's. They found at least 10 percent whom they labeled "bystanders," people who said they seldom voted and rarely followed politics. We have at least a similar population of bystanders or disaffected citizens in Colorado, and for presentation purposes cluster them in with "independents."

The Pew national poll found that those in the middle of these typologies have little in common, aside from their consistent avoidance of partisan and ideological labels. They also found a large ideological gulf between the most conservative Republicans and the most liberal Democrats. The gulf was larger than in previous surveys at the national level.[11]

These data suggest the following. Republicans usually campaign, indeed they have to campaign, to their fairly sizeable conservative base (or campaign "to the right," as consultants put it). They also have to try to appeal to the independents or moderates in both parties. Republicans have sometimes hurt their general election chances by nominating candidates whose conservatism hampers their chance of winning the general election in November (as happened both in 2006 and 2010).

Conversely, Democrats may occasionally consider possible liberal candidates. In fact, however, they fare better in November with moderate-leaning pragmatic liberals who can appeal to moderates and at least some pragmatic conservatives. Gov. Roy Romer, who grew up in rural Colorado and became a successful businessman, was the type of moderate Democrat who could win. Indeed, he won five statewide elections, two for state treasurer and three for governor.

Ken Salazar was yet another acceptable moderate Democrat who could appeal to moderates and transcend being labeled a "liberal Democrat." The fact that he came from a family of long-time rural Coloradans and was a Catholic helped to broaden his appeal.

John Hickenlooper, who understood better than most people that Colorado had become a purple state, mostly identified himself as an independent, a businessperson, and an entrepreneur. He seldom described himself as a Democrat in his 2010 campaign for governor or later. A year or so into his governorship, some Democrats even wondered whether he was one of them, though his base is plainly Democratic, especially Democrats and moderate-leaning independents in the Denver metropolitan area. But what was important was that the likeable Hickenlooper had successfully earned branding as a probusiness, pro-jobs, promilitary centrist.

The larger point is that the center plays a crucial, pivotal role in Colorado politics, and Democratic strategists know this. If anything, Democrats, because of the numbers, are keenly aware that it is nearly impossible for them to win statewide elections by only cultivating and attracting those who call themselves liberal Democrats.

Colorado Democrats were fortunate that from 2006 to 2010, moderate and so-called unaffiliated voters leaned toward the Democratic side in statewide elections. This had not been the case in George W. Bush's 2000 and 2004 election years.

Another way to assess Coloradans and their political outlook is to place large numbers of Coloradans in two general camps. We call them (1) liberty-loving libertarian individualists and (2) communitarian civic moralists. Not everybody, to be sure, fits neatly into those two political camps. But our survey suggests Coloradans often divide over questions of liberty and equality, or notions of individual versus governmental responsibility.

Coloradans are split. Many dislike the state and national governments. Yet many others believe, at least occasionally, government can be a positive problem-solving agent serving the common good.

We make the case, as we suggested in chapter 1, that Colorado politics can often be understood as a clash of rival political cultures. The usual dominant political culture in the state, as it usually is in the nation, is an individualistic or moderately libertarian philosophical orientation. It is an ideology that evolves from a deep-seated preference for liberty and a constrained, limited role for state government. In a sense, although a simplistic one, it is the spirit of Reaganism combined with TABORism.

The usual minority political culture in Colorado also prizes liberty, but it acknowledges at least an equal preference for equality, fairness, and social justice. This somewhat more communitarian civic moralism understands that the state has to be a problem solver, that "taxes are the rent we pay for civilization," and that an enviable quality of life is an important goal for government. In a sense, again to simplify, this is part New Dealism, part progressivism, and part environmental conservationism.

Understanding these diverse political cultures helps us, we believe, to understand many of the ongoing political conflicts, contests, and motives that frame Colorado politics.

Below are a handful of questions that show marked differences in the general policy and political principles Coloradans hold. The perspective shared here doubtless encourages our respondents to align with one position rather than another or to vote one way as opposed to another. No one of these questions makes this case in a compelling way. But the series of them builds a case that Coloradans divide when it comes to generalized libertarian versus generalized communitarian points of view.

We asked people to indicate their agreement (which one do you agree with most?) with either an individualistic perspective or a decidedly more communitarian political prospective. The results were: (A) "Each individual should take care of him or herself" (55% agreed), and (B) "Government should work to make people's lives—and community life—better" (34% agreed).

The statements were randomly rotated so as not to bias the response. Five percent ducked committing by volunteering "both" as their response. Six percent had no opinion or did not respond.

True, many people might at least partially agree with both these principled propositions. Yet we forced the issue by asking which one they most preferred. And the responses, we believe, are another indication of the individualistic, liberty-loving, take-care-of-yourself ethic that is widespread in Colorado. Still, there is a division. At least one-third responded with communitarian or civic-moralistic sentiments.

We also asked those we polled whether they believed liberty is more important than equality. Our 2010 results are shown in Figure 8.

Coloradans, in common with Americans throughout the country, have been raised and educated to revere liberty as well as the principle of equality before the law, equality in voting, and the more generalized idea of equality of opportunities. But when forced to choose liberty over equality, most Americans give their vote to liberty. And, not surprisingly, such is the case in Colorado by about a two-to-one margin.

Next we asked our sample to speak to the issue of whether government should have the responsibility to sponsor programs to assist people who cannot take care of themselves. Forty-five percent said they do not see this as the responsibility of government. These dissenters apparently believe charities or churches have that responsibility. Or that needy people need to shape up and take responsibility for themselves. In any event, they did not want to be taxed to provide social welfare benefits to those who lack initiative or fall through the cracks. It reminded us of the message-sending bum-

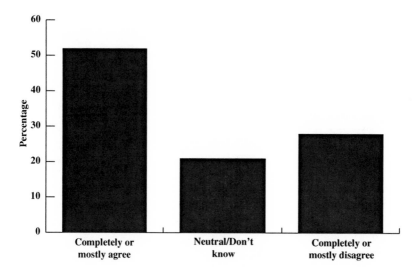

Figure 8. Liberty vs. Equality

STATEMENT: "I believe liberty is more important than equality."

*Source*: Colorado College Citizens Poll, April 2010 (*N* = 603).

per sticker we occasionally see in El Paso County that reads "Work Harder, Millions on Welfare Are Depending on You!" On the other hand, 48 percent responded that welfare was an appropriate responsibility for government.

We also asked whether Colorado, as a state, should be spending more of its tax dollars on buying open spaces and developing parks and recreational areas. Here again, Coloradans are divided. Forty-four percent of the presumably more communitarian and liberal respondents agreed to such spending, even in the midst of a major recession. Forty-three percent of the more libertarian-leaning Coloradans opposed spending tax dollars on open space and parks, suggesting these may be nice public benefits but were not, they believed, necessary.

One question did evoke a more communitarian response. This question raised the issue of the role of government in ensuring fairness and equity to minorities. Most, by a nearly two-to-one margin, find racial discrimination unacceptable and agree it is a proper function of government to make certain minorities are treated fairly. See Table 5.

This is an issue that both state and national courts have presumably settled over the past four generations. What may be significant in the response

Table 5. Government Role in Discrimination

QUESTION: "If minorities are not receiving fair treatment when it comes to jobs and housing, is it the responsibility of government to step in and make sure minorities are treated fairly?"

|  | April 2010 |
| --- | --- |
| Agree | 60% |
| Disagree | 33 |

*Source*: Colorado College Citizens Polls, April 2010 (*N* = 603).

to this question is that there were still a third of Coloradans who opposed government intervening in the housing market or private-sector hiring processes to promote fairness and minimize racial or ethnic discrimination.

Who are they? There are no tidy or easily identifiable dissenters here. But in general, those who do not favor a government role on this issue of discrimination or fairness are far more likely to be conservatives, Republicans, and live in rural areas. They are also, unsurprisingly, more likely to be white rather than racial and ethnic minorities. Finally, they are a bit more likely to be male than female, have less formal education, and view their economic situation as less favorable now then it was in earlier years.

We do not want to overstate our generalization here. But Coloradans are plainly divided on the proper role of government. Politics and governing involves making choices. There are choices about taxes, regulations, and the priority one places on community, efficiency, equality, liberty, prosperity, and security. People differ, sometimes strongly, about these choices and priorities. That is why, of course, we have politics, elections, parties and ongoing and often-heated political arguments. And the arguments will plainly continue because of the persisting divisions in political philosophy we have outlined here.

## DISLIKE TAXES YET WANT MORE SERVICES

Coloradans, like citizens everywhere in the United States, believe their taxes are too high. They also believe their state government should be providing more and better services. This sounds contradictory, and it is, yet this ambivalence is nothing new in America or elsewhere. Life is full of contradictions. Also, few people really understand the cost of public services or see clearly that there is a direct connection between the taxes they pay and the amount and quality of government services provided.

Our polling reveals Coloradans consider themselves heavily taxed and want lower taxes. Thus, 70 percent said the state government is doing only a fair or a poor job of "keeping state taxes down." Fifty-six percent agreed that "taxes in Colorado are too high, and the state legislature has got to do something about cutting the state's tax burden."

Even a majority of Democrats faulted the state for not doing enough to keep taxes down. Republicans, predictably, were even more upset by their tax burden. The message is clear: there is widespread antitax sentiment across the ideological spectrum.

Although most of those surveyed in our recent polls said the state is doing at least a decent job of providing parks and recreational facilities, they were mostly critical of the job the state is doing on most other programs. Thus 70 percent complained, probably correctly, that the state was doing a poor or only fair job of maintaining the state's roads and highways. Sixty-two percent faulted Colorado for not doing enough to promote economic development. A solid majority (57 percent) said Colorado needs to do more to plan and regulate land use. A plurality (47 percent) said the government should be doing more to regulate and control the economy and big business.

All of this is, of course, a painfully familiar refrain for state legislators and governors. "Do more, yet tax us less!" This is a second cousin to the old saying that every elected official has to live with: "What have you done for me lately?"

Most citizens believe more (and presumably better) services and benefits can be rendered, and at the same time taxes could go down. Antitax voters believe there are always more waste, fraud, and inefficiency that can be eliminated. A little problem often arises, however. One person's waste is often another person's vital service or indispensable benefit.

What makes these antitax sentiments noteworthy is that state taxes are relatively low in Colorado. Indeed, Colorado has had the second-lowest state tax collections ($48.91 per $1,000 of personal income) in the United States. And this has been true for some time. "Colorado's combined state and local taxes of $98.01 per $1,000 of personal income were the fifth lowest in the nation in fiscal year 2005–06," according to a report issued by the Colorado Legislative Council staff. They explained: "Colorado's tax structure has had a long tradition of having a strong decentralized local government tax system that has resulted in state taxes that continue to rank among the lowest in the country while local government taxes rank among the highest."[12] The Colorado state sales tax, as of 2012, was only 2.9 percent. The state personal income tax was 4.6 percent. Moreover, this state income tax was a flat tax and not a progressive tax.

Still, the bottom line is that most Coloradans believe more "fat and waste" must be cut in state programs. Current governor John Hickenlooper hears this sentiment all the time. And he has repeatedly pledged to "scrub" all the waste out. He implies that he will only be able to support tax hikes when the people really think their government is run efficiently. It is unlikely, however, that given the data we are examining here, and given Colorado's seemingly engrained political culture, that the day will come when Coloradans think "fat and waste" have been seriously eliminated.

Coloradans, on occasion, are willing to pay increased targeted taxes if they can be assured the funds will be well spent on a clearly designated priority. Thus, in 1986, two-thirds of Coloradans favored a small increase in the state sales tax to build a new medium security prison. Voters in and around Denver have voted to tax themselves to support the zoo, the symphony, the library system, and to construct a stadium (Coors Field) to help bring a major league baseball team to Denver. They also voted to build a new Mile High Stadium for the Broncos and to increase taxes to expand the Denver "light rail" commuter train system. And many local governments have supported targeted tax increases for schools or special projects.

Generally, however, Coloradans are opposed to having their property or income taxes go up. If additional revenues are needed, Coloradans would rather see a modest hike in casino revenue taxes, taxes on liquor sales, or increases of various user fees or penalties.[13]

One final note on taxes. Our poll of Coloradans found that a majority (54 to 39 percent) believe "upper income people in this country do not pay their fair share of taxes." No one will be surprised by the high correlation here with income levels, with nearly two-thirds of lower-income Coloradans concurring that the tax system is unfair. Lower-income folks may not understand all the details of the tax system, yet they doubtless know they cannot afford the accountants, tax attorneys, and tax shelters that are often more available to the wealthy.

## REPUBLICANS AND DEMOCRATS: HOW THEY DIFFER

In recent years, as mentioned, Coloradans have been almost equally divided in their party registration. More than a third are Republican, nearly a third are Democratic, and the rest are independents. In Colorado, independents are technically called "unaffiliated." As of this writing, Republicans had edged up a bit and unaffiliated voters were down a bit, but over the long haul registration remains pretty even at around one-third Republican, one-third Democrat, and one-third unaffiliated.

Pollsters and political scientists believe that about two-thirds of the so-called independent or unaffiliated registrants actually vote on a fairly regular basis for one of the two parties. Indeed, these so-called independents may even have a moderate to strong tie or regular leaning toward that party.[14] Nonetheless, for a variety of professional, personal, or even idiosyncratic reasons, they register as unaffiliated.

In our 2010 survey, we asked the 90 percent of our interviewees who were registered to vote whether they were registered as a Republican, a Democrat, unaffiliated, or some other party. Our Colorado response: Republican, 37 percent; Democrat, 33 percent; unaffiliated, 29 percent. Only 1 percent said "other."

But later we asked a more open-ended question of those registered to vote. The findings are especially interesting when contrasted to responses we had in earlier years to the same question. See Figure 9.

In a four-year period, from 2006 to 2010, both Colorado Republicans and Democrats have lost some support, but the shifts were to the decidedly more conservative Tea Party and Libertarian factions. Note that this survey was conducted at about the same time as major debates over federal health insurance and economic stimulus programs had divided the nation. Both programs were controversial and triggered some backlash to the Democrats, who were then in control of both the White House and the Congress.

Not all Libertarian Party or Tea Party supporters always vote for Republicans. Some do not vote at all. But their default choice typically is to vote for the Republican. In which case, even though the percentage telling us in 2010 that they considered themselves as Republicans declined modestly, the ranks of the right-of-center political forces expanded, especially when compared to the center left.

Who are the Republicans? How do they differ from Democrats? There are a few demographic differences. We know that Denver, Boulder, Pueblo, and Adams Counties are home to many more Democrats than Republicans. In El Paso and Douglas Counties and most rural areas of the state, however, Republicans tend to outnumber Democrats by at least a two-to-one margin. Democrats are least likely to live on the Eastern Plains.

But there are no significant differences between the two major parties in terms of age, income, and how long one has lived in Colorado. Note that, contrary to some stereotyping, Republicans come almost proportionally from all income groups. The same is mostly true for Colorado Democrats, though there is a slightly increased presence of Democrats at higher-income levels.

Democrats enjoy a slight edge among those with postgraduate degrees.

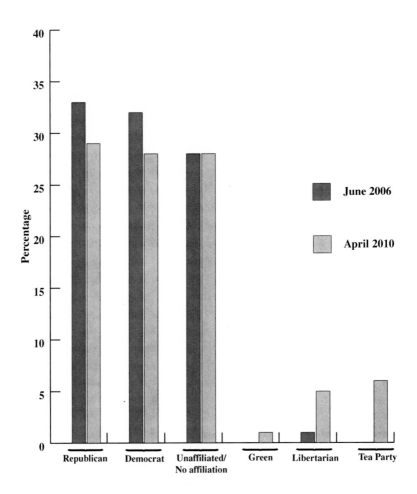

Figure 9. Coloradans and Their Party Loyalties

QUESTION: "Regardless of how you are registered to vote, do you consider your-self to be a Republican or a Democrat, unaffiliated or closer to some other party like the Green Party, the Libertarian Party, or the Tea Party?"

*Source*: Colorado College Citizens Polls, 2006, 2010.

Republicans do poorly in attracting Hispanics and other minorities. Democrats attract more support from women than men, and this has been the case for several years. In 2010, for example, both John Hickenlooper and Democratic U.S. Senate candidate Michael Bennet won about 56 percent of the female vote yet only about 44 percent of the male vote.

Upper-income voters, particularly those in Denver's inner-suburban areas, continued in the early years of the first decade of the twenty-first century to shift from Republican to Democratic loyalists, and indeed, in 2008 Arapahoe and Jefferson Counties voted Democratic for U.S. president for the first time in many decades. Similarly, in 2010 the Democratic candidates for governor and U.S. senator narrowly carried these two pivotal suburban counties.

Presented in Figure 10A–H are a number of notable differences between Colorado Democrats and Republicans on specific policies or political principles.

In sum, Republicans viewed themselves as conservative, gave a higher preference for liberty as opposed to equality, prized the right to own guns, and were much more disapproving of taxes and then Democratic governor Bill Ritter. They were also much less likely to say they were "environmentalists." Republicans were more likely to be "creationists" and more likely than Democrats to say religion plays a significant role in their personal lives. Republicans sharply disagreed with their partisan opponents on whether gay and lesbian marriages should be legalized in Colorado. Two-thirds of Republicans say same-sex marriages should be illegal. Only 15 percent of Democrats shared this view.

Nearly two-thirds of Colorado Republicans say they would vote again for TABOR-type tax restrictions. Only 41 percent of Democrats favor this.

While there are major differences between Republicans and Democrats in Colorado, one has to be careful not to make sweeping generalizations. For example, nearly a third of Republicans consider themselves environmentalists, and a majority of Democrats say religion is important in their lives. A majority of Democrats in Colorado affirm that "gun ownership is a basic right of all Americans." (Indeed, the Colorado Constitution affirms that basic right.) And while 52 percent of Democrats say they are liberal in political outlook, 30 percent call themselves middle-of-the-roaders, and at least 16 percent of Democrats think of themselves as conservatives. On the other hand, virtually none of the Republicans said they were liberal in political outlook.

Democrats and Republicans were in general agreement, as were men and women, on the historic 1990 referendum on a slight increase in the sales tax in the greater Denver area in order to build Coors Field baseball

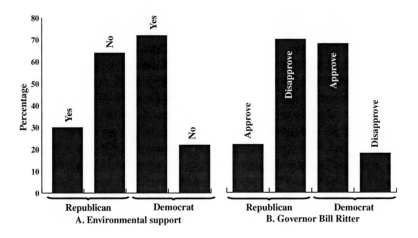

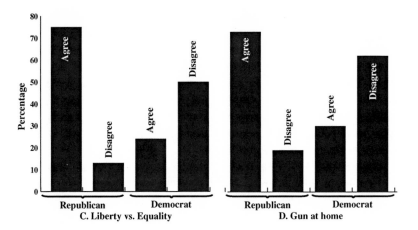

Figure 10. Coloradans' Party Ties and Policy or Philosophical Differences

A. QUESTION: "Do you consider yourself an environmentalist?"
B. QUESTION: "Do you approve or disapprove of the job Bill Ritter is doing as governor?"
C. STATEMENT: "I believe liberty is more important than equality."
D. STATEMENT: "It is a good idea to keep a gun in your home for protection."

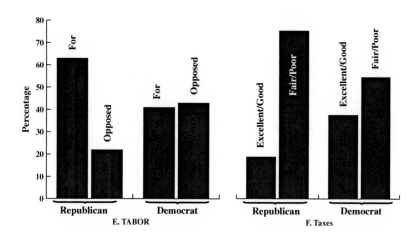

E. TABOR

F. Taxes

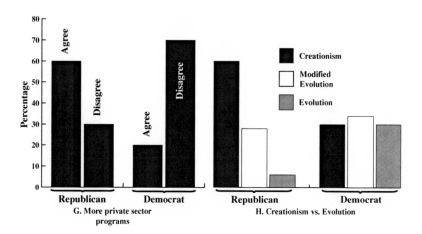

G. More private sector
programs

H. Creationism vs. Evolution

E. QUESTION: "Would you again vote for TABOR tax restrictions if they were on the ballot?"

F. QUESTION: "How well is the state (tax) policy keeping taxes down?"

G. QUESTION: "Could taxpayer money be saved if we contracted out more programs to the private sector?"

H. General view on "Creationism" vs. "Evolution."

*Source*: Colorado College Citizens Poll, 2010.

stadium. That stadium was planned to lure a National League expansion team to Denver. It admirably succeeded.

But sharp partisan differences exist in Colorado. These differences are sharpest on Election Day every two years when sometimes as many as 90 percent or more of Republicans vote Republican and nearly as high a percentage of Democrats vote for most of the Democrats on the ballot. As a rule in Colorado, Republicans turn out to vote in higher numbers and are more loyal to their fellow partisans. This was not the case in 2006 and 2008 when Bill Ritter and Barack Obama won handily. But it is usually the case.

Those who are unaffiliated are less likely than Republicans and Democrats to mail back their ballots or turn out and vote on Election Day. This has long been the case both in Colorado and across the country. But Colorado is among the states with the highest percentage of unaffiliated or independent voters, so theirs is often the crucial difference in competitive statewide elections in Colorado.

### THE TEA PARTY AND THE LIBERTARIANS

As we conducted our 2010 statewide survey, we found a small yet feisty group who called themselves Tea Party supporters. This term had only come into use in mid-2009, yet 6 percent of our sample identified themselves as Tea Partiers. Most of them said they were conservative and vote as Republicans. More males and longer-term Colorado residents say they support the Tea Party, which is more a state of mind, or a protest movement, than a real political party. Our sample was small. But the shared political sentiments of the Tea Party were clear. They disliked taxes, government intrusiveness, or social welfare policies.

Here is what Tea Party people told us:

1. 100 percent said the U.S. government is going in the wrong direction.

2. 94 percent said elected officials do not think like me.

3. 93 percent said gun ownership is a basic American right.

4. 91 percent preferred local government as opposed to state and national governments.

5. 87 percent said state taxes are too high.

6. 82 percent said Colorado is headed in "the wrong direction."

7. 66 percent said "America's best years are behind us."

Around the same time as our poll, a national Gallup Poll of Tea Party supporters nationwide found similar antigovernment and anti–Democratic Party sentiments.[15]

In our Colorado statewide poll, we had another 5 percent of respondents calling themselves libertarians. Libertarians, as the label implies, love liberty and are generally suspicious of government intrusion and regulation. They differ from most Republicans and Tea Partiers in that they are also staunch advocates of personal liberties and personal freedom. They are more likely to favor decriminalization of recreational drugs and are much more open than traditional Republicans to abortion and same-sex marriages.

"The Libertarian Party is more of a discussion group than a viable political force," says Denver conservative radio talk-show host Mike Rosen. "As libertarian candidates propose to eliminate one government program or activity after another, as they promise to slash defense spending or legalize prostitution or drugs, what they imagine will be a sea of potential libertarian voters is reduced to a puddle." Pragmatic libertarians usually settle on voting for Republicans candidates as the lesser of two evils. "Impractical libertarians don't care about election outcomes," notes Rosen. "They revel in righteous purity of thought and wear their political martyrdom as a badge of honor."[16]

## ENVIRONMENTALISTS AND CONSERVATIONISTS

The economy and the environment, often in that order, head the list of major public concerns in Colorado. In boom economic years, more Coloradans view the environment, and Colorado's quality of life, as top worries. But in years such as 1989 and 1990, or 2008, 2009, and 2010, when Colorado was in one of its periodic economic downturns, the economy and jobs plainly came first, and the environment and quality of life concerns were in the runner-up spot.

Even the question of whether one is or is not an environmentalist elicits a different response during varying economic times. See Table 6.

Most Coloradans definitely care about the environment and maintaining the natural beauty of the Centennial State. Yet we noticed a decline in those calling themselves environmentalists over a fourteen-year period from 1996 to 2010. We also asked whether state government should be doing more to regulate land use in Colorado: in 2006, 64 percent said yes. Four years later, only 56 percent agreed. Next we asked whether people agree or disagree that "we have to protect the environment no matter what

Table 6. Environmentalism

QUESTION: "Do you consider yourself an environmentalist?"

|                       | 1996 | 1999 | 2006 | 2010 |
|-----------------------|------|------|------|------|
| Environmentalist      | 66%  | 64%  | 53%  | 51%  |
| Not environmentalist  | 30   | 32   | 44   | 46   |

*Source*: Talmey-Drake Polls, 1996, 1999; Colorado College Citizen Polls, 2006, 2010.

the costs." Fifty-four percent agreed in 2010, 8 percent less than the 62 percent who agreed with this idea four years earlier.

"Should Colorado be spending more of its tax dollars on buying open space and developing parks and recreation areas?" The 53 percent positive response in 2006 dropped to 44 percent in 2010. Finally, we pitted the environment and the economy against each other in our question "[Does] Colorado needs stronger laws to protect the natural environment, even if the laws endanger jobs and economic growth in the state and elsewhere?"

Forty-nine percent agreed with that statement in good economic times in 2006. This support fell 11 points to just 38 percent who concurred in the aftermath of the Recession of 2008–10.

Most Coloradans want both economic growth and to protect the magnificent environmental grandeur that is part of their state's iconic signature. Yet these twin aspirations are sometimes in conflict, and economic prosperity, or the lack thereof, affects public opinion.

Those who say they are environmentalists are more likely to say they are liberal and identify themselves as Democrats rather than as conservatives and Republicans. They are somewhat more likely to have more formal education, but age and income level have no correlation with whether one is an environmentalist. Women and longer-term residents in Colorado are slightly more likely to say they are environmentalists than men and relative newcomers to the state.

Environmentalists in our survey indicated they are more "communitarian" than "libertarian" in their views about government, and they were more approving of the job Gov. Bill Ritter was doing at that time. Governor Ritter had made environmentalism and his "green economy" initiatives one of his top priorities, so it is understandable that, even though his negative approval ratings were high in 2010, those saying they were environmentalists were 50 percent less likely to be negative about Ritter's performance as their governor than the "nonenvironmentalists." Thirty-one percent of environmentalists were negative toward Ritter compared to 60 percent of "nonenvironmentalists."

The words "environmentalism" and "environmentalist" have become somewhat politicized over the past generation. This may be partly due to the aggressiveness of national environmentalists who developed the image of opposing oil and gas exploration and perhaps overreaching in their zeal to protect all kinds of endangered species. As Republican talk-show hosts and candidates turned negative on these ardent environmental activists, the support for environmentalism clearly declined, especially among those who see themselves as loyal Republicans.

But public opinion polling done in 2011 by the Hewlett Foundation found that most Coloradans still favor a broad variety of "conservationist" principles and values. Thus, the vast majority of registered Colorado voters agreed that "even with state budget problems, we should still find money to protect the state's land, water, and wildlife."

Similarly, most Coloradans want their state and the nation to enforce existing laws that protect clean air and clean water. They also say that "we need to do more to ensure oil, gas, and mining companies follow laws protecting our land, air, and water."

The vast majority of Coloradans say they regularly visit state and national parks. Nearly 40 percent of Coloradans say they occasionally hunt or fish, or do both.

About three-quarters (75 percent) say they consider themselves "a conservationist." This drops to less than 50 percent when asked if they consider themselves "an environmentalist."

Party affiliation accounts for some of these differences. Republicans, whether highly conservative or more moderate, are less comfortable with the environmentalist label than are Democrats.[17]

Coloradans will continue to want economic growth and preservation of the environment in the decades to come. But with the state's population likely to double in the next fifty years, these sometimes-colliding concerns will pose additional challenges, both for Colorado citizens and Colorado's political leadership.


### THE ROLE OF RELIGION IN COLORADO POLITICS

Religious beliefs are generally viewed as a personal matter in Colorado. Most residents do not know the religion of their neighbors. Veteran journalist Carl Miller, formerly of the *Denver Post*, once said the difference at cocktail parties in Colorado, as opposed to such places as Texas, is that instead of asking new acquaintances where they go to church, people in Colorado are more likely to ask: "Where do you and your family ski?"[18]

Another longtime columnist and editor, Vincent Carroll, who has worked for both the *Rocky Mountain News* and the *Denver Post*, said Coloradans are conservative "yet not in the Bible Belt sense. People here are tolerant of religious practices and the religious beliefs of others."[19]

National surveys suggest Colorado is among the lowest states in terms of religiosity (church attendance and regular praying).[20] But precise information on religious identity and religious participation by Coloradans is difficult to obtain. One 2001 survey suggested that of Colorado churchgoers, about 39 percent were Protestants, another 39 percent were Catholic, and a much smaller percentage were Mormon, Jewish, Muslim, or "Eastern religions."

An entry on Wikipedia in 2011 estimated at least 25 percent of Coloradans are nonreligious, perhaps about 20 percent are Catholic, about 40 percent are Protestant (with about half of that being evangelical), and small percentages being Mormon, Jewish, or other.

Census data do not include religious affiliation. And, as is well known, what a person says is their religious affiliation is imperfectly correlated with whether they are regular practitioners or attendees of that particular faith. Our best estimate is that perhaps two-thirds of Coloradans are actively involved with their faiths and about a third of Coloradans do not regularly attend church services. Yet, as we will discuss, most people here say religion is important in their lives.

While most Coloradans believe religion and "faith" are private concerns that do not belong in partisan political debates, Coloradans are divided when it comes to issues such as abortion and same-sex marriages. For example, we asked Coloradans in our 2010 poll whether or not gays and lesbians should be allowed to be legally married in Colorado. Fifty-five percent indicated it was okay with them, 11 percent were neutral, but 42 percent disagreed. Those who said religion is very important in their lives strongly opposed same-sex marriage. People under forty-five are rather supportive of legalizing same-sex marriage in Colorado, while those over fifty-five are noticeably less in favor of this social reform.

On another lifestyle issue, Rasmussen polls have found that between 50 and 60 percent of likely Colorado voters favor legalizing and taxing marijuana.[21]

The Colorado Springs area has won national attention as a home to scores of evangelical Protestant ministries including Focus on the Family and megachurches such as New Life Church, founded by Ted Haggard.

Most of the leadership of these ministries is pro-life, pro–school prayer, and anti–same-sex marriage. Sometimes these religious leaders take these stands vociferously. Not surprisingly, evangelical Protestant leaders favored candidates like Ronald Reagan, George W. Bush, Sarah Palin, and Rick Santorum.

Religion is not unimportant to Coloradans. Religion is, in fact, important to most of the state's residents. Nearly 85 percent of Republicans say religion is important to their lives, and over 60 percent of Democrats share this sentiment.

Our Colorado College Citizens Polls in both 2006 and 2010 found that about 50 percent of Coloradans say "religion plays a very important role" in their lives. Twenty-three percent say religion plays a "somewhat important role" in their lives. Seventeen percent say religion plays just a minor role, and only 11 percent say religion plays no role in their lives.

Other surveys reinforce that religion is important to Coloradans. Thus 74 percent told Talmey-Drake pollsters that they received "comfort and support from [their] religious beliefs." And a majority affirmed that their religious faith "is the most important influence" in their life.[22]

Coloradans are divided when it comes to the creation versus evolution debate. Yet a plurality of respondents (43 percent) agreed with the essentially creationist view that "God created man in his present form all at once within the last 10,000 years." Only 17 percent agreed with the more narrowly evolutionist view that "mankind developed over millions of years from less advanced forms of life, and God had no part in this process." About one-third (34 percent) indicated an evolutionist perspective yet credited divine guidance. They agreed to the statement "Mankind developed over millions of years from far less advanced forms of life, but God guided this process." See Table 7.

Coloradans who tell us that religion is "very important" in their lives also say they are very conservative. People of Latino ethnicity indicate religion is important in their lives, as do residents of the Eastern Plains and in the Colorado Springs region. The numbers are lower among Denver Metro residents.

Earlier surveys of Coloradans indicated that most (61 percent) do not think "it is important to know about a candidate's religious beliefs before voting for him." About 73 percent agree that when a person dies "some part of that person lives on, either in a next life on earth, in heaven, or elsewhere."

This 2000 survey also asked people to respond to this "new age" state-

Table 7. Creationists versus Evolutionists

|  | Estimated percentage |
|---|---|
| God created man in his present form all at once within the last 10,000 years. | 43% |
| Mankind developed over millions of years from far less advanced forms of life, but God guided this process. | 34 |
| Mankind developed over millions of years from less advanced forms of life, and God had no part in this process. | 17 |

Source: Colorado College Citizens Poll, 2010 (N = 603).

ment: "The best religion would be one that borrowed from all religions." Thirty-three percent agreed. Another 23 percent were not sure or did not know. But 45 percent disageed.[23]

### CONCLUSIONS

Coloradans love their state, their country, and the Rocky Mountains, and are more conservative Republican and antigovernment than Americans in general. Coloradans are a fascinating mix of philosophical conservatism and political pragmatism. They are more progressive on lifestyle or personal human issues yet more conservative on fiscal matters than citizens elsewhere. But, in common with most Americans, Coloradans say they would love to see lower taxes and less waste in governmental operations. Besides the mountains, they like the Broncos, Nuggets, Rockies, and Avalanche sports teams more than they will ever like politicians.

Coloradans, compared to the nation, are slightly less diverse, slightly younger, slightly more conservative, somewhat less religious, and more likely to have been born elsewhere.

Several things divide Coloradans. First, there are several geographical divides. The Continental Divide runs north to south near the middle of the state. Interstate 70 (east to west) and Interstate 25 (north to south) also divide the state in intriguing ways, but the main significance of these highways is that about 90 percent of the state live within twenty-five miles or so of either side of them.

Political consultant Eric Sondermann joked with us that "Coloradans live on I-25 and play on I-70."[24]

In addition, there is a psychological divide of sorts between Denver

Metro residents and the rest of the state. Denver dominates the state financially, politically, and culturally. And nearly two-thirds of the state live in or can easily commute to the Denver area. In many ways, then, as the Denver area goes, so goes the state. The rest of the state knows this and they sometimes resent it.

But there are other more subtle divides as well. Coloradans are divided over the role of government. A large number of Coloradans view government and politicians as a problem, perhaps even as *the* problem. But another smaller yet still sizeable block of Coloradans is more hopeful and more trusting of government and like to think of government as at least a selective problem-solving "Hamiltonian agent" rather than just as a problem.

Colorado, as mentioned, is also divided almost in thirds when it comes to party loyalties: one-third Republicans, one-third Democrats, and the last third independents. In voting patterns Colorado has become one of the most competitive and purple-leaning states in the nation.

Effective political leaders are forever trying to find common ground, continually emphasizing shared values and shared aspirations. They try to build bridges across these multiple divides. It is sometimes an exacting challenge.

Two key factors shape Coloradans and their political attitudes. Their partisan allegiances greatly influence how they evaluate officeholders and state and national government. When Republicans controlled the Colorado governorship, the U.S. Congress, and the White House (as was the case in the Gov. Bill Owens and the President George W. Bush era), most Republicans held a more rosy view of the state and U.S. governments. This contrasted with harsher verdicts by Democrats during the same time period.

But the exact reverse held true when Democrat Bill Ritter was Colorado's governor and Democrats controlled both the U.S. Congress and the White House. Democrats were almost twice as likely to approve these officials and praise their general leadership of state and national governments. Thus, which party is in office, along with partisanship and political ideology, plays an important role in the shaping of political attitudes.

One's religious views also influence political views. As noted, religion nowadays may not play a big role in our day-to-day relations with neighbors or in business. But most Coloradans consider themselves at least somewhat religious. How fundamentalist one is and how important religion is in one's life shape political ideology and party loyalties. Those saying religion is a very important part of their life are far more likely to be conservative and Republican.

And there is at least some evidence in recent years to suggest that people with conservative or fundamentalist religious views shifted to the Republican Party as that party welcomed people who were disappointed in the *Roe v. Wade* abortion case and related lifestyle and prayer-in-schools public policies.

To know about a person's ideological leanings and the role of religion in their life is to know, with some reliability, how that person stands on a wide number of political, partisan, and policy issues.

Party affiliation both shapes and reinforces ideological values. While most of us inherit party affiliations from parents, our communities, or ethnic ties, people do occasionally shift from one party to another. "People have stereotypes in their heads about what Democrats are like and what Republicans are like," writes *New York Times* columnist David Brooks, "and they gravitate toward the party made up of people like themselves." And once they have moved toward red or blue, "people bend their philosophies and their perceptions of reality so they become more and more aligned with members of their political tribe."[25] This seems to be the case in Colorado.

Because Colorado has so many new residents who have moved here and such a large percentage of independent voters, there is somewhat more flux and unpredictability in the Colorado political culture than elsewhere in the United States.

Elected officials constantly have their work cut out for them here as they try to negotiate and navigate toward common ground. It is a challenge to unify this divided and somewhat more politically polarized state. But Coloradans, overall, share more in common than is generally believed. Most Coloradans want prosperity and to conserve the natural beauty of their state. Most Coloradans want leaner, more efficient, and more effective state institutions. They all generally want clean air, safe water, and strong public schools. Coloradans, like people everywhere, complain about taxes, yet they love living here.

# CHAPTER THREE

# A Brief Sociopolitical History of Colorado

Among the first permanent residents of what is now Colorado were Native Americans living at Mesa Verde in the southwest corner of the state. Called Prehistoric Puebloans or Anasazi, they first occupied the area in the first century AD. Initially they lived in pit houses dug into the earth and covered with a thatched roof. Later, they built masonry-style pueblo villages on the mesa tops. They then moved to cliff dwellings, elaborate structures built in large niches halfway up the walls of canyon cliffs. Frequently, high solid-rock overhangs protected these cliff communities from the elements. To most people, these early Coloradans are known as the cliff dwellers.

For some unknown reason, the cliff dwellers departed Mesa Verde by AD 1300, and what was once a booming area was abandoned.[1] The cliff dwellings at Mesa Verde, the first of Colorado's many ghost towns, today are preserved as Mesa Verde National Park.

Up until the late 1800s, nomadic Native Americans were moving in and out of present-day Colorado. The Apaches, Navahos, Comanches, Pawnees, Kiowas, Cheyennes, and Sioux all hunted and lived in the area at one time or another. The most permanent Native American residents were the Utes, whose language was similar to the Shoshonis. The Utes were not agricultural, living instead by hunting and enjoying the spoils of war making. They inhabited and in effect possessed the major mountain areas of Colorado at the time of the earliest European explorations, and they remained there for many years to come.

### SPANISH EXPLORATIONS

The first European nation to claim a portion of what is now Colorado was Spain. After conquering Mexico under the leadership of Hernando Cortez, the Spaniards explored and colonized to the north, working their way up the Rio Grande River through what is now New Mexico to Santa Fe and Taos.

Probably one of the first persons of European origin to enter Colorado was Juan de Archuleta. Sometime between 1664 and 1680, he traveled through southeastern Colorado while searching for runaway Native Americans who had escaped from their Spanish masters in Taos. Archuleta found his way to the Arkansas River and explored the general area along the Colorado-Kansas border.

### LOUISIANA PURCHASE

By the year 1800, domination of North America by Europe was coming to an end. The thirteen British colonies on the Atlantic seaboard had won their Revolutionary War and established the United States as an independent nation. Napoleon Bonaparte, the ruler of France, was having trouble maintaining control of France's many possessions in the New World, so he offered to sell all of his Louisiana Territory to the United States. The Louisiana Purchase, completed in 1803, brought the vast lands west of the Mississippi and north of the Arkansas River under U.S. control. Because the Arkansas River runs through Southern Colorado, the Louisiana Purchase brought approximately one-half of what is now Colorado into the United States.

On July 15, 1806, U.S. army lieutenant Zebulon Montgomery Pike and a party of men set out from Fort Belle Fontaine, north of St. Louis. They were on an unofficial expedition to explore the southwestern portion of the Louisiana Purchase.

Pike traveled by horseback across what is now central Kansas and then advanced up the Arkansas River to present-day Pueblo. As he crossed the prairie, he noticed a mountain peak to the northwest that stood alone as a majestic landmark.

By this time, it was late November of 1806. For two and a half days Pike and his party attempted to climb the great mountain, but eventually they had to give up because of their light clothing and the waist-deep snows surrounding the mountain top. Since Pike was the first American to describe the mountain and attempt to climb it, those who came after him called it Pike's Peak.

Pike continued his explorations in the general area of Southern Colorado. His party eventually encountered Spanish soldiers from Mexico, who detained and questioned them, but after taking them to Mexico, eventually released them.

## BEAVER TRAPPERS AND BUFFALO HUNTERS

Throughout the early 1800s the area that is now Colorado belonged to the "mountain men," the beaver trappers and fur traders who explored the Rocky Mountain regions but did not settle in them. It was European fashions that brought these "lone explorers" to the edge of the mountain frontier. Hats made from beaver pelts were popular with European men at the time.

The trappers worked out of Santa Fe and Taos in New Mexico. Many of them were French, and they gave French names such as St. Vrain and Cache La Poudre to many of the rivers in northern Colorado. The closest the beaver trappers and fur traders came to settling in the Rocky Mountains was holding periodic "rendezvous," large encampments where they would sell and trade furs, restock their provisions, and socialize, mainly by telling stories of their explorations and exploits in the mountains. The fur trade faded when beaver hats were no longer popular in Europe.

## SANTA FE TRAIL

In 1820 Mexico revolted from Spain and became an independent nation. Unlike the Spanish, who wanted to keep United States commercial interests out of New Mexico, the newly independent Mexicans welcomed trade with the United States. Wagon trains set out from Independence, Missouri, carrying U.S. goods to Santa Fe where they could be sold for large profits.

The shortest route of the Santa Fe Trail crossed Oklahoma into New Mexico, but the "Mountain Branch," which was longer but had more reliable water supplies and less danger from Native Americans, crossed through southeastern Colorado. In 1833, between the present-day cities of La Junta and Las Animas, the trading firm of Bent, St. Vrain and Company built Bent's Fort on the Mountain Branch of the Santa Fe Trail. The fort, constructed of thick adobe with high watchtowers at two corners, served buffalo hunters and beaver trappers as well as wagon traders traveling the Mountain Branch of the Santa Fe Trail. Bent, St. Vrain and Company later built Fort St. Vrain on the South Platte River near the present town of Platteville to serve as a trading post for northeastern Colorado.

Although the trappers, traders, hunters, and trading post operators did not found permanent settlements in the area, they made significant contributions. The valleys and passes of the mountain regions were explored by these "mountain men," and their maps and stories would help guide other men and women into these once remote regions. Contact had been made with the Native American tribes of the area, and in many instances trade had been established between the Native Americans and the newcomers. Most important, they demonstrated the mountain and prairie wilderness of Colorado was liveable.

SAN LUIS

In 1845 the United States annexed Texas from Mexico, thereby gaining the land south of the Arkansas River claimed by Texas. Following the Mexican War, at the Treaty of Guadalupe Hidalgo in 1848, the United States gained from Mexico virtually all the remaining land that comprises the southwestern United States, including southwestern and western Colorado. From 1848, the entire land area of what is now the state of Colorado belonged to the United States.

In 1851 New Mexican settlers came up the Rio Grande River valley and established a permanent settlement at what is now San Luis, Colorado. Of Spanish origin, these settlers probably were from the Santa Fe and Taos area. They constructed homes and public buildings of adobe. They also dug the San Luis People's Ditch, the oldest irrigation canal in Colorado in continuous operation. The oldest water rights recognized in Colorado were claimed by these first settlers at San Luis. In 1858 the first church in Colorado was constructed at the nearby town of Conejos.

Other New Mexican settlers soon followed the founders of San Luis. They brought with them the Spanish names, architecture, and lifestyle that had come from Spain through Mexico to New Mexico. Towns were given Spanish names, such as Alamosa, Antonito, and Conejos. A distinctive and rich Spanish influence still exists in Southern Colorado.

San Luis is the oldest permanent settlement in the state. It is noteworthy, however, that almost two hundred years passed between the time Juan de Archuleta entered Colorado in the middle 1600s and the time when the first permanent Euro-American settlement was established in 1851.

GOLD

The Colorado region was a relatively quiet place in the mid-1850s. The fur trade had faded almost completely, and most of the trading posts on the Arkansas and Platte Rivers were abandoned. The only permanent settlements of European origin were the small New Mexican colonies in Southern Colorado. The vast area of mountains and plains surrounding Pike's Peak mainly belonged to the mountain Utes and the nomadic Native Americans on the Eastern Plains.

In February 1858 William Green Russell and his two brothers, Oliver and Levi, left their home in Georgia with the intent of prospecting for gold in the Rocky Mountains. William Russell had found and mined gold both in Georgia and in the California gold rush of 1849. He and his brothers accumulated a sizeable party of would-be miners and came up the Arkansas River into present-day Colorado. They continued north until coming to the spot, just east of the Rocky Mountains, where Cherry Creek flows into the South Platte River.

There was no gold at Cherry Creek. A short distance away, however, at the mouth of Dry Creek, the Russell party panned out several hundred dollars' worth of gold dust. The small pocket was soon exhausted. "The quantity was insignificant, but it was, perhaps, the most important discovery ever made within the region, for from this meager showing the great Pike's Peak gold rush developed."[2]

Word of the Russell party's discovery quickly spread eastward, and Colorado's first great mineral rush was underway. It was called the Pike's Peak gold rush because the prominent mountain seventy miles to the south served to guide the prospectors to the mining areas. In 1859 additional and more lucrative gold strikes were made along Clear Creek and Boulder Creek (South Platte River tributaries) at Central City, Idaho Springs, and Boulder.

To serve these booming mining areas, supply towns were built at the eastern foot of the Rocky Mountains. The most important of these supply towns, Denver, grew up at Cherry Creek and the South Platte River. Denver was near where gold was first discovered, and therefore Denver was where everyone went to get started looking for gold of their own. Other important supply towns were founded at Golden (west of Denver), Colorado City (now part of Colorado Springs), and Canon City (on the Arkansas River west of Pueblo).

The importance of the Russell brothers striking gold near the present-day city of Denver cannot be minimized. The major effect of the strike was to draw large numbers of people into what is now Colorado from the eastern, midwestern, and southern United States. Although not so numerous or famous as California's "Forty-Niners," Colorado's "Fifty-Niners" came in large numbers and began the process of populating a previously remote and forbidding area. The number of people from the East, Midwest, and South who came to search for gold, or service those who were doing the searching, soon greatly outnumbered the people of New Mexican origin settled in Southern Colorado.

It was the miners who were generally responsible for the way the Utes and other Native Americans were pushed out and away from the mineral-rich mountains and the prairie and foothill trails that led to the mountains. The Utes were pushed ever westward, particularly when more minerals were discovered on lands allocated to the Utes by the U.S. government. For the miners it was "the Ute Problem," and eventually the cry of the day became "The Utes Must Go!" "Wherever Anglo-Americans contended with the Indians for land, conflicting interests led to disputes and the triumph of the former's overwhelming numbers, resources, and superior technology."[3]

At the time of the 1858 gold strike in Colorado, the "agricultural frontier" was still back in the general area of the Missouri River. Homesteaders, those sturdy farmers who took virgin lands, broke them with the plow, and turned them into productive agricultural areas, had not advanced anywhere near Colorado. This meant that Colorado was not founded as a rural-agrarian community of farmers, which is the way most states in the United States were first populated and developed.

The people who rushed to Colorado in and shortly after 1858 were interested in pursuing an urban-industrial process, the mining of precious minerals. Instead of founding small rural towns, as happens in rural-agrarian areas, they founded towns and cities (i.e., urban areas) that served as either mining camps or supply towns. Except in San Luis and the other Spanish-oriented towns of Southern Colorado, where the lifestyle was rural-agrarian, Colorado bypassed the rural-agrarian stage and, through mining and city founding, proceeded directly to the urban-industrial stage.

The increase in population caused by the Pike's Peak gold rush led almost immediately to various proposals for the area that is now Colorado to be organized as a territory. In 1861, only three years after gold was discovered at Dry Creek, the U.S. Congress enacted the necessary legislation creating the Territory of Colorado. Fifteen years later, in 1876, Colorado became a state.

## BOOM AND BUST

Gold mining in Colorado boomed throughout the early 1860s, and Colorado gold stocks boomed on the New York Stock Exchange. At one point the stocks of more than two hundred Colorado mining companies were being traded on major eastern stock exchanges. Adding to the Colorado gold euphoria, which was turning into investment madness, was the fact that gold found in Colorado during this period was largely free gold, chemically separate from other elements. Only a minor amount of crushing and washing was required to redeem the gold and prepare it for sale.

By early 1864, however, the rumor began to spread that the gold-bearing ores were beginning to dwindle in Colorado. Further, it appeared that the "easy" gold had run out. Now the ores being brought out of the ground had their gold mixed with other elements, and simple mechanical procedures were no longer sufficient to set the gold free. In April of 1864, the Colorado gold mining "bubble" burst. The price of Colorado gold mining stocks collapsed on the eastern stock exchanges. Colorado, famous for its giant "boom," was experiencing its first major "bust."

Colorado's first mineral depression began to ease in 1868 when Nathaniel P. Hill, a professor of chemistry at Brown University, developed an efficient and profitable process for separating gold from gold ore. He organized Colorado's first ore reduction company, the Boston and Colorado Smelting Company, and built the state's first gold smelter at Black Hawk, a mining town adjacent to Central City. As Colorado entered the 1870s, the gold mining industry began to revive.

### SILVER

In the 1870s the renewed gold boom in Colorado was joined by a silver boom. Similar to the deeper gold ores, the problem with silver was that it was tightly mixed with other materials. By 1870, however, working silver smelters were in operation, and one mountain town after another boomed as silver discoveries were made and publicized. With each new find, the word spread, excitement built, and people rushed to the new "El Dorado." There seemed to be a promise of wealth for everyone. This process repeated itself in the silver areas of Colorado over and over again. As the mines and enthusiasm played out in one area, another strike somewhere else would reinitiate the entire process.

The first of the "silver queens" was Georgetown, located west of Denver in a scenic valley just east of the Continental Divide. Soon silver camps were everywhere in the mountains of Colorado, from Ward, in Boulder County northwest of Denver, to Aspen, in the central mountains, to Silverton, in southwestern Colorado. Another major silver area was Creede, which boomed in the early 1890s. Yet another silver mine blossomed just south of Crestone at the eastern edge of the San Luis Valley. Perhaps the most notable silver strikes of all, however, were in Leadville, in the mountains nearly one hundred miles southwest of Denver. Lucky finds and smart deals made many new millionaires.

As the years passed, the day of the individual prospector rapidly gave way to corporate mining operations. Solo prospectors with picks and shovels were displaced by mining companies using expensive steam and electrical appliances, especially steam drills. Wrote Emma Langdon, an activist historian in Cripple Creek: "The speculators and capitalists came to get that which the prospector had found, and from then until now every inch of valuable ground, staked as a claim by the miner, has in some manner found its way into the hands of corporation capital."[4]

### RAILROADS

The famed mining era in Colorado corresponded to the railroad era. In 1869 the Union Pacific and Central Pacific joined their rails at Promontory, Utah, thereby completing the first transcontinental railroad. Because of the high mountain barrier west of Denver, the railroad had been built to the north of Colorado, through Cheyenne, Wyoming, on a route with a lower and easier crossing of the Continental Divide. Suddenly it appeared that Cheyenne, on the Union Pacific's transcontinental mainline, and not Denver, which had no railroad at all, was going to be the major metropolis of the Rocky Mountain region.

Not to be outdone, Denver political and business leaders organized a Board of Trade and began raising the money to build a branch line off the Union Pacific from Cheyenne to Denver. The project was linked with a plan to lay rails east from Denver and connect with the western terminus of the Kansas Pacific Railroad in western Kansas. The Union Pacific and Kansas Pacific Railroads supported the combined plan, both hoping to profit by serving the mining industry in Colorado.

In June 1870 the Cheyenne to Denver line was completed, and in August 1870 the final spike was driven on the Denver to Kansas City route. Colorado now had two railroad connections to the rest of the United States.

With each new gold or silver strike, the various railroad companies in Colorado would race to see which one could build the first rail line into the new mining camp. The company that reached a major strike area first would reap handsome profits hauling in people and supplies and hauling out the mineral ore. Railroaders became prospectors themselves, laying tracks into the mountains of Colorado and gambling that sometime in the near future a major gold or silver strike would be made close to their line.

The Denver and Rio Grande Railroad and its founder, General William J. Palmer, seemed particularly bold and adventurous in this regard. "It was a railroad with a master prospector at the helm, one that followed the miner and his burro, bound for where they were headed, looking for the same thing, wherever it was."[5]

The coming of the smelters and the railroads added to the urban-industrial character of early Colorado. Denver in the north and Pueblo in the south became major rail junctions on the Front Range, and their urban populations increased accordingly. Because of the smoke and cinders of puffing steam engines, and the smoke pouring from the smokestacks of the smelters, many Colorado cities and towns developed a decidedly industrial look.

## LABOR UNREST

Along with the mines, the smelters, and the railroads came labor unions, and with the unions came labor strikes and labor unrest. Some of the union strikes at the gold and silver mines were particularly bitter, resulting in violence on the part of both strikers and strikebreakers and attracting national attention. In one incident in 1904, thirteen people were killed when a railroad station was dynamited during a miners' strike at Cripple Creek, a booming gold camp southwest of Colorado Springs.[6] On April 20, 1914, striking coal miners clashed with the state militia at Ludlow, a coal mining area north of Trinidad. As many as two dozen people were killed and unknown numbers were wounded.[7] A poignant United Mine Workers of America memorial, less than a mile from Interstate 25, marks the burial area of those who died at Ludlow. In less than two decades, 1884 to 1912, mining accidents claimed the lives of more than seventeen hundred Colorado miners.

The Cripple Creek and Ludlow episodes were only two among many clashes between the mineworkers and the mine owners. Whom one favored in these struggles usually shaped one's political values and election preferences. State politics for nearly fifty years was affected by the politics of mining and the political and economic struggles between workers and their employers. During much of this time Republicans, aided by mining money, controlled state government.

A different approach was taken by Josephine Roche, a mine heiress who had seen firsthand the indecent conditions of the miners. She vowed to be a fair-minded and responsible mine owner and set out to prove one did not have to mistreat mineworkers as other absentee mine owners regularly did. She paid her miners seven dollars a day, a high wage at the time, and they responded with high rates of production. In 1934 Josephine Roche was a candidate for governor (the first woman to run for governor in Colorado) but she failed to be elected.[8]

CATTLE

As prospectors and miners poured into Colorado, closely followed by merchants and railroaders, there suddenly was a market for agricultural produce. As the various gold and silver strikes changed the mountains, they also changed the Eastern Plains, because it was there that some of the new arrivals began attempting to grow food to take to market in the mountain mining camps and the supply cities on the Front Range.

At first it was not believed that the high, dry prairies in eastern Colorado could support large cattle herds. A popular legend holds that many prospectors and freight wagon drivers, after arriving in Denver or Colorado City, would turn their oxen loose on the Eastern Plains, certain that the animals would meet an early death from starvation. The oxen flourished on the native grasses of the high prairies, however, thus demonstrating that Colorado's Eastern Plains had the potential to be good cattle country.[9]

Almost from the moment of the first gold strike at Dry Creek, Texas cattlemen began driving cattle northward from Texas to supply meat to the gold and silver camps. The first official report of a Texas herd reaching what is now Colorado was in 1859. By the 1870s, when the railroads reached as far west as Denver, Texas cattlemen would drive their herds north into Colorado, fatten the animals on the prairie grasses of the Eastern Plains, and then ship the cattle eastward to market by rail. Two of the best-known cattle-drive trails entering Colorado were the Dawson Trail and the Goodnight Trail.

As farmers began to fence the open range, cattle growers began to do the same thing. What once was "cattle ranging" on public land became "cattle ranching" on private land. Although giant herds grazing on vast stretches of public land are a thing of the past in Colorado, the cattle industry still remains an important part of the state's economy.

IRRIGATION AND DRY FARMING

Colorado lies well west of the one-hundredth meridian, that north–south line in western Kansas and Nebraska that marks the boundary between the Midwest and West. In most of the area west of the one-hundredth meridian, annual rainfall is so low that it becomes a major problem for agriculture.

In Colorado the rainfall averages only sixteen to seventeen inches a year, considerably less than the minimum requirements for "traditional farming" as it is practiced in the more humid sections of the United States.

The first Europeans to settle in Colorado, those of Spanish origin who moved into the San Luis Valley from New Mexico, had little difficulty adjusting to farming under "water-short" conditions. They copied the dams and irrigation ditches that were used to irrigate crops throughout the Rio Grande River Valley in New Mexico. If there had been more contact between the two groups, the Hispanic settlers of Southern Colorado could have taught their new northern neighbors much about successful irrigation techniques.

In northern Colorado many disappointed prospectors and miners, failing to strike it rich in either gold or silver, turned to agriculture, the trade they had grown up with. Having learned farming in the East, however, they had to "unlearn" much of their previous agricultural knowledge and "begin anew."

In 1859 David K. Wall diverted water from Clear Creek near the town of Golden and successfully grew two acres of vegetables. Others soon copied this idea of irrigating nearby lands with diverted river water, and lands accessible to both the South Platte and Arkansas Rivers were dotted with small irrigation systems and small farms.

Soon farmers were banding together to form cooperatives and corporations for building more elaborate irrigation systems in which larger and longer canals could irrigate the "table" or "bench" lands a considerable distance from the river beds. Large reservoirs were constructed to store the precious river water so that it could be released for irrigation at exactly the time in the growing season that the farmers needed it.

As might be expected, water regulation and water law became a crucial part of early Colorado legal history. A doctrine of "prior appropriation," the idea that water in a river or stream "belonged" to the first person who found and used it, was written into the new state constitution when Colorado Territory became a state in 1876.

Although irrigated agriculture became widespread in Colorado, millions of acres of land on the Eastern Plains remained high and dry prairie grass. Many attempts to plow and plant these lands were made during the 1880s and 1890s, particularly in small communities located along and promoted by the various east–west railroad lines. In periodic "wet" periods when rainfall would increase, prairie farmers would bring in a grain crop or two and make some money. The wet periods were soon followed by dry periods and widespread crop failures, however, and disappointed farm families would attempt cattle ranching or give up and move away. Boom and bust became a part of life on the dry prairies, just as it was in the gold and silver camps.

In the early 1900s, however, farmers made a new assault on the task of "dry farming" the prairies of Colorado. The state agricultural college at Fort Collins experimented with various methods and techniques of getting crops to survive on low amounts of annual rainfall. The Colorado state dryland experiment station, founded at Cheyenne Wells in 1893, aided in the development of drought-resistant crops.

Farmers learned to plow and till their lands in ways that prevented the evaporation of precious moisture. By 1910 the Eastern Plains, particularly the high prairie between the South Platte and Arkansas Rivers, had became a successful dryland farming area with wheat one of the principal crops.

The need to feed the miners, and the merchants and railroaders who came close behind them, led to relatively rapid agricultural development in Colorado. The rise of the cattle industry, irrigated agriculture, and dryland farming in Colorado was not as spectacular and well-publicized as the gold and silver strikes. Still, agriculture developed steadily in the state. Yet the rural-agrarian lifestyle on the Eastern Plains generally developed after, not before, the development of an urban-industrial lifestyle in the mining areas in the mountains and the supply towns on the Front Range.

### EARLY TWENTIETH CENTURY

The situation quieted down in Colorado as the twentieth century began. In the 1890s the U.S. government refused to set an official price for silver, with the result that the price fell dramatically, and silver mining ceased to be a highly profitable enterprise. Major gold discoveries at Cripple Creek and Victor, two mining camps located on the south slopes of Pike's Peak, brought a gigantic mining boom to that area. The millionaires created by this great gold strike lavished their civic affections on Colorado Springs, the neighboring supply town located at the eastern foot of Pike's Peak. As the U.S. government moved away from gold money and began to emphasize paper currency in the twentieth century, however, even the boom and glory of Cripple Creek and Victor began to fade.

Like many states, Colorado experienced a period of progressive political reform in the years between 1900 and 1920. In 1907 the legislature adopted the state's first civil service statute for state employees. The legislature also created a state railroad commission to regulate railroads in Colorado. Other major reforms of the period included the adoption of the initiative and the referendum, a primary election law, child labor laws, and laws requiring state safety inspections of factories. A state soil conservation commission also was created. Plainly the moralistic political culture with its "communitarian" values was in the ascendancy in Colorado between 1900 and 1920, as several progressive reforms were adopted.

Prohibition of the sale and use of alcoholic beverages was an issue in early twentieth-century Colorado. Statewide prohibition of alcoholic beverages was defeated at the polls in 1912, but two years later statewide prohibition was adopted by the voters.

Colorado rose to the challenge when the United States entered World War I. The state sent its share of young men to fight in Europe, but no major war industries or military bases were located in the Centennial State during the "Great War." Similar to the rest of the nation, Colorado experienced an upsurge in anti-German feelings that evolved into antiforeigner sentiments during the post–World War I period.

## THE TWENTIES AND THIRTIES

By the 1920s the mining era was about over. Agriculture had become important, and so had the manufacturing industry, particularly in Denver and Pueblo. With the rise of the automobile and the development of national and state highway systems, tourists began coming to the mountains of Colorado in their automobiles rather than on the train. As automobiles became more dependable and the state highway system improved, auto tourism would become a vital part of the Colorado economy.

The 1920s were the years in which Colorado, and the Colorado lifestyle, became similar to the rest of the United States. The gold and silver mines had played out, most of the booming mining towns were ghost towns, and the "roaring and bawdy" life of the mining era was mainly a treasured memory. Most Coloradans now worked on the farm or in the factory or in the office building. The only mining towns with a future were those few, such as Central City and Aspen, that would become either tourist attractions or ski resorts in the latter part of the twentieth century.

Along with the rest of the United States, Colorado suffered economically during the Great Depression of the 1930s. There was little change, however, in the character of the state. The years from 1919 to 1939 thus were relatively quiet ones. Population growth was slow, and both mining and agriculture had fallen upon hard times. "Observers might understandably predict that the glorious days of the Centennial State had passed; and never again would excitement like that generated by a Leadville or a Cripple

Creek lure the fortune-seekers and fortune-makers."[10] Colorado had been in one of its "bust" periods, and as always happened at such times, people wondered if it would ever "boom" again.

WORLD WAR II

World War II witnessed a major turning point in Colorado history, almost as great a turning point as the discovery of gold on the banks of Dry Creek near Denver in 1858. The Japanese attack on Pearl Harbor plunged the nation into a major war. In the all-out effort to win, the U.S. government sought to expand both military and industrial capacity. Colorado benefited greatly from this process, more so than most states. The war brought military installations and industrial expansion that completely changed the state, not only during the war itself but long after it ended.

In 1941 the U.S. government built the Denver Arms Plant, a large arsenal and ammunition works manufacturing cartridges, shells, and fuses. In 1942, on open land just to the northeast of Denver, the Rocky Mountain Arsenal, a chemical warfare plant, was constructed. A medical depot was built in northeast Denver and an ordnance depot at Pueblo.

The army air force operated an instruction center for pilots at Lowry Air Base just east of downtown Denver. In Colorado Springs, Peterson Air Field trained bomber crews. Also in Colorado Springs, Camp Carson, later Fort Carson, became a major army training center, particularly for tank warfare. Wounded soldiers recuperated at Fitzsimons Army Hospital in Denver.

One effect of the large number of military production and training facilities in Colorado was to expose hundreds of thousands of war workers and military personnel and their families to the attractive climate and the recreational potential of the Centennial State. People stationed in Colorado during the war found they liked the sunny, dry climate and the hiking and skiing in the nearby Rocky Mountains. Consequently, after the war was over, many of the wartime visitors moved to Colorado and expanded the state's postwar population.

Along with these many military installations came a budding scientific and defense research industry. Military technology advanced rapidly during World War II, and there was money to be made by firms that specialized in carrying out military research and technological development. Wishing to locate close to the military installations they served, many of these research and development firms chose to locate in Colorado.

The development of the Cold War between the United States and the Soviet Union immediately following World War II sustained the military-industrial boom in Colorado. Fort Carson became a large and active army training center, thereby continuing the population boom in Colorado Springs. The North American Aerospace Defense Command, the air force facility charged with defending the United States and Canada from attacking bombers and guided missiles, was located in Colorado Springs, as was the new United States Air Force Academy. Also during the Cold War, west of Denver, the U.S. government built Rocky Flats, a major nuclear weapons facility.

Most of the military-industrial expansion in Colorado during and after World War II was centered along the Front Range, particularly in Denver and Colorado Springs. In the Denver area, many of the new facilities were located in the Denver suburbs rather than in the city itself, thus contributing to rapid suburban growth in the Denver metropolitan area. World War II not only led to increasing population growth in Colorado, it centered that population growth along the Front Range.

In the years following the war, therefore, Colorado rapidly changed from an urban-industrial society into a metropolitan-technological society. In the sprawling suburbs of Denver and the quiet residential neighborhoods of small cities such as Boulder and Colorado Springs (Colorado Springs is sometimes called a suburb without a city), Coloradans were able to have the pleasures of small-town life combined with the convenience and economic opportunity of being close to a major city.

### ENDURING EFFECTS OF WORLD WAR II

By the time World War II was over, the typical Coloradan no longer was a miner or an industrial worker in Denver or Pueblo. The typical Coloradan now was a Denver suburbanite, living in a ranch house and working either in an office building in downtown Denver or in one of the many "office parks" being built in the Denver suburbs.

The U.S. Army had built Camp Hale high in the Rocky Mountains in the Holy Cross National Forest. Here the famed Tenth Mountain Division U.S. Army ski troops were trained in the deep powder snow of the Colorado winter. After the war, many of these ski soldiers returned to Colorado and played a leading role in the development of major ski facilities and ski communities at places such as Aspen and Vail.

Like the gold and silver boom in the late nineteenth century, the World War II military boom attracted new residents with an individualistic political culture to Colorado. As hundreds of thousands of service personnel and war plant workers poured into Colorado, enterprising investors found considerable wealth to be made in real estate, shopping center construction, and other consumer-related enterprises. Business boomed along with the military bases and the military-industrial plants, drawing to Colorado thousands of new residents who were committed to the individualistic philosophy of rapid economic development and free-market profit making. Colorado was once again attracting prospectors, but these new prospectors were coming with blueprints for housing developments and shopping centers rather than picks and shovels.

### ENVIRONMENTALISM

As the Front Range continued to boom in the years following World War II, so did recreational developments in the nearby mountains. Well-to-do Coloradans, and people from other states as well, began buying second homes in the Colorado mountains. Some were condominiums or chalets in ski areas. Others were "hideaway" homes in more remote areas of the state. In addition to urban sprawl on the Front Range, Colorado was experiencing "resort sprawl" in the mountains.

By the late 1960s and early 1970s, the idea began to grow among a number of Colorado citizens that the concept of "Sell Colorado" had been oversold. People who had moved to Colorado for blue skies, bright sunshine, and exhilarating clear air began to notice that, many days of the year, certain Colorado cities were covered by a brown cloud of air pollution. Except where national parks and national forests protected them, the formerly pristine mountainsides of Colorado were being cluttered up with vacation homes. Traffic congestion was making Denver almost as unpleasant to drive in as major cities in the Midwest and on the coasts. People began talking about "quality of life" in Colorado as well as "economic opportunity."

The rise of environmentalism as a political issue in Colorado was sharply posed in 1972 when the electorate voted against holding the 1976 Winter Olympics in the state. Both the business community and the political leadership had worked hard to get Denver selected over a host of competing cities as the site of the 1976 winter games. Critics, including a young state representative named Richard Lamm, charged that the Winter Olympics would overdevelop mountain recreation areas, cause mammoth traffic problems, and increase air pollution. Opponents petitioned the question of holding the 1976 Winter Olympics in Colorado onto the 1972 general election ballot, and the Olympics were defeated statewide by more than 180,000 votes.

The actual ballot question was a constitutional amendment that prohibited the expenditure of state funds. There also was a Denver city charter amendment that prohibited the expenditure of city funds. "This was the only way we could get a handle on the issue that would actually 'stop' the Olympics," said John Parr, a key organizer of this pro-environment drive.[11]

Concern for conserving the environment fit perfectly into the moralistic stream of political culture in Colorado. Environmentalists were willing to limit the right of individuals to develop their land in any manner they saw fit.[12] Environmentalists emphasized the unique yet fragile natural beauty of Colorado and said this natural beauty should be preserved for the common good. In the moralistic culture tradition, conservationists and environmentalists turned to government and urged better planning, government-designated wilderness areas, and more national parks and forests as ways to keep Colorado in a more natural state.

CONCLUSIONS

The history of Colorado is the history of boom and bust. The discovery of gold in the Denver area ignited a mineral boom that was truly spectacular in the later decades of the nineteenth century and lasted for several years into the twentieth century. In most cases, however, boom towns became ghost towns, and during the 1920s and the 1930s Colorado became a quiet place.

World War II launched Colorado's second great boom. This boom was based on the military needs of the United States during World War II and the Cold War period that followed. Military research and development became a major part of the Colorado economy in the post–World War II years. Skiing and tourism "ramped up" in the 1950s and 1960s.

Following the discovery of gold and silver in Colorado, both the individualistic (somewhat libertarian) and the moralistic (somewhat communitarian) political cultures helped frame attitudes about public policy and government in Colorado. Prospectors, miners, and farmers were strong representatives of individualistic culture. Conservationists, with their emphasis on community values and cooperation, symbolized the moralistic culture.

These two political cultures continue still to compete for the political mind of Colorado. The individualistic political culture calls for developing the state's economy and attracting new businesses and more people. The moralistic political culture shows more concern for conservation and quality-of-life issues. It calls on government to adopt programs that will preserve the natural beauty and enjoyable ambiance of the state, for new-comers as well as old-timers, and for the common worker and middle class as well as the well-to-do.

These clashing political approaches of the individualistic culture and the moralistic culture have clashed throughout the history of Colorado. They clash still.

# CHAPTER FOUR

# The Colorado Constitution
# and Its Politics

Colorado, like every state, has a constitution. It represents, at least in theory, the basic agreement of the citizens about the shape of state government and the distribution of power between citizens and state government. The Colorado Constitution is a political compact that structures state government and specifies how government power is to be divided and constrained.

Colorado's constitution, in common with other state constitutions in the United States, is a product of Colorado's politics and political culture. It is a set of "rules of the game" that attempts to shape politics and political processes. It is both fundamental law and a highly political document that has major consequences for who gets what political opportunities. Through the amendment process, Colorado's constitution is periodically questioned, challenged, and changed in an effort to redefine basic political rights, values, and opportunities or to rearrange the relationship of citizens and their state.

A major purpose of the state constitution is to establish the basic organization of government and to assign various powers and responsibilities to the three branches of government. Equally important, however, and very much in the American political tradition, the framers of the Colorado Constitution used their written constitution to limit and restrict the power of public officials and to prevent the abuse of public power.

State constitutions contain more detail and more restraints than the U.S. Constitution. They are longer, less flexible, and as a result, require more amendment. Colorado's constitution is the third-longest state constitution of the fifty states. At around seventy-five thousand words, it recently ranked behind only Alabama's (340,136 words) and Texas's (90,000 words).

It does not have to be that way. New Hampshire gets along with a state constitution that is only ninety-two hundred words long. Another state with a much shorter constitution than Colorado's is Indiana at 10,379 words.[1]

Why is Colorado's constitution so long?

The main reason is the constitution is filled with "statutory-type provisions," which are minor matters of government that could be state laws rather than constitutional principles. Also, the Colorado Constitution is long because the state has the citizen initiative. This is the ability of average citizens to circulate a petition, get a certain number of signatures, and then have the entire state electorate vote to adopt or reject a proposed constitutional amendment. Over the years, the Colorado Constitution grew longer as citizen initiatives adopted by the voters put new ideas and programs into the constitution.

Constitutional amendments are quite easy to initiate in Colorado. The number of signatures required to put an initiated amendment on the ballot is quite low. Coloradans know that the state constitution is not "sacred." Initiated constitutional amendments have become a widely approved and frequently used way of effecting political change in the state.

The state legislature further contributes to this process, periodically referring constitutional amendments of its own to the voters for approval or denial. A two-thirds vote of each house of the legislature is required to put a constitutional amendment on the ballot.

In 2006 Colorado tied for thirteenth place (with North Dakota) among the fifty states in terms of the number of times its state constitution had been amended. The amendment count began with the adoption of the state constitution in 1876.[2]

## THE COLORADO CONSTITUTIONAL CONVENTION

The Colorado Constitution was drawn up at a state constitutional convention that met in Denver in early 1876. In many ways, that Colorado constitutional convention is still in session. Whether it was woman suffrage or railroad regulation back then or environmental or abortion issues today, Coloradans have amended their fundamental law with regularity.

Colorado's constitution does much more than establish a democratic form of government. It calls upon the state to build prisons and reformatories and to provide a uniform system of free public schools. It specifies that Colorado will have colleges and universities, to be located in Boulder, Colorado Springs, Denver, Fort Collins, Golden, and other cities as provided by law.

The constitution defines how the state shall collect taxes and borrow money. It establishes how counties, cities, and towns will be created and how mining and irrigation projects shall be protected and regulated. The result is that most of the basic institutions of Colorado state government are required by and provided for in the state constitution.

Most Coloradans know little about the constitution of their state and have only a vague grasp of the importance of the constitutional principles contained within it.

## AT THE CONSTITUTIONAL CONVENTION

The Colorado constitutional convention, with thirty-nine delegates, gathered in Denver's Odd Fellows Hall beginning in December 1875. Twenty-four of the delegates were Republicans and fifteen were Democrats, thus giving the Republicans partisan control. The debating and voting at the Colorado constitutional convention did not break down on Republican-Democratic lines, however. Most of the arguments were tied to political controversies of the time rather than disagreements over established principles of government.

By 1875 there was general agreement throughout the United States on what a state constitution should include and how a state government should be structured. As a result, there was little debate and rapid agreement at the Colorado constitutional convention on the basic structure of the proposed state government.

### Boundaries and Bill of Rights

Article I established the boundaries of the proposed state. By mandate of the U.S. Congress in the enabling act for Colorado statehood, the boundaries were the same as Colorado Territory.

Article II provided for the state's bill of rights, which was listed near the beginning of the proposed state constitution, rather than as amendments at the end as is the case with the U.S. Constitution. The state bill of rights was placed in a prominent position, immediately after the preamble and the boundaries, and was given a preamble of its own. The preamble says the purpose of the bill of rights is "to assert our rights, acknowledge our duties, and proclaim the principles upon which our government is founded."

The Colorado Bill of Rights is much longer than the U.S. Bill of Rights, consisting of twenty-eight sections compared to the U.S. Constitution's ten amendments. In essence, it is a statement of timeless doctrines that transcend government yet which government is obliged to guarantee and protect.

This bill of rights clearly states that Colorado will be governed by the people. Section 1 asserts "all political power is vested in and derived from the people, . . . is founded upon their will only, and is instituted for the good of the whole."

Section 2 further elaborates this idea with specific reference to the proposed state constitution. It declares "the people of this State have the sole and exclusive right of governing themselves, as a free, sovereign and independent State; and to alter and abolish their Constitution and form of government."

The drafters of the Colorado Constitution drew upon the Declaration of Independence and various provisions from other states' declarations of rights as well as the U.S. Bill of Rights. They made explicit the property rights that are only indirectly referred to in the Declaration of Independence. Section 3 of the Colorado Bill of Rights declares: "All persons have certain natural, essential and inalienable rights, among which may be reckoned . . . acquiring, possessing and protecting property."

The Colorado Constitution deals with freedom of speech more explicitly than the U.S. Constitution, but an effort was made to protect those who might be harmed by abuse of freedom of speech. Section 10 of the Bill of Rights states: "Every person shall be free to speak, write or publish whatever he will on any subject, being responsible for all abuse of that liberty."

The remaining sections of the Colorado Bill of Rights closely parallel the protections found in the U.S. Constitution. Ex post facto laws, self-incrimination, double jeopardy, and unreasonable searches and seizures are forbidden. A fair trial, religious freedom, free and open elections, due process of law, and freedom of conscience are all expressly guaranteed.[3]

### Separation of Powers

Separation of powers, a concept only indirectly referred to in the U.S. Constitution, is explicitly provided for in most state constitutions. Colorado directly proclaims separation of powers as a principle of government in Article III.

The powers of the state are allocated among executive, legislative, and judicial departments. "No persons, or collection of persons, charged with the exercise of powers properly belonging to one of these departments shall exercise any power properly belonging to either of the others" except as the constitution expressly permits.

The Colorado Constitution next establishes the office and powers of an elected governor, thereby placing the gubernatorial article ahead of the state legislative article. This is the reverse of the U.S. Constitution, where the legislative article is placed in the prior position. This style change probably reflects that the distrust of executive power, which was so strong when the U.S. Constitution was written in 1787, had faded somewhat by the time the Colorado Constitution was being written almost ninety years later.

In addition to the governor, a number of other executive officials were to be elected by the people. They included the lieutenant governor, attorney general, treasurer, and secretary of state. Similar to most state constitutions at the time, the Colorado Constitution weakened the power of the governor by having other principal executive officers elected by the people rather than appointed by the governor.

The legislature is called the General Assembly and, similar to the national Congress, has two chambers. The Colorado Senate, with thirty-five members, is roughly one-half the size of the sixty-five-person Colorado House of Representatives. Members of the House of Representatives are elected every two years for a two-year term of office. One-half of the members of the Senate are elected every two years to a four-year term, the other half of the Senate being elected two years later, also to a four-year term.

The Colorado Constitution established a third branch of state government, the judiciary. Unlike the judicial article in the U.S. Constitution, which is short and general, the Colorado judicial article carefully structures the entire state judiciary. State constitutions as a rule are more detailed about courts because they have to establish a wide variety of courts and because even today state courts handle at least 95 percent of all judicial business in the United States.

Thus a county court was provided for each county, and a district court system was established to try major offenses against state law. Final appeal was to a state Supreme Court of three members elected for nine-year terms. The terms were staggered, and the justice with the least amount of time left to serve automatically would be the chief justice.

One other difference from the U.S. Constitution is that the Colorado Supreme Court can give "advisory" opinions when requested to do so by the state legislature or the governor. Several other states also provide for such advisory opinions. Unlike the U.S. Supreme Court, which only renders decisions on actual court cases, Colorado's highest court does not have to wait for a trial and an appeal before being able to render its judgment on important state issues of jurisprudence.

It should be noted, however, that the Colorado Supreme Court is not required to give advisory opinions when requested to do so by the legislature or governor. In practice, the Colorado Supreme Court rejects more requests for advisory opinions than it accepts.[4]

## CONTROVERSY AT THE CONVENTION

The basic structure of state government, so familiar and well tested in the other states by the 1870s, was readily agreed upon. Major debates and disagreements at the Colorado constitutional convention of 1875–76 erupted, however, over four hotly debated political issues of the day. They were economic regulation, the vote for women, state aid to parochial schools, and whether to mention God in the preamble.

### Regulation

Government regulation of railroads and other private business corporations presented a major dilemma to the convention delegates. Nearby midwestern states were combating monopoly abuses by railroads and grain storage elevators by passing laws limiting railroad rates and grain storage charges. On the other hand, Colorado was at the frontier and badly needed the capital investment that major railroads and similar large corporate enterprises could bring to the area. Convention delegates sought to provide a measure of state regulation of private business, yet not so much that it would stop private corporations from wanting to invest in the state.

The proposed constitution required a general incorporation law, thereby reducing the prospect of private corporations receiving special privileges from the state legislature. Irrevocable corporation charters were prohibited, and railroads were forbidden to merge competing railroad lines or discriminate unjustly or unreasonably between customers. A prohibition on "special legislation" was included to prevent the legislature from exempting certain classes of people from obeying a law without a reasonable basis for so doing.

Government regulation went no further than these general principles, however. No state agencies were created to regulate railroads or other public utilities, and no provision was included to give the state specific powers to set corporate charges and prices.

### Votes for Women

The woman suffrage movement was well underway at the time of the Colorado constitutional convention. Supporters of giving women the vote collected thousands of signatures and presented them to the delegates convened in Denver. Pressure was exerted to make Colorado the first state in the United States to grant the vote to women in the state constitution.

A few delegates, including Judge Henry Bromwell of Denver and Agipeta Vigil representing Huerfano and Las Animas Counties, wanted to take this historic step, but most were not ready. By a twenty-four-to-eight vote the convention denied women suffrage.

After considerable discussion, a compromise was fashioned. Women would not get the right to vote, except in school elections, but delegates agreed to put the question of full suffrage for women to a vote of those then eligible to vote. All eligible voters at the time were, of course, male.

The promised referendum was duly held a year later. Colorado's first state governor, John Routt, endorsed woman suffrage. Noted suffragists Susan B. Anthony and Lucy Stone campaigned actively in Colorado for a positive vote, but the state's male electorate rejected full voting rights for women.

It would take another fifteen years, until 1892, for Colorado's male voters to approve woman suffrage in all elections. The winning vote for woman suffrage that year was 35,798 for and 29,451 opposed.

Colorado would, at this later date, become the second state to grant full suffrage to women, but it was the first state in which woman suffrage was established by a separate vote by an all-male electorate. Wyoming women were given the right to vote by the Wyoming territorial constitution of 1868, and that right carried over when Wyoming became a state in 1890.[5]

## Church and State

In the enabling legislation for Colorado statehood, Congress provided for two sections of land in each township to be reserved to finance schools. The land was to be sold and the proceeds used to build and maintain school facilities.

The Colorado constitutional convention debated heatedly the question of whether church-related private schools could receive a portion of these school land monies. Many Roman Catholics wanted parochial schools to receive school land funds. Protestants tended to argue that school land funds should be for public schools only. The Protestant viewpoint prevailed as the proposed constitution denied state aid, other than exemption from taxation, to "any sectarian institution."

The U.S. Constitution makes no reference to God, but by the 1870s a number of the states had included some mention of the deity in their constitutions. Convention delegates discussed at length whether to put God in the proposed Colorado Constitution. Once again, controversy was settled with something of a compromise. The preamble refers to "the Supreme Ruler of the Universe."[6]

### THE FINAL DOCUMENT

The Colorado constitutional convention of 1875–76 produced a twenty-three-thousand-word final document that was five times as long as the 4,543 words of the unamended U.S. Constitution. It included considerable detail not found in the U.S. Constitution, yet it was not substantially longer nor more detailed than other state constitutions written close to the same time.

The delegates mainly were interested in achieving statehood. Plainly they were not trying to invent new, or more innovative, forms of state government. Nor were they trying to institute a more egalitarian or progressive "new state."

These were practical people primarily wanting to win statehood and guided by the widely accepted models of the existing states. The writers of the Colorado Constitution turned mainly to proven constitutional principles. They willingly compromised when this was necessary, as on the woman suffrage matter. They relied on proven and familiar constitutional language rather than attempting political innovation or constitutional creativity.

The convention adjourned on March 14, 1876. The delegates apparently had done a pleasing job of writing a popular constitution. On July 1, 1876, the voters of the Colorado Territory overwhelmingly voted for statehood and the proposed constitution by a vote of 15,443 to 4,062. On August 1, 1876, a date officially designated as Colorado Day, President Ulysses S. Grant proclaimed Colorado a state.

The constitutional convention's handiwork became the constitution of Colorado. Although considerably amended over the years, this same constitution is still in effect.

Because Colorado voted for statehood and was proclaimed a state almost exactly one hundred years after the United States' Declaration of Independence on July 4, 1776, the new state was nicknamed the Centennial State.

### AMENDING THE COLORADO CONSTITUTION

The original Colorado state constitution has been amended many times over the years. The first amendment was adopted in 1878, only two years after the constitution itself was adopted. Between 1876 and 2010, more than 120 amendments were added, doubling the length of the document and causing the present-day Colorado Constitution to be much more detailed than the 1876 original.

Nowadays there are twice as many sections of the Colorado Constitution as there were in 1876. Technically, Colorado is still operating under the 1876 constitution as revised, yet there are important differences between the constitution adopted in 1876 and the much amended constitution that governs Colorado today.

The 1876 Colorado Constitution provided only two methods for amending the constitution. Under the first method, which has never been used, a *constitutional convention* is proposed by a two-thirds vote of all the members of both houses of the state legislature. The constitutional convention actually convenes, however, only if it is approved by a majority vote at the next general election. If approved, the constitutional convention consists of seventy members, two elected from each of Colorado's thirty-five state senate districts.

Between 1876 and 2012, Colorado legislators and other political leaders made more than twenty attempts to persuade the state legislature to propose to the voters the question of calling a state constitutional convention. An 1899 proposal failed to gain approval in the state legislature by only one vote. Three times in the early twentieth century, in 1916, 1922, and 1930, the Colorado legislature submitted proposals for a state constitutional convention to the voters, but voters rejected all three.[7]

The second method of amending the Colorado Constitution is regularly used. A *referred amendment* must pass both houses of the state legislature by a two-thirds majority (currently 44 of 65 votes in the state House of Representatives and 24 of 35 votes in the state Senate). The amendment then is referred to the voters at the next general election and must receive a majority vote to be adopted.

In 1910 yet another method of amending the Colorado Constitution, the *initiated amendment*, was adopted. The initiative process was first proposed by Populist Party leaders and endorsed by Colorado's Populist governor Davis Waite back in the early 1890s. The idea later was vigorously championed by the Progressives. The initiative allows voters to propose a legislative measure or a constitutional amendment by filing a petition bearing a required number of valid signatures.

Supporters of an initiated amendment circulate petitions and obtain the signatures of registered voters equal to 5 percent of the votes cast in the last general election for Colorado secretary of state.[8] If a sufficient number of signatures are collected, the proposed amendment is placed on the ballot at the next general election and must receive a majority vote to become part of the state constitution. (Both legislatively referred measures and citizen-initiated measures can be used for statutory as well as constitutional changes.) Initiated amendments are popular in Colorado and have been used to make significant and important changes in the state constitution.

In Colorado, as in a few other states, the final battles over whether or not to adopt the initiative process pitted Democrats, who had been converted to the cause by Populists and labor interests, against Republicans, who generally held a more traditional view favoring representative government. At the time, Colorado's Democratic governor John F. Shafroth said that if he could have only one reform, it would be the initiative.[9] The fact that citizens could initiate laws and constitutional amendments, Shafroth believed, would make state legislators more careful and accountable.

Opponents of the initiative in Colorado, notably the Republican Party, said direct democracy measures such as the initiative would be alien to representative government and harmful to the financial and social welfare of the state. According to the *Denver Republican*: "The initiative and referendum both conflict directly with the representative principle, and to the extent to which they may be applied, representative government will be overthrown. . . . Cannot the people of Colorado do a little sober thinking for themselves and on their own account? Must they adopt every newfangled notion that may be adopted or experimented with in some other state? . . . Let Colorado always be sober and sane."[10]

But Colorado adopted the initiative, and this had a significant effect on opening up the political process. Many initiated constitutional amendments would not have been adopted by the more traditional method of amending the Colorado Constitution by referral from the state legislature. Populist groups on the left and right, good government groups, and occasionally even an impatient legislator or governor have used the initiated amendment procedure to bring about constitutional change in Colorado.

The amendment process, both referred and initiated, has had a major impact on government in Colorado. Significant constitutional amendments *referred* by the legislature, and subsequently adopted by the voters, have included the state income tax, reorganization of the governor's office, four-year term of office for the governor, and equal rights for women.

*Initiated* amendments that made important changes include the recall, appointed rather than elected judges, home rule for cities and towns, the state civil service system, repeal of state prohibition, a reapportionment commission to draw state legislative districts, limiting the power of cities to annex territory without a favorable vote of the people who live in the territory to be annexed, low-stakes gambling in historic mining towns, eight-year term limits for all state elected officials, taxing and revenue limits on state and local government in Colorado, limits on election campaign contributions, the required use of wind power for generating electricity, and constitutionally mandated expenditures on kindergarten through high school (k–12) education.

Critics point out that it is easier for Colorado citizens to amend their state constitution by initiative than it is in just about any other state. The signature level required to initiate an amendment on to the ballot is low and a mere majority of state voters is required to approve the amendment.

### Housecleaning Amendments

The amendment process has generally been used in Colorado to make the state constitution longer and more detailed, but there are some exceptions. A 1974 amendment deleted language that required listing and publishing the number and amount of every warrant paid by the state treasurer.[11] In 1988 an amendment removed or shortened dated provisions concerning suffrage for women, selection of the site for the state capital, and appropriations for the state capitol building.[12]

In 1990 a "housecleaning" amendment, among other things, removed an obsolete provision that a person who fights in a duel, or is a second in a duel, or assists in a duel, may not hold office in the state.

In 2010 an update to the state constitution of a housecleaning sort provided for removal of the state government from the state capital of Denver in case of a major emergency. The original constitution specified that only Denver could be the seat of government.[13] The amendment, Amendment Q, was noncontroversial and passed with broad support.

Over the years, the state legislature has periodically sent housecleaning amendments to the voters to shorten, clarify, and update the state constitution.

### Principle Amendments

Similar to other states, Colorado has had its share of "principle" as well as "programmatic" amendments to the state constitution. Principle amendments establish an idea or concept rather than being directly concerned with the way government is structured and operated. In 1972 Colorado adopted an amendment, referred to the voters by the state legislature, guaranteeing equal rights on the basis of sex (Equal Rights Amendment).[14] An initiated amendment to repeal this Colorado ERA was defeated in 1976.[15]

People debate whether such principle amendments make any difference in the actual conduct of state and local government. Whatever its meaning, the Colorado ERA was strongly supported by its proponents and adamantly fought by its opponents when it twice appeared on the Colorado ballot.

An equally controversial principle amendment was petitioned to the voters of Colorado in 1988. It stated that "the English language is the official language of the State of Colorado."[16] Part of a nationwide movement to establish English as the "official" language of the United States, the "Official English" amendment immediately came under fire from Hispanic political leaders in Colorado, who viewed it as hostile to the large number of Spanish-speaking citizens in Colorado. Opponents attempted to rename the amendment "English Only" and launched a major campaign to defeat it.

Of the eight constitutional amendments on the Colorado general election ballot in 1988, the Official English Amendment was one of the most controversial. It was frequently pointed out that English was required by statute in all written proceedings in Colorado courts of law and therefore the amendment would have no practical effect.[17]

Colorado voters settled the issue by voting in the Official English amendment by a vote of 829,617 for the amendment to 527,053 against.[18] As time passed, the Official English provision in the Colorado Constitution became a statement of principle and nothing more. No laws were passed to further implement the provision, and it received little if any subsequent attention.

### Antiabortion Amendments

As in other states, the linking of the state constitution with the initiative process in Colorado has encouraged various groups with political "causes" to use the constitutional amendment process to enact their version of social, economic, or political reform. In 1984 antiabortion groups in Colorado petitioned onto the ballot a constitutional amendment forbidding the use of state funds to pay for abortions. The amendment was narrowly adopted.

Four years later, in 1988, prochoice groups initiated a constitutional amendment that would repeal the amendment and permit state-subsidized abortions.[19] Public opinion in Colorado apparently was moving in the direction of antiabortion supporters, however, because the 1988 attempt to repeal the ban on state-financed abortions failed by the substantial margin of 809,078 votes against the amendment to 534,070 votes for.[20]

As elsewhere in the United States, the abortion issue refuses to get finally settled in Colorado. In 2008 a young woman from El Paso County (Colorado Springs area) led a successful drive to petition a "personhood" amendment on to the statewide ballot. Opponents saw this initiative as a backdoor attempt to ban abortion. The personhood amendment was easily defeated at the polls.

Two years later, in 2010, the effort to make abortions illegal in Colorado came back to the ballot in a slightly reworded form of the "personhood" amendment.[21] Once again, the proposed amendment was resoundingly rejected by the voters.

### TAX-LIMITATION AMENDMENTS

Colorado has had a long history of antitax groups initiating proposed amendments to the state constitution to require a vote of the people every time the state or a local government proposes to raise taxes. For instance, in 1976 a group of "fiscal conservatives" collected enough signatures to put such a "vote on all tax increases" amendment on the Colorado ballot. The idea did not fare well in the general election, however. A powerful alliance of elected officials, public employee associations, and lobby groups representing city and county governments (the Colorado Municipal League, Colorado Counties, etc.) strongly opposed the proposed amendment. It was overwhelmingly rejected by the electorate.[22]

The possibility of initiating constitutional amendments on to the ballot in Colorado has resulted in a wide variety of tax-limitation proposals coming before the voters. An initiated amendment in 1978 would have required a vote of the people on any state or local tax increase that exceeded the rate of inflation. It was defeated by the voters by almost a three-to-two margin.[23]

In 1988 an initiated amendment once again called for a public vote on most state and local government tax increases. It, too, was easily defeated by 778,075 votes against the amendment to 567,884 votes for.[24] In 1990 a similar though slightly modified measure was put before the voters, but this time the vote was much closer. Tax limitation was defeated by a vote of only 515,234 against to 493,456 for.[25]

### TABOR AMENDMENT

In 1992 a major tax- and revenue-limitation amendment, known as TABOR (Taxpayers' Bill of Rights), was narrowly adopted by the Colorado electorate. Passage of the amendment was helped by the independent candidacy for U.S. president of Ross Perot, a billionaire computer magnate. He received more than 20 percent of the vote in Colorado and in the process brought out a strong antitax vote.

The TABOR Amendment was long and complicated, but it was mainly sold to the voters on the point that it would require a vote of the people on any tax-rate increase.

Hidden within TABOR, and almost never discussed during the election campaign in which it was adopted, were provisions strictly limiting government revenues to the previous year's allowable revenues plus percentage adjustments for population growth and monetary inflation. Any money that came to state government above these revenue limits had to be returned to the taxpayers. Voters could, however, decide by a public vote to let the state government retain the excess revenue.

TABOR also applied to local governments in Colorado such as cities, counties, and school districts. All local tax-rate increases had to be submitted to a vote of the people before taking effect. The revenue limits applied to local governments as well, but with a difference. City and county revenues could be adjusted from the previous year only by changes in the value of real property in the city or county. School district revenues could vary only with changes in student enrollment in the district.[26]

Got all that?

TABOR was page after page of complicated legal language cemented into the state constitution. Very few average citizens really understood exactly how it worked and what its long-term effects would be on government finances in Colorado.

TABOR quickly became the most controversial part of the Colorado Constitution. Elected officials were reluctant to put needed tax increases on the election ballot, fearful that the antitax sentiments of voters might subsequently end their own political careers with a defeat for reelection. The result was that government services began slowly shrinking as many elected officials cut budgets rather than take the political risk of asking the voters for a tax-rate increase.

Throughout the 1990s, when the Colorado population was growing rapidly and the national economy was booming, the revenue limitations in TABOR were a major problem. To a number of observers, the revenue limitations in TABOR were taking critically needed funds away from state and local governments in Colorado. That was preventing the state and the localities from adequately maintaining public infrastructure. As roads, bridges, park facilities, and public buildings fell into disrepair in Colorado, critics blamed TABOR.

With the economic downturn that hit the national economy in 2000, the revenue limitations in TABOR became less of a problem. With state and local tax revenues falling rather than increasing rapidly, the TABOR revenue caps no longer applied. Throughout the 1990s, however, TABOR revenue limitations had denied a great deal of money to state and local governments in Colorado that could have been used to better maintain public infrastructure.

We should note, however, that TABOR does permit voters to increase taxes. According to the Colorado Municipal League: "Since 1992, voters have approved tax increase or tax extension questions 55 percent of the time." On the other hand, in 2011, voters in seven Colorado cities, including Aurora and Cañon City, rejected proposed tax increases or extensions. The only tax increase approved was in the city of Fort Lupton, northeast of Denver.[27]

The TABOR Amendment was the work of Douglas Bruce, a Colorado Springs landlord and tireless antitax advocate. After TABOR was adopted by the statewide electorate, Bruce made it his business to protect the amendment from its many vociferous critics.

Douglas Bruce filed lawsuits whenever he thought state or local politicians were failing to follow TABOR's requirement for a public vote on all tax-rate increases. He was equally zealous about seeing that state and local officials strictly followed TABOR's revenue limitations. In addition, Bruce strongly opposed any effort to amend the Colorado Constitution so as to remove or weaken any TABOR provisions. In the process, Douglas Bruce became a strong defender of the initiative in Colorado and fought any and all attempts to make it more difficult to petition reforms on to the ballot.

Because of his key role in the adoption of TABOR in Colorado, and because of the amendment's widespread effects on the financing of government in Colorado, Douglas Bruce was among the most influential political figures in Colorado in the 1990s. His importance waned after 2000 as a slowing economy reduced the impact of TABOR's revenue caps. During the same period, the Colorado electorate voted to take a "time out" from TABOR revenue caps for five years. The requirement for a public vote on all tax-rate increases remained in effect, however, and had a chilling effect on the willingness of public officials to propose tax-rate increases to the voters.

### Citizen Bruce

Born on August 26, 1949, in Los Angeles, California, Douglas Bruce grew up and was educated in southern California. He attended Hollywood High School, Pomona College, and received his law degree from the University of Southern California in 1973. He then worked six years as a Los Angeles County deputy district attorney, a position he resigned in 1979.

Bruce subsequently had a number of tax disputes with the Internal Revenue Service. This struggle may have either generated or strengthened his strong dislike for taxes and his apparent mission to use the initiated constitutional amendment to limit the taxing abilities of state and local governments.

As a longtime resident of California, Bruce had ample opportunity to witness and study the functioning of the constitutional initiative in that state. He also was present in California when antitax advocates used an initiated constitutional amendment to severely limit property taxes.

### Antitax Sentiment in Colorado

Colorado qualifies as an exceptionally attractive place for using the citizen initiative to oppose high taxes. Similar to California, Colorado has the citizen initiative in its state constitution. And better than California, Colorado has an even lower requirement for the number of citizen signatures needed to put an antitax or revenue-limiting constitutional amendment on the ballot.

It is well known that Colorado Springs, the second-most populous city in Colorado, is strongly Republican, conservative, and antitax in its voting behavior.

### The Douglas Bruce Technique

In 1986 Douglas Bruce moved from the Los Angeles area to Colorado Springs, Colorado. Colorado Springs would prove fertile ground in which Douglas Bruce could begin his campaign to use the initiative to severely limit the taxing ability of state and local governments in Colorado.

People who observed Douglas Bruce at work understood that he used the following techniques to get his antitax and limited-revenue amendments adopted by the voters.

1. He gathered signatures for his initiatives well ahead of Election Day. That way there was little media attention paid to his initiatives when he put them on the ballot, because the day they were voted upon was so far in the future.

2. Instead of running a campaign in favor of his initiatives, Bruce remained in the background and at times even seemed to be hiding from the news media. The strategy here seemed to be that if there was no one campaigning for the constitutional amendment, there would be no controversy and thus the news media would not cover it.

3. Most voters never saw or heard about most constitutional amendments until they actually went to vote on them. In such a case, most voters decided their vote on what they read in the short paragraph, or *ballot title*, describing the constitutional amendment. Key words such as "cutting taxes" or "revenue caps" that appeared in the ballot title thus become critical to whether a particular constitutional amendment passes. Bruce understood the importance of what appeared in the ballot title to the constitutional amendment, because he struggled mightily with election officials over exactly which words would appear in the ballot title.

4. Last and definitely not least, Bruce was relentless with his initiated constitutional amendments limiting taxes and capping revenues. He apparently did not mind losing time after time with a ballot proposal, because he knew that sooner or later conditions would be right for his proposal to be adopted. As previously noted, it took three tries (in 1988, 1990, and 1992) before Bruce finally got his TABOR Amendment passed by the voters of Colorado.

Bruce was a savvy Tea Party libertarian populist long before the Tea Party activism of 2010. Supporters of his achievements love him. Critics say he is a Machiavellian *initiative demagogue* engaged in "ballot-box budgeting. He has perfected techniques for putting his personal preferences about state and local government finance on the ballot in subtle packages that voters will vote for, even though few understand the long-term implications of those financial changes on taxes and revenues.

### *Douglas Bruce's Imitators*

Other interest groups in Colorado, observing Bruce's skillful use of the initiative to achieve his particular goals where taxing and revenue limits were concerned, learned to imitate his techniques. A conspicuous case in point was Amendment 23, which was petitioned on to the statewide ballot in order to constitutionally mandate increased spending on kindergarten through twelfth grade (K–12) education in Colorado.

Amendment 23 required state funding for public schools to rise at the rate of inflation plus one percentage point. This mandated spending was to be in effect from 2001 through 2011. After 2011 state funding for public schools was only to rise with the rate of inflation.[28]

The voters adopted Amendment 23, little realizing that it and TABOR were in conflict with each other. Amendment 23 required spending on

K–12 education at the same time that TABOR was setting strict limits on state tax revenues.

## THE GALLAGHER AMENDMENT

The situation is also complicated by the Gallagher Amendment, which had been referred onto the ballot by the state legislature. This amendment, adopted by the voters in the early 1980s, set the ratio statewide at which property taxes on residences could be collected compared to all other property taxes, mainly business property taxes. The ratio ended up being 45 percent from residential property and 55 percent from commercial property. The intent of the Gallagher Amendment was to lower property taxes on residential property.

The Gallagher Amendment allowed the local contribution to schools to float upward with property values, but TABOR said all such increases in taxes had to be subject to a vote of the people. The result was the state had to make up the local share of school taxes that prior to TABOR had floated upward with property values.[29] Once again a state constitutional provision was forcing the state to spend money on K–12 education at the expense of other important programs and services provided by the state.

## THE CONTINUING STRUGGLE

In 2010 three new financial provisions were petitioned onto the Colorado general election ballot. Although Douglas Bruce at first denied any connection to the three, the newspapers in Denver and Colorado Springs eventually ferreted out that Bruce had organized and financially supported all three initiatives.[30]

Amendment 60 mandated the lowering of property taxes and the shifting of school taxes from local communities to the state government. Amendment 61 forbade all borrowing by the state government and limited local government bonds to a term of no more than ten years. Proposition 101, among other things, greatly lowered car registration fees, thus denying the state badly needed funds for highway improvements.

The financial implications of these three initiatives for the State of Colorado were viewed by the Legislative Council of the state legislature as potentially catastrophic. Amendment 60 "would commit almost all the state's general operating budget to . . . K–12 education, leaving little for other government services." Amendment 61 would, by eliminating public borrowing, remove "the only way governments can afford to build and maintain safe bridges, roads, and other public infrastructure." Proposition 101 would cut the state's operating budget by "$1.6 billion, or about 23 percent, . . . an amount greater than what the state currently spends on prisons, courts, and the Colorado State Patrol combined."[31]

Not wanting to be caught off guard as they were when TABOR was adopted by the voters in 1992, more than six hundred public and private organizations actively campaigned against Amendments 60 and 61 and Proposition 101. Indeed, over $6.8 million was raised and spent against this Bruce attempt to further constrain state and local government in Colorado. On Election Day in November of 2010, voters solidly rejected all three initiatives by a two-to-one vote.[32]

When this arduous and expensive struggle over what should be in the Colorado state constitution was over, Douglas Bruce's opponents noted that, for all their effort and money, they had only succeeded in maintaining the status quo. These opponents wrote: "It is a shame that so many resources and so much energy were being devoted to simply maintaining the status quo in Colorado. Rather than moving our state forward, millions of dollars and hours were spent just to ensure that things didn't get worse."

"What is needed," Bruce's opponents argued, "is a substantial effort to restrict the ways in which Colorado's cluttered constitution can be amended, without eroding the right to direct democracy that Coloradans value."[33]

How expensive has this struggle become? Former governor Dick Lamm wrote in the *Denver Post*: "Over the past decade, Coloradans spent $177 million fighting ballot issues. This money could have been invested in moving our state forward. . . . Hundreds of groups—businesses, associations, non-profits—were forced to spend their resources fighting ballot measures . . . instead of focusing on their core missions."[34]

### SINGLE SUBJECT REQUIREMENTS

In their efforts to remedy the crippling financial effects of TABOR on government finances in Colorado, Douglas Bruce's opponents actually ended up making the situation worse. Because the TABOR Amendment included a variety of provisions on many different subjects, the state legislature in 1994 referred a state constitutional amendment to the voters that limited any future proposed constitutional amendment to only one subject. This "single subject" amendment, as it was called, was designed to make it impossible to change a wide variety of provisions in the state constitution with a single constitutional amendment, as the TABOR amendment had done. The amendment was adopted by the electorate.

In the end, the single subject requirement backfired on the opponents of Douglas Bruce and the TABOR Amendment. As a state constitutional law-yer at the state capitol put it: "However, the single subject requirement has had the unintended consequence of making it impossible to repeal TABOR in its entirety (since it contains more than one subject) or to take a compre-hensive approach to unraveling the fiscal mess caused by conflicting con-stitutional provisions such as TABOR, Amendment 23, and the Gallagher Amendment."[35]

TABOR critics began looking for a way to temporarily suspend the single subject requirement so that TABOR could be taken out of the constitution with a single constitutional amendment. There also were hopes the single subject rule could be waived in order to overhaul completely the many con-flicting financial and budgetary provisions in the state constitution with a single vote. None of these proposals, however, came close to being referred by the legislature or initiated by citizens onto the ballot.

There is an important overall summary point here. More and more in Colorado, political struggle is taking place in battles about what is in the state constitution, mainly put in by popular initiative, than in battles be-tween Democrats and Republicans in the state legislature and the gover-nor's office.

## TO THE UNITED STATES COURTS

In May 2011 a group of state legislators and local government officials in Colorado filed a lawsuit in the United States courts that sought to have TABOR declared unconstitutional because it denied the citizens of Colorado a "republican" form of government.

The U.S. Constitution guarantees each state a "republican" government, which means a government in which power is held by elected representa-tives rather than being based directly in the voters. The suit argued that TABOR, by centering the taxing power in the voters (direct democracy) rath-er than the state legislature and the governor (representative government), was clearly unconstitutional. The suit described TABOR as creating "a slow, inexorable slide into fiscal dysfunction" in state and local government in Colorado.

Would this "judicial" solution to the TABOR problem actually work? No one could say for certain. The lawsuit faced a long and tortuous pathway upward through the federal courts, probably taking years, before the U.S. Supreme Court might weigh in on it.[36]

### INITIATED SPENDING PROGRAMS

On the same ballot with TABOR in the 1992 November election was the Great Outdoors Colorado (GOCO) initiative. It provided that the major part of state proceeds from the Colorado Lottery, a series of state-run lottery games such as Lotto, Powerball, and Megamillions, must be devoted to purchasing open space for parks, recreation, and conservation in Colorado.

The situation was grimly ironic. The voters had adopted the initiated amendment for TABOR, which severely limited the power of the state and local governments to tax. At the same election, however, the voters took a reliable new source of income, the state's share of the state lottery, and mandated that most of it be spent for the specific purpose of purchasing open space.

The result was predictable. As the more traditional parts of state government, such as highways and public higher education, began to slowly starve financially under TABOR, state and local open space programs thrived under Great Outdoors Colorado. By 2008 Great Outdoors Colorado had raised $570 million that had been spent on more than twenty-eight hundred state and local park and recreation projects. These included purchasing almost six hundred thousand acres of open space, building or restoring seven hundred miles of biking and hiking trails, and creating or enhancing more than one thousand parks, ball fields, and playgrounds.[37]

The riches for open space just kept on coming. By 2010 over thirty-one hundred projects had received lottery funds totaling $642 million. The total acreage of open space in Colorado had climbed to 774,000 acres.[38] Of course, because both TABOR and GOCO were locked into the state constitution, there was nothing the state legislature or the governor could do, without a vote of the people, to allocate state fiscal resources more strategically.

Voters subsequently voted in an initiated amendment that provided for low-stakes gambling (slot machines, poker, etc., with a low bet limit) in the three historic gold-mining mountain towns of Central City, Black Hawk, and Cripple Creek. In this case, the state tax money earned was directed specifically to historic preservation in Colorado. As expected, historic preservation projects began to thrive as other, less-protected functions of government began to wither on the vine under TABOR.

In 2008 Colorado voters passed yet another gambling initiative. It increased the hours of operation and removed the betting limits on gambling in Central City, Black Hawk, and Cripple Creek. The increased state share of this expanded gambling was earmarked solely for Colorado's community colleges. Due to the effects of the 2008–10 economic recession, however, this constitutional change did not immediately result in significant amounts of new money for community colleges.

But there was irony. While the state's flagship universities, such as the University of Colorado at Boulder and Colorado State University in Fort Collins, continued to struggle for adequate financing because of TABOR, the state's community colleges, it was hoped, would sometime in the future reap some benefits from gambling tax money.

### MEDICAL MARIJUANA

In 2000 the voters of Colorado approved an initiated constitutional amendment that allowed for the drug marijuana to be provided to medical patients in order to relieve pain. The voters did this despite the fact U.S. laws continued to declare possessing and using marijuana to be illegal.

Until the year 2009, this initiated constitutional amendment appeared to have little effect in Colorado. Then, in November 2009, U.S. attorney general Eric Holder instructed U.S. government prosecutors not to pursue cases against medical marijuana patients in states where voters had legalized medical marijuana. In issuing the instruction, Attorney General Holder was fulfilling a campaign promise made by President Barack Obama in his 2008 campaign for president.[39]

As one of fourteen states with voter-enacted medical marijuana, Colorado was directly affected by Attorney General Holder's instructions. Medical marijuana dispensaries mushroomed throughout the state, particularly along the Front Range. Under the leadership of then state senator Chris Romer, the state legislature quickly took up the problem of regulating the rapidly expanding medical marijuana business in Colorado.[40]

The state legislature wrote regulations for the medical marijuana business in Colorado, providing for "dispensaries" to sell the drug in local communities. The term "dispensary" was not in the constitutional amendment providing for medical marijuana. The legislature also required these new marijuana dispensaries to register with and be licensed by the state. The marijuana bill was signed into law by then governor Bill Ritter.

On the first round of applications in August 2010, more than two thousand people filed to get a "pot license" to sell marijuana at a dispensary in Colorado.[41] Moreover, it became relatively easy for people, with the flimsiest claims, to qualify as marijuana patients.

As Colorado continued its apparent march toward de facto legalization of marijuana, one could question whether state voters intended this to happen when they voted for medical marijuana solely for the seriously sick and in pain. By 2011 it had become obvious to many observers that voters had been tricked into legalizing marijuana in Colorado for a wide variety of consumers, even though the specific constitutional amendment had only promised it for medical purposes.

In any event, the entire issue was headed for the courts as well as more ballot decisions. Marijuana supporters challenged the constitutionality of the regulations that had been imposed on the fledgling industry by the Colorado House and Senate and the governor.

The state legislature was required to implement the de facto legalization of marijuana in Colorado. John Morse, a Democratic state senator from El Paso County (Colorado Springs), who was state senate majority leader and a former police chief, noted: "When the voters put something in the state constitution through the initiative, no matter how ridiculous, the state legislature has no choice but to go ahead and implement it."[42]

Morse's views were echoed by Colorado attorney general John Suthers, a Republican from Colorado Springs. Suthers described the initiated marijuana amendment as leading to "government-sanctioned fraud" because what was supposed to be marijuana for medical purposes was being turned into marijuana for all. He explained that as attorney general, he has to go into court and defend what he called "indefensible voter initiatives" no matter how legally questionable they might be.[43]

As groups with political causes have learned to do in Colorado, marijuana supporters turned to the initiative to push their industry even further toward full legalization. By 2012, eight initiatives had been filed with the state to legalize marijuana and authorize the state legislature and governor to enact laws regulating the new industry. Two of the eight initiatives were sweetened up with provisions to make them more attractive to the voters. One included a wholesale tax on marijuana that would generate up to $35 million a year for the state treasury. A second earmarked marijuana revenues for constructing public school buildings and athletic fields.[44]

### REFERRED VS. INITIATED AMENDMENTS AND LAWS

The necessity of a two-thirds vote in both houses of the Colorado legislature to refer a constitutional amendment probably is one of the reasons the initiative is frequently used in Colorado. The number of signatures required (5 percent of the most recent vote for secretary of state) is low when compared with the number of signatures required in other states that use the constitutional initiative. In Colorado, gathering petition signatures appears to many to be an easier alternative than persuading two-thirds of both houses of the legislature.

Many groups, even those formed for no other purpose than to initiate a particular constitutional amendment, have demonstrated that, with determination and an appealing cause, the necessary signatures can be gathered. Following through with a successful campaign to win a majority of the statewide vote for a citizen-initiated amendment can be an enormous challenge, however. It requires either money for advertising or the support of interest groups that can recruit large numbers of volunteer election workers.

How one views the role of citizen-initiated amendments depends on a number of factors, including one's political vantage point and ideological outlook. The initiative process especially appeals to activists on the left and right, to people who do not generally win at their state capitols, and to people who are either outside the mainstream or who grow impatient and frustrated by the incremental and brokerage practices of the state legislature.[45]

Such activists often wish to stop progress or to push things forward fast. As one longtime aide to the Colorado legislature put it: "The conservatives most often use initiated constitutional amendments to try to stop people and government from doing things. The liberals are more likely to use initiated constitutional amendments to try to get things going."[46]

The U.S. Supreme Court gave a boost to those who initiate constitutional amendments when it ruled the State of Colorado could not outlaw the use of paid workers to gather signatures for an initiative petition.[47] This decision increased the opportunity for persons and groups with substantial financial resources to be able to get their favorite idea or reform for the state constitution initiated on to the general election ballot. A staff member in the Colorado secretary of state's office speculated that special interests in the state might begin using paid petition-signature gatherers in an effort to initiate constitutional amendments that would provide them direct economic benefits.[48]

The initiated constitutional amendment sometimes becomes a not too subtle element in the partisan competition between the Democratic and Republican parties in Colorado. For instance, in 1966 an initiated constitutional amendment mandated single-member legislative districts in Colorado, a reform generally acknowledged to have helped the Republicans.

## CHANGING THE AMENDMENT PROCESS

In 2010 state senator Abel Tapia from Pueblo proposed a constitutional amendment that would require 60 percent voter approval before a citizen-initiated constitutional amendment could pass in Colorado. A *Denver Post* editorial endorsed his effort, noting that the state constitution was already a cluttered mess of often-conflicting mandates that have made it hard to govern the state.

The *Denver Post* said: "Amending the Colorado constitution, the operating manual for state government, ought to be tough to accomplish. The public should have an abiding interest in an issue of civic importance before this document is changed. That's why we are generally supportive of ideas embodied in this draft measure."[49]

Yet other groups and legislators have proposed increasing the number of signatures required for constitutional amendments as well as stipulating that signatures be collected throughout the state.

A campaign to reform the ballot and constitutional amendment process in Colorado has been championed by a group called Colorado's Future. Another advocate for reform was Reeves Brown. He was the executive director of Club 20, a civic advocacy group that has been a stalwart representative of business, agricultural, and government leaders on Colorado's Western Slope. In 2011 Brown was appointed by Gov. John Hickenlooper as executive director of the Colorado Department of Local Affairs.

Brown said his efforts to reform the initiative process were separate from his Club 20 responsibilities. He acknowledged support from various business groups, such as Colorado Concern. Indeed, Dan Ritchie, chairman of Colorado Concern, enthusiastically praised Brown's efforts.

Brown organized a number of community forums across the state to test the depth of interest in reforming selective aspects of the state constitution.

These "civic engagement" meetings, mostly attended by invited civic and community leaders, found a working consensus of those in attendance for the following recommendations:

1. Ballot language should be clear and concise (readable at an eighth grade level).

2. Make the financial disclosure requirements for ballot initiative campaigns just as strict as the requirements for candidate campaigns.

3. Require petitioners to collect signatures from various locations around the state.

4. Require more signatures for constitutional amendments than for statutory amendments [laws].

5. Require that constitutional amendments secure a super-majority of votes while continuing to allow statutory amendments to be adopted

with a simple majority, but allow anything that is ALREADY in the constitution to be amended OUT with a simple majority vote.

6. Establish a Constitutional Review Commission the meets periodically to review the [state] constitution and recommend to voters changes in conflicting provisions.[50]

Brown and Ritchie and their allies understand how much Coloradans prize the rights of citizens to have the safety valve of an occasional citizen-initiated law. But they believe the overly lenient Colorado method of amending the state constitution had taken too great a toll on both the integrity of Colorado's representative government processes and on the state's capacity to deal comprehensively with major issues of the budget and taxes, and thus provide adequately for critically important state infrastructure.[51]

Brown and Ritchie believe strongly that this process has undermined representative democracy and handicapped Colorado state government.

They and like-minded allies, especially in Denver business and political circles, believe the initiative process fails to provide for the give and take of debates, deliberations, and compromises that a well-functioning legislative process provides.

They do not think a constitution is the proper place for a detailed set of specific legal requirements (often containing thousands of words). These constitutional requirements affect highly technical and arcane matters such as educational spending, tax policy, campaign finance regulation, and the like.

Legislators and veteran attorneys who have worked in and around the state legislature realize how hard it is to get legislative policy making right the first time. These experienced hands remind us that law is an evolutionary and incremental process. But a statutory law passed by the legislature, as opposed to a constitutional amendment, can be brought up at the next legislative session and repaired or rescinded. Mistakes added to the constitution, however, are far more difficult to amend and very often have to be lived with for years, in some cases many years.

Properly done, a bill or amendment in a legislature gets subjected to critically important scrutiny and public hearings. This generally results in thoughtful consideration of costs as well as concern for those citizens who are going to be affected by the measure.

There is no doubt that this new breed of constitutional reformers understands the effects of TABOR, Amendment 23 (K–12 education), the lottery amendment, the mountain-town casinos amendments, and others. These initiated constitutional amendments have reshaped the fiscal and governing landscape of Colorado. A growing number of well-informed Coloradans share these concerns. Yet it will be an uphill battle to win voter approval, even though many observers, including the present authors, believe these measures deserve serious consideration.

CONCLUSIONS

Average citizens of Colorado are either ill informed about or even indifferent to their state constitution. On the other hand, many elected officials and business leaders acknowledge a need to reform various sections of the Colorado Constitution, particularly those portions dealing with the initiative process and state and local government finance.

Many elected officials worry about the relatively easy process by which private citizens and special interest groups initiate amendments that alter the constitution. Yet most of these same officials are reluctant to lead any effort to take that power away from the people. (Of course, only a majority of the people by a positive vote could so amend the existing constitution). A few attempts have been made to make the initiative more difficult in Colorado, mainly by increasing the number of signatures required to launch an initiative, but all have failed with the electorate.

Most legislators and most political scientists have long favored relying on elected officials for lawmaking and for amending constitutions, contending there is an important difference between public opinion and the public interest. They cite the difference between direct democracy and representative democracy. But it is also clear that most American voters, and most Colorado voters, still want to have at least an occasional voice in the shaping of laws and in the reshaping of their constitution.

The Colorado Constitution continues to grow. It has been amended about forty times in the past four decades. Some would say it is appropriately a living institution adapting to new needs and changing demographic and political values. Others bemoan the needless amount of new detail in this ever-lengthening document.[52]

Central participants in the lawmaking process in Colorado have managed to live with the state constitution, in all its revised and expanded annotations and amendments. Many prefer to cope with the constitution as it is rather than take any chances on a constitutional convention that might weaken government or alter the strategic balance of power in the state.

Still, a number of reformers want to overhaul the constitutional system in the Centennial State. Invariably this is because they believe a different set of policies might be produced by a differently written "improved" and "streamlined" state constitution.

# CHAPTER FIVE

# Political Parties and Elections in Colorado

The Centennial State has long been characterized as a Republican state, yet Democrats have always competed successfully for a number of state-wide and congressional offices, and especially for governor. Indeed, there have been more Democratic than Republican governors, and Democrats have held the governorship for several more years than the Republicans. The Populist Party held the Colorado governorship for one two-year term from 1893 to 1895.[1]

## A PARTISAN STATE

State law carefully spells out how the two major political parties in the state will be organized and will nominate candidates for office. Many cities and towns, including Denver and Colorado Springs, have exercised the option of holding nonpartisan municipal elections. Otherwise, the overwhelming majority of elected offices in Colorado are held by either a Democrat or a Republican. In most cases, those who wish to function effectively in Colorado politics and government must first learn how to function effectively in one of the two major political parties.

## REGISTERING TO VOTE

To vote, citizens must register to vote. In rural areas voter registration takes place at the county courthouse. In the more populated counties, there is usually a county election office located near the courthouse in the county seat.

Coloradans may register in one of the two major parties, Republican or Democratic. They also may register in one of the minor or so-called third parties, such as the Libertarian Party, the Green Party, or the American Constitution Party. If a prospective voter does not want to state a party affiliation, he or she is registered as unaffiliated. Unaffiliated voters can participate in political party primary elections in Colorado, but they must register in the party at the polling place on primary election day to do so. Unaffiliated voters cannot participate in party caucuses, including presidential nominating caucuses.

In the 1980s Colorado adopted "motor voter" registration. Coloradans are asked if they want to register to vote whenever they obtain or renew their driver's license. "Motor voter" has proven to be a convenient way to get newcomers and younger citizens registered to vote.

Although historically Colorado has been regarded as a Republican state, voter registration recently has shown an almost even match between the two major political parties and unaffiliated voters. In other words, as noted previously, roughly one-third of Coloradans register Democratic, one-third register Republican, and one-third register unaffiliated. The simplest analysis of Colorado elections has always been that unaffiliated voters swing the balance of power between the two major political parties. This may be even more the case since Colorado has become, at least for the time being, a "purple" state.

Why do one-third of Colorado voters choose to register as unaffiliated and not bother to join one of the two major political parties? One reason is that large numbers of people move into Colorado every year from elsewhere and want to wait a few years before making a commitment to one political party or the other. A second reason is that our survey data show that most unaffiliated voters are moderate and centrist on policy issues.

The almost equal balance in Colorado between Democratic, Republican, and unaffiliated voter registrants inspired former *Denver Post* political columnist Fred Brown to say this about Colorado: "A state that was once reliably Republican is now a delicately balanced political toss-up."[2]


### THE NOMINATING PROCESS

Colorado has an ingenious and detailed system for nominating party candidates. There are party primary elections, one in the Republican Party and one in the Democratic, and these primary elections are held in June prior to the November general election. To qualify for the primary election ballot, however, would-be party candidates must receive 30 percent or more of the delegate votes at a party convention held previously. Delegates to party conventions are initially selected in party precinct caucuses.

## The Precinct Caucus

Political and electoral activity in Colorado begins at the precinct level. The precinct is the smallest-size voting unit in the state, consisting of approximately a thousand registered voters who live in the same neighborhood. On Election Day, the registered voters in a precinct often can vote at the precinct polling place, usually a public school, public library, or other public building in or near the precinct. Voters also can vote at the county election office, in vote centers, or by mail. Some elections, usually local elections, are held exclusively by mail.

Voting by mail has proved increasingly popular in Colorado. More than 50 percent of the state's electorate votes by mail rather than in traditional polling places or at the county election office. It is probably only a matter of time until all Colorado elections are held exclusively by mail.

Statewide elections for political offices are held every two years. Early in each election year, precinct caucuses are held in every precinct. The precinct caucus is the beginning of the party nominating process.

There are two separate caucuses in each precinct, one for Republicans and one for Democrats. The caucuses are held in the home of a loyal party worker or in a meeting room at a local elementary school, a church, or some other public or semipublic place.

Only registered Democrats can vote at the Democratic precinct caucus, and only registered Republicans can vote at the Republican precinct caucus. Colorado thus has a "closed" caucus system in which only registered party members can actively participate.

One suggestion for increasing voter participation in Colorado party politics is to allow unaffiliated voters to attend either the Republican or the Democratic precinct caucus. This would give unaffiliated voters a say in which candidates receive a particular party's nominations for office. It also would bring unaffiliated voters into the party process, perhaps encouraging a percentage of them to join one of the major political parties.

Critics of this suggestion, however, claim that only loyal party members, those who care enough about the party and its policies to register in the party, should participate in something as important to the party as nominating candidates for office.

In each party precinct caucus, two precinct committee persons are selected to organize the precinct and to turn out the party vote on Election

Day. In the past, one committee person was a man and one was a woman, and in many precincts in Colorado it is still customary to select a man and a woman to handle party chores. The two committee persons are selected every two years at the precinct caucus.

The major event that takes place at the precinct caucus is the election of delegates from the precinct to the party county convention.[3] This is important because the county convention will begin the process of nominating party candidates for county offices, including county commissioner, county clerk, and county assessor.

The county convention also will select delegates to the party's state convention, where the first steps will be taken in nominating party candidates for statewide elected offices, including governor, attorney general, U.S. senator, and state treasurer. In presidential election years, a party's state convention also will select those party members who will serve as delegates to the party's national convention.

The party precinct caucus is important in Colorado because it is the first step in a lengthy nominating process that eventually decides the party nominees for important offices, including the state's governor and U.S. senators. In many cases, candidates for major office in Colorado begin campaigning at the precinct level, urging their supporters to go to the caucus and elect delegates who support the candidate to the various party conventions.

When a candidate does a good job of turning out supporters to a precinct caucus, he or she is said to have "stacked the caucus."

There is great variety in the way party precinct caucuses are conducted in Colorado. Some are well attended and there is much discussion of the various party candidates and the issue positions they have taken. In some of these lively caucuses, elections may be required to determine the precinct's delegates to the county convention.

For the 2008 presidential election, Colorado held its first-ever presidential precinct caucuses. The exciting contest between Barack Obama and Hillary Clinton for the Democratic Party nomination for president resulted in Democratic precinct caucuses in Colorado that were unusually lively and well attended. Indeed, the 2008 Democratic precinct caucuses set caucus attendance records.

The various candidates for delegate to the county convention may or may not identify themselves with the various candidates running for county, state, or national nominations for office, but many of them do.

Many other party precinct caucuses are poorly attended, however, and there is little or no discussion of party politics or the various candidates for party nominations. Every person who attends the party precinct caucus will likely be offered the opportunity to serve as a delegate to the county convention, since there are often more delegate spots at the county convention for the precinct than people in the precinct who want to go.

In many precincts, committee persons must recruit party members to serve as delegates to the county convention, using arguments about "good citizenship" and "party loyalty" to get people to undertake the task.

Some critics say the party precinct caucus is a poor way to begin the party nominating process in Colorado. Every registered member of a political party can attend his or her party precinct caucus, yet relatively few bother. In some cases, there can be lively discussion and competition between candidates for delegate to the county convention at precinct caucuses, but that is a rare occurrence.

In many of the precincts, probably a majority, the same party stalwarts dutifully attend the precinct caucus, vote themselves and their friends a trip to the county convention, and adjourn, often without ever discussing which of the various candidates might make the better nominees for office.

Those who like the current precinct caucus system point out that it places power right where it belongs, and that is in the hands of faithful party members who are sufficiently committed to the party to take the time to attend precinct caucuses, county conventions, and, periodically, state conventions.

Moreover, it is said, people should vote for county convention delegates because they trust the delegate's judgment, not because they are committed to one candidate or another.

Candidates for political office in Colorado have learned how to win with the precinct caucus system. It is known that in many precincts the same people go to the precinct caucus year after year and frequently are elected delegates to the county convention. Candidates for office get lists of these "party regulars" and contact them by mail, e-mail, telephone, or occasionally in person. Many candidates will set up Internet websites where regular caucuses attendees can get detailed information about the candidates' backgrounds and issues positions.

Candidates make an effort to get the votes of these party regulars at the county and state party conventions. In most cases, it is easier and more productive to campaign for the votes of these party regulars than it is to try to elect your own people to the county and state conventions. Working the party regulars tends to be a more fruitful endeavor than attempting the considerably more difficult task of turning out supporters at the precinct caucuses.

The candidates who are most likely to work to bring new people to precinct caucuses are party newcomers who are challenging an incumbent party officeholder for the party nomination. It is well known that the party "loyalists" who regularly attend precinct caucuses are most likely to support party incumbents. "Upstart" candidates challenging an incumbent thus will work to get large numbers of new party members to the precinct caucuses in an effort to outvote the party regulars.

## The County Convention

In each of the sixty-four counties in Colorado, usually on a Saturday in early spring, the delegates elected at the precinct caucuses meet and hold the county convention. Customarily the convention is held in the auditorium of a high school in or near the county seat, but in larger counties the convention may be held in a hotel, a convention center, a sports arena, or other large public facility.

The number of persons eligible to attend the county convention varies with the population of the county, with roughly three to eight delegates and three to eight alternates for each precinct in the county. Alternate delegates qualify to vote at the county convention when one of the regular delegates fails to attend or leaves before voting is completed.

The county convention can be an important party event. Ample time is usually provided before the convention begins for party members to socialize and renew political acquaintances. Candidates for nomination greet convention delegates, handing out campaign buttons and bumper stickers and signing up supporters.

Also present will be incumbent officeholders, even those who are not up for reelection that year. The county convention is a perfect opportunity for party officeholders to shake hands with the party faithful, hear what their constituents are concerned about, and demonstrate that they are loyal, hard-working party members themselves.

The first item of business at each party's county convention is electing delegates to the party *state* convention. In certain cases, as they check in, delegates to the county convention are asked if they want to be delegates to the state convention. Those who say they do are put on a list. A group of county party leaders will meet and examine the list, deciding on those who will be nominated as delegates and alternates to the state convention.

In other cases, would-be delegates to the state convention put their names in a hat and are chosen by lot. Whichever method is used, the list of names is then presented to the county convention and in most cases readily approved.

In some instances candidates for important statewide offices will be competing for delegates to the state convention. Often county party leaders will work to resolve disputes by balancing the recommended list of state convention delegates among competing candidates. If things cannot be worked out in that manner, delegates at the county convention may have to choose between competing lists of state convention delegates, with each list committed to a different candidate.

The second order of business at the county convention will be the nomination of party candidates for county offices. Following brief speeches by the candidates for the office being voted on, a secret ballot will be conducted. All candidates who receive 30 percent or more delegate votes will be eligible for the August party primary election.

The candidate with the highest number of votes will be listed first on the primary election ballot, the candidate with the second highest number of votes will be listed second, and so forth.

Candidates for party nominations work hard to get the most delegate votes and qualify for "top line" designation on the primary ballot, but that does not necessarily mean they are going to win the primary election. No one knows exactly what "top line" designation is worth in added votes, but it is sometimes said to be worth 10 percent of the vote.

Colorado election laws provide one last option to those would-be candidates who believe they will fail to get at least 30 percent of the delegate vote at the county convention. If they wish, they may go door to door and collect the signatures of registered party members on a petition supporting their candidacy. Once they have gathered a minimum number of authenticated signatures, they will have "petitioned" their way onto the primary election ballot.

In most instances, however, aspiring candidates take their chances at the county convention. If they fail to get 30 percent or more of the vote at the county convention, they quietly accept the judgment of their fellow party loyalists and withdraw from the competition.

In addition to electing delegates to the state convention, the county convention also will elect delegates to the congressional district convention, where the party's nominees for the U.S. House of Representatives will be voted on. Delegates will also be elected to the judicial district convention, where the party's nominees for district attorney will be selected. These conventions are similar to the county convention in that any candidate who receives 30 percent or more of the convention vote is automatically placed on the primary election ballot.

For party members who want to be actively involved in party affairs, it is relatively easy to become a delegate to the county convention. Once there, one can get involved in the democratic process, mingling with office-holders and party leaders, listening to speeches by prospective party candidates, and voting for one's choices among the various candidates for nomination to a number of important local offices.

County conventions are usually successful in building party "spirit" as well as beginning the process of nominating candidates for public office.

## The State Convention

Each of the two major parties holds a state convention, customarily in late spring in general election years.[4] Historically, state conventions have been held in one of the larger cities on the Front Range, including Denver, Boulder, Colorado Springs, or Pueblo.

In recent years, however, both the Republican and Democratic state conventions have become such large gatherings that they are usually held in Denver, either at a big downtown hotel, the Pepsi Center sports arena, or the Colorado Convention Center. Democrats, however, occasionally meet in the large Colorado University Events Center in Boulder.

After a large new venue, the World Arena, opened in Colorado Springs, both parties began periodically holding their state conventions in Colorado's second-most populous city.

The state convention is primarily an enlarged version of the party's county convention. There is much talking and socializing, as well as a great deal of speech making by statewide officeholders and party candidates for statewide offices.

As at the county convention, those candidates whose names will appear on the party ballot in the June primary election must receive at least 30 percent of the delegate vote, and the person who receives the most votes gets the valued "top line" designation.

Also, as at the county level, those who do not like their chances of getting 30 percent of the vote at the state convention, and thus getting in the party primary that way, have the option of petitioning their way onto the statewide primary ballot.

Thus, at the 2010 Republican state convention in Colorado, a major candidate for the Republican nomination for U.S. Senate, Jane Norton, elected to make certain she was listed on the Republican primary ballot by petitioning on. Her opponent, Weld County district attorney Ken Buck, won at the state convention and received top line on the Republican primary ballot. In a somewhat close and very hard-fought primary election, Ken Buck, the convention favorite, defeated Jane Norton, who had petitioned on.

Little attention is paid to third parties in Colorado, such as the Libertarian Party or the Green Party. The candidates nominated by them have only a remote chance of winning the general election and holding office. One exception to this happened in 2010. Tom Tancredo, a former Republican member of the U.S. House of Representatives from Colorado, received the American Constitution Party's nomination for governor and succeeded in winning almost four times as many votes as the weak Republican nominee. It was not enough, however, and Tancredo lost to Democrat John Hickenlooper.

It should be noted that the national Libertarian Party got its start in Colorado in 1971 when a group led by David Nolan gathered in Westminster, a northern suburb of Denver. David Nolan bolted from being a Republican because of his opposition to Republican president Richard Nixon's policies on wage and price controls and the U.S. war in Vietnam. Nolan and a few of his friends in the Denver area and in Colorado Springs were influenced by the writings of Ayn Rand and Robert A. Heinlein.[5]

### Party Differences

Our Colorado College political polling highlighted the differences between Democrats and Republicans in Colorado. See Figure 11A–D.

The overall results of our polling indicate that there are sharp disagreements between Democrats and Republicans in Colorado over some of the major issues of the time. Figure 11A shows that Democrats favor equality while Republicans want liberty. Figure 11B reveals many more Republicans than Democrats think that taxes are too high. Figure 11C shows that Democrats want to protect the environment at all costs, but Republicans are much less supportive of that idea. Figure 11D highlights that Democrats support gay and lesbian marriage while Republicans are opposed.

There were no surprises in Table 8. Colorado Republicans are much more likely to describe themselves as conservatives. Colorado Democrats see themselves as mainly liberals. Those with no affiliation preferred to say they were mainly in the moderate middle ideologically, halfway between conservative and liberal.

The clear message of these surveys is that Colorado voters are separated from each other along ideological lines as well as partisan (political party) lines. This leads to the conclusion that Colorado Democrats and Republicans in recent years have become more strongly ideological (conservative or liberal) in their politics and thus are more polarized (separated from one another) along conservative or liberal lines.

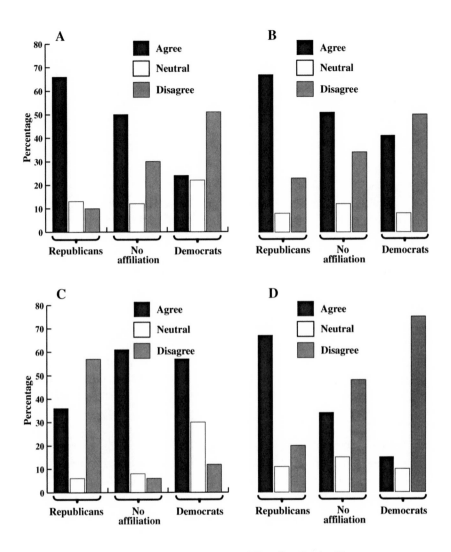

Figure 11. Partisan Views on Liberty and Equality, Cutting Taxes,
the Environment, and Same-Sex Marriage

A. STATEMENT: "I believe liberty is more important than equality."
B. STATEMENT: "Taxes are too high. The state legislature has got to do something
about cutting the state's tax burden."
C. STATEMENT: "We have to protect the environment no matter what the costs."
D. STATEMENT: "Gays and lesbians should not be allowed to be legally married in
the state of Colorado."

*Source*: Colorado College Citizens Poll, 2010.

Table 8. Political Outlook of Coloradans Correlated with Party Affiliation

|  | Very conservative | Somewhat conservative | Neutral | Somewhat liberal | Very liberal |
|---|---|---|---|---|---|
| Republicans | 61% | 37% | 23% | 6% | 0% |
| No affiliation | 7 | 28 | 42 | 25 | 28 |
| Democrats | 2 | 15 | 28 | 62 | 65 |

*Source:* Colorado College Citizens Polls, Spring 2010.

Colorado's liberal Republicans and conservative Democrats are not quite the endangered species that they are in the U.S. Congress, yet even in Colorado there are declining numbers of liberal Republicans and conservative Democrats.

### The Primary Election

The nominating process in Colorado concludes with the June primary election. Colorado has a "semiclosed" primary. Only registered Democrats can vote in the Democratic primary. Only registered Republicans can vote in the Republican primary. However, on primary election day, unaffiliated voters can go to their polling place, announce they want to join one political party or the other, and vote in that party's primary election.

Relatively few unaffiliated voters exercise their right to declare a partisan affiliation on primary election day and then vote in the appropriate primary. It happens occasionally, however, particularly when there is a hotly contested and well-publicized primary. Those unaffiliated voters who declare a partisan affiliation on primary election day remain registered in that political party. If they wish to be unaffiliated again, they must go to the county election office and formally change their registration back to unaffiliated.

As previously noted, over the past several years the two major political parties in Colorado have been fairly evenly balanced in terms of party registration. Because of this relatively even party balance among registered voters and the high proportion of unaffiliated voters, party primary elections do not attract great attention in Colorado.

There are local areas in the Centennial State, of course, where one political party wins the general elections so regularly that winning that party's primary is tantamount to winning the general election. The Democratic Party tends to be so dominant in Denver and Pueblo that, for those seeking political office, winning the Democratic primary is a bigger challenge than winning the general election.

On the other hand, in heavily Republican areas, such as Douglas County, south of Denver and in Colorado Springs, the Republican primary usually determines the eventual officeholder.

In recent years both political parties in Colorado have had some hard-fought primary elections. Often these bruising contests have helped the opposition party, particularly when the other party did not have a tough primary fight.

Primary elections have become so destructive to party candidates, in fact, that leaders in both parties maneuver to avoid primaries. They do this by pressuring fully qualified candidates to defer to the party leaders' first choice and voluntarily drop out of the race.

A case in point occurred in 2004 when Mark Udall, the U.S. representative from the Boulder area, was encouraged to exit the race for the Democratic nomination for U.S. senator. He was persuaded to step down to smooth the way for state attorney general Ken Salazar, who was the pick of party-leader Democrats in both Colorado and Washington DC. After his primary victory over a relatively unknown competitor, Salazar went on to win the U.S. Senate seat for the Democratic Party.

In 2010 Andrew Romanoff, the former Democratic speaker of the Colorado House of Representatives, ran in the Democratic primary for U.S. senator against Michael Bennet, the incumbent, who had been appointed to fill a vacancy. It was something of a classic showdown, with Romanoff having strong support among rank-and-file Democrats but little money to spend on his campaign. Bennet, on the other hand, was backed by Democratic president Barack Obama and Democratic Party leaders in Washington DC, and was well financed. Bennet won the primary and went on to narrowly retain his seat against a strong Republican challenge.

Similar to most other states, voter turnout in primary elections in Colorado is approximately 30 percent of the total number of voters registered in the particular political party. In those primary elections where a race is hotly contested and well publicized, however, the percentage increases.

### Nominating Process Evaluated

The nominating process in Colorado is a combination of both party conventions and the primary election. In effect, a system of caucuses and conventions is used to narrow the field of candidates that eventually run against each other in the primary election.

Under this system, party regulars, people dedicated enough to the party to attend caucuses and conventions, make the "first cut" in the pool of candidates available for party nomination to elected office. The "final cut" to a single party nominee is made by the "rank and file," those persons registered in the party who take the trouble to vote in the primary election.

The nominating process thus retains the strengths of both the convention and the primary election. The party convention provides the opportunity for face-to-face politics, bringing party members together to both socialize and begin the nominating process. The primary election, however, provides the opportunity for less-committed party members to participate by voting for their first choice from a final list of candidates selected by the caucus convention process.

There is in the eyes of some, however, a major drawback to the nominating process used in Colorado. The people most likely to participate in precinct caucuses tend to come from the ideological extremes of the two major political parties rather than from the moderate center. Thus right-wing social conservatives tend to dominate Republican precinct caucuses, and left-leaning social liberals occasionally prevail in Democratic precinct caucuses. Since the precinct caucuses choose the delegates to the county conventions, and the county conventions then select the delegates to the state conventions, the system now and then is biased toward the more conservative (Republican) and liberal (Democratic) wings of the two parties, rather than the center. These biases extend all the way up to the state conventions.

Conservative Republicans and progressive Democrats thus often have had a bias in their favor from the very start of the party nominating process in Colorado. The more moderate and centrist candidates in both parties have to hope they can make it to the party primary in which more moderate and centrist voters will be participating. Moderate and centrist candidates in both political parties, but most notably the Republican Party, often choose to petition onto the primary ballot by gathering signatures rather than take their chances at an extremely conservative Republican state convention or an extremely liberal Democratic state convention.

In recent years the Democrats have done a better job than the Republicans of nominating centrist, moderate candidates for statewide office, despite the bias of the nominating process toward more extreme candidates.

## The 2008 Presidential Caucuses

In 2008 Colorado Democrats used their control of both houses of the state legislature to schedule presidential caucuses for both the Democratic Party and the Republican Party. The major attraction of presidential caucuses was the fact that they are paid for by the political parties, unlike presidential primaries, which are expensive to conduct and must be paid for by the state. In the age of severe TABOR restrictions on state spending, presidential caucuses were the obvious choice for Colorado.

Barack Obama easily defeated his main opponent, former First Lady and New York U.S. senator Hillary Clinton, in the 2008 Colorado presidential caucuses. The delegation to the Democratic National Convention from Colorado was divided up between the two candidates in accord with the proportion of votes each received at the presidential caucuses. Barack Obama went on from his Colorado caucuses victory to win the 2008 Democratic presidential nomination, and the following November, to win the White House.

For the Republicans in Colorado in 2008, former Massachusetts governor Mitt Romney beat U.S. senator John McCain of Arizona in the GOP presidential caucuses. In 2012 Rick Santorum ran against Romney, Gingrich, and Ron Paul in the Republican nominating caucuses. Santorum, backed by evangelicals and the Tea Party, won a surprising victory over Romney.

The 2008 Democratic National Convention was held at the Pepsi Center in Denver, Colorado. For one politically fascinating week, Denver and Colorado became the center of national political attention. Barack Obama elected to accept the Democratic Party's presidential nomination outdoors at Mile High Stadium, where the Denver Broncos professional football team plays.

THE GENERAL ELECTION

General elections in Colorado are overwhelmingly a two-party affair. Independent candidates are almost never elected to political office in Colorado, even though access to the general election ballot by independent candidates is relatively easy. Only a minimal number of petition signatures are required. The result is that noticeable numbers of independent candidates and third parties, such as the Libertarian Party and the Prohibition Party, show up on the general election ballot in Colorado.

The most successful third-party candidate to run for president in Colorado in recent years was billionaire Ross Perot, who petitioned onto the Centennial State ballot in both 1992 and 1996. Although Perot did not win Colorado's electoral votes either year, he garnered 23 percent of the Colorado presidential vote in 1992. He doubtless took enough of those votes from incumbent Republican president George H. W. Bush that it enabled

Democrat Bill Clinton to win Colorado on his way to a national victory and the presidency.

This analysis has made clear the major role of political parties, particularly the Democrats and the Republicans, in Colorado elections and Colorado government. This is a good point at which to remember that there is no democracy without politics, no politics without political parties, and no effective parties without bargaining, compromise, and patient agreement building.

## A Relatively Balanced State

Prior to 2004, most observers classified Colorado as a Republican state, mainly because the Republicans consistently did well at winning Colorado's electoral votes in presidential elections and at controlling both houses of the Colorado legislature. A more recent look, however, shows Colorado to have a definite two-party flavor, one that began trending toward the Democrats in the 1990s and early in the first decade of the twenty-first century.

Recent figures suggest that Colorado currently is neither a Republican state nor a somewhat Republican state. Rather, it is nearly evenly divided between the two major political parties when it comes to voting in statewide elections for major offices such as U.S. president, state governor, and U.S. senator.

## Regional Voting Patterns

Voting analysis in Colorado makes one point clear. The Denver Metropolitan Area, and the Front Range of which it is a part, are the major political battlegrounds in Colorado. They are where more than 80 percent of the vote is cast in statewide elections. Denver Metro and the Front Range steadily increased their percentage of the state electorate throughout the last half of the twentieth century, and they appeared likely to continue to do that in future years.

The Denver Metropolitan Area is one of the most Democratic parts of Colorado. Denver Metro contains almost 60 percent of the state's voting population, and it is clearly the biggest Democratic vote producer in the state.

Southern Colorado also is Democratic, yet it contains too few voters to make a substantial impact on statewide voting results. Still, in close elections, Democrats need Southern Colorado to win.

It is important to note that, as the Denver Metropolitan Area became increasingly Democratic in recent decades, two populous counties outside Denver Metro, El Paso and Weld Counties, became increasingly Republican.

The Eastern Plains of Colorado, which have the most agriculture in the state, are the most Republican part of Colorado. This does the Republican Party little good, however, because the Eastern Plains cast so few votes compared to those cast on the Front Range.

The same is true of the Eastern Foothills region. It is solidly Republican but has almost the same small number of voters as the Eastern Plains.

The Western Slope is one of the more notable regions in terms of its politics. Back in the 1980s, it was one of the more Republican parts of the state. By 2004, however, it had become almost evenly balanced between the two political parties, with a slight edge to the Republicans.

That suggests the Western Slope joined the Denver Metropolitan Area in becoming significantly more Democratic in the three decades from 1980 to 2010. One reason for this was the Democratic-leaning character of the destination ski areas located on the Western Slope.

Recent election returns make it clear that the wealthy, trendy, and outdoor-oriented persons who settled down permanently and become voters in Colorado's stylish destination ski resorts have shifted heavily Democratic. In fact, the Colorado ski country now is one of the most heavily Democratic sections of the state. Keep in mind, however, that the seven ski counties comprised only a small percentage of the state's electorate in 2008 when compared to votes cast on the Front Range.

It is the decidedly Democratic character of the voters living in the destination ski counties that has pulled the Western Slope increasingly toward the Democratic Party. When the ski counties are removed from the Western Slope, that region of Colorado becomes almost as distinctly Republican in 2010 as it was in the 1980s.

Map 4 identifies the most Democratic and most Republican counties in Colorado in major statewide elections from 1989 to 2008. It also identifies the counties that swing back and forth between the major parties.

### Voting Shifts in Denver Metro

With more than 60 percent of Colorado voters living in the Denver Metropolitan Area, and more than 80 percent living on the Front Range (which includes Denver Metro), there is no question that these are the crucial areas for understanding partisan voting behavior in Colorado.

Denver, which is both a city and a county, clearly is the most Democratic portion of Denver Metro. This is typical of United States cities. Denver has the largest African American and Hispanic populations in Colorado, two groups that tend to favor the Democratic Party. In addition, upscale

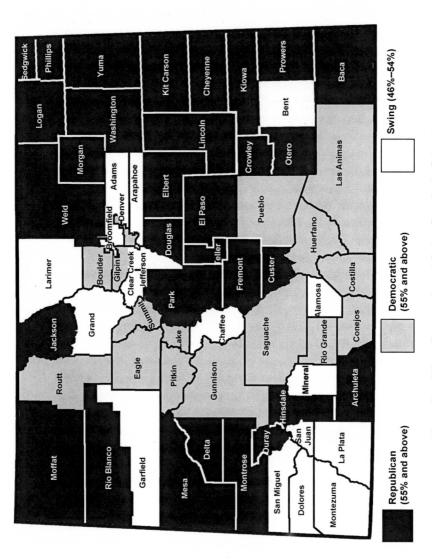

Map 4. Republican, Democratic, and Swing Counties in Colorado

Republican
(55% and above)

Democratic
(55% and above)

Swing (46%–54%)

voters have been moving into Denver, and that group has been voting more Democratic.

The next most Democratic county in the Denver Metropolitan Area is Boulder County. This upscale county is located northwest of Denver and is home to the University of Colorado, a leading state public university. The county also contains several U.S. government research institutions. Boulder is almost as strongly Democratic as Denver.

Thus Denver and Boulder are the two most important counties in Colorado when it comes to producing votes for the Democratic Party. The two counties' large populations coupled with their strong preference for voting Democratic make them the "bedrock" of the Democratic Party in Colorado.

Because of its many factories and warehouses, Adams County has been pro–labor union and thus slightly Democratic in voting behavior.

Adams County is located northeast of Denver and fits the definition of an industrial suburb. Adams County is only slightly Democratic, however, while the City and County of Denver and Boulder County vote dramatically for the Democrats.

Arapahoe and Jefferson Counties have traditionally been the swing counties in Colorado elections. The candidate who carries Arapahoe and Jefferson Counties, whether a Democrat or a Republican, has consistently been elected to statewide office.

These counties, noted for their upscale inner-suburban voting populations, have been slowly but steadily shifting to the Democrats. Forty years ago, Arapahoe and Jefferson Counties were considered reliably Republican in most elections, but in recent statewide contests they have been barely Republican at all.

There are two explanations for these two populous Denver suburban counties shifting steadily away from the Republicans. One is that the voting populations for which these counties were famous, upscale suburbanites with high incomes and good educations, were somewhat antagonized by the increasing social conservatism of the Republican Party during the 1980s, 1990s, and early years of the first decade of the twenty-first century. These former liberal Republicans, or "Eisenhower Republicans," did not share the antiabortion, antienvironment, and antigay and antilesbian views of many national Republicans, particularly those in leadership positions in Congress in recent years. They progressively shifted their votes to the Democrats, particularly during and after the presidency of conservative Republican George W. Bush.

A second explanation is that many minorities, primarily Hispanics, began settling in suburban Arapahoe and Jefferson Counties rather than in Denver. Their Democratic votes coupled with those of the upscale suburbanites shifting toward the Democrats weakened Republican voting patterns in Arapahoe and Jefferson Counties.

Of the counties in the Denver Metropolitan Area, Douglas County is one that is somewhat more distant from center-city Denver. It lies south of Denver, with Arapahoe County in between Douglas County and Denver.

Douglas County might best be defined as an outer suburban county or as an "exurb." It has many expensive homes on very large lots. Some of the lots are five acres or more in size. The county sports a large number of country "estates" with stables for horses for recreational horseback riding. In addition, there are planned communities and golfing communities in which large numbers of spacious homes have been constructed. Douglas County has long been the most Republican part of Denver Metro.

Overall, however, the Denver Metropolitan Area has been trending toward the Democrats, and that is the principal reason Colorado has been trending more Democratic.

### Front Range (Minus Denver Metro)

After the Denver Metropolitan Area, which contains more than 60 percent of the voting population in Colorado, the second-largest region in the state is the Front Range (minus Denver Metro). These four populous counties contain just a little bit more than 25 percent of the Colorado electorate.

El Paso County, which contains Colorado Springs, the second-largest city in Colorado, remains the Republican Party powerhouse in the state. Indeed, El Paso County is shifting ever more strongly Republican. In many statewide elections, it casts more than 60 percent of its ballots for the Republican candidate. El Paso County is the driving force of Colorado Republicanism in the same manner that Denver Metro is the mainspring of the Colorado Democratic Party.

Larimer County includes the city of Fort Collins, home of the main campus of Colorado State University. The southern edge of the county has the city of Loveland and is starting to get some of the more distant suburban growth of the Denver Metropolitan Area. Larimer County has always been comfortably Republican, and by 2010 Larimer County was still Republican, but by closer margins.

It will be disappointing news for the Colorado Republican Party if Larimer County, with its growing population, continues to shift more Democratic.

Weld County also is located north of Denver Metro. Similar to Larimer County, it has been receiving substantial amounts of distant suburban growth from the Denver Metropolitan Area. The county seat is Greeley, a major agricultural center and the location of the University of Northern Colorado. Weld County is reliably Republican and is becoming more Republican. Weld County has joined Douglas County and El Paso County as one of the most Republican counties in Colorado.

Pueblo County historically has joined Denver as one of the most Democratic counties in Colorado. Lately, however, Pueblo County has been nudging slightly more Republican. Pueblo contrasts sharply with Denver, which became much more strongly Democratic.

One way to view Colorado voting is to see the Denver Metropolitan Area, with its strong Democratic proclivities, as locked in political battle with the Front Range (minus Denver Metro), with its demonstrated preference for the Republican Party.

This is something of an oversimplification, however, because one of the strongest Republican counties, Douglas County (the Castle Rock, Parker, and Highlands Ranch areas) is located in the Denver Metropolitan Area. On the other hand, historically Democratic Pueblo County (Pueblo City) is located in Front Range (minus Denver Metro).

The "mother lode" or key to winning Colorado elections for the two major political parties is Arapahoe and Jefferson Counties in Denver Metro. These two upscale Denver inner-suburban counties are populous and have a past history of swinging from one major political party to the other and then back again. They thus swing the balance of power in Colorado statewide elections.

The political equation in Colorado is as follows: Denver and Boulder are becoming more solidly Democratic. They are offset in their Democratic support, however, by the increasing Republicanism in El Paso (Colorado Springs), Douglas (Castle Rock), and Weld (Greeley) Counties. This essentially leaves the swing electoral role in the state to Arapahoe and Jefferson Counties.

The real question in Colorado is whether Arapahoe and Jefferson Counties will continue their pronounced shift toward the Democratic Party. If the two counties do so, the Democrats can look forward to a bright electoral future in Colorado. Republican hopes for the future rest in the possibility that, having shown the ability to vote strongly Republican in the past, Arapahoe and Jefferson Counties might switch their loyalty back to the Republican Party.

When it is a close statewide race, however, regions of Colorado outside

Denver Metro and the Front Range (minus Denver Metro) come into play. Rural Colorado (farming and ranching country) is strongly Republican, Southern Colorado leans Democratic, and the ski counties on the Western Slope lean Democratic.

## The 2010 General Elections

Due to the unpopularity of some of President Barack Obama's policies and a high national unemployment rate of 9.6 percent, a Republican wave swept across the United States in the 2010 general elections. In Colorado, however, the Republican wave hit two Democratic sandbars that greatly reduced its impact on the state.

One Democratic sandbar was John Hickenlooper, the popular mayor of Denver. Aided by a strong third-party candidacy that split the Republican vote, Hickenlooper won the Colorado governorship for the Democrats. See Map 5.

The other Democratic sandbar was incumbent U.S. senator Michael Bennet, who eked out a whisker-thin victory and thus held his U.S. Senate seat for the Democrats. Bennet beat off the Republican wave by criticizing his opponent, Weld County district attorney Ken Buck, for being an extremist, mainly on the pro-life issue.

Farther down the ballot, however, the Republican wave hit Colorado and hit it hard. The Republicans picked up two of Colorado's U.S. House of Representatives seats that had formerly been held by Democrats. The Republican wins were in District 4, mainly on the Eastern Plains, and in District 3, mostly on the Western Slope and in Southern Colorado. Those Republican wins shifted the state's balance in the U.S. House from five Democrats and two Republicans over to four Republicans and three Democrats, a more normal situation for Colorado.

The Republicans also won big in the three statewide races below the level of the governorship. They elected neophyte candidates to the positions of state treasurer and secretary of state, unseating incumbent Democrats. The Republicans also reelected the incumbent Republican state attorney general.

The surge of the Republican wave reached well into the Colorado state legislature. The Republicans took enough seats from the Democrats in the state House of Representatives to win a one-vote majority after six years out of power. The Republicans made gains in the state Senate, but not enough to win the majority away from the Democrats. In the 2011 session, the state legislature was under split control, with the Republicans narrowly

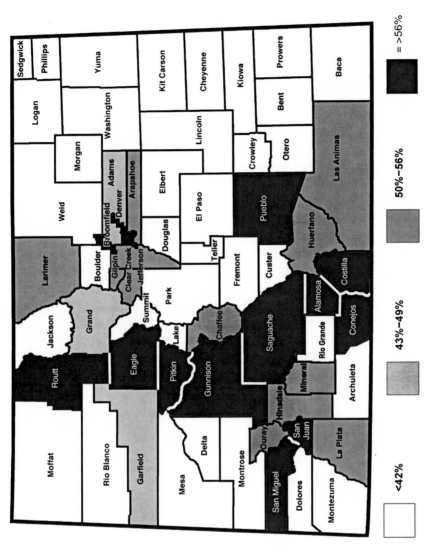

Map 5. Gubernatorial Vote for Democrat John Hickenlooper in Colorado in 2010 by County

*Source:* Updated from the *Denver Post,* November 3, 2010, 15A.

= >56%

50%–56%

43%–49%

<42%

controlling the state House of Representatives and the Democrats dominant in the state Senate.

One way of seeing the impact of the 2010 elections on Colorado was this: Democrats got their feet good and wet in the Republican wave because they lost badly at the bottom of the ticket, but Democrats kept their heads above water because they won the two top spots, the governorship, and a U.S. Senate seat.

Because the U.S. Senate race between Democrat Michael Bennet and Republican Ken Buck was especially close, that election provided an opportunity to study Colorado's electorate in an evenly balanced situation. Notably, Colorado's two most famous swing counties, Jefferson and Arapahoe Counties in the Denver suburbs, voted for Michael Bennet, the Democrat, but only narrowly so. Yet these two bellwether counties shifted statistically back toward the Republican Party from the strong Democratic preference the two counties had shown in the 2008 presidential election. The rule still held that Jefferson and Arapahoe Counties were the major swing counties in the state. Thus, as a popular Colorado adage nowadays has it, as Jefferson and Arapahoe Counties go, so Colorado is likely to go.

The blunting of the 2010 Republican wave in Colorado in 2010, particularly at the top of the ticket, reinforced for us, and most political analysts, that Colorado was neither red (Republican) or blue (Democratic) but a deep shade of purple (evenly divided between the two major political parties).

## CONCLUSIONS

The practical results of the recent trend toward the Democrats in Colorado have been evident in recent elections. Barack Obama won Colorado's nine electoral votes for president in 2008. Two Democrats, Mark Udall and Michael Bennet, are Colorado's two U.S. senators, Udall elected in 2008 and Bennet in 2010. The Democrats elected the state governor, Bill Ritter, in 2006, and won the governorship again with John Hickenlooper in 2010. But the Republicans' modest comeback in 2010, electing Republicans to minor offices and regaining control of one house of the state legislature, suggests Democrats do not dominate Colorado elections.

Colorado has become a competitive two-party "purple" state, delicately balanced on the edge between the two parties. Colorado thus has undergone a gradual electoral metamorphosis. It shifted from generally Republican to one of the more competitive two-party states in the United States.

While Democrats have had successes, Republican will undoubtedly win a share of future Colorado state races. Both some of the ideological find-

ings in our state polls and a number of Colorado political analysts suggest
Colorado is still a "Republican default" state. That means statewide races
are still most likely to be won by Republicans. It's just that in the Udall,
Salazar, Ritter, Hickenlooper, and Bennet years, Republicans seemingly
found ways to lose.

But stay tuned.

# CHAPTER SIX

# Electing Colorado Legislators

Former Democratic state representative Jerry Kopel of Denver was a veteran door-to-door campaigner. He invariably asked constituents if he could help them in any way. In one campaign, one woman told him, "Yeah, you can water my petunias." Kopel said, "Sure," went outside, turned on the hose, and watered the petunias.[1]

Coloradans have, as the late former Representative Kopel found out, a pragmatic approach to their state legislators. They want them to be honest and responsive. They also want them to keep taxes down. Yet most Coloradans do not know their legislators' names and few attend "meet the candidate" forums or write or otherwise contact their legislators.

Our statewide surveys indicate that Coloradans' opinion of their state legislature has declined over the past twenty years. A lot of that decline occurred in the four years from 2006 to 2010, when the Recession of 2008–10 created voter disaffection with all levels of government in the United States. See Figure 12.

For forty years, from the early 1960s to the early 2000s, the Colorado state legislature mainly was controlled by the Republican Party. At times, the Republican-dominated legislature operated in a highly partisan manner with the majority party working to exclude the minority party from the legislative process. At other times, the two parties functioned in a more cooperative manner, although the majority Republicans were always clearly in control.

In 2004 the Democrats won comfortable majorities in both houses of the Colorado legislature. They maintained those majorities through the 2006 and 2008 elections. Suddenly, after many years out of power, it was the Democrats' turn in Colorado to run the legislature. The Democrats elected the president of the Senate and the speaker of the House, and the Democrats named all the committee chairs.

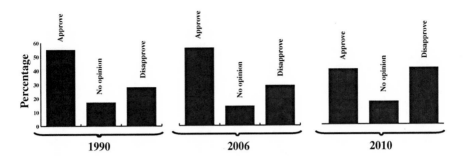

Figure 12. Approval/Disapproval of State Legislature

QUESTION: "What about the state legislature? Do you generally approve or disapprove of the job the Colorado state legislature is doing?"

*Source*: Colorado College Citizens Polls, 1990, 2006, 2010 (*N* = 614, 613, 603).

In 2010, however, control of the Colorado state legislature changed again, but only partly so. The Democrats maintained control of the state Senate, but the Republicans won the state House of Representatives by a majority of only one representative. Clearly, in the early twenty-first century, either major party had a good shot at winning a majority of either house of the Colorado state legislature.

Colorado has had a two-house state legislature since its inception. Only Nebraska has a one-house legislature. Occasionally a legislator or a citizens group proposes a unicameral legislature for Colorado. For example, state Representative John Carroll in 1974 urged this. He said having a senate and a house of representatives at the state level was "expensive duplication, an unneeded luxury."[2] His resolution produced discussion in the press yet failed to win much support in Colorado's two legislative chambers.

### STAGGERED SENATE TERMS

General elections for the Colorado legislature are held on the first Tuesday in November of even-numbered years. Ever since the state constitution was adopted, state representatives have been elected every two years to a two-year term of office.

Things are different in the Colorado Senate. One-half of the state senators are elected every two years to a four-year term of office, and the other half are elected two years later, also to a four-year term of office.

This staggered reelection system has a definite effect on the partisan composition of the Colorado legislature. With only one-half of the Colorado Senate up for reelection at any one time, it is difficult for the minority party in the state Senate to gain a majority of Senate seats in only one election. Usually the party out of power in the Senate will have to make gains in two or three consecutive elections before it can become the majority party in the upper chamber.

This contrasts with the situation in the Colorado House of Representatives, where every seat is up for election or reelection every two years. If the party out of power is popular at the time of a particular election, it has the opportunity to win a large number of seats in the House.

That is how it happened when the Democrats won control of both the state Senate and the state House of Representatives in 2004. The Democrats began improving their position in the Colorado Senate in the 2000 election. As a result, when the Democrats had a big state legislative election year in 2004, the state Senate as well as the state House of Representatives went majority Democratic.

By 2010, however, it was the Republicans, and not the Democrats, who were suffering from the effects of staggered state Senate elections in Colorado. The Republicans had become the party that would need two or three winning election cycles to gain back control of the state Senate. The 2010 elections bore this reality out clearly. As a Republican tide swept across the nation, the Republicans gained narrow control of the Colorado House of Representatives, where every member was up for reelection. In the state Senate, however, where only one-half of the thirty-five members had to face the voters, the Democrats retained their majority.

## REQUIREMENTS AND LIMITS

A candidate for either house of the Colorado legislature must be a U.S. citizen and at least twenty-five years old. Candidates must have been a resident of their district for at least twelve months prior to the general election.

Until 1990 there was no limit on the number of times a person could be reelected to the Colorado legislature. A citizen-initiated constitutional amendment, adopted by the voters at the 1990 general election, limited Colorado elected officials to eight years in office. This "term limits" amendment passed by a wide margin of 71 percent of state voters in favor to 29 percent against.

A citizen-initiated constitutional amendment approved in 1966 set the total membership of the Colorado legislature at one hundred. There are thirty-five state senators and sixty-five state representatives. The same constitutional amendment required that state legislators be elected from single-member districts.

### REDISTRICTING

Every ten years the U.S. government conducts a census. The Colorado Constitution requires that district lines for the Colorado Senate and Colorado House of Representatives be redrawn every ten years to conform to the latest census figures. This process of redrawing legislative district lines every ten years is known as *redistricting*. As a result of a series of U.S. Supreme Court decisions in the early 1960s, the population of state senate districts must be "substantially equal," and the population of state House of Representatives districts must be "substantially equal."

Prior to 1980, redistricting in Colorado was implemented by passing a bill through the state legislature and obtaining the governor's signature. Under that system, if a political party had a majority in both houses of the legislature, the district lines usually were drawn in such a way that the majority party had a better chance of winning legislative elections. If the governor at the time was a member of a different political party than the one that enjoyed a majority in both houses of the legislature, the governor could veto the redistricting plan, thereby forcing the legislature to come up with a plan that created less-partisan legislative districts.

In 1974 Colorado voters approved an initiated constitutional amendment establishing a new procedure for redistricting the state legislature. Instead of the legislature and the governor drawing legislative district boundary lines, an eleven-member Colorado Reapportionment Commission is appointed to do the job. In an effort to reduce the partisan character of the redistricting process, no more than six of the eleven members of the reapportionment commission can belong to the same political party.

The Colorado Reapportionment Commission is misnamed. It should be called the redistricting commission. It redraws state legislative districts every ten years. The apportionment, the number of voters per district, is required by court decision to be equal for every district in the state House and every district in the state Senate.

An important part of this redistricting system is that members of the commission are appointed by all three branches of Colorado state government. Four members of the commission are appointed by party leaders in the state legislature, three members are appointed by the governor, and four members appointed by the chief justice of the state Supreme Court.

The four members of the commission appointed by party leaders in the state legislature are named in the following fashion: one commission member is selected by the speaker of the state House of Representatives. A second member is selected by the majority leader of the state Senate. Because they are the elected leaders of their respective houses, the speaker of the House and the majority leader of the Senate are always members of the majority party in that house. If they prefer to do so, the speaker of the House and the majority leader of the Senate can name themselves to the reapportionment commission.

The other two legislatively appointed members of the reapportionment commission are from the minority party, one selected by the Senate minority leader and the other selected by the House minority leader. If they wish, the minority leaders can appoint themselves to serve on the commission.

Once appointed, the Colorado Reapportionment Commission operates under a tight time schedule. Using U.S. Census materials, maps, voting returns, and special computer programs, the commission has ninety days to draw up a preliminary redistricting and reapportionment plan for the state.[3]

The commission then holds public hearings on its preliminary plan, after which it draws up a final plan. This final plan is then submitted to the Colorado Supreme Court, which carefully reviews it. The court makes certain the new legislative districts meet constitutional requirements concerning equal population of districts, compactness of districts, respect for city and county boundary lines, and preservation of traditional communities of interest in the state.

In addition, to meet U.S. government requirements, the redistricting cannot have a negative impact on minority voters.

### Redistricting 2001

In 2001 the Democrats succeeded in gaining majority control of the Colorado Reapportionment Commission. With the help of sophisticated computer technology, the Democrats redistricted so as to give their party maximum advantage in state legislative elections.

A case in point was El Paso County, Colorado, the most Republican county in Colorado, which includes the city of Colorado Springs. When the Republicans were doing the redistricting in Colorado, the Democrats were hardly ever able to elect even one Democratic state representative or one Democratic state senator from El Paso County. The Republican voting strength in the county was too great for the Democrats to win anything there.

With the Democrats drawing the district lines, however, El Paso County soon elected a Democrat to the state House and a Democrat to the state

Senate. In the 2008 election, the Democrats surprised everyone by electing a *second* Democrat to the state House of Representatives from El Paso County.

One of the contributing factors often cited for the Democrats gaining control of both houses of the Colorado state legislature in 2004 was that the Democrats gained control of the state legislative redistricting process in Colorado following the 2000 U.S. census.

### *Redistricting 2011*

The 2011 Colorado Reapportionment Commission was completely different from the 2001 commission. Instead of being biased toward one political party or the other, it was evenly divided along partisan lines (five Democrats and five Republicans) with an unaffiliated voter serving as chairman and frequently casting the deciding vote.

This situation came about because Gov. John Hickenlooper, a Democrat, declined to pack the commission with members of his own party but instead appointed a Republican to create an even balance. Hickenlooper was joined in this effort to help create a bipartisan commission by Chief Justice Michael Bender of the Colorado Supreme Court.

The reapportionment commission operates in the following fashion. Redistricting plans are drawn up by each party and presented as partisan alternatives. In the age of computers, these highly partisan plans, for the most part, are not drawn by the commission members themselves but by professional computer experts employed in behalf of the political parties. As the commission votes on plans for the seven major regions of the state of Colorado, it adopts either the Democratic plan for the region or the Republican plan.

As would be expected under such a system, the five Democrats routinely voted for each Democratic regional plan and the Republicans mainly voted for each Republican regional plan. The end result was that the unaffiliated commission chairman, Mario Carrera, got to cast the deciding vote for each regional plan. The result was a preliminary plan that favored the Democrats in some areas of the state and the Republicans in others.

Following the required statewide hearings on the preliminary plan, Chairman Carrera took that combined Democratic-Republican plan and began to mold it into a compromise bipartisan plan. It was a plan that strongly emphasized the creation of as many state House and state Senate seats as possible that would swing back and forth between the two major political parties from one election to the next.

The Colorado Supreme Court rejected the "Carrera plan," with its swing seats, on the grounds that the plan did not sufficiently follow city and county boundary lines.

At this point Chairman Carrera joined with the Democrats, giving the Democrats a six-to-five-vote majority. The Democrats proceeded to gerrymander ten Republican state legislative seats into only five legislative seats, thus forcing five Republican legislators out of office.

The final plan, which was approved by the state supreme court, had a bright spot for reformers. Of the one hundred seats in the Colorado legislature, thirty-eight were swing seats that did not favor one political party over the other.[4]

### Redistricting Evaluated

Despite its tendency to be more partisan than originally intended, the Colorado Reapportionment Commission is generally admired by political commentators. But in 1997 Chuck Berry, a Republican who was speaker of the Colorado House of Representatives at the time, summed up the great difficulty of getting politics out of the legislative redistricting process. "You can't take politics out of [redistricting]," he said. "It is an inherently political process."[5]

One major reform for the reapportionment commission would be to have the various regional plans proposed by a neutral group of computerized districting experts employed by the state rather than by computer geniuses working in behalf of the Democratic and Republican parties. That way the final plans adopted would not be strongly biased toward one of the two major parties, which is what happens under the present system where the parties prepare competing plans.

Another reform would be to legally mandate the evenly balanced commission which Governor Hickenlooper and Chief Justice Michael Bender voluntarily created in 2011. Requiring an equal number of Democrats and Republicans on the commission, with an unaffiliated voter serving as chair, might over the decades guarantee redistricting plans that will be less biased toward one political party or the other.[6]

#### REDISTRICTING FOR THE U.S. HOUSE

The Colorado Reapportionment Commission, however, *only* redistricts the state legislature. Colorado's congressional districts, which elect Colorado's members of the U.S. House of Representatives in Washington DC, still are drawn by the state legislature and signed into law by the governor.

This process is highly political and often results in heated arguments between a legislature dominated by one political party and a governor from the other party. Following the 2000 U.S. Census, the Democrats sued the Republicans and succeeded in getting U.S. House redistricting in Colorado decided in the Denver district court.

The court adopted a plan favored by the Democrats, and within six years three Republican U.S. House seats in Colorado switched to the Democratic Party. In the 2010 congressional elections, however, the Republicans gained back two of those U.S. House of Representatives seats. It seemed as though court-ordered redistricting in Colorado had produced two safe seats for the Democrats, two safe seats for the Republicans, and three seats that either party had something of a chance of winning.

The pattern described above was repeated following the 2010 U.S. Census. The Democrats took the Republicans to court, and a Denver district court judge preferred the Democratic congressional redistricting plan. As expected, the Democratic plan took a strongly Republican U.S. House seat and made it a swing seat either party could win.

It can be argued that U.S. House of Representatives district lines as well as state legislative district lines should also be drawn by the Colorado Reapportionment Commission.[7] Another idea is that, since judicially ordered redistricting after the 2000 census produced a more evenly balanced Colorado delegation to the U.S. House of Representatives, judicial redistricting for U.S. House districts should be permanently instituted in Colorado.[8]

SAFE SEATS

In terms of general elections, seats in the Colorado legislature can be classified into three categories. There are safe Democratic seats, safe Republican seats, and swing seats.

Safe Democratic seats are those easily won by the Democratic candidate. Often Republicans cannot find a challenger or do not even bother to find an opposition candidate. Safe Democratic districts in Colorado are located in center-city Denver, Adams County (an industrialized area northeast of Denver), the city of Pueblo, the city of Boulder, and in the San Luis Valley in Southern Colorado.

One Democratic member of the state House of Representatives, Wayne Knox of south-central Denver, had such a safe seat in the legislature for thirty years. Term limits of eight years, adopted in 1990, put an end to such lengthy careers.

Safe Republican seats are those easily won by the Republican candidate. Just as Republicans have trouble finding candidates to run in safe Democratic districts, Democrats often have trouble recruiting candidates to run in safe Republican districts. Most of the safe Republican seats in the Colorado legislature are found in El Paso County (Colorado Springs), Douglas County (Castle Rock), Weld County (Greeley), and many of the rural areas of the state.

Chuck Berry, the speaker of the Colorado House of Representatives during the late 1990s, sat in a seat so safe that, even the first time he ran for the legislature, no Democratic candidate could be found to oppose him. No Democrat opposed him the three times he ran for reelection. It was term limits, not a successful Democratic challenger, that forced Berry out of the legislature.[9]

## SWING SEATS

Swing seats are legislative districts that, based on their voting records and demographic characteristics (average income, average educational levels, percentages of minorities, etc.), can vote either Democratic or Republican in the next election. As expected, both political parties put forth their greatest electoral efforts to win and retain the swing seats in the state Senate and state House of Representatives.

A swing seat is most likely to switch from one political party to the other when it is an "open" seat, that is, when one party or the other does not have an incumbent legislator running for reelection. Because the average voter does not pay much attention to legislative elections, and because name familiarity is one of the biggest factors in winning elections, incumbent members of the state legislature generally have an easy time getting reelected.

When an incumbent is not running for reelection in a swing seat, however, each party will have the opportunity to win the seat in the next general election, and each party will "target" the seat and make an extra effort to win it.

Political parties traditionally have done three things to establish which swing seats to target with extra campaign efforts and extra campaign funds.[10] First the party will study the *voting history* of the various legislative districts, noting how Democratic and Republican candidates for U.S. president, U.S. senator, governor of Colorado, and so on, have done in each district. If the political party's candidates for national and statewide offices have done well in a particular district, it becomes a possible target district.

The second factor is the *demographics* of the various districts. Prior to

2000, the lower the educational levels and income levels in a legislative district, the more likely it was considered to vote Democratic. After 2000, when upscale, well-educated voters began voting more Democratic, districts with higher education and income levels also became Democratic targets. Republicans did best in middle-class districts, particularly if they were far away from Denver.

Precincts with high percentages of black voters and Hispanic voters also are more likely to vote Democratic. Other demographic factors that can help Democratic candidates are high percentages of older voters and large numbers of labor union members in the district. Republicans do best with white voters and nonunion workers.

The third factor in establishing target districts is *candidate strength.* Political parties will pay particular attention to those legislative races in which the party candidate appears to be particularly popular with the voters and is proving to be a strong and energetic campaigner. At the same time, the parties look for legislative races in which the opposing candidate appears to be a weak campaigner with little voter appeal.

Both parties in Colorado concentrate their efforts on target seats. As a result, in any given general election, a mere twelve to fifteen of the total eighty-two or eighty-three legislative races are regarded as important by the two political parties. This concentration of effort on a small number of seats occurs because both political parties in Colorado target the same way and pour most of their money into the same legislative races.

## LEGISLATIVE ELECTION CAMPAIGNS

Both parties start with a long list of thirty or so swing seats that have potential for being targeted, but the list narrows as it gets closer to Election Day. In some races, a candidate gets way ahead and the party no longer feels the need to target the race. In other cases, the opposition candidate develops a big lead and the party decides it would be wasted effort to emphasize that district.

Once they have decided which legislative races to target, the two major political parties in Colorado provide essentially the same kind of campaign help for their respective candidates. The parties provide voting data that campaigns can use to identify voting precincts in which there are large numbers of voters favoring the political party. The assumption is that party candidates will campaign heavily in these precincts, working hard to turn out known party supporters to the polls on Election Day. Both parties encourage their legislative candidates to make extensive use of direct mail, sending their campaign materials to computerized mailing lists of frequent voters.

Colorado now has early voting and mail-in voting, and these two forms of voting grow in popularity with each succeeding election. As a result, candidates running for the state legislature have most of their mailings in the mail and the bulk of their political ads running on television as much as a month before Election Day.

### *"Walking"*

Candidates who can afford them purchase street listings with information as to whether residents are registered to vote and how they are registered. Armed with this information, candidates for election or reelection can make better use of their time. They concentrate on getting to know and win the support of their own partisans and also try to win over the unaffiliated voters to their cause.

A popular method of campaigning for the state legislature is called "walking," as in walking your legislative district. Candidates go door to door, using their street listings as a guide to where the registered voters are and in which party those voters are registered. The hope is that a five-minute chat with a prospective voter at the doorstep will produce another vote on Election Day. Candidates also walk their district because they want to develop a reputation for walking, thereby furthering the idea that they are really committed to getting to know and more fully represent the voters.

A Denver Democrat in the Colorado House of Representatives, Andrew Romanoff, was famous for going door to door in his district each time he ran for office.

### *Competitive Character*

Prior to 2004, legislative elections in Colorado were often described as uncompetitive. The fact that the Republicans maintained almost uninterrupted control of both houses of the legislature for more than forty years, from the early 1960s to 2004, suggested that the Democrats were never really able to challenge the Republican domination of both legislative chambers.

The dramatic takeover of both the Colorado House and the Colorado Senate by the Democrats in 2004 provided direct evidence that state legislative elections in Colorado after 2000 had become competitive. There was only one question to consider. Were legislative elections in Colorado now truly competitive, with the Republicans likely to win back control of one or both houses in the near future? Or were the Democrats, by maintaining control of the redistricting process, going to rule the Colorado legislature for many years, in much the same manner as the Republicans had previously done.

The question was at least partly answered in the 2010 legislative elections in Colorado. It was a big Republican year nationally, and the Republicans won enough seats in the Colorado House of Representatives to gain control of that one house. The Republicans also made a slight gain in the state Senate in 2010, but it was nowhere near enough to win a majority. Clearly, there are enough swing seats in the Colorado state legislature that party control is likely to shift back and forth from election to election, particularly in the state House of Representatives.

But how many seats are truly "swingable?" The *Denver Post* suggested one indication in the form of its editorial endorsements in 2010. Out of the total of sixty-five state House of Representatives seats (all up for election), the *Denver Post* found only ten to be contested enough to merit the newspaper going to the trouble of making an endorsement. Thus it was the judgment of Colorado's leading newspaper that less than one out of every six seats had a reasonable prospect of shifting from one political party to the other.[11]

In the state senate, where senators serve a four-year term and only one-half come up for election every two years, there are only sixteen or seventeen seats on the ballot in any one election year. In 2010 the *Denver Post* decided only five were competitive enough to rate the newspaper recommending a choice. That was a ratio of less than one out of three in the swing category.[12]

So, in the *Denver Post*'s opinion, only fifteen of the eighty-plus legislative seats up for election in 2010 had any real competition between the Democrats and the Republicans. Still, that was enough for at least one house of the Colorado legislature, the House of Representatives, to switch from Democratic to Republican control.

Targeting of a limited number of swing seats in the Colorado legislature by both political parties has one unfortunate side effect. Targeting severely reduces the number of voters who have a meaningful vote to cast in legislative general elections.

We described the 2011 Reapportionment Commission as producing a new high of thirty-eight swing (or competitive) seats in the Colorado state legislature. Reformers, including some members of the commission, hoped this increased figure would result in more targeted legislative seats and more genuinely contested state legislative campaigns.

*Primary Elections*

Because Colorado election laws provide for party primaries, incumbent state legislators in both political parties occasionally are defeated in their party primary rather than the general election. Primary elections are held in June, five months before the November general election.

Legislative primary elections most often occur when there is an open seat (no incumbent running for reelection) and two or more party members want to try for the party nomination. Because voter turnout is much lower in primary elections than in general elections, candidates running in a legislative party primary will emphasize highly "personal" campaign techniques, such as telephoning registered party members who have a record for voting in primary elections.

The primary election process has its greatest effect on state legislators who represent safe Democratic or safe Republican seats. Such legislators probably will not face a serious reelection challenge from the other party in the general election, yet they may be challenged in their own party primary.

As a result, legislators from safe seats often become more concerned about the voters who vote in their party primary, a relatively small number of people, rather than the much larger group of voters who vote in the general election.

This phenomenon of legislators from safe seats caring more about the primary election than the general election has ideological effects. The people who vote in Republican primaries tend to be more conservative than the general electorate. A Republican legislator sitting in a safe Republican seat thus will have relatively more conservatives voting in the Republican primary than vote in the general election. The result is to encourage the Republican legislator to be more conservative than he or she might otherwise be.

The ideological effects are the opposite in the Democratic Party. A Democratic legislator from a safe Democratic seat will have relatively more liberals voting in the Democratic primary than vote in the general election. A safe-seat Democrat thus will often be more liberal than he or she might otherwise be.

### POLARIZING EFFECT OF SAFE SEATS

Are safe Republican and safe Democratic seats good or bad for the Colorado legislature? In one sense they are good, because they provide a solid base for each of the two political parties. No matter how badly a party might lose any particular general election, it will still have its safe seats, and thus have some representation in the state legislature.

On the other hand, safe party legislative seats can be viewed as problematic for the legislature. Because safe-seat Republicans tend to be very conservative, and safe-seat Democrats tend to be liberal, one effect of safe seats is to polarize the legislature and create core groups in each of the two political parties that tend toward philosophical extremes.

Plainly, the major effect on the state legislature of safe seats and primary elections is to create more partisanship, more ideology, and more polarization. As safe-seat Republicans become more ideologically conservative, and safe-seat Democrats become more ideologically liberal, moderate and middle-of-the-road voices have greater difficulty being heard in the Colorado state legislature.

## THE DEMOCRATS GAIN CONTROL

One of the most memorable days in Colorado political history was the day after the 2004 general election. Coloradans woke up and learned that, for the first time in forty years, the Democrats had won control of both houses of the Colorado state legislature. Most political observers, even the most skilled, were flabbergasted. These results sparked rethinking about whether Colorado really was "a generally Republican state."

There were many reasons the Colorado legislature went strongly Democratic in 2004. Some of those reasons were changes in procedural rules that greatly affected the election process in Colorado. Other reasons were simple shifts by certain groups and localities from voting Republican to voting Democratic.[13] For example, there was greater participation by younger voters and independents, and an increasing Latino vote. Then, too, Republicans were probably caught napping.

*Democrats gained control of the redistricting process.* At the time of the 2000 U.S. Census, the Democratic Party gained a one-vote majority on the appointed commission that redistricts the Colorado state legislature. Once they gained this advantage, the Democrats rigorously applied the same gerrymandering techniques against the Republicans that in previous years the Republicans had used against the Democrats. By creating a small group of very Republican House and Senate districts, the Democrats were able to create a large number of more moderate districts that the Democrats would have a better chance of winning.

Although this pro-Democratic redistricting plan went into effect at the time of the 2002 legislative elections, the Republicans retained control of both houses of the Colorado legislature that year. The Democrats made gains, however, and those gains set the stage for the Democrats to win solid control of both houses in 2004.

As it turned out, 2004 was not only a one-time win for the Democrats. They maintained solid control of the Colorado legislature in both the 2006 and the 2008 elections.

*Democrats were better than Republicans at Internet politics.* Following in the footsteps of Howard Dean's Internet-oriented campaign for the Democratic Party nomination for U.S. president in 2004, Colorado Democrats were quick to adopt and master the Internet as a better way to communicate with supporters, turn out crowds at rallies, and raise campaign funds. Both nationally and in Colorado, the Democrats were ahead of the Republicans in using the Internet as a key part of their campaign infrastructure.[14]

*Term limits.* At least a dozen efforts were made during the 1970s and 1980s to impose limits on legislative terms of office in Colorado. None won the required two-thirds vote for a constitutional amendment in the Colorado legislature.

In 1990 state senator Terry Considine, a Republican from a wealthy suburb south of Denver, proposed another such measure to the legislature. It failed once more. This time, however, Considine and a group of political allies started an organization called Coloradans Back in Charge, or CBIC. They launched a campaign to collect the needed number of citizen signatures to qualify their term limitation measure for the November 1990 ballot.

Considine and his organization succeeded in putting on the ballot a constitutional amendment limiting legislative terms. On November 6, 1990, term limits were approved by Colorado voters 707,114 to 289,046.

There were many theories as to why term limits were adopted so overwhelmingly in Colorado. Some believed it was the result of the general antigovernment attitude found among voters in the state. Others argued that Coloradans liked the idea of a "citizen" legislature rather than a "professional" legislature.

Moreover, some observers noted that despite several legislators making statements to the news media questioning the wisdom of term limits, there was no organized campaign against their adoption.

The Considine-initiated amendment on term limits was one of the most sweeping measures of its kind. It limited all elected state officials to eight years in the same office. In most cases, that meant two four-year terms. In the Colorado House of Representatives, of course, the term limit was four two-year terms.

The term-limits amendment was adopted in 1990, but it only applied to members of the state legislature who were elected in 1990 or thereafter. That meant that no incumbent legislators would be forced out of office until eight years later, in 1998.

There was an unanticipated effect of term limits. The majority of the legislators who were forced out of office by term limits, beginning in 1998, were Republicans. This was logical, because the Republicans held large majorities in both houses in 1990, when the eight-year term limits "clock" began ticking.

Without term limits, many of the Republicans who were "term limited" in 1998 would have stayed in the legislature and been easily reelected. They were forced to leave office, however, and their Republican safe seats suddenly became open seats that the Democrats had a better chance of winning.

This process of term-limited Republicans being forced out of office continued in 2000, 2002, and 2004. Many of them were influential incumbents certain to be reelected, but they were forced to step aside. The Democrats took advantage of the increased number of open seats, many of them fair game for either party, that were being created for the Democrats to take a shot at.

There was irony in this development. Terry Considine, the key supporter of term limits for the Colorado legislature, was a staunch Republican. In the end, however, term limits pushed a large number of strong Republicans out of the legislature. This is yet another example of the "law of unintended consequences" that often characterizes political reforms.

In the long run, term limits slowly began to work against the Democrats. As Democrats increased their numbers in the state legislature, and elected majorities in both houses in 2004, the Democrats became the party with the largest number of legislators who would eventually be subjected to term limits. A conspicuous example was Andrew Romanoff, a widely admired Democratic speaker of the House of Representatives, who was forced by term limits to leave the legislature, and the speakership, in 2008.

*Campaign finance reform.* Prior to the 1998 elections, the state's voters initiated and adopted an extensive campaign finance reform program. Strict limits, some of which were quite low, were placed on individual contributions to election campaigns. This reform, which was strongly supported by the lobby group Common Cause, greatly curtailed the amount of money available to candidates' *official* campaigns for state office.

Campaign finance reform in Colorado, however, placed no limits on the amounts of money that could be contributed to so-called *independent expenditure groups*, also known as "527s" for the section of the law that allowed them. Committees could be formed that took in unlimited amounts of money, and these funds could be used to buy campaign advertising lauding a particular candidate or discrediting his or her opponent.

There were two major restrictions concerning these independent expenditure campaigns. The first was that the *magic words* "vote for" or "vote against" could not be used in the campaign materials. The second was that the independent expenditure campaigns could not be coordinated with the candidates' *official* campaigns.

The Democrats turned much of their campaign finance and expenditures over to four 527s, thereby enabling the Democrats to pour all the money they could raise into state legislative campaigns and bypass campaign contribution limits completely.[15]

When campaign finance reform took effect in Colorado, Democrats proved more adept than Republicans at using independent expenditure campaigns to run negative radio and television advertisements against Republican candidates for the state legislature. (Democrats would say they were running "comparative ads," not negative ads.) Republicans formed their own independent expenditure campaigns, but Republicans usually seemed to be a step behind the Democrats in exploiting this newly developing way of financing election campaigns.

What happened was that many Republican candidates for the state legislature adhered to campaign finance reform restrictions and did not develop parallel independent expenditure campaigns. These Republicans were outspent by their Democratic opponents, most of whom had independent expenditure campaigns operating in their behalf.

The net effect was, at least for a while, to give Democratic candidates for the state legislature a monetary advantage over Republican candidates. That monetary advantage paid off in the form of more Democrats being elected to the legislature.

Republican frustration with the manner in which campaign finance reform had ended up favoring the Democrats was expressed by Steve Durham, a staunch Republican who served in the state legislature and then became a leading lobbyist at the state capitol. He said: "There are not very many Republican incumbents, no matter how safe a seat they sit in, who can withstand the kind of money the Democrats are now able to spend against them. Control is shifting away from the political parties. The candidate and the party are increasingly irrelevant to the campaign. The 527s, because they have the most money now, are slowly taking charge of the entire process."[16]

This view of the reduced impact of political parties on legislative election campaigns was supported by Tom Tancredo, a former Republican member of both the state legislature and the U.S. House of Representatives. Tancredo grumbled to the *Denver Post* about the rise of the 527s: "We have to figure out a way to get Republicans elected because the state party can't do [anything]. It's been neutered."[17]

*The gang of four.* Another reason cited for the Democrats winning majorities in both houses of the Colorado legislature in 2004 was the influence of four super-wealthy Democratic Party contributors. Just at the time when the rise of independent expenditures provided a way of funneling large amounts of money into Democratic campaigns, four donors came along with the wherewithal to put Colorado Democrats in a strong position financially.

The four multimillionaire contributors were Jared Polis, Pat Stryker, Tim Gill, and Rutt Bridges. Most of the money contributed by this so-called gang of four was spread around to 527s supporting Democratic campaigns for the legislature throughout the state.[18]

*Skillful use of negative attack advertisements.* Armed with money raised from 527s, much of it contributed by the gang of four, supporters of Democratic candidates for the state legislature began hitting their Republican opponents with negative television ads and mailed brochures that many observers considered over the top in terms of lacking fairness and honesty.

Vincent Carroll, a columnist for the *Denver Post*, described two of the Democrats' better efforts at defaming opponents in the 2010 state legislative elections. Bob Boswell, a Republican candidate for the state House from Weld County, noted on his Web site that he favored "allowing the new-generation nuclear plants to be built." The response from the Democrats was a mailed brochure showing a nuclear bomb's mushroom cloud over northern Colorado with text saying that Boswell wanted to "bring all of America's nuclear waste to Colorado."

Carroll deemed this brochure so overstated that no other ad "could possibly out-smear" it.[19]

According to Carroll, another newspaper came up with a similar story. The *Pueblo Chieftain* criticized the Democrats for unfair attacks on a Republican candidate for the legislature named Keith Swerdfeger. Although one of Pueblo's leading businessmen and a leader in local economic development programs, Swerdfeger was labeled by the Democrats as comparable to "Ponzi scheme criminal Bernie Madoff."[20]

The *Colorado Springs Gazette* noted a Democratic brochure criticizing Republican state House candidate Karen Cullen for cutting $140 million in education spending. Democrats later admitted that they had no record that Cullen had ever said anything about cutting education spending.[21]

Of course the Republicans were running similar negative attack advertisements against the Democrats. The Republicans were as usual a bit behind the Democrats at taking up these negative techniques. One major concern was that an emphasis on negative ads would produce "a race to the bottom" in which both parties would saturate state legislative general election campaigns with negative attack ads.

*Social conservatism hurt the Republican Party.* Beginning with the presidency of Ronald Reagan in the 1980s, the Republican Party in the United States and Colorado became more than just an *economically* conservative political party. The Republican Party also became a *socially* conservative political party. Particular tenets of this new social conservatism included making abortion illegal, opposition to expanding gay and lesbian rights, and placing limits on stem cell research.

These socially conservative positions were less popular with upscale, well-educated Republicans, many of whom previously had been reliable supporters of the Republican Party. By the early years of the past decade, well-to-do Republicans were voting for Democrats for the Colorado state legislature whenever the opposition Republican candidate was a strong and outspoken social conservative.

*Democrats started doing better in presidential elections.* Another reason the Democrats took control of both houses of the Colorado state legislature in 2004 was that, starting in 1992, the Democrats nationally began doing better in presidential elections than they had done in the 1980s.

Republican domination of the Colorado legislature, particularly in the 1980s, was partially attributed to Republican presidential candidates, such as Ronald Reagan and George H. W. Bush, having strong coattails where Colorado legislative elections were concerned. Throughout the 1990s and after 2000, however, the Democrats started doing better nationally in presidential elections.

Denver political consultant Eric Sondermann believes Colorado voters experienced "buyers' remorse" following the 2004 presidential election, and support for George W. Bush and the Republicans dropped precipitously, both in the nation and in Colorado. The 2006 and 2008 elections thus became referendums on the Bush presidency, and that helped as much as anything else to keep the Democrats in control of both houses of the Colorado legislature.[22]

By 2010, though, there was an incumbent Democratic president dealing with a prolonged economic recession. Thus the shift of the lower house of the Colorado legislature back to the Republicans might have been attributed to a sitting president's unpopularity rather than any Colorado issues. One conclusion appears to be that Colorado state legislative elections are greatly influenced by two things. One is which party is winning presidential elections in presidential years. The other is the popularity, or the unpopularity, of the sitting president in nonpresidential years.

### THE ROUNDTABLE

Adam Schrager and Rob Witwer write about an organization created by the Democrats to coordinate legislative candidate campaigns with 527s that was known as the Roundtable. In May 2004 two members of the gang of four, Pat Stryker and Tim Gill, met at Gill's home in Aspen, Colorado, to get the ball rolling.

Subsequent meetings were held throughout the summer of 2004 in the Columbine Room at the headquarters building of the Colorado Education Association across from the state capitol in Denver. It was at these meetings that the legal techniques for avoiding Colorado's strict campaign finance laws and funneling millionaires' dollars into Democratic legislative campaigns were developed.[23]

### CONCLUSIONS

For four decades, the Republicans dominated state legislative elections in Colorado. One reason was the growing size and voting strength of upscale, well-educated voters living in Denver's suburban counties, which at that time were reliably pro-Republican. Another was the powerful coattails of victorious Republican presidential candidates. Structural factors, such as the requirement of single-member legislative districts and the rise of incumbency advantage, also helped to explain why the Republicans won most of the state legislative races.

Things changed in Colorado in the early years of the first decade of the twenty-first century. Structural changes, such as a shift in control on the redistricting commission and the adoption of term limits, enhanced the position of the Democrats in Colorado state legislative elections. The rise of independent expenditures in political campaigns, particularly as a way to avoid campaign finance limitations, further aided Democrats, as did the unpopularity of Republican social conservatism in formerly Republican upscale, well-educated areas.

Democrats, it should also be noted, increased their fund-raising capabilities and mastered the use of the Internet and similar technologies for political campaigning.

Republican gains in the 2010 state legislative elections, however, suggested the Democrats were going to have to work hard to preserve their new position of strength in the Colorado state legislature.

Overall, the challenge of encouraging party competition and voter turnout and voter interest in state legislative elections is a continuing one. Many Coloradans are too laid back or preoccupied with their jobs, families, and leisure-time pursuits to take an interest in which party dominates the state legislature and why. This, of course, is not much different from other states.

There is an enduring paradox about the Colorado legislature, a paradox found in other states and the Congress. Colorado's state legislators are regularly returned to office by the same voters who routinely complain (as we noted in chapter 2) about high state taxes and express frustration with the overall performance of the legislature.

# CHAPTER SEVEN

# Legislative Politics and Processes

Colorado's legislature is officially called the General Assembly, but it is commonly referred to as the state legislature. Back in the 1980s and 1990s, Colorado was described by scholars as having one of the more influential state legislatures in the United States, particularly in relation to the state governor. As one scholar put it: "The fifty American states vary in the relative power of their legislative and executive branches, but in Colorado, the relationship is clear: Ours is a system of legislative dominance [over the executive]."[1]

By the early years of the twenty-first century, however, the power of the Colorado legislature compared to the Colorado governor was beginning to wane. There were two major reasons for this. One reason was the impact of term limits on legislators, a reform that was adopted by the voters of Colorado in 1990 and that had its first effects in 1998.

A second reason was TABOR, the Taxpayers' Bill of Rights, which limited the legislature's ability to raise taxes and increase state expenditures. Similar to term limits, TABOR was imposed on the Colorado state legislature by passage of a citizen initiative.

## THE LEGISLATIVE ROLE

What do Colorado legislators do? They enact laws that support public education, build state parks and highways, specify salaries for state officials, determine the number and quality of state prisons, and much more. State legislators oversee the administration of state programs. Although they do not administer programs directly, legislators influence the way programs are carried out through hearings, investigations, audits, and direct involvement in the budgetary process.

State legislators have the twin responsibilities of lawmaking and representation. While they do most of their lawmaking at the statehouse, they spend even more time acting as representatives of their local constituencies, a year-round job.

A good state legislator is constantly listening, learning, and trying to find out what people like and dislike about state programs. State legislators try to make themselves accessible, often holding "open house" or "town meeting" gatherings in their home communities. "A good legislator will 'bond' with the voters in his or her district, learning their interests and concerns and letting them know he or she will look out for those interests and concerns up at the state capital."[2]

## GENDER

The typical American state legislator is a white, male Protestant of Anglo-Saxon origin. This is also pretty much the case in Colorado. The Colorado legislature, however, has a long tradition of having a high number of women members.

For instance, at the start of the 2011–12 session, forty-one of the one hundred seats in the Colorado state legislature were held by women. That meant the legislature was 41 percent female. It also meant that Colorado had the highest percentage of women in any state legislature in the United States. The top-ranked states for female state legislators in 2011 were Colorado, 41 percent; Vermont, 38 percent; Arizona, 34 percent; and Hawaii, 34 percent.

Having more women state legislators than any other state in the nation was not a first-time event for Colorado. The Centennial State also won that honor at the start of the 2009–10 session.[3]

In fact, at the time of this writing, the state Senate, the upper house of the state legislature, is almost evenly split between the genders. There are seventeen women and eighteen men. The Democrats are the majority party in the Senate, and there are fourteen women Democrats and six men Democrats. The Democratic caucus in the state Senate, the majority party caucus in that house, is thus comfortably dominated by women members. See Table 9.

The Republicans previously had more women members of the legislature, but many of them were defeated in Democratic Party sweeps in the 2004, 2006, and 2008 elections, said House Republican leader Amy Stephens of Monument.[4] As the number-two Republican in the Colorado House of Representatives, Amy Stephens held the highest leadership position of any woman in the 2011–12 state legislature.

Table 9. Women in the Colorado State Legislature in January 2011

| House | Women | Men | Total | Percentage of women |
|---|---|---|---|---|
| Republicans | 9 | 24 | 33 | 27 |
| Democrats | 15 | 17 | 32 | 47 |
| House total | 24 | 41 | 65 | 37 |

| Senate | Women | Men | Total | Percentage of women |
|---|---|---|---|---|
| Republicans | 3 | 12 | 15 | 20 |
| Democrats | 14 | 6 | 20 | 70 |
| Senate total | 17 | 18 | 35 | 49 |

| House and Senate | Women | Men | Total | Percentage of women |
|---|---|---|---|---|
| Republicans | 12 | 36 | 48 | 25 |
| Democrats | 29 | 23 | 52 | 56 |
| House and Senate total | 41 | 59 | 100 | 41 |

Source: Denver Post, January 5, 2011, 3B; additional calculations by R. Loevy.

Hispanic women enjoyed good representation in the state Senate in the 2011–12 session. There were three Hispanic women serving in the Colorado upper house. This was the first time there had ever been more than one. Overall, there were eight Hispanics in the legislature in 2011, double the number in the previous session.

Another highlight for women in 2011 was the presence in the state capitol of state representative Rhonda Fields from Aurora. She was the first black elected to the legislature from Arapahoe County, located south and east of Denver. At one time a predominantly upscale white county, Arapahoe County now is much more diverse. The election of Rhonda Fields gave further credence to the observation that more minorities in Denver were moving out of the city into the surrounding suburban counties.[5]

## A PART-TIME JOB

Serving in the Colorado legislature is a "part-time" job. The legislature meets in formal session only four months of the year. Most members use the time available during the eight months the legislature is not in regular session to work in other professions.

Members of the Colorado House and Senate received a salary of thirty thousand dollars a year in 2012, and this was regarded as a part-time salary. Colorado state legislators also receive funds to help meet living and travel expenses while the legislature is in session. In addition, they are re-imbursed for expenses when they attend to legislative business when the legislature is not in session.

More than a few former legislators have said that serving in the Colo-rado state legislature is a "sure-fire way of going broke."

### RULES AND REGULATIONS

Once elected to the Colorado legislature, senators and representatives en-ter what appears to be a highly regimented world. Because the legislature meets for only a limited amount of time each calendar year (120 days), bills theoretically must be introduced and advanced according to a detailed legislative deadline schedule.

Enforced somewhat in both houses, the deadline schedule is designed to provide for an orderly flow of work under tight time constraints. On paper at least, Colorado's carefully scheduled legislature is far more "tidy" than the "freewheeling" processes in the U.S. Congress.

But this tight scheduling has been breaking down in recent years. Al-though most bills follow the regular process, the majority leaders in both the state House and the state Senate have taken to waiving deadlines and granting "late bill status," that is, letting state representatives and state sen-ators introduce brand-new bills late in the session.

"These days," said Senate Democratic leader John Morse, "the only real deadline is the 120th day of the session, when both houses of the legisla-ture adjourn."[6]

This ability to waive deadlines and grant late bill status has greatly in-creased the power of the leadership. Legislative leaders in Colorado "can make some members and their casts of supportive lobbyists happy by giv-ing them permission to introduce bills after the deadline."[7]

Nominally, Colorado state lawmakers are limited as to the number of bills they can introduce at any one session of the legislature. They can in-troduce no more than five bills. Also, any bill that requires an increase in the expenditure of money has to be reviewed by the Appropriations Com-mittee in the house in which it is introduced. Many bills die in the appro-priations committees because there is no money available to fund them.

Since the adoption of the strict taxing and spending limits in TABOR, the requirement that bills which increase spending be automatically reviewed by the appropriations committees has become a particular threat to legislators' bills. "The noose of the TABOR spending limit . . . turned the Appropriations Committee in both chambers into killing fields for bills with costs attached."[8]

Here again, however, House and Senate leaders can waive the five-bill limit if they wish. They also can do away with the fiscal impact designation if it suits them. The end result is more power for the leadership in each house and more success for those legislators who make it a point to "play ball" with their leaders.

## HOUSE LEADERSHIP

Every two years, shortly after the November general elections, the two major political parties in the Colorado legislature hold their respective organizational caucuses. In the House of Representatives, the majority party selects its candidate to be the speaker of the House. In addition, the majority party elects the House majority leader, the assistant House majority leader, and the chair of the House majority caucus.

The minority party, meeting separately, elects the House minority leader, the assistant House minority leader, and the House minority caucus chair.

The speaker of the House has been described as "the power center in the Colorado House of Representatives."[9] The speaker is elected by majority vote of all the members of the House, but the candidate chosen by the majority-party caucus invariably wins the office.

The speaker presides over meetings of the Colorado House, preserving order and recognizing state representatives who wish to address the House. The speaker appoints the chairpersons and majority party members of the major House committees. The speaker also decides the number of members on each committee and the number from each political party, carefully making sure there are always more members of the majority party on a committee. The speaker also decides which bills will be considered by which committees.

The minority leader in the House of Representatives appoints members of the minority party to committees.

Members of the majority party in the Colorado House of Representatives may submit their preferences for committee assignments to the speaker, but the speaker is not bound to honor those requests. In the same manner, the speaker may or may not consult with veteran members of his or her political party when deciding on majority party committee appointments.

It is the powers to appoint committees, determine the partisan balance on committees, and route bills to particular committees that make the speaker of the House important. Speakers generally appoint a number of reliable partisans in the majority party to three or four major committees, thereby creating a majority in these committees that will, within reason, do what the speaker desires.

Speakers then route major or controversial bills to one of these three or four committees, confident that the bills will be processed with the speaker's views in mind.

If the speaker especially wants a bill voted down in committee, the speaker sends it to one of these three or four committees. These committees thus become a convenient instrument for eliminating bills that the speaker considers frivolous, inappropriate, or untimely. Because of the utility of these committees for voting down bills opposed by the House majority-party leadership, they are often referred to as the "killer committees" or "death committees."[10]

One such committee in the Colorado House of Representatives has been the State, Veterans, and Military Affairs Committee. It is "known as a kill committee composed of members in safe seats," writes *Denver Post* reporter Tim Hoover.[11]

The speaker of the House has the power to run things, or not run them, as the speaker sees fit. The speaker of the House has the power to exclude the minority party from much of the legislative process in the House, or the speaker can give the minority an expanded role to play. The choice clearly is the speaker's, and that makes the speaker, whether ruling with a tight hand or a loose one, the most powerful member of the Colorado House of Representatives.

When the Democrats took control of the Colorado House of Representatives in 2004, they opted for a looser style of leadership. There were few complaints from the Republicans about being unfairly excluded from the legislative process. In addition, from 2004 to 2006 the Democratic House in Colorado worked well with Republican governor Bill Owens.

When the Republicans retook control of the Colorado House of Representatives in 2010, they got off to a partisan start. They renamed some of the House committees to better suit Republican tastes and philosophies. Words such as "labor" and "human services," with their Democratic Party connotations, were dropped from committee names. The new Republican names for committees were flavored with more conservative words such as "business development."

## An Inexperienced Speaker

The incoming Republican speaker of the House for the 2011–12 session was Representative Frank McNulty of Highlands Ranch, an upscale suburb south of Denver. Speaker McNulty illustrated the impact of term limits on the legislative leadership in Colorado. At the time of his election as speaker, McNulty had served only four years in the Colorado House of Representatives. He was elevated to speaker without ever having served in a leadership position in the Republican Party in the House. And, similar to most of his Republican colleagues, for the first time in his legislative career he was seeing the Republicans in control of a legislative chamber in Colorado.

McNulty came to the speaker's chair with a reputation for being "loud." The Republican majority leader, Representative Amy Stephens of Monument gave the reason: "You can hear Frank's voice from down the street. You always know when Frank's near the chamber. You can hear that laugh." Speaker McNulty had a different explanation: "I came from a family of six kids. If you're not loud, you're not heard."

Frank McNulty is a graduate of Denver's J. K. Mullen High School. He did his undergraduate work in college at the University of Colorado at Boulder and earned his law degree at the University of Denver.

Before being elected to the state House of Representatives, McNulty was best described as a professional political operative. He worked in the office of U.S. senator Wayne Allard, Republican from Colorado, and specialized in water law while serving in the Colorado Department of Natural Resources.

Despite his previous reputation for loudness, incoming Speaker McNulty promised he would use a softer tone as the top Republican in the House of Representatives. He was well aware that there was split party control between the state House (Republican) and the state Senate (Democratic). He remarked: "Anything we seek to accomplish now, by definition, has to be Republicans working with Democrats."[12]

*Other House Leaders*

The majority leader and the minority leader in the House work to develop the positions of their respective parties on the various bills that are under consideration by the legislature. They are aided by the assistant leaders, who are often referred to as "party whips" because of their task of "whipping party members into line" to support bills the party leadership wants passed and to oppose bills the party leadership wants defeated.

The majority leader and the minority leader also direct floor debate for their respective political parties. The two leaders are often called upon to serve as spokespersons for their party, explaining to the public what bills and positions the party is backing and why. Because the majority leader and the minority leader play the roles of partisan disciplinarians, the speaker of the House can, if the speaker wishes, stay above the open partisan fight and attempt to play a mediator role.

SENATE LEADERSHIP

Although a number of the positions and functions of the Senate leadership are similar to the House leadership, there are differences. The Senate is a smaller body, with thirty-five members rather than sixty-five. This smaller size permits the Colorado Senate to operate somewhat more informally than the House, and with less discipline and less centralized control.

The top officer in the Senate is the president of the Senate. Similar to the procedure used to select the speaker of the House, the members of the majority party in the Senate caucus and choose their party candidate for Senate president. The majority party choice then is generally elected on the first day of the session. The Senate president has the power to assign bills to committee.

The second-ranked person in the state Senate, the majority leader, determines the number of Democrats and Republicans on Senate committees. The majority leader also appoints the majority party members to the committees. The minority leader appoints the minority party members to Senate committees.

The Senate elects a president pro tempore to preside over Senate sessions when the president is absent. Similar to the president of the Senate, the president pro tempore is nominated in the majority party caucus and elected in a partisan vote.

### A "Club" Atmosphere

Speaking generally, the majority party leadership in the Colorado Senate is friendlier to the minority party than is the case in the Colorado House of Representatives. The reason for this is doubtless the smaller size of the state Senate. With fewer people available, majority party senators perhaps are thankful that minority party senators are willing to help do some of the work.

Also, there is more of a "club" atmosphere in the state Senate. Senators get to know one another better, and that typically makes the majority somewhat more cooperative with the minority. Because of the longer term in office (four years) and the fact that a number of state senators have previously served in the Colorado House, senators as a group are more independent of the party leadership than state House members. "Not surprisingly, then, it has been more difficult for leadership to keep the troops in line in the Senate."[13]

When the Democrats took control of the Colorado Senate in 2004, they continued the accommodative and bipartisan ways that developed previously under the Republicans. Colorado state senator John Morse, the Democratic majority leader in 2011, noted that in the state Senate, "personality and not politics determines friendships. Above all, do not burn your bridges. Five minutes from now, you may need that state senator's vote on a different issue. And make it a point to never surprise your friends in the state Senate."[14]

### Other Senate Leaders

The other Senate leaders are the assistant majority leader, the minority leader, and the assistant minority leader. Elected at party caucuses, these leaders play the same role in the Colorado Senate that their counterparts play in the Colorado House. They work to establish party positions on bills and then line up party members to support those positions. As in the House, the assistant party leaders often are referred to as whips.

### Majority Leader John Morse

A good example of a party leader in the Colorado legislature is state senator John Morse of Colorado Springs, who served recently as the Senate majority leader (Democratic leader).

Morse was a resident of Colorado Springs from the age of nine, graduating from Mitchell High School. He majored in accounting at the University of Colorado at Colorado Springs and also trained as a paramedic. He went into police work and rose to the position of police chief in Fountain, Colorado, a small suburban city south of Colorado Springs. Along the way, Morse earned a PhD in public policy at the University of Colorado at Denver.

In 2006 Morse was recruited to run as the Democratic candidate in a state senate district in Colorado Springs. He had no previous experience in elective office. The seat he was running for had been targeted by the state Democratic Party for possible victory, and considerable money from independent campaign organizations (527s) was spent on his behalf. He won election following a bruising campaign, filled with negative advertising against an incumbent Republican.

Similar to Speaker McNulty in the state House of Representatives, John Morse advanced rapidly thanks to term limits, which forced more experienced legislators to depart the legislature. In his first four years in the state Senate, he served for a time on the powerful Joint Budget Committee and then was elected majority leader. Although one of the top two Democrats in the state Senate, he possessed none of the long years of service and deep "institutional memory" that characterized legislative leaders prior to the adoption of term limits.

John Morse fit a leading scholar's definition of the state legislature, after term limits, as "an institution of rookies and novices." But, having been a police chief, Morse was at least a well-educated "rookie" with extensive experience in government.[15]

## HOUSE AND SENATE COMMITTEES

Committees that meet and work during regular sessions of the Colorado legislature are known as *committees of reference*. All bills are referred to committee shortly after they are introduced in a house (the house of origin) or after they move from one house to the other (the second house).

The real work of the Colorado legislature, similar to the pattern in the U.S. Congress, takes place when bills are in committee. The details of bills and the advisability of enacting them are carefully considered by the various committees. Committee meetings are open to the public, and interested citizens have the opportunity to express their views on proposed legislation.

After studying a bill and hearing public comment on it, a committee can recommend the bill for passage, amend the bill and then recommend it for passage, refer the bill to another committee, postpone consideration indefinitely, table the bill for consideration at a later date, or kill it outright by voting it down. Because of the careful scrutiny given to bills by committees of reference, the debate on bills when they reach the House or Senate floor is often brief.

Each house of the legislature has ten committees of reference. House and Senate committees have somewhat similar names. Thus, the House has a Health and Environment Committee, the Senate has a Health and Human Services Committee, and both committees review and vote on health and social services programs. See Table 10.

Partisanship is a factor in committee work in the state legislature. Although the majority party has a majority of the members on each committee, all committee members from both political parties share in the work and participate in discussions. Most important, amendments pro-

Table 10. Colorado Legislative Committees in January 2011

| House committees | Senate committees |
|---|---|
| Agriculture, Livestock, and Natural Resources | Agriculture, Natural Resources, and Energy |
| Appropriations | Appropriations |
| Economic and Business Development | Business, Labor, and Technology |
| Education | Education |
| Finance | Finance |
| Health and Environment | Health and Human Services |
| Judiciary | Judiciary |
| Local Government | Local Government |
| State, Veterans, and Military Affairs | State, Veterans, and Military Affairs |
| Transportation | Transportation |

*Source*: Colorado General Assembly, "Committees," under "Current Regular Session Information," http://www.leg.state.co.us/ (accessed October 6, 2011).

posed by minority-party members of committees sometimes are adopted in committee.

An unusual situation developed in 2011 when the Republicans took control of the Colorado House while the state Senate remained in Democratic hands. Democratic bills tended to be rejected in Republican-controlled House committees. Republican bills were axed in Democratic-controlled Senate committees. The end result was a legislative session distinctive for its low output of bills.

The committee chair is a member of the majority party, which meant that as of 2012, the committee chairs in the Colorado House were all Republicans and their opposite numbers in the Colorado Senate were all Democrats. The most important formal functions of the committee chairs are calling meetings, determining the order in which bills are reviewed, and scheduling votes on bills.

### The GAVEL Amendment

Prior to the adoption of the GAVEL Amendment to the state constitution in the 1988 general election, committee chairs in the state legislature had the power to "pocket veto" bills. This meant that a chair could single-handedly kill a bill sent to the committee by "putting it in his or her pocket," that is, refusing to schedule a hearing or a committee discussion of the bill.[16]

Adoption of the GAVEL Amendment made it a constitutional requirement in Colorado that every bill sent to a legislative committee be voted upon in committee. GAVEL is an acronym that stands for "Give a Vote to Every Legislator."

The adoption of the GAVEL Amendment by the voters illustrated the extent to which the initiative is such a big part of state government in Colorado.

Despite GAVEL, committee chairs still find ways to quickly kill insignificant or illogical bills that come before the committee. The most popular way is to have the committee majority vote down large numbers of bills at marathon "bill killing" sessions. Two committees that do a great deal of bill killing, as noted, are the appropriations committees in each house.

The GAVEL Amendment also eliminated another tool of majority party control in the legislature. That was the House of Representatives Rules Committee. Prior to the adoption of GAVEL, the House Rules Committee could refuse to send to the House floor bills that had been reported out by committees of reference. The speaker of the House controlled the House Rules Committee and often used it to prevent unwanted bills (usually minority-party bills) from reaching the House floor. Once the GAVEL Amendment removed the ability of the House Rules Committee to kill bills, the House abolished the Rules Committee.

### THE HOUSE AND SENATE IN SESSION

The regular time for the House and Senate to begin meeting is 10:00 a.m. on Mondays and 9:00 a.m. on Tuesdays through Fridays. If they want, however, the speaker of the House or the president of the Senate can schedule different starting times. Both houses begin each meeting by calling the roll to make certain a quorum, a majority of all members of the particular house, is present. If a quorum is not present, no legislative business can be transacted until enough members are present to constitute a quorum.

Debate is limited in both houses of the legislature. Unless consent is given to speak longer, members of the state House of Representatives must limit their speeches to ten minutes. In the state Senate, speeches are limited to one hour. As a result, senators cannot filibuster, which is an attempt to kill a bill by giving never-ending speeches against it.

A voting machine is used to record votes on bills and amendments in the Colorado House of Representatives, and two big boards on opposing walls of the chamber instantly report the results. In the Senate, however, the roll is still called to record each senator's yea or nay.

In line with the Senate's more informal atmosphere, when the Senate president suspects the great majority of senators in the chamber favor the bill, only the small number in opposition will be asked to raise their hands to have their negative votes counted. All other senators present automatically will be counted in the affirmative.[17]

### Conference Committees

When there are differences between the text of a bill passed by the House and the text of a bill passed by the Senate, a conference committee is appointed. Each house sends three members, two from the majority party and one from the minority party, as its delegation to the conference committee. Because the Democrats took control of both houses in the 2004 elections, conference committees from 2005 to 2010 always consisted of four Democrats and two Republicans.

The Republicans won control of the Colorado House in the 2010 elections, but the Democrats retained the majority in the state Senate. That meant that during the 2011–12 session, conference committees were evenly balanced at three and three. There were two Republicans and one Democrat from the state House, and there were two Democrats and one Republican from the state Senate.

When the conference committee meets, the six legislators, called conferees, work to resolve the differences in the two versions of the bill. If the conference committee succeeds in writing a compromise version of the bill, it is sent back to each house for a vote on final passage without amendment.

### Joint Sessions

Periodically both houses of the legislature meet for a joint session. These sessions are held in the House chamber with the Senate president presiding and House rules in effect. The best-publicized joint session occurs at the beginning of each annual meeting of the legislature when the governor presents a "State of the State" address. Customarily the governor comments on the condition of the state's economy and presents the highlights of the proposed budget and related new initiatives.

The legislature also meets in joint session to receive a report from the chief justice of the Colorado Supreme Court on conditions in and needs of the state court system.

### Carrying a Bill

At the time a bill is introduced in either house of the legislature, it is assigned a bill number. In the Senate bills start with number 1. In the House they start with number 1001. A bill has both a House and a Senate sponsor, and it is these two legislators who shoulder the major responsibility for steering the bill through their respective houses of the legislature. The sponsor of a bill in a particular house is said to be "carrying" the bill in that house.

Legislators are generally eager to carry important bills before their house. It represents their best opportunity to show how effective they are and to have their names and accomplishments reported in the news media. A legislator carrying a bill will line up favorable testimony before the committee of reference, lead the debate in favor of the bill on the House or Senate floor, and if necessary, work to see that a compromise version of the bill is agreed upon in conference committee.

### INTERIM COMMITTEES

Starting in 1989, annual sessions of the Colorado legislature were limited to 120 days. Even before that limitation took effect, however, the legislature was having trouble getting all necessary work, particularly research and bill writing, completed during the regular session. In order to get things accomplished while the legislature is not in session, special committees of legislators are appointed to work during the "interim," the eight-month period between the adjournment of one session and the beginning of the next. Such committees are called "interim committees."

### THE JOINT BUDGET COMMITTEE

Back in the 1980s and early 1990s, the budget process in Colorado was centered in the legislative branch. It was the legislature's Joint Budget Committee and their staff, not the governor's budget director, who shaped the major recommendations as to how much money was to be spent and for what purposes. According to a respected student of state legislatures, Colorado in 1989 was third on the list of states where the legislature exerted "enormous control through the budget." Only the Texas and South Carolina legislatures were viewed at that time as having stronger budgetary powers than the Colorado legislature.[18]

The same two initiated reforms that reduced the power of the legislature overall were critical to reducing the stature and importance of the Joint Budget Committee. Those reforms, as noted at the beginning of this chapter, were term limits and TABOR, the Taxpayers' Bill of Rights. Opponents of these voter-sanctioned reforms often refer to them as the "Terrible Two."

## Structure and Operations

The Joint Budget Committee of the Colorado legislature is noted for its small size. There are three members from the House of Representatives (appointed by the speaker) and three members from the Senate (elected in party caucuses). The delegation from each house consists of the chairman of the Appropriations Committee (always a member of the majority party) plus one majority party member and one minority party member.

When one political party controls both houses of the legislature, four members of the Joint Budget Committee are from the majority party and two members are from the minority party. When the Democrats were the majority in both houses of the state legislature from 2005 to 2010, they controlled the Joint Budget Committee over the Republicans by a four-vote to two-vote margin.

Of course, as in 2012, when the Republicans held a majority in the Colorado House of Representatives but the state Senate remained Democratic, the Joint Budget Committee, similar to all the other joint committees, was evenly split with three members from each party. There were two Republicans and one Democrat from the House, and two Democrats and one Republican from the Senate.

The chair of the Joint Budget Committee alternates back and forth between a House member and a Senate member. When a Senate member is chair, a House member serves as vice chair, and vice versa.

The Joint Budget Committee, commonly referred to by the initials JBC, works year round and has a full-time staff of at least fifteen analysts. Committee members work three days a month from June to October but then work almost every day during November and December and during the January to May session of the legislature.

The committee occupies a suite of offices in the Legislative Services Building (located immediately south of the state capitol building).

Former state senator Mike Bird of Colorado Springs liked to tell the following story. On the wall in one of the rooms where the committee sits, in full view of those requesting funds, is a photograph of about fifteen men, members of Woodmen of the World, their lumber axes at the ready. The symbolism of the photograph—this is the room where budget requests get "chopped"—was often remarked upon, said Bird.

One day the Joint Budget Committee was surprised to discover that someone had taken red ink and painted "blood" dripping from the firemen's fire axes. After an appropriate amount of time for this act of humorous vandalism to be properly appreciated, the red ink was removed. The axes remained, Bird noted, both in the photograph and in the budget-slashing hands of the Joint Budget Committee.[19]

The JBC was created in 1959, a time when Democrats controlled both the legislature and the governorship. The committee has been influential for several reasons. Over the years it has been led by strong personalities, such as former state senators Joe Shoemaker and Mike Bird. They worked hard to expand the committee's influence.[20] It is the only committee of the state legislature that has a large professional staff of its own.

The budget cycle traditionally begins in the executive branch, yet it does not stay there. Budget proposals from state departments and agencies are generated under the direction of the Office of State Planning and Budgeting, which sees that those requests are in line with the policy objectives of the governor and also makes certain that the total budget request is in line with projected revenues. Sometimes the governor will hold a final cabinet meeting or a retreat to make final decisions on the budget request. The finished product is then sent to the Joint Budget Committee.

This is done by November 1, two months before the legislature convenes in early January, so that the JBC members and their staff can have several weeks to work on the budget prior to the next legislative session.

There is much discussion, and a number of humorous stories, about exactly how much attention the Joint Budget Committee has paid to the budget requests that come from the governor and the executive departments. Most observers believe that the JBC gives a governor's budget more than just a casual glance, yet plainly the JBC reserves the right to prepare its own budget rather than merely "review" the governor's recommendations.

Although no one seems certain whether the story is true or not, it is said that one chairman of the Joint Budget Committee actually picked up the book of gubernatorial budget requests and publicly threw it in the wastebasket. One expert on state politics wrote: "The executive budget prepared by the governor in Colorado is said to have as much status as a child's letter to Santa Claus."[21]

In fact, however, the governor's budget in recent years is given serious attention, and especially in hard economic times, both governors and legislators do not have much leeway when it comes to state spending.

During the months of November and December each year, the JBC and its staff carefully review departmental budget requests. JBC staff members prepare a recommended series of issues to be discussed by the JBC. Spokespersons for the departments of state government, often department heads and top budget officers, attend these meetings and defend their requests before the JBC.

Once the legislative session begins in January, the Joint Budget Committee begins writing the long appropriations bill, customarily referred to as the "long bill." This giant piece of legislation contains the entire budget for the State of Colorado for the following fiscal year.

The Colorado Constitution prohibits deficit spending and thereby requires a balanced annual state budget. Hence, before the JBC can write the long bill of expenditures, it must know how much money the state is going to collect in taxes and fees during the fiscal year. *Revenue estimates* are presented to the committee by both the Office of State Planning and Budgeting and the Legislative Council staff. The JBC begins its work by adopting the revenue estimates for the coming fiscal year. These estimates become an integral part of the final budget the JBC recommends to the legislature.

Because of all the extra work, and because they spend so much time together, members of the JBC often develop an esprit de corps and loyalty to the committee that, much of the time, can be as significant as political party membership.

In early February the Joint Budget Committee begins the most important part of its work, which is known as "figure setting." Item by item, the committee goes through the budget and "sets" the actual amounts of money that will be spent during the next fiscal year.

These meetings are open to the public. Early in the morning, from 7:30 to 9:00 a.m., any citizen can come in and address the JBC concerning budget matters. Later in the day, people directly affected by the budget, such as department heads and lobbyists for key interest groups (or their personal representatives), often are sitting in the audience and watching closely as pet programs are voted up or down.

The long bill then moves to the majority party caucus and the minority party caucus in both the House and the Senate. The budget is discussed and debated at length in the various caucuses. Amendments proposed in the majority and minority party caucuses may or may not be adopted on the House or Senate floor.

Once the party caucuses are finished with it, the long bill moves simultaneously to the House and Senate appropriations committees. Approval by these two committees is typically a mere formality since the chairs of the House and Senate appropriations committees are both on the Joint Budget Committee.

If different versions of the long bill are adopted in the House and Senate, as almost always happens, *the JBC serves as the conference committee* for ironing out the differences between the two houses. During this process the majority party caucuses will meet and approve the settling of differences. Similar to any bill emerging from a House-Senate conference, the long bill cannot be amended when it returns to each house for final passage.

Notice that, sitting as the conference committee, the Joint Budget Committee gets to "dot the final *i*" and "cross the final *t*" in the writing of the Colorado state budget.

### IMPACT OF TERM LIMITS

As noted, term limits were adopted in Colorado in 1990 but did not begin ending legislative careers until eight years later, in 1998. The result, clearly evident by the early 2000s, was to greatly diminish the experience, and thus the expertise, of legislators serving on the Joint Budget Committee.

No longer were members of the once vaunted JBC some of the longest-serving and best-informed members of the state legislature. Under term limits, state House and state Senate members were appointed to the Joint Budget Committee early in their careers when they knew little about the state and its financial needs. Also because of term limits, legislators did not stay on the JBC for a long time and build up a great depth of knowledge about the state's fiscal affairs the way they once did.

The end result was to enhance the power of the governor at the expense of the JBC. State senator John Morse of Colorado Springs explained this dramatically changed situation. "Term limits robbed the Joint Budget Committee of experience. In 2011 the six members of the committee had a total of just three years' experience on the committee between them. All that happens now is that the JBC just tweaks the governor's budget. Ninety-nine percent of the governor's budget is adopted unchanged. Term limits weakened the legislators and empowered the [governor's] staff and the lobbyists."[22] Term limits also increased the power of the Joint Budget Committee staff.

### IMPACT OF TABOR

The second initiated change in Colorado that reduced the power of the Joint Budget Committee was TABOR, the Taxpayers' Bill of Rights. TABOR so tightly constricted taxing and revenues in the state that the JBC had little money to work with. As money became scarce for state government, the JBC had little money to appropriate. Managing the budget became more a job of cutting rather than giving. The problem was further enhanced when the Recession of 2008–10 greatly added to the state's fiscal woes that had initially been created by TABOR.

A longtime business lobbyist at the Colorado state legislature, Steve Durham, summed up the situation this way: "Who wants to be on the JBC anymore? They have no real power anymore. They have no money to spend."[23] State senator John Morse added: "How much budgeting can anyone do with the effects of TABOR and [the economic downturn]?"[24]

By 2011 it was obvious that the Joint Budget Committee, in a time of economic distress, was willing to step back from its traditional leading role in Colorado budget matters and let the governor and his staff do the dirty work of making unpleasant and unpopular budget cuts. But the Joint Budget Committee paid a price for this. This once illustrious and respected interim committee of the Colorado legislature lost influence as Governor Ritter, and then Governor Hickenlooper, bore the brunt of making the severe budget cuts required by both TABOR and a major economic downturn. As the JBC lost power, there was an equivalent increase in the power of the governor's Office of State Planning and Budgeting.

That raised an interesting question. Would the JBC regain its former power and prestige if the TABOR restrictions were modified and the economy revived? When there is more state money to be appropriated rather than just a budget to be cut, how will the Joint Budget Committee try to regain the power it had ceded to the governor's office? With term limits remaining popular with the people of Colorado, and TABOR proving politically difficult to even modify let alone completely remove, it may be hard for the Joint Budget Committee to reclaim the influence it once enjoyed.

The Joint Budget Committee celebrated its fiftieth anniversary in 2009. There was an awareness, however, that the tight financial conditions forced on the state by the TABOR Amendment and a faltering economy had taken most of the fun out of being on the JBC. Representative Jack Pommer, a Boulder Democrat, noted that any state legislator "would love to be on the powerful JBC and hand out wads of cash to every constituency, but we don't have wads of cash."[25]

### LEGISLATIVE EFFECTIVENESS

How effective is the state legislature at providing policy leadership for the state of Colorado? The answer is the state legislature has gradually relinquished at least some of its power to govern the state of Colorado by not resisting more strongly citizen initiatives that put policy in the state constitution rather than the state legislature.

TABOR, the Taxpayers' Bill of Rights, had not been a major problem in the 1990s when the Colorado economy was expanding rapidly. A major economic downturn after 2001, however, produced what was called the *ratchet effect.* As the economy declined, so did state income from sales taxes and property taxes. Those declines lowered the base figure on which the small increases in revenues allowed by TABOR were calculated.

The result was that even by the time the economy had recovered a bit by 2004 and 2005, the total Colorado state budget, adjusted for inflation, was smaller than it had been in 2002. The state's population was growing, resulting in a greater demand for state services, but the final result of TABOR was to force Colorado to have less money to spend than it had two or three years earlier.

In an effort to eliminate the *ratchet effect*, Republican governor Bill Owens and Democratic speaker of the House Andrew Romanoff created Referendum C, a referred measure from the state legislature to the voters. Ref. C, as it was called, based the TABOR budget increase limits on "the highest previous state budget year" rather than the previous year's budget, which during a recession was usually much lower than "the highest previous state budget year." After a hard-fought statewide campaign, Ref. C was narrowly adopted by the voters in November 2005.

In 2008 the U.S. economy went into the second and even worse decline in less than a decade. Prospects were that, as state income from sales taxes and property taxes once again went sharply down, there would be a tremendous shrinking of the Colorado state budget. For example, about $1 billion had to be cut out of the state budget in fiscal year 2011–12.

There has been little or no incentive for the Joint Budget Committee to recommend a tax increase to the state legislature as a way of getting more money to ease the budget woes in Colorado. Under the provisions of TABOR, such a tax increase could not go into effect without a majority vote in a statewide election. Most observers agreed that a major increase in state taxes would not be approved during an economic recession. Indeed, a citizen-initiated tax increase targeted to help education was on the ballot in 2011 and was readily defeated.

## CITIZEN BRUCE GOES TO THE LEGISLATURE

During the 2007–2008 session of the Colorado state legislature, Douglas Bruce of Colorado Springs was appointed to a vacancy in the state House of Representatives. This rather routine political event received great publicity, however, because it was the same Douglas Bruce who was the author and chief supporter of the TABOR Amendment that severely limited taxation and government revenues in Colorado.

Douglas Bruce's career in the Colorado House got off to a rocky start. When Representative Bruce saw that a press photographer was about to take his picture during the morning prayer, Bruce allegedly kicked the photographer on the foot. An event that under ordinary circumstances would have been laughed off was turned into a major news-media exposé.

A short time later, Bruce voted against a resolution commemorating the sacrifices of Colorado's military veterans in defending the United States. Bruce patiently explained that he thought all such resolutions, not having the force of law, were meaningless and thus not worthy of his support.

By this time the legislative leadership of both political parties had experienced enough of Douglas Bruce. He was censured for his actions. Political scientist John Straayer noted: "I think the Democrats disliked him for TABOR, the Republicans were upset because he was an embarrassment to the Republican Party, and everyone disapproved of his confrontational demeanor."[26]

These actions against Bruce by the news media and the state legislature produced the desired effect. When Douglas Bruce ran for reelection to his legislative seat in the Republican primary in Colorado Springs, he was narrowly defeated by a relatively unknown opponent.

There was great irony in these events. The state legislative leadership undoubtedly sought to make an example of Bruce because of its dislike for how Bruce's TABOR Amendment had greatly reduced the financial options of the state legislature. The leadership may have diminished Bruce's personal reputation, but the legislators lacked the political courage to do anything in the way of changing TABOR in the state constitution and mitigating its damaging effects on the legislature's taxing and revenue-raising abilities.

### LEGISLATURE LOSING POWER

A concern for many political observers in recent years was the extent to which the state legislature (along with the governor) was losing power to voter-initiated constitutional amendments that locked state financial procedures into the state constitution. TABOR was the most obvious example of this process, but certainly not the only one. Initiatives that dictated regular yearly increases in K–12 school finance, historic preservation spending, and open space acquisition with lottery funds all reduced the legislature's (and the governor's) ability to set tax and revenue policy for the state.

### Three Go Up and Two Go Down

By the 2011–12 fiscal year, Colorado's financial situation looked like this. There were five major areas of state expenditures, three of which were going steadily up and two of which were moving drearily down.

The three constantly increasing state expenditures were (1) constitutionally mandated annual increases in K–12 education; (2) the U.S. government program mandating state spending for Medicaid, which provides funds for medical services for the poor; and (3) the increasing cost of operating state prisons, which was going up as the state's population increased. Since letting hardened criminals out of prison and back onto the streets was unacceptable in the light of safety concerns, increases in prison expenditures had to be made.

As a result of the above three expenditure areas always going up, the following two areas were going constantly down: (1) the state's contribution to higher education (state universities and colleges), which was falling to lower budget levels with every passing fiscal year; and (2) all other functions of state government (state highways, state parks, state mental hospitals, the state contribution to welfare services, etc.).

The Colorado state legislature seemed unable to find any solutions to this "three go up and two go down" conundrum. As the legislature struggled, powerful interest groups, seeing that the legislature had no funds with which to help them, toyed with trying to sell the voters an initiated constitutional amendment that would put a permanent annual appropriation for their particular cause in the state constitution.

### A BUSINESS LOBBYIST

Colorado has about 650 registered lobbyists, but perhaps only about fifty or so work full-time and interact with each other at the state capitol on a daily basis. About a dozen are former state legislators. Many lobbyists are "contract lobbyists" and have just one or two clients. These contract lobbyists are only at the state capitol when a client has a bill of importance to the client being considered by the legislature.[27]

Lobbyists perform several of the same functions as state legislators. They represent citizens and interest groups. They research and prepare legislative bills and amendments to bills. They fight to enlarge or to cut various parts of the state budget. They care a great deal about who wins and who loses state legislative elections.

One influential Colorado lobbyist is Steve Durham, who is often characterized as Colorado's foremost business lobbyist. Durham works full-time at lobbying. Two of his major clients have been the Denver Metro Chamber of Commerce and the Colorado Association of Homebuilders. Other clients have included doctors, realtors, a major telephone company, and insurance companies.

Steve Durham grew up in Colorado Springs, graduated from Cheyenne Mountain High School, and then went to what is now the University of Northern Colorado. Elected to the state House of Representatives at a relatively young age, he later served as the Region 8 administrator for the Environmental Protection Agency under U.S. president Ronald Reagan. After a second stint in the state legislature, this time as a state senator, he became a professional full-time lobbyist.

"This is a tough business to get started in," said Durham, "even for a former legislator. If you're a beginner, you need at least one 'anchor client' to get you started."

"An anchor client," Durham explained, "is a major firm or organization that has a big interest in the state legislature and is willing to pay you close to a living wage to lobby for it. After you have your anchor, you can start signing up other clients as you go along. The anchor client that launched my lobbying career was the Colorado Cable Television Association."

"It's a tough life physically as well as mentally," said Durham. "When the legislature is in session, you have to be in the halls of the state capitol buttonholing state legislators anywhere you can find them. You try to visit them in their offices. You sometimes are on your feet twelve hours a day, working in a building where you have no office."

"You do most of your work when bills are being considered by a legislative committee," Durham continued. "It is much harder to get a bill moving in the legislature than to kill it. You have to watch your time carefully. You cannot follow everything that is happening on the state House floor and the state Senate floor at the same time. That's one reason I prefer to work the state Senate, which is smaller, rather than the state House. You only need a few votes to kill or move out a bill in the state Senate."

As expected of a business lobbyist, Durham holds conservative views on most issues. He supports term limits, he says, because untalented legislators are automatically forced out of office. But term limits create problems in his work. He is required to build new relationships all the time with all the new representatives and senators that come into the legislature under term limits.

Durham likes the TABOR limits on taxing and revenues. He argues those limits have kept Colorado state government from spending itself into even more serious budget deficits than the ones the state is facing now. He qualifies his support for TABOR, however. "There need to be taxing and revenue limits," he said, "but TABOR might not be the right limits. Some modifications to TABOR would be acceptable."

"Be careful when dealing with a client," Durham warned. "You want to keep your client informed about what is happening in the legislature that might help or hurt your client, but the final decision on whether to back or fight a bill rests with the client. Even if you disagree with what the client wants, you have to do what the client says and support or oppose the bill accordingly."

Steve Durham acknowledges that the real power in Colorado politics and government now often rests in the citizen initiative rather than the state legislature. As a result, he advises clients on initiative campaigns and often goes out and gives speeches for or against various initiatives, generally supporting the conservative side of the issues.

He points out to clients that it is much easier and cheaper to get an issue referred to the voters by the state legislature than having to collect the requisite number of signatures for a citizen initiative. Durham also informs his clients that they will need to spend at least $3 million (in 2012 dollars) to pass a contentious referred or initiated constitutional amendment.

## AN INTEREST GROUP LOBBYIST

Wade Buchanan is president of the Bell Policy Center, which he describes as "a progressive public policy research and advocacy group." He adds for simplicity: "We are a progressive interest group that lobbies."

Buchanan grew up in Boulder, graduated with honors from Colorado College, and won a prestigious Rhodes scholarship to do graduate studies at Oxford University. He notes that his group's allies at the state legislature are not business organizations but other left-leaning interest groups pursuing social-improvement agendas. Among these groups are the Colorado Children's Campaign and the Civic Engagement Roundtable. Another like-minded group, the Colorado Fiscal Policy Institute, works to develop fiscal reforms in Colorado that will produce more state money for health, education, and welfare programs.

Buchanan had earlier in his career worked on Gov. Roy Romer's staff. Although he originally spent considerable time lobbying at the state capitol for the Bell Center, Buchanan now dispatches other people to do the actual buttonholing and office visiting. He said the biggest change he has observed in the state legislature has been the disappearance of the moderate Republicans. "They've been replaced by conservative Democrats," Buchanan explained, "and that makes it harder to get progressive bills passed even when the Democrats are in the majority."

As for the Republicans in the legislature at the start of the 2011–12 session, Buchanan sees them as sharply split between what he calls "business and industry Republicans," who are mainly interested in economic issues, and "archconservative Republicans," who are opposed to abortion, are critical of gay and lesbian rights, and believe in major tax cutting.

Buchanan previously supported the eight-year term limits for state legislators, but he has subsequently changed his mind. "I voted for term limits back in 1990," he said, "but now I am against them. The cast of characters changes too quickly. There are a lot fewer wise old hands in the legislature, most noticeably on the Joint Budget Committee."

Buchanan noted that the Democrats in Colorado ironically suffered the handicap of taking over the legislature in 2004 and the governorship in 2006, which meant they were just in time for the economic recession that began in September 2008. "It's the economy that kept the Democrats from being Democrats," he explained. They were not able to spend money to expand existing government programs and create new ones. "The Democrats came to power in a period when state government was being constrained fiscally rather than expanding."

Along with other politically active progressives in Colorado, Buchanan is concerned about the use of the citizen initiative to cement fiscal policy into the state constitution. He remarked tartly: "These initiated constitutional amendments have taken tax and revenue policy away from the state legislature and put them on autopilot."

"Colorado has become a direct-democracy state," he added. "We therefore need more responsible voters, but I do not know how you go about getting them."

Buchanan sees one favorable side effect from conservatives, such as Douglas Bruce, using the initiative to hold down taxing and spending in Colorado. "At least TABOR unified business interests and the liberals," he explained. These two groups, he notes, though not usually allies, now are meeting together to see what might be done to create more secure revenue streams for state government.

Buchanan was asked whether his group might turn away from the state legislature and begin using citizen-initiated constitutional amendments to achieve its various social goals. His response was that it would still focus on the legislature. Yet he noted that increasingly, "the system is set up to drive people to use the initiative if they want to advance their cause."[28]

### LOBBYING EVALUATED

Is lobbying necessary and valuable? "Definitely," wrote Roger Walton, one of the leading Colorado lobbyists in the 1980s in Colorado. "Members of the legislature cannot possibly have the depth of information they need to

make sound decisions on all pending legislation. Lobbyists can readily provide information on certain issues and also represent the views of specific
segments of the electorate."[29]

Lobbyists seek to influence the legislature with campaign contributions
at election time. Many people are understandably suspicious of these contributions, but campaign contributions are a form of free speech and thus
are a protected right of every citizen under the U.S. Bill of Rights.

### AN UPDATED EVALUATION OF TERM LIMITS

By 2012 term limits had been implemented for two decades in Colorado,
and the effects had been widely studied by political scientists. One study
found that term limits, by reducing the time that legislators from both parties were together in the state legislature, resulted in a loss of "collegial
bipartisanship and moderation."[30]

Term limits also caused legislative committees to lose power to political parties in the legislature. Legislators had less time to gain committee
expertise and thus found it easier to simply vote along party lines. Parties
began to replace committees as the major source of legislative proposals.

Another study found that committee expertise was a victim of term limits and that committee chairs no longer possessed deep knowledge of the
committee's subject area. "Committees are no longer expert in a policy domain," the study said. "In the term-limited states they exhibit a 'knowledge
deficit.'" The study concluded that because of term limits "legislators have
less confidence in committees in . . . Colorado; their recommendations are
ignored on the floor."[31]

Still another consequence of term limits has been the frequent turnover
of those in top legislative leadership positions. Speakers of the House or
Senate presidents now turn over every two years or so. Some of these leaders come to their positions with a lot less expertise and experience than
used to be the case, and then they leave after relatively brief tenures. Even
those who favor term limits are troubled by this downside of term limits.

Josh Penry, a former Republican state senator from Grand Junction,
Colorado, still supports term limits but now believes a twelve-year rather
than an eight-year limit would be preferable.[32]

### CONCLUSIONS

Major conclusions can be drawn about the Colorado legislature. First, it
has lost some of its power to govern the state to the citizen initiative pro-

cess. Second, term limits, initiated by the voters, have turned the majority of legislators into newcomers and rookies who have limited knowledge of what they are doing. Third, power is more centralized in the hands of the majority party leadership in both houses of the state legislature. Fourth, the legislature is more partisan. Finally, however, the Colorado General Assembly somehow gets its job done. It represents the people and is able to collaborate, at least some of the time, across party lines.

An example of the recent centralization of power in the legislature is the decline in the influence of the Joint Budget Committee, both over the state budget and within the legislature. Much of state politics is about who controls the budget, and in Colorado this has been the legislature in general and the JBC in particular. When hard economic times hit Colorado following the major recession that began in 2008, however, the JBC seemed to step back and let the governor take the leading role in announcing unpleasant budget cuts.

Further, many observers of Colorado politics worry that the power of the state legislature in Colorado government is being eroded by initiated constitutional amendments, particularly the TABOR Amendment and Amendment 23 guaranteeing high K–12 public school spending. According to this argument, ballot issue by ballot issue, the voters are shifting control of state finances away from the legislature and into the hands of the electorate.

Thus Colorado has the only state legislature in the United States that cannot raise taxes without a vote of the people. The state legislature also must operate within strict limits on the growth of state revenues. The Joint Budget Committee can no longer be characterized as "powerful," these critics argue, when it cannot increase taxes without first going hat in hand for a vote of the people.

Put another way, in Colorado every voter is virtually a government budget official, because tax increases have to be approved by the electorate rather than the legislature. Perhaps the most important characteristic of the Colorado legislature is what it cannot do, and that is raise taxes whenever the legislature, and only the legislature, deems it necessary.

A major critic of this development is Fred Brown, veteran political columnist for the *Denver Post*. He laments the decline in the power of the state legislature and the rise of conducting so much of state government by state initiatives and referendums. Brown reminds us regularly, in his columns and other commentary, that Colorado was designed as a representative government and not a direct democracy.

But on a more positive note, state legislators work hard as representatives of their constituents. Occasionally there is a sharp partisan divide and breakdown. This was the case with a civil unions proposal that the Republican leadership refused to bring to a vote at the end of the 2012 legislative session. But, more typically, there have been a fair number of legislators in both parties who reach across party lines and make sure the legislative and budgeting for the state get done. Senate president Brandon Shaffer (Democrat from Longmont), taking a broader view of life in the Colorado legislature, put in this way: "You know, the political dialogue here at the state capitol does not have to be a zero-sum game. It doesn't have to involve winners and losers. . . . I'm about trying to solve problems and figuring out how to make things work."

Shaffer continued: "If I've learned one thing over the course of the last seven years, it's that the process works. It's not always pretty, but it is a very thorough process for vetting legislation. And, with very few exceptions, when a bill finally makes it to the governor, it is in pretty good shape."[33]

# CHAPTER EIGHT

# The Colorado Governorship

Colorado governors get a big office with a view of the Rocky Mountains on the first floor of the majestic if cramped state capitol building at 200 East Colfax Avenue in Denver. The capitol was built of Colorado granite in 1886. As of 2013, governors get paid a meager $90,000 for overseeing about a $20 billion state budget and about sixty thousand state employees.[1] That is the second-biggest workforce in the state, second only to U.S. government employees. Colorado governors point out, however, that only about thirty thousand of the state employees are directly under their purview.

Everyone expects a governor to balance the budget, improve highways, upgrade higher education, help recruit new businesses, help create new jobs, protect the environment, reduce crime, plan for the future, and much more. We want governors to fight for our state's share of federal monies but resist unneeded and unwanted federal regulations. Further, the governor is the state's chief troubleshooter when emergencies or natural disasters occur, such as floods, droughts, prison riots, massive forest fires (as in 2002 and 2012), high school shootings (such as at Columbine High School in Colorado in 1999), or blizzards (as in Colorado in 2007).

As former governor Bill Owens put it: "When disaster happens, a fire or flood, the public looks to you [the governor]."[2] If that's not enough, governors get politically attacked regularly by the opposition party and occasionally even from some in their own party. And, if this wasn't enough, in mid-July of 2007 an undoubtedly deranged thirty-two-year-old armed gunman who was threatening the Colorado governor's life was fatally shot right outside the governor's office.

Colorado's legislative branch, discussed in the previous chapter, occupies the second floor of the state capitol. It is as if they literally oversee the governor's every move from right upstairs. And as discussed, legislators justifiably believe they are the state's lawmakers, and they cherish their prerogative as at least a coequal policy- and budget-making leader for Colorado.

Still, governors play a central and highly visible role in both the politics and the governing of the state. Constituents expect the governor to serve as chief administrator, symbolic and ceremonial head of the state, chief economic officer, chief innovation officer, chief tourism booster, head of a political party, and on and on. The public expects the governor to take the lead on at least two or three dozen major public-policy fronts. A governor found wanting, especially in emergencies or at tough economic times, rarely recovers politically.

Do we expect too much? Yes, we do. But hope (and Colorado Promises)[3] spring eternal. Just as with American presidents, we are highly unlikely to lower our demands on Colorado's chief executive.

A leading Republican state legislator from Grand Junction, Josh Penry, considered running for governor in 2010 but dropped out of the race. He told us that "who becomes governor in Colorado really matters." One of the hardest realities for the governor, Penry added, is that Colorado has "more permanent spending programs than it has permanent, reliable revenue streams."

Penry's Republican Party vision of an effective conservative governor was of a chief executive who "makes tough choices, works closely with business leaders in creating new jobs, cuts taxes, and is willing to lay off more state employees when necessary. He or she is also willing, at least on occasion, to take on his or her political base."[4]

Article IV, section 2, of the Colorado state constitution may overstate the case when it proclaims: "The supreme executive power of the state shall be vested in the governor who shall take care that the laws be faithfully executed."

In fact, Colorado governors have to share power, not only with a typically feisty state legislature but also with several other separately elected executive officials. The list includes the state attorney general, the state treasurer, and the state secretary of state (who maintains state records and regulates state elections). A separately elected Board of Regents governs the University of Colorado system. A separately elected state Board of Education helps supervise the state Education Department.

The powers of the Colorado governor might better be described as "potential" rather than "supreme." Democratic governor Bill Ritter found these so-called supreme powers inadequate if not illusory when Colorado was faced with the Great Recession of 2008–10. Republican governor John

Love, who was chief executive from 1963 to 1973, once suggested: "Colorado governors have the responsibility but not the authority to run the state."[5]

### TERM LIMITS, SALARY, HOUSING, ETHNICITY

Gov. John Hickenlooper, inaugurated in January 2011, is technically Colorado's forty-second governor, yet only the thirty-seventh person to serve in the office. This is because three former governors served two nonconsecutive terms and a fourth served on three different occasions.

Twenty of Colorado's governors have been Democrats, one was a Populist (Davis Waite, who served 1893–95), and sixteen were Republicans. Democrats, as of 2013, have occupied the office for seventy-nine years, the Populists held it for two years, and Republicans served for fifty-eight years. Looking back, Democrats consider Governors John Shafroth, Stephen McNichols, Dick Lamm, and Roy Romer as their favorite governors. Republicans generally rank Ralph Carr, John Love, and Bill Owens as among their favorite governors.[6]

Until 1958, Colorado governors served a two-year term of office. The gubernatorial term in Colorado is now four years. Until 1990 there was no limit on the number of times the Colorado governor could be reelected. A constitutional amendment adopted by the voters in 1990 limited the Colorado governor to eight years (two terms) in office.

Putting an eight-year limit on serving as governor did not change things much. Prior to the 1920s, no Colorado governor had ever served more than four years in office. Only three Colorado governors, John A. Love in the 1960s and 1970s, Richard D. Lamm in the 1970s and 1980s, and Roy Romer in the 1980s and 1990s, served more than eight years in office.

John Love occupied the governor's chair for ten years. Richard Lamm was in office three full four-year terms for a total of twelve years. Roy Romer, similar to Lamm, served three four-year terms. Romer might have served a fourth four-year term, but he was the first Colorado governor to have to give up the office because of term limits.

The governor's salary has increased over the years yet has always been modest compared to what successful professionals in other fields are paid. In fact it is among the lowest in the nation for a governor's salary—the forty-seventh lowest of the fifty states. Colorado's first governor in 1877 earned $3,000 a year. By 1930 the gubernatorial salary had increased to only $5,000 a year. The 1960 yearly salary was $20,000, and in the early 1990s it was $76,000 a year. It is now $90,000.

In addition to a decidedly low salary, the Colorado governor receives certain fringe benefits associated with being the chief executive of one of the fifty states. One of these is the supposed "privilege" of living in the Governor's Mansion, the former home of a "millionaire," located in Denver's Capitol Hill neighborhood six blocks south of the capitol building. The home is lavish, containing twenty-seven rooms spread over twenty-five thousand square feet. The house that later became the Governor's Mansion was built by an important early resident of Denver, Walter Cheesman. Next it was occupied by Claude Boettcher, the owner of a prosperous Denver stock brokerage and investment firm. Boettcher was a "mover and shaker" in Colorado politics.

Colorado has had a Governor's Mansion since 1960. Prior to this, governors who were not from the Denver area were expected to live in hotels or apartments near the capitol during their term in office. Perhaps that helps to explain why, before the 1960s, no Colorado governor ever served more than six years in office. William "Billy" Adams, who was governor from 1927 to 1933, lived and took his meals at the Brown Palace, the most prominent hotel in Denver. Gov. Ralph L. Carr lived at his own home at 747 Downing Street with the quaint listing in the Denver telephone directory of: "Carr, Ralph L., Governor, State of Colorado."

In recent years, neither the family of Gov. Bill Owens nor Gov. Bill Ritter enjoyed living in the Governor's Mansion. Gov. John Hickenlooper, elected in 2010, decided that he, his wife, and young son would remain in their own private home in the Park Hill section of Denver.[7] In mid-2012, however, Governor Hickenlooper moved into the Governor's Mansion alone after he and his wife separated.

Because it was one of the later states to be settled and granted statehood, Colorado did not have a Colorado-born governor until Teller Ammons, a Democrat, was elected in 1936. All the state's governors have been white males, although women have been elected and have served as lieutenant governor, attorney general, secretary of state, and state treasurer.

Half the American states have elected a woman governor, and this includes most of Colorado's neighboring states such as Arizona, Kansas, New Mexico, Oklahoma, Nebraska, and Texas. One woman, Democrat Gail Schoettler, came close to winning the Colorado governorship in 1998. She was nosed out in a tight election by Bill Owens, her Republican opponent.

Colorado has had two African American lieutenant governors. And it currently has in Joe Garcia a lieutenant governor with Hispanic heritage. Before being elected to the state's highest office, Colorado's governors have worked in a wide variety of occupations reflecting the state's history.

They have been miners, smelter men, farmers, ranchers, newspapermen, and most recently a district attorney and a geologist turned restaurant owner and brewmaster.

## FORMAL POWERS

Governors and their staffs complain a lot about the alleged weakness of the office and the seemingly permanently contentious state legislature, but Colorado's constitution gives every governor considerable formal powers. Perhaps their most important power is the authority to appoint most of the heads of the state administrative departments.

Colorado governors also get to appoint a few dozen people as personal staff assistants to the governor, such as chief of staff, chief legal counsel, and press secretary. They also get to name top budget, planning, and policy advisers as well as a chief operating officer.

The Colorado governor has a broad power to appoint judges and justices from the county level all the way to the state supreme court. Former governors Roy Romer, Bill Owens, and Bill Ritter, who collectively served from 1987 to 2011, appointed four hundred state, district, and county justices and judges. Governors, however, must select judicial appointees from among three people nominated by merit selection panels, though governors have an important role in shaping those panels. Moreover, unlike at the federal level and in many of the states, Colorado's gubernatorial appointments to the bench need no legislative confirmation. Once appointed by the governor, judges and justices begin a two-year term after which they have to win retention in nonpartisan elections at varying intervals depending on the level of the court.

A Colorado governor also has the power to appoint a large number of volunteer boards and commissions that shape public policy and oversee the operation of various state administrative functions. These include the State Highway Commission, the Colorado Lottery Commission, and the Wildlife Commission. The governor appoints the Colorado State University Board of Governors, which supervises the Colorado State University campuses at Fort Collins and Pueblo. Many of these nominees have to be confirmed by the state Senate, yet most win confirmation.

Colorado governors also have the authority to fill vacancies when they occur in statewide offices. Thus Republican governor Bill Owens appointed fellow Republican John Suthers to be state attorney general when Democratic attorney general Ken Salazar was elected to the U.S. Senate in 2004. Four years later Democratic governor Bill Ritter appointed Democrat Michael Bennet to a U.S. Senate seat when Senator Salazar was appointed and confirmed as secretary of the U.S. Interior Department.

We'll discuss later that nearly every governor wishes he or she had even greater leeway in appointments, but it is clear that Colorado's chief executive has many major appointments to make. The best governors make the most of this power and recruit and appoint wisely.

A second formal power, at least on paper, is to initiate the annual state budget. The governor has a small budget staff and an executive budget director. They, together with the governor, gather and assess executive branch budget requests for the upcoming fiscal year. This is done every fall, and the governor presents a proposed budget on November 1. This proposed budget is immediately reviewed and scrutinized by the legislature's Joint Budget Committee and its staff.

A governor can put a cap, or upper limit, on the amount of money any agency can request from the state legislature. Many governors would prefer to set a higher rather than a lower figure for spending, but sometimes that has not been possible due to constitutional budget constraints and economic downturns.

Another important constitutional power of the Colorado governor is the general veto authority. When a governor disapproves of a bill passed by the state legislature, he or she can veto the entire bill. The legislature can override such a veto by mustering a two-thirds vote in both the state Senate and the state House of Representatives. In most instances, however, governors will have enough members of their own political party in at least one chamber of the legislature to prevent a legislative override of the veto.

Former governor Bill Owens brags that as governor, he vetoed more bills than any of his predecessors. During his last two years in the governor's office, Owens, a Republican, faced a state legislature in which both houses were solidly controlled by the Democrats. Owens vetoed forty-seven bills in the 2005 session of the legislature and forty-four bills in 2006. In eight years as governor, Bill Owens vetoed more than 150 bills. His successor, Democrat Bill Ritter, who had a Democratic legislature sending him bills, vetoed only twenty-four bills during his four years in office.[8]

A Colorado governor also possesses the "item veto" on fiscal appropriations, a power American presidents do not have. Thus the Colorado governor can strike individual appropriation items out of spending bills without killing the entire bill. This presumably provides the governor the chance to kill "pork barrel" and "special interest" earmarks in major appropriation bills. The item veto, or partial veto, is not widely used by Colorado governors, however. From 2000 to 2010 the partial veto was never used more than four times in any one legislative session.[9]

The veto and item veto make the governor a legislative actor and can, when used effectively, help strengthen a governor's hand in negotiations over both budgetary and general legislative matters.

Article IV, section 7, of the Colorado constitution stipulates that each governor shall have the power to grant reprieves, commutations, and pardons (after conviction by the courts) for all offenders, except in cases of "treason or impeachment." A pardon is an executive granting of a release from the consequences of a criminal act. A commutation is a reduction of a penalty to a less severe one.

But if the governor uses the reprieve, commutation, or pardon powers, he or she is required to send a transcript of the petition to the legislature to inform the legislators of the reasons for the executive action.

A State Parole Board, along with a more recently established Juvenile Parole Board, makes recommendations to the governor about pardons and related issues. The two boards are assisted by a pardon specialist in the Department of Corrections. These recommendations for pardons come to the governor through the governor's legal counsel. The number of pardons in recent years is fewer than in the past, partly because of several reforms having to do with sentencing guidelines. Gov. Bill Owens pardoned thirteen and Gov. Bill Ritter pardoned forty-two offenders.

As in the rest of the American states, the Colorado governor is made commander-in-chief of the state's military forces except when those forces are called into national service by the president of the United States. Section 5 of Article IV adds, "He [the governor] shall have the power to call out the militia to execute the laws, suppress insurrection, and repel invasion."

Governors nowadays not only take care "that the laws be faithfully executed," but they also view it as one of their chief responsibilities to advocate improvements or revisions in past laws. Governors also see it as their duty to propose new ideas for new programs that would promote economic development, energy conservation, more efficient administrative practices, and a whole host of similar legislative and constitutional amendment initiatives.

The Colorado governor, like the American president, also has authority to issue *executive orders* such as when Governor Hickenlooper closed down the Office of Homeland Security and transferred its coordinating role to the Colorado Department of Public Safety. Hickenlooper issued about two dozen executive orders in his first couple of years.

Colorado governors present a state-of-the-state address early in January of each year. This is a theatrical and almost regal occasion. It is staged before a joint session of both the state Senate and the state House of Representatives.

The locale for this is the impressive state House of Representatives chamber on the second floor of the state capitol. State senators and state representatives are nearly all present along with the governor's cabinet members, other statewide elected officials, members of the state supreme court, and often the mayor of Denver. Up in the balcony are scores of lobbyists, county commissioners, guests, family members, visitors, and an occasional professor of political science.

For example, on January 8, 2009, Democratic governor Bill Ritter gave a rather somber thirty-three-minute state-of-the-state address. He reviewed the tough economic times facing the state along with a pitch that "we must not give in to partisan politics." Declining tax revenues and rising unemployment forced the governor to talk about "tough choices."

"We are committed in a bipartisan manner to protect jobs, help stabilize the economy, and make our roads and bridges safer," Ritter said. Like most governors in any state, he emphasized the need for creating jobs, managing the state budget, and making government more accountable and efficient.

But the weak economy in 2009 forced the governor to limit his advocacy of new programs. Indeed, he and the assembled state legislators fully understood they soon would be cutting programs, trimming staff, and undertaking other, often drastic measures in order to deal with recent shortfalls and balance the state budget.

On January 13, 2011, John Hickenlooper gave his state-of-the-state address at the capitol at a time Colorado faced the possibility of having to slash nearly another billion dollars from an already lean state budget. His was an upbeat and even optimistic twenty-five-minute talk, yet he offered few specifics. Colorado needs, he urged, "very direct, very pragmatic conversations about what we can and cannot afford."

He was acknowledging cuts he and the legislature would have to make. On a more somber note, Hickenlooper added that "no one in this room took office to cut programs that are needed and used by some of our most vulnerable citizens. No one wants to vote to support a budget that cuts education when clearly we need to instead find ways to better support our school districts and colleges."[10]

In more prosperous times, governors boldly call for more spending on higher education, for investments in environmental protection, and major initiatives in transportation, corrections, economic development, and tourism.

### INFORMAL POWERS

The list of formal powers suggests the Colorado governor is a relatively strong chief executive. But when compared with the formal powers governors have in other states, Colorado ranks just above the middle of the fifty states.[11] Stronger governors, in terms of formal powers, are found in states such as Illinois, Maryland, New York, and Washington. Illustrative weaker governorships are found in Texas, Nevada, and in the Carolinas.

Colorado's weak, or mixed, governorship in terms of formal powers is explained in part because Colorado governors have considerably less leeway in appointing executive branch officials below executive directors (cabinet heads). Colorado's weaker ranking is also due to the fact that, as discussed in the previous chapter, the legislature has often played a stronger role in shaping the state's budget than is the case in most states.

But effective Colorado governors learn to maximize their informal resources and husband their "political capital." Recent Colorado governors have expanded their policy and advisory staffs. Several of these have come about because of U.S government funds or money provided by Colorado foundations. Thus there are expanded offices on energy, economic development, trade policy, and water issues. In addition, information technology responsibilities have been centralized in the governor's office.

Here briefly are some of the informal powers or resources of a Colorado governor: becoming a confident and effective crisis manager; exploiting the "bully pulpit" opportunities for passionately celebrating both Colorado's and their policy agenda; becoming a "power listener" with an extensive "kitchen cabinet;" visiting all sixty-four Colorado counties at least once a year (it is tempting to be just an I-25 governor rather than governor for the whole state); skillfully promoting Colorado's exports and Colorado's support for entrepreneurial innovation; working closely with business leaders to recruit new business and new federal installations to the state; artfully lobbying the U.S. government to obtain needed and deserved funding; scrubbing harmful regulations; and creatively learning from the successes as well as the mistakes that other states have experienced.

Patricia Limerick, a historian at the University of Colorado at Boulder, understands that the Colorado governor's formal powers are mixed. Yet she mused that in a way that makes the governor all the more powerful when speaking passionately to an issue. "But being governor here does give someone the chance to improve lives," she says. "It's a great opportunity to bring out people's 'better angels.'"[12]

Colorado governors who want to can serve as the primary agenda setters for the state. An effective Colorado governor also uses negotiating abilities, public relations campaigns, coalition-building skills, and patronage to cultivate critical swing votes in both chambers of the state legislature.

Governors have to hire highly professional press secretaries, speechwriters, and special liaisons for legislative and U.S. government relations. They also have to be both effective political party leaders and equally effective at building coalitions across party lines. Little gets done in Colorado unless a governor and legislative leaders from both political parties can collaborate and negotiate agreements.

This calls for great dexterity and navigation skills on the part of governors. They learn, as all good politicians learn, that a political opponent today may be a crucially needed ally tomorrow. The "no permanent enemies" motto thus becomes a strategically important one. The best governors learn how to disagree without becoming disagreeable.

Governors must be tough poker players in their dealings with state legislators. Understandably, legislators believe they are the constitutionally designated lawmakers for the state. But governors and state legislators both have to know when to fight and when to compromise. The art of compromise and agreement building is the essence of politics.

Governors learn that people in both parties have good ideas. Governors reach out to those, regardless of party loyalties, who come up with ways to make programs more effective and efficient.

Effective governors learn to improvise, invent, and adapt to constantly changing political and economic environments. "Politics is like surfing," said former governor Dick Lamm. "You have to look where the waves are coming from."[13]

Gov. Bill Owens said he was caught off guard and rather unprepared when the tragic April 20, 1999, Columbine High School shooting took place that killed twelve students and one teacher. "I was a brand-new governor and did not know what to do," Owens said. But he quickly called former governors Dick Lamm and Roy Romer as well as President Bill Clinton in Washington. They gave useful advice. He had to learn, as Hickenlooper learned after the equally tragic 2012 Aurora theater shootings, that governors have to serve as the face of Colorado and display strength as the state mourns, grieves, and conducts memorials and investigations.

Owens also learned, by mistake, that everything a governor says can have consequences. During one summer of intense drought and extensive forest fires, Owens was quoted on national television as saying that "all Colorado is burning." The tourist industry, among others, did not much like that. At a party for incoming Gov. John Hickenlooper, Owens was asked to give some gubernatorial-type advice. "Never, never," he joked, "say 'all Colorado is burning,' even if it is."[14]

Every governor is faced with some combination of floods, droughts, forest fires, tornadoes, and their own Columbines. The state constitution does not provide for what needs to be done on such occasions, yet the public expects strength, confidence, and prudent leadership from the governor.

Governors get flooded with invitations to cut ribbons at new buildings, march in parades, and speak at dinners, conventions, and charity roasts. They have to do far more of these events than they want to do. But they must use these occasions to meet people and listen to the concerns of average people. Most Coloradans, as discussed in chapter 2, do not think their elected officials are good listeners and do not think politicians adequately care about or understand the average citizen. It is a demanding job when you are governor of a state of 5.5 million or more constituents, most of whom think big business executives and Denver-based campaign contributors get most of the governor's attention.

It is easy for a governor to become isolated and arrogant. "The Achilles heel of most people in power is arrogance," said former Colorado governor Roy Romer. "Arrogance is what does us in."[15]

Governor Lamm shared this advice: "The hardest but most necessary thing to do in politics is to be able to say no to your friends."[16] He was not saying a governor should reward enemies and punish friends, but rather that a governor in a highly pragmatic state such as Colorado has to act strategically, especially when negotiating coalitions that necessarily have to include Democrats, independents, and Republicans.

Governor Owens spoke to this as well when he said: "You sometimes have to go against your base. . . . Some things are good for the state but not good for you politically."[17]

GOVERNING COLORADO

There is a perception that the Colorado governor lacks power. This gubernatorial weakness has been enhanced by various TABOR and TABOR-related budgetary laws and constitutional amendments. So how does a governor get things done in Colorado?

First, even though governors are plainly the most visible and most central source of leadership in the state, Colorado's is a three-branch system of government. A chief justice presides over the judicial branch and the Judicial Department and oversees various agencies such as the public defender program and the Commission on Judicial Discipline. Legislative leaders do the same for the state legislature and offices such as the Legislative Council and the Joint Budget Committee.

Then, too, a separately elected attorney general and separately elected secretaries of state and treasury head up and oversee the administration of major offices, such as the solicitor general's office and the state's election bureau.

Still, an effective governor is expected by everyone not only to ably manage existing operations but to identify emerging problems and opportunities, propose general policy solutions, and help frame the larger public-policy agenda for the state. Every governor knows that the opposition party and scores of well-organized interest groups, such as the AFL/CIO, chambers of commerce throughout the state, teachers' unions, oil and gas lobbies, Colorado Concern business leaders, contractors, county commissioners, home builders and similar industry groups, among others, will have their own usually contending agenda.

That is all part of the democratic process of give and take, deliberation, and compromise. It is always far easier to propose new ideas than it is to get them approved, funded, and effectively implemented.

One helpful study of an effective Tennessee governor summarized both his and his management consultant's advice: "Hire good people. Give them authority to make decisions. Get them the resources they need. Leave them alone. Support and protect them. If they make too many mistakes, remove them."[18]

Colorado governors get plenty of advice along these lines from former governors of Colorado and of other states and from the National Governors' Association.[19]

Roy Romer was a recent Colorado governor who worked hard at finding areas of strength in Colorado's allegedly weak governorship. B. J. Thornberry, Romer's deputy chief of staff, described these techniques for getting the most influence available. "This governor is an activist and a populist," she said. "He effectively uses the publicity powers of the governorship to set a vision for the future of the state."

Thornberry noted that Romer liked periodically to get out of the Denver area in order to learn what people all over the state were thinking. She concluded: "He listens to the people. Then he articulates what they tell him as goals for the future. When you mobilize your constituents behind ideas and programs in this way, eventually the changes you want will be implemented."[20]

Another Colorado governor who made reasonably good use of his publicity powers was Bill Ritter, who served from 2007 to 2011. Ritter traveled the state talking up wind-generated electrical power and other forms of "green energy" that would create "green jobs" in Colorado. Working with the U.S. government, Ritter invested big chunks of federal stimulus funds in what he called "Colorado's New Energy Economy." Still, the major responsibility for developing green energy rested with private industry rather than state government.

As a spokesman for change, a governor works to influence more than just the legislature. Governors also will endeavor to provide leadership on local government issues to the cities and counties in the state. For instance, when the public schools in Denver were about to be closed by a teachers' strike, Gov. Roy Romer personally intervened, mediated, and eventually produced an agreement that was acceptable to both the teachers and the school board.

Colorado governors provide leadership and vision to the wide variety of boards and commissions that govern so many of the activities of state government. Often a governor will meet with a board or commission, making his or her views clear to the members and urging various plans of action, or inaction, on them. "If the governor keeps after the various boards and commissions he appoints, his policies will likely be implemented by them."[21]

Observers point out, however, that the publicity powers used effectively by many Colorado governors have limitations. "Drumming up public support for ideas and legislation is a technique that only works occasionally," said a Romer aide. "The daily verbal hammering the governor has to do on issues and programs takes a long time to take effect."[22]

Romer himself was well aware that a governor's powers were often fragile and that getting public opinion behind him was a primary way, as a Democrat, he could have an impact on a Republican legislature. "And it is unfortunate," notes Romer. "You'd have better government if you had more governor's involvement in the budget and the education process. [Mobilizing public opinion] is a very tough way to organize power."[23]

On balance, Colorado governors are effective only to the extent they are able to persuade others to join them voluntarily in various state programs and projects. The role of the governor is, above all, that of a communicator, negotiator, and persuader. To get the job done the governor must influence administrators, state legislators, federal officials, local officials, party leaders, business leaders, the press, and the public. But persuasion has its limits. Governors also have to be strategic in setting their priorities.

Over the last two decades, Colorado governors began to realize that a big part of their job was getting the Colorado electorate to vote for or against particular statewide ballot proposals. This was true of proposals referred to the voters by the state legislature as well as proposals initiated onto the ballot by the general public. Overall, Colorado governors have done a better job of drumming up support for what they considered good proposals than they have for mobilizing opposition to what they considered bad proposals.

In the early 1990s Gov. Roy Romer expressed his opposition to three initiated ballot issues. One was the TABOR Amendment, which limited both tax increases and government revenues in Colorado. A second prohibited local governments in Colorado from passing laws that favored gays and lesbians. A third provided for low-stakes gambling in three Colorado mountain towns (Central City, Blackhawk, and Cripple Creek).

All three of the ballot issues passed, much to Governor Romer's chagrin. He probably wished he had more actively campaigned against them rather than just opposing them verbally.

Bill Owens provides the best illustration of a governor winning voter support for key ballot issues. He gave both his time and his voice to backing a statewide bond issue to improve roads (including the T-REX project on I-25 south of Denver) and to pushing for a five-year timeout from the expenditure limitations in TABOR. In addition, Owens pressed for voter enactment of a Denver metropolitan area "light rail" line to parallel the T-REX highway project. All three measures were adopted by the voters, and all three became highlights in Bill Owens's career as governor.

Despite his success with ballot issues, however, Bill Owens was well aware of his limitations as governor of Colorado. He once said: "[Coloradans have] a long history of liking their governor but not following [the governor's] lead on issues."[24]

Gov. Bill Ritter tried to follow the Owens model. He put before the voters in 2008 a proposal to reduce tax breaks for oil and natural gas producers and use the money for scholarships to state colleges and universities. Despite Governor Ritter's vigorous efforts, the proposal was easily defeated at the polls, mainly because of an effective and well-financed opposition campaign by oil and natural gas interests that bitterly attacked Governor Ritter in some of its television advertisements.[25]

## WEAKNESSES OF THE COLORADO GOVERNOR

As mentioned, perhaps the chief constitutional weakness of the Colorado governor is limited appointment powers. A governor can appoint fifteen department heads, *and these are among the few administrative appointments that he or she can make in state government.*

Department heads in state government are generally known as executive directors. For example, an executive director heads the state Department of Corrections and another heads the state Department of Natural Resources. A commissioner of agriculture heads up the Department of Agriculture.

Four department heads are not appointed by the governor. Three of the four are elected by the voters. They are the attorney general for the Department of Law, the state treasurer for the Department of Treasury, and the secretary of state for the Department of State. In a fourth case, the Department of Education is presided over by a commissioner selected and appointed by the State Board of Education rather than the governor.

In recent years, executive directors of state departments have been paid about $150,000 per year. The number of employees per department varies considerably from a few hundred to several thousand. The Department of Transportation, for example, has about 3,000 employees and oversees more than 9,000 miles of state highways and hundreds of state bridges. It also plans and monitors ongoing construction projects.

Gov. John Hickenlooper appointed his lieutenant governor, Joe Garcia, to serve simultaneously as executive director of the Higher Education Department. This gave the lieutenant governor more responsibility and more to do. Garcia was well qualified for the post, and the double job saved money, as Garcia was paid only for his heading up the Higher Education Department.

Below the level of department head, the governor has few appointive powers. There are more than one hundred agencies, and each one is presided over by an agency head, or division director, who is a civil service employee in the state bureaucracy. The agency heads are appointed to office on the basis of civil service tests and job performance evaluations. Their selection as agency head is not under the direct control of the governor.

A state legislator said of this heavy bias toward the civil service system: "Rather than get rid of the spoils system, it created another kind of spoils."[26]

Even in those major departments where the department head is appointed by the governor, there will be agencies over which the governor's department head has no effective control. These agencies, called Type 1 agencies, report to an appointed board or commission. Although the governor, and previous governors, may have had a hand in appointing the board or commission, the governor will not have direct control.

Gene Petrone, a former executive director of the Office of State Plan-

Table 11. Departments of Colorado State Government

|  | Personnel | Spending ($) |
|---|---|---|
| Higher Education | 21,500* | 3,000,000,000 |
| Corrections | 6,750 | 730,500,000 |
| Human Services | 5,200 | 2,150,000,000 |
| Transportation | 3,300 | 1,040,000,000 |
| Revenue | 1,525 | 705,000,000 |
| Natural Resources | 1,475 | 245,000,000 |
| Military and Veterans Affairs | 1,400 | 225,000,000 |
| Public Safety | 1,350 | 260,000,000 |
| Public Health and Environment | 1,230 | 440,000,000 |
| Labor and Employment | 1,050 | 160,000,000 |
| Regulatory agencies | 580 | 77,800,000 |
| Education (commissioner selected by elected State Board of Education) | 550 | 4,400,000,000 |
| Personnel and Administration | 400 | 170,000,000 |
| Health Policy and Financing | 300 | 4,600,000,000 |
| Local Affairs | 175 | 320,000,000 |
| Agriculture | 290 | 40,000,000 |
| Governor's office and staff | 1,050 | 200,000,000 |

| *Independent branches or departments* | | |
|---|---|---|
| Judicial (courts) | 4,100 | 460,000,000 |
| Attorney General/Law | 430 | 50,000,000 |
| Legislature | 275 | 36,000,000 |
| Secretary of State | 135 | 21,500,000 |
| Secretary of Treasury | 30 | 350,000,000 |

*Source*: Joint Budget Committee, Appropriation Report, 2010–11.

*Notes*: Numbers for personnel and spending are rounded off. These personnel figures are for full-time equivalents and may understate the number of people who work part-time for the state such as adjunct professors and others who consult with the state or are paid indirectly by the federal government. The governor's staff was greatly expanded in recent years because information technology personnel were consolidated under the governor's office.

*This figure for higher education, we believe, greatly underestimates the real numbers of those employed either full-time or part-time in the state's colleges and universities.

ning and Budget, said the limited number of direct gubernatorial appointments erodes executive authority in Colorado. He explained: "The way things are in Colorado, classified civil service employees are driving policy rather than appointees of the governor. The result is a very rigid system under which the governor cannot have the personnel he wants running the various agencies."

Because the governor has little or no control over them, Petrone pointed out, the agency heads learn to bypass the governor and go directly to the legislature for what they want. "Often, the only real control there is of the civil servants who run the individual agencies is the legislature's control of their appropriations [the amount of money they will have to spend each year]."[27]

This view that the governor's lack of appointive powers weakens the office was confirmed by Larry Kallenberger, former executive director of the Colorado Department of Local Affairs. People assume the Colorado governor has powers that he or she really does not have, Kallenberger said. Putting so many agency heads under the merit system [civil service] creates a bureaucracy that is responsible to the legislature, not the governor.

Kallenberger concluded: "Even the governor's own department heads get savvy and start playing ball with the legislature and pay less attention to the governor."

Having such a powerful civil service bureaucracy, Kallenberger argues, weakens control of state government by the voters. Too much power is given to people who are not elected, he said, or who are not directly responsible to people who are elected. "A person can be governor for many years and never get the reins of bureaucratic control firmly in hand."[28]

There have been periodic attempts in Colorado to have the more than one hundred agency heads (division directors) appointed by the governor rather than remain under civil service. Proposals for this kind of personnel reform were on the general election ballot in the 1970s and again in the 1980s, but a well-organized opposition, led by the Colorado state employees' labor unions, succeeded in defeating both proposals at the polls.

Several people who worked for recent governors said that good management practices as well as an effective governorship required greater control over personnel. Gene Petrone, who worked as budget director for Governor Love as well as Governor Romer, said it made sense to allow the governor the authority to appoint every agency head. That would give the governor some real clout.[29]

Gov. Roy Romer's chief of staff, Stewart Bliss, agreed. He told us governors need the flexibility to move people around at the agency head level.

"We really ought to be able to move the best talent to where it is needed. I wouldn't want a return to the spoils system, yet there is no real system that allows for effective management of the executive branch bureaucracy."[30]

Former governor Richard D. Lamm (1975–87) also noted this was a chief weakness of the governorship. He said he would settle for just being able to replace a handful or so of agency heads. "I'd wait until they proved to be deliberately undermining a program and then I'd fire them or transfer them out. Heck, you'd only need to do that in a limited number of cases to gain better influence over the sprawling bureaucracy."[31]

One "reform" in recent years created a senior executive service for about 125 people in the upper reaches of the state's civil service. In some ways it parallels similar efforts in the U.S. government civil service. In Colorado's case, top civil servants can opt for increased salaries and more responsibilities for leadership yet have to agree to contracts that only last for a year or so. This allows for some terminations, and in the Ritter administration there were several terminations (and some lawsuits).

All this was intended to create greater flexibility for governors and department executive directors. Still, aides to recent governors continue to echo complaints that Lamm, Romer, and their aides made twenty and thirty years earlier. One senior executive office aide, referring to the seemingly permanent career civil servants in Colorado, said: "We call them 'WEBIES.' In effect, they tell us: '*We be* here before you came, and *we be* here after you all leave.'"

Recent governors have held regular cabinet meetings, usually once a month, to coordinate their activities and provide cohesion for the governor's policy agenda. Governor Ritter held cabinet meetings at the Carriage House adjacent to the Governor's Mansion. After a brief buffet breakfast and social conversations beginning at 7:30 in the morning, the cabinet meeting would generally take place from 8:15 to 9:30 a.m. Hickenlooper held his monthly cabinet meetings in conference rooms at the capitol. His cabinet had working groups on issues such as water, economic development, and government efficiency that met more frequently depending on the issue.

The governor would usually outline his priorities and projects. Executive directors sometimes were called on to give updates on their departments. Senior aides to the governor were present and treated as equals to the department heads. These senior aides included the chief operating officer, the chief of staff, the governor's legal counsel, the head of the Office of State Planning and Budget, and similar policy advisers.

A quiet growth of the executive office and gubernatorial advisory system resembles similar expansions in staff for the U.S. president at the White House in Washington DC. In both cases, it is an understandable response to the greater policy and emergency responsibilities that come with growing populations and greater expectations for economic development and effective management of expanded state government operations.

Another weakness of the governor's office in Colorado is its lack of control over state education programs. This weakness is particularly notable because a majority of the state's general-fund budget is devoted to education (kindergarten through twelfth grade [K–12] plus state colleges and universities). Much of the control over public education rests with two boards that are elected by the voters. They are the state Board of Education and the regents of the University of Colorado. Governors, as a result, sometimes lament that they have limited influence over how education funds are spent.

The Colorado governor also has minimal control over the state highway program. Governors appoint the State Highway Commission, yet they must appoint commission members from specified regions of the state. The state constitution requires that neither the governor nor the state legislature can make major changes in the amounts of money the highway commission specifies for various highway projects in Colorado.

Former state senate president John Andrews, a prominent conservative spokesman and a former unsuccessful Republican candidate for governor, told us he too would like to see a fundamental upgrade in the executive authority of the Colorado governor. "It is too weak of an executive," said Andrews. "I'd have a single executive [as does the U.S. government]. I wouldn't have a separately elected attorney general or treasurer. Further, I'd give the governor the right to name all of the cabinet and go a few levels below the cabinet. All this would make the governor's office more efficient and accountable."[32]

PLANNING AND BUDGET POWERS

The extensive influence over the state budget in Colorado by the legislature was described in chapter 7. The Joint Budget Committee and its staff have assumed the budget powers that elsewhere are considered more of an executive responsibility. As a result, a small group of people, the six members who comprise the legislature's Joint Budget Committee, are often, in effect, setting the priorities for the administrative branch of Colorado's government. That is a job many people believe should primarily be the responsibility of governors and their direct political appointees.

The already mentioned item-veto power rarely provides much real power to a Colorado governor. If the legislature was a notoriously big spender, often adding more funds to programs than the governor wished to have spent, then Colorado governors would find the item veto an especially helpful weapon in their arsenal. But as discussed earlier, the Colorado legislature is usually known more for its cutting than its spending habits. "I never found a way to imaginatively use the item veto authority," former Governor Lamm said. "If you have a tightfisted penny-pinching legislature as we have, then the item veto power isn't really much of a power. In my case, when we differed, I usually wanted to spend or invest a bit more, not a bit less."[33]

### POLITICAL PARTY COMPETITION

Under normal circumstances, the two-party system in Colorado should periodically strengthen the position of the governor vis-à-vis the state legislature. From time to time, the same political party that elected the governor should have comfortable working majorities in both houses of the state legislature. The governor could then use party loyalty and a spirit of party cooperation to get the legislative majorities in both houses to support his or her programs for the state.

But, for much of the past two generations, Democrats controlled the governorship and Republicans controlled the legislature. During that period, Democrats charged that the Republican majority in the legislature opposed the governor's programs not because they were bad programs, but because the Republicans did not want to enhance the political image and influence of a Democratic chief executive.

In 1999 Bill Owens became the first Republican governor of Colorado in twenty-four years. For the following six years, from 1999 to 2005, he mainly worked with a Republican state legislature. As noted earlier, however, Owens was a small-government conservative and did not present a large number of bold expenditure proposals to the state legislature.

The takeover of both houses of the Colorado legislature by the Democrats in 2004, coupled with the winning of the governorship by the Democrats in 2006, gave the Democrats the opportunity to have *unified partisan government* in Colorado. But the nation's and Colorado's fiscal woes became so great in the ensuing years that the Democrats could do little with their newfound powers except to cut the state budget and the many important state programs and institutions that budget supported.

Governor Hickenlooper had to work with a Republican-controlled state House of Representatives yet had a Democratic state Senate. This divided legislature resulted in few controversial bills reaching his desk. Bold budget cuts earned him Republican praise, and he generally won bipartisan support for his modest program initiatives.

As would be expected, recent governors and their friends and associates criticize the effects of restricted gubernatorial power in Colorado. Governors McNichols, Love, and Lamm all lamented the rise in power enjoyed by the Joint Budget Committee of the state legislature and the governor's limited appointment powers.

Former legislative lobbyist and department head Larry Kallenberger shares this verdict: "The real result of a weakened governorship is that the governor is not able to move state government." Bureaucrats and legislators tend to resist change, he explained, so giving them so much power means that issues do not get addressed, problems do not get resolved, and people who want things to happen get frustrated and alienated. In the end, Kallenberger noted, "the state loses the ability to react to public concerns with good public programs."

With the governor relatively weak in this regard, Kallenberger continued, state government does not change much. The bureaucrats and legislators only add a little here and subtract a little there. "The public ends up with little confidence that state government can solve problems. The final conclusion is that the system is not functioning in the best interests of democracy."

Kallenberger compared the Colorado state bureaucracy to a headless snake. "It moves. It winds around. When you first look at it, you see motion. Due to the weak governorship, however, the Colorado state bureaucracy has no head and thus never goes anywhere."[34]

### LIEUTENANT GOVERNOR

Colorado's lieutenant governor has two constitutional duties. One is to act as governor when a governor is out of town. The other is to succeed as governor if the governor retires, dies, or is impeached. At least four lieutenant governors became governor because of this succession provision (in 1905, 1937, 1950, and 1973). A few former lieutenant governors, such as Stephen McNichols in 1956, ran for and won the governorship in their own right.

Until 1974 Colorado's lieutenant governor presided over the state Senate, but this practice was ended by constitutional amendment.

Recent lieutenant governors, by statutory (legislative) provision, have chaired the Colorado Commission on Indian Affairs. They have also served in the governor's cabinet and been assigned various ambassadorial special assignments. Barbara O'Brien, Gov. Bill Ritter's lieutenant governor, took on several roles as an advocate for children and public education priorities in Colorado. Joe Garcia, Hickenlooper's lieutenant governor, spearheaded efforts to champion childhood literacy programs.

As of 2001, party nominees for governor personally select their lieutenant governor running mate, and the two run as a team in the November general election. The position may only be "a heartbeat away" from being governor, but its $68,000 annual salary is meager.

A debate arises from time to time as to whether Colorado really needs a lieutenant governor. Supporters of keeping the lieutenant governor position contend it nicely solves the problem of succession and provides a well-briefed and experienced successor should a vacancy occur. Further, supporters say the lieutenant governorship provides for an additional person to represent the state to the state's many constituencies. Finally, the office can provide additional diversity. Several women and minorities have ably served as lieutenant governor in recent decades.

On the other hand, seven states (including Colorado's neighboring states of Utah and Arizona) do not have this office and seem to get along just fine. Former Colorado lieutenant governor Ted Strickland called it "a useless office" that costs taxpayers money yet fulfills little purpose except its ceremonial functions. Stickland repeatedly called for abolishing the office.

Former Democratic governor Dick Lamm agreed with Republican Strickland's urging to end this position, saying it would be a good way to save money. Colorado historian Duane Smith favors doing away with the post. Political scientists Robert Lorch and James Null wrote that "the office of lieutenant governor could probably be abolished with no damage at all to the state of Colorado because there is almost nothing for the lieutenant governor to do."[35]

The Colorado general public is largely unaware of this office and thus lacks an opinion about whether it should be kept or abolished. Our own 1990 Colorado College Citizens Poll found plurality support for doing away with Colorado's lieutenant governorship. Forty-four percent favored eliminating the office, 31 percent wanted to keep it, and 8 percent were neutral. Our 2010 poll found a slight plurality in favor of abolishing the office (33 percent for abolishing it, 32 percent for keeping it, and almost an equal amount of respondents unsure, neutral, or having no response to the issue).

The value of this office continues to be debatable. Yet it is likely to remain, just as the U.S. vice presidency is likely to be kept. States without a lieutenant governorship provide for succession by passing the gubernatorial reins to either the secretary of state or a member of the leadership in the state legislature.

## ATTORNEY GENERAL

An attorney general is elected by Colorado voters every four years. This statewide official does not report to the governor nor is he or she even an informal or unofficial member of the governor's cabinet.

In practice, however, most of Colorado's attorneys general have worked closely with governors and their legal counsels, even when they come from different political parties.

One of the jobs of an attorney general is to represent state agencies in cases before the Colorado state court of appeals and the state supreme court. In effect, the attorney general and his or her staff are the lawyers for the state and provide legal advice for other statewide officials and the state's executive departments.

The attorney general's office and staff are located in the Ralph Carr Judicial Center. The attorney general is paid a low annual salary of $80,000 as of this writing, about half of what a beginning lawyer earns at a good Denver law firm.

As of 2012 John W. Suthers, the current attorney general, presides over more than 430 employees, of which about 250 are attorneys. In recent years his office handled more than ten thousand separate legal matters each year, including more than fifteen hundred cases in the state and federal courts. It also handles at least one thousand water rights cases each year.

Attorney General Suthers and his deputies regularly used statewide grand juries to investigate major criminal cases impacting multiple jurisdictions in Colorado. They also regularly investigated white-collar crimes, particularly insurance and securities fraud.

By 2012 the attorney general's office had grown into a large public law office that was probably the largest "law firm" in Colorado. Its scope covered a wide range of public policy issues from crime and water to campaign finance reform and immigration controversies. John Suthers, like attorneys general elsewhere, spent some of his time overseeing litigation with nearby states over water. He also monitored cases involving energy companies and natural resource damages. Suthers joined fellow attorneys general from other states in legally disputing some aspects of the controversial Patient Protection and Affordable Care Act of 2010.[36]

One of the best ways to understand the Colorado governorship is to review the careers and accomplishments of recent governors. Each of Colorado's elected governors in the past generation brought his own approach and style to the job. The governors were Dick Lamm, Roy Romer, Bill Owens, Bill Ritter, and John Hickenlooper. Their governorships were different from each other in terms of tone and accomplishments.

### Richard Lamm

Richard Douglas Lamm was born in Wisconsin and raised in Illinois and Pennsylvania. An accountant and attorney, he moved to Colorado in the early 1960s. He served as a state legislator from 1967 to 1975.

Lamm first attracted attention in 1969 when as a legislator he challenged then Governor Love's efforts to "sell" Colorado and bring new industry and new people into the state. He suggested Colorado might do better to limit population growth, thereby preserving the state's great natural beauty and avoiding the problems of overcrowding and overbuilding that afflicted many other parts of the United States.

If attracting new industry and new people produced the good life, Lamm said, then "Los Angeles must truly be one of America's most liveable cities."[37]

Richard Lamm also gained statewide attention by leading the fight to prevent the 1976 Winter Olympics from being held in Colorado. When in the 1972 general election the state's voters rejected state financing for the Olympics, Lamm emerged as a principal Colorado spokesman for environmentalism. He ran for governor in 1974 on environmental conservation issues and was easily elected.

Lamm served three four-year terms. The entire time he was governor, however, either one or both houses of the state legislature were in firm control of the Republican Party. But Lamm's popularity seemed to grow the longer he was in office. He won his first election by 53.2 percent of the vote, his second by 58.7 percent, and his third by a remarkable 65.7 percent of the vote.

As Lamm came more and more to symbolize environmentalism and controlling population growth in Colorado, the Republican-dominated state legislature became more committed to strengthening the business community and stimulating economic growth. The result was wrangling between Democratic governor Lamm and a Republican state legislature.

Throughout the late 1970s and early 1980s, Governor Lamm became particularly concerned about the effects of the energy crisis on Colorado. As the U.S. government inaugurated a major program to extract large amounts of oil from large deposits of oil shale in the western part of the state, Lamm gave increasingly dire warnings about how such large-scale energy projects would threaten the natural beauty of Colorado.

"We are going to have to be a region with synfuel plants and wilderness areas side by side," Lamm said. "Our streams must support fish and wildlife, agriculture and industry. It's going to require a good deal of creative planning to bring about that balance and harmony."[38]

But Lamm's repeated calls for better state planning and control of population growth often fell on deaf legislative ears. Colorado's population and industrial base expanded rapidly throughout the late 1970s. Cities on the Front Range, primarily Denver and Colorado Springs, became larger and more crowded. The ski resort areas of Breckenridge, Aspen, and Vail also expanded rapidly.

Throughout it all, Lamm argued with the state legislature about the state's future. In the end, less was accomplished in the way of state programs for controlling population growth and protecting the environment than he had wanted, yet environmentalists have remained a major political force in Colorado.

One of Lamm's few environmental "victories" later came back to haunt him. He opposed the construction of an interstate highway, to be built with U.S. government funds, that would have formed a "beltway" around the entire Denver metropolitan area. The environmentalist governor believed the new interstate beltway would encourage further population growth and commercial development in a portion of the Denver suburbs that was already overdeveloped and overcrowded.

Lamm stated he would drive "a silver stake" in the heart of the giant suburban highway project, and he used his appointive powers on the state highway commission to accomplish his purpose. Lamm never heard the end of this, especially from real-estate developers and residents in the parts of suburban Denver where the highway would have gone.

Ironically, a portion of the belt-highway around southwestern and western Denver (Colorado 470) was subsequently constructed using state rather than U.S. government funds. Also constructed was a toll road around southeastern, eastern, and northern Denver, with a major interchange right at Denver International Airport.

Lamm was credited by many for recruiting scores of talented young professionals to his cabinet and to his state capitol office. He often said that whatever else historians may say, he believed his most significant accomplishment was having surrounded himself with gifted and talented people. Lamm opined: "The governor's most important responsibility is putting together a team to govern the state."[39]

Lamm also opened up state government to large numbers of women and minorities, appointing the first woman and first Hispanic justices to the state supreme court and hiring the first black and Hispanic department heads.

In 1975 Lamm called for and later signed into law the nation's first sunset law. This law terminated programs and bureaucracies unless they were specifically reauthorized by the state legislature after a specified time such as five or seven years. The law helped eliminate fifteen agencies and countless unneeded regulations. Lamm also appointed consumer advocates to all regulatory boards and commissions and initiated the creation of the Office of Consumer Counsel. That office, first funded by federal funds and subsequently funded by the legislature, helped represent consumers in utility rate proceedings.

By the time Richard Lamm was serving his third term as governor, population growth and rapid economic development were less pressing as Colorado public-policy problems. As the energy crisis eased, the U.S. government abandoned its expensive attempts to produce oil from western Colorado oil shale. An economic downturn in the electronic industry and cuts in U.S. military spending further weakened the Colorado economy. Controlling growth and preserving the environment receded somewhat as major issues in Colorado politics.

At the end of his tenure as governor, Lamm began using the bully pulpit of the Colorado governorship to draw attention to what he believed were major problems facing both the state and the nation. He began publishing books and giving speeches both inside and outside the state on such subjects as the environmental destruction of the West, the welfare problems being created by immigration of foreign nationals into the United States, and the rapidly increasing cost of public health care.[40]

In one particularly famous 1984 speech, Lamm sparked a national controversy when he appeared to say that terminally ill older medical patients had a "duty to die" and thereby save the government the high medical cost of prolonging their lives. He said: "We've got a duty to die and get out of the way with all of our machines and artificial hearts and everything else like that and let our society, our kids, build a better life."

Richard Lamm decided not to run for reelection as governor in 1986, even though political observers thought he could have easily been elected to a fourth term in office. Lamm gave his support to Roy Romer, a long-time political ally in the Democratic Party who was serving as state treasurer. Romer easily defeated his Republican opponent in the 1986 general election.

Lamm's career as governor was controversial. He often was criticized for being confrontational with the Republican leadership in the state legislature. Some observers suggested he might have done better by working with the legislators and being more willing to compromise. Many others say he was one of the best governors Colorado ever had. Veteran journalist Ed Quillen believed Lamm was as close to being one of Plato's "philosopher-kings" as is possible in public life. "He really thought deeply about the challenges the state was facing."[41] Conservative Republican Steve Durham, a lobbyist, also told us he thought Lamm was one of Colorado's best governors.

Speaking many years after he left office, Richard Lamm pointed out that he had to deal with a state capitol press corps that had been made super-critical by the Watergate scandal in Washington DC. In that environment, Lamm joked, "the news media often did not appreciate my genius."[42]

Lamm's lengthy tenure as governor illustrated the point that if a governor cannot persuade the Colorado legislature to adopt his programs and policies, most of those programs and policies are never going to be implemented.

Speaking of the state legislature, Lamm recommended that Colorado change its redistricting system so that there are not so many safe Democratic and safe Republican seats. "Change the redistricting system," Lamm said, "so safe seats are not producing archconservative Republicans and left-wing liberal Democrats. The moderates are losing out at the state legislature."[43]

Even those who disagreed with him admired his strength of conviction, his intelligence and integrity, and his celebration of the beauty and majesty of Colorado. On balance Lamm felt the need to "save" and not to "sell" Colorado. He wound up doing some of both.

### Roy Romer

Roy Romer was born in Garden City, Kansas, but raised in Holly, Colorado, a small agricultural community, complete with grain elevators, located close to the Colorado-Kansas border. "I never let people forget my roots were on the Eastern Plains of Colorado," Romer said. "That's why, even when governor, I always wore my leather jacket and my mountain boots."[44]

Romer also liked to demonstrate that he was originally a country boy by always eating oatmeal for breakfast.

He was a successful businessman before serving in the state legislature and as state treasurer. He was a close ally and adviser to his predecessor, Gov. Richard Lamm, serving at different times both in Lamm's cabinet and as his chief of staff.

When Democrat Romer was inaugurated governor of Colorado in 1987, he faced a much different situation from that faced by Richard Lamm when he was inaugurated twelve years earlier. Instead of rapid population growth and an economic boom, which Lamm contended with, Romer found a state in a major economic slump. Unemployment rates were rising, more people were moving out of the state than were moving into it, and both Denver and Colorado Springs were "overbuilt" and had large numbers of vacant offices, apartments, houses, and shopping centers.

Roy Romer made economic development the major theme of his governorship. He appointed a Colorado Springs business executive, Stewart Bliss, as his chief of staff. Romer also put Bliss, a Republican, in direct charge of the state's economic development efforts. Romer himself began touring the United States and foreign countries, carrying the message to all that would listen that Colorado was "open for business." Once again, a governor had felt the need to "sell" Colorado, or at least to aggressively promote it.

Democratic governor Romer took a more collaborative approach with the Republican state legislature. He highlighted general areas that needed action rather than sending specific bills to the House or the Senate. In something of a contrast with his predecessor, Romer let it be known that he was available to work with and compromise with the legislature. Instead of making Republican legislative leaders come down to the governor's office, as Governor Lamm had done, Romer would sometimes climb the stairs in the capitol building and meet with legislative leaders in their offices.

Romer won praise from many legislators and lobbyists for his willingness to work with them. One lobbyist said Romer was his own best lobbyist because he was never timid about meeting with legislators and coming to them and asking for their help. The fact that he had been around state government for nearly thirty years obviously was an asset.

"I can be the point man and political leader on some issues," said Romer, "but not on every issue. [This] particular office doesn't have a lot of constitutional power, but it has a lot of power if you know how to use it. You need to pick your issues and pick good people. I pay a lot of attention to appointments. Finally, my philosophy is that popularity is not something you put in the bank. You use it."[45]

Perhaps no governor in Colorado history has made better use of the bully pulpit of the governorship than Roy Romer. He earned a reputation for being willing to travel the state and attend almost any event that would be enhanced by the presence of the governor. He proved adept at appearing and giving speeches at county fairs, local parades, and annual dinners.

Under his "Dome on the Range" program, Roy Romer and key members of his staff would travel to outlying parts of the state and visit with those citizens who were having problems and wanted to talk to the governor about them.

Governor Romer also worked to become identified with major projects that would enhance the state economic climate. He strongly supported the construction of a new Denver Convention Center and a new Denver regional airport (DIA). After a long struggle with the legislature, he succeeded in implementing a major portion of his plan for improving the state highway system. He also took a lead in the successful effort to bring major league baseball to Denver. That task included helping to secure financing for a new baseball stadium in Denver, Coors Field.

Not every project Romer supported was a success. In cooperation with Denver officials, he worked to get United Airlines to locate a major airplane maintenance facility near the new Denver airport. In the end, United decided to locate the new facility in Indianapolis, then later decided not to build it at all. Romer also used up a great deal of his political capital in 1992 by pushing for a 1 percent state sales tax increase to support K–12 public education. The ballot issue lost, 54 to 46 percent.

Backed by a number of business leaders and Republicans, Governor Romer was easily reelected in 1990 by 62 percent of the vote. In his second term, Romer became increasingly involved in the National Governors' Association as a spokesperson for educational reform in the states. By mid-1991 he was co-chairing a national panel on educational goals and won recognition from fellow governors as one of the top governors in the nation.

Romer was reelected to a third term in office in 1994, joining Dick Lamm as one of only two Colorado governors to each serve twelve years in the governor's chair. It was a significant victory, because Romer was a Democrat, and on that particular election day the Republicans won every other governorship up for election and took control of both houses of the U.S. Congress.

In his third term Romer branched out into national politics. For a brief period, he served as cochair of the Democratic National Committee as well as governor of Colorado. After leaving office in 1999, Roy Romer extended his political career by serving as the head of the Los Angeles public school system.

Romer, similar to Lamm before him, attracted a number of talented young leaders to work in his administration, including Ken Salazar and Joe Garcia. Salazar recalls that "what I always remember about [Romer] was that he was so caring about the people around him. . . . He had a genuine authentic care for all of Colorado and I think in particular for the rural areas of the state."[46]

After he left the governor's office, Roy Romer expressed three concerns about the Centennial State. First, he worried that "arrogance was the biggest problem facing public officials, because they were too likely to forget the intelligence and the concerns of the people they were dealing with." Second, he pointed out that large amounts of money were required to win statewide office in Colorado, and "that means elected officials have to please their contributors" and not their constituents. Third, he viewed with alarm "the growing antigovernment sentiment in Colorado that is becoming a very big problem."[47]

### Bill Owens

William Forrester Owens—always called Bill Owens—was born in Fort Worth, Texas. Owens got a taste of politics at an early age as a congressional page working at the U.S. Capitol in Washington DC. This was at age seventeen. He went to college at Stephen F. Austin State University in Texas. He also earned a master's degree in public administration from the University of Texas.

He moved to Colorado in 1977 and almost immediately went into Republican politics. He became executive director of the Colorado division of the Rocky Mountain Oil and Gas Association and lobbied the state legislature on that organization's behalf.[48]

Owens served in the state legislature for eight years. He then was elected the state treasurer in 1994. He was elected governor in the 1998 general election, becoming the first Republican to be governor of the Centennial State in twenty-four years.

Bill Owens was a small-government conservative, yet he quickly appreciated upon taking office that something had to be done about the woeful condition of the state's highways. Because of the TABOR Amendment and other restrictions in the Colorado Constitution, Governor Owens first had to win the approval of state voters in order to finance his comprehensive highway-improvement program.

Owens stumped the state to win support for his highway plan, which cost $1.7 billion and provided for twenty-eight major highway projects throughout Colorado. The highlight of the project was T-REX, a widening of I-25 south of Denver to more than eight lanes in places. The expanded expressway would run from the Denver Tech Center, a major employment center in the south Denver suburbs, to downtown Denver. This project would relieve what many considered to be the worst traffic bottleneck in Colorado, and it earned Owens the nickname "Ten-Lane Bill."

Because statewide voter support was required, Bill Owens's highway plan involved much more than Denver. I-25 through Colorado Springs would be widened to six lanes and also improved in other Front Range cities such as Pueblo. All over the state, local and regional highway projects would give all voters an immediate reason to support the statewide plan.

When Bill Owens's highway project was approved by a solid majority of Colorado voters, it was the first major victory of his governorship. During the remainder of his eight years in office, Bill Owens saw his highway plan come into existence in the form of cement and steel. "It really is a jewel," Owens said of T-REX near the end of his governorship.[49]

A second major goal for Governor Owens was to improve CSAP, the Colorado Student Assessment Program. This educational reform had been instituted by Owens's predecessor, Gov. Roy Romer, yet Owens greatly added to it. Owens pushed for a statewide plan to test every public school student in Colorado and make the composite test scores for each school available to the public. These "accountability reports" would permit the parents of Colorado public schoolchildren to see how their child's school was doing and whether the school needed to be improved.

This expanded CSAP program, with its school and classroom "report cards," was controversial, particularly with public schoolteachers' unions in Colorado. It was passed into law, however, and soon public school ratings were being printed in all the state's newspapers.

Bill Owens had a ready explanation as to why CSAP was so unpopular with public schoolteachers. "CSAP measured teachers' teaching abilities," he said, "and teachers do not want to be measured."[50]

Another accomplishment of Bill Owens's governorship was lowering the Driving Under the Influence (DUI) standard from .10 percent alcohol in the bloodstream to only .08 percent. He also signed a new law banning drinking alcoholic beverages from open containers in automobiles.

In 2004 the Democrats gained control of both houses of the Colorado state legislature. For the first time, Bill Owens faced a legislature controlled by the opposition party. Unlike some similar situations in the past,

Bill Owens did not let Colorado state government degenerate into backbiting and polarizing competition between the Republican governor and the Democratic legislature. Owens worked with the Democrats and was able to move the state forward.

The economic downturn that gripped the United States in 2001 had proved financially challenging for Colorado. As the economy weakened, state income tax receipts and sales tax receipts dropped precipitously. The situation was exacerbated by the TABOR Amendment, which restricted the ability to raise state taxes and state revenues once the economic recession was over.

Bill Owens joined with the Democrats in the state legislature to promote Referendum C. The legislators put on the statewide ballot a five-year time-out from the crippling revenue restrictions of TABOR. As he had done with his statewide highway program, Governor Owens campaigned throughout Colorado in behalf of Referendum C, joining with Democratic legislative leaders and many major business leaders in promoting its adoption.

The voters gave narrow approval to Referendum C, and for the next five years the restrictive revenue chains of TABOR were removed from Colorado state government. It was one of Bill Owens's greatest achievements as governor, and it demonstrated his ability to function effectively in a bipartisan manner when he needed to.

"The Democrats in the state legislature came to me with a plan that was going to limit TABOR for twenty years," Bill Owens recalled. "As governor, I told them I would only accept a plan that put the brakes on TABOR for five years. My viewpoint prevailed, and I and the Democrats moved forward with Referendum C together."[51]

Yet there were some failures. Governor Owens strongly supported a plan, called the "Big Straw," that would take water from the Western Slope and bring it to new housing developments and shopping centers on the Front Range. Once again statewide voter approval was required, and Owens did his best to sell the project, but Colorado voters said no.

Owens's "water policy misfired more for political reasons than policy reasons," said former U.S. senator Bill Armstrong of Colorado. "It was a better proposal than it got credit for."[52]

Some critics of Owens fault him for pushing through both income and sales tax cuts when times were good. These were revenues Colorado could never get back except via statewide vote.

Bill Owens told a reporter for the *Economist* magazine that he had one major regret about his time in the governor's office. It was that he presided over the slow but relentless shift of Denver's two most-populous suburban counties, Arapahoe County and Jefferson County, from the Republican Party to the Democratic Party.

Owens was originally a supporter of legislative term limits, but he changed his tune after seeing them in operation for ten years. "I would do away with term limits on the legislature," he said. "I was wrong on it. Because of terms limits, we are losing our best legislators."[53]

Although he might not acknowledge it, Bill Owens was the first Colorado governor to behave as though he understood the changed role of the governor in a state in which the initiative and the referendum had become the major avenues of governmental change. It was no longer sufficient for the governor to only lead the state legislature. It had also become necessary for the Colorado governor to lead the voters at the ballot box into authorizing and financing needed programs for the state.

Bill Owens succeeded twice in this new role of leader of the voters as they, the voters, governed the state through the initiative and referendum. Governor Owens won with his statewide highway referendum, which included T-REX, and he got his Referendum C expenditure reform. He lost with the Big Straw statewide vote, but that did not diminish his historical role as the first Colorado governor to play a key role in leading the voters to pass much-needed initiatives and referendums.

Bill Owens had a succinct statement for why he worked to lead the voters where initiatives were concerned. He explained: "In Colorado, the governor and the legislature have less power because of the initiative."[54]

### Bill Ritter

August W. Ritter Jr., known all his life as Bill, grew up in a large Catholic family. His childhood home was on Chambers Road east of Aurora, Colorado, on a small wheat and dairy farm. He was raised as a country boy yet spent his youth close to Denver and the Front Range.

When Bill was thirteen years old, his alcoholic father left home, forcing the family to survive sometimes on government aid. Bill Ritter won a scholarship to go to a local Catholic high school, and he took out student loans to get through Colorado State University in Fort Collins and the University of Colorado Law School in Boulder.[55]

Ritter often said he had been helped through tough times in his own life, so he went into politics as a way of "giving back" to all those who had supported him in his youth.

"Giving back" also included interrupting his promising career as a young attorney in Denver and, with wife, Jeannie, and one-year-old son, operating a nutrition center for poor people in Zambia for three years. Back in the United States, now with four children of their own, Bill and Jeannie Ritter welcomed an eight-year-old boy, the son of a crack-addicted mother, into their home and cared for him for more than two years.[56]

Bill Ritter served as Denver's district attorney from 1993 to 2006. In 2006 he was elected governor by a 57 percent majority.

Ritter was often described as soft-spoken and "oddly reticent for a politician." In his opposition to abortion, he was at odds with most Democrats. "Nor is Ritter a particularly magnetic politician. In a party that is now defined by the youth and energy at the top of the ticket, Ritter . . . is a sort of anti-Obama," wrote Ryan Lizza in an approving 2008 *New Yorker* magazine profile. Lizza added: "A self-described policy wonk, [Ritter] reaches a pitch of excitement when he talks about the benefits of highly efficient photovoltaic cells or when he recalls what he learned from glaciologists on a recent trip to the Arctic. Rather than charisma, he exudes a beguiling genuineness."[57]

The main theme of Ritter's 2006 election campaign was labeled the "Colorado Promise." It included programs such as fixing the state's transportation, health care, and higher education problems. He added to this list making Colorado a leader in the "new energy economy," by which he meant encouraging energy conservation and the promotion of solar, wind, and other *renewable* sources of energy.

To Ritter's credit, he was able to promote a whole range of energy initiatives. "Among the accomplishments of Ritter's energy strategy were passage of laws requiring [electric utility] Xcel Energy to convert three coal-fired power plants to natural gas, the first legislation of its kind in the country, and requiring utilities to generate at least 30 percent of their energy from renewable sources by 2020."[58]

Ritter was applauded by environmentalists, yet his proposed mineral severance taxes and stricter environmental rules on oil and gas drilling won him heated political resistance from business groups. His help for unionized state employees also earned stern criticism from business as well as the *Denver Post* editorial page.

Ritter created a number of "blue ribbon" panels or commissions to study transportation, health care, and higher education needs. Whatever the recommendations of these "blue ribbon" groups, they were usually quietly disregarded by Ritter because of the effects of the economic recession that began in 2008. There was little or no state money, save for some much-needed U.S. government stimulus money, to be used to implement Governor Ritter's "Colorado Promise" pledges. Still, these panels and task forces at least pointed out critical needs and the necessary revenues that would someday have to be raised to address those problems.

Thus Bill Ritter, who enjoyed public approval ratings as high as 70 percent his first year in office, soon had a steady decline in approval to 50 percent his second year. He fell still lower in his third and fourth years. By winter and spring of 2010, his disapproval ratings were higher than his approval ratings (45 percent disapproved, 40 percent approved), according to our 2010 Colorado College poll.

As the Great Recession developed, unemployment shot up, as did home foreclosures and business bankruptcies. State employees had to take twelve days of unpaid leave in fiscal 2009. In fiscal 2010, state employees in effect took a 2.5 percent pay cut because they were forced to make increased payments into their retirement program, known as PERA (Public Employees Retirement Association). These payments also were increased by Ritter's successor as governor, John Hickenlooper.

In many ways, Ritter was a political casualty of the recession. He was also, of course, restricted by TABOR taxing and revenue restraints.

Republicans generally liked Bill Ritter as a person, but they faulted him for being indecisive and too pro-labor. Republicans criticized many of his programs and proposals as "job killers." Some Democrats said Ritter was overly cautious and lacked the hardball political savvy necessary to forge crucial political coalitions. He was, some pointed out, the first Colorado governor in more than three decades who had not served in the state legislature.

One benefit for Bill Ritter was that he was the first Democratic governor in many years who enjoyed Democratic majorities in both chambers of the state legislature. But many observers, including aides to the governor, believe this was at best a mixed blessing. Democratic activists like teachers and union leaders pushed the state legislature and Ritter to enact some of their pet projects that could not have been adopted during periods of divided government in Colorado. This had the effect of pushing Ritter more to the left than he may have wanted to go. What first appeared to be a strength—Democratic control of both the legislature and the governorship—may have become a liability.

Whatever the cause, Bill Ritter's lower job ratings were "at least partially a reflection," said pollster Floyd Ciruli, "of growing criticism about many unfulfilled expectations, most of which he [Ritter] raised, and his association with controversial or thwarted initiatives."[59] Political strategist Eric Sondermann added that Ritter, unlike Governors Lamm, Romer, and

Owens, never developed what might be called a Ritter "brand." The failure to do that became a political drag on him.[60]

Governor Bill Ritter and the Democratic majorities in the state legislature had bold plans, yet these cost money. TABOR and the 2008–10 recession took away most of the money that might have been available for new programs.

By late 2009 Ritter was mostly relegated to slashing state budgets and laying off state workers. The fun of being a governor, especially a Democratic governor, seemed to be gone.

Still, it was a surprise when Ritter announced in early 2010 that he would not stand for reelection. He did not say that his reelection prospects seemed grim or that he was disheartened by his rising disapproval ratings. Instead, he simply said his family needed him and that the job had caused an apparently painful imbalance in his life. "My family needs me. My wife needs me," said Ritter. He explained: "I have not found the proper balance where my family is concerned and I have not made them the priority they should be. . . . So today I am announcing that I am ending one of my roles. I am no longer a candidate for reelection."

Ritter's final year working with the state legislature may have been his most productive one. Together he and the legislature improved kindergarten through twelfth grade (K–12) education with measures that should enhance student learning and teacher effectiveness, increased Colorado's renewable energy requirements, developed job training and workforce development programs, and several other similar initiatives.

We asked Bill Ritter in October of 2010: "What unites Colorado?" He replied that "K through 12" education is the issue that unites people. He added: "But there is not much else that wins unity around here [referring to the state capitol]."[61]

Ritter retired with considerable respect for his integrity and dedication. Wilderness and wildlife activists honored Ritter as "the best friend Colorado sportsmen have had" in recent decades. Environmentalists hailed him for his "green energy" initiatives that made Colorado a model for other states. Progressives admired him for greatly expanding health care coverage by working with the legislature to enact the Healthcare Affordability Act of 2009. Ritter also promoted better counseling for special needs youngsters in public schools. Wade Buchanan of the Bell Policy Center told us that Ritter was, in fact, one of the best recent governors on progressive issues. Other Ritter supporters credit Ritter with helping to modify some of the ways TABOR revenue numbers are calculated.

Still, he is likely to be ranked as one of the less successful governors in recent times in light of his (and the state's) inability to achieve many of his policy aspirations. The economic times, to be sure, were a major impediment to progress. Polarization also played a role as did the ongoing divide between those who hate government and those willing to approve sensible government problem solving.

Did Bill Ritter's personality and political style hurt him? Some people thought so. Some said he was too timid. Others said he was not enough of a fighter. Still others thought he lacked the communication skills needed to work with legislators. It may be that he did not compensate for his political weaknesses by hiring advisers who had those skills.

Ironically, some if not many conservatives liked the fact that Governor Ritter faced frequent gridlock. In their view gridlock, if it stops government from taxing, borrowing, and spending, is more of an achievement than a problem.

### John Hickenlooper

John Wright Hickenlooper was born and raised in suburban Philadelphia, Pennsylvania. Educated at the Haverford School, he later earned an AB in English and an MS in geology at Wesleyan University in Middletown, Connecticut.

He came to Colorado in 1981 to work as a geologist, but he was unceremoniously laid off in one of the state's periodic energy industry slowdowns. He jokes that he is a "recovering geologist" and that he came to Colorado "to study rocks and wound up selling beer." He became a successful entrepreneur in Denver as well as a nimble squash player. He was twice handily elected mayor of Denver.

Gov. Bill Ritter announced in January 2010 that he would not be a candidate for reelection. The Democratic Party turned to Denver mayor Hickenlooper for its gubernatorial candidate. Hickenlooper was unopposed for the Democratic nomination and thus did not have to endure the strain and expense of a primary election.

Meanwhile, the Republicans had difficulty finding a candidate to run against Hickenlooper. The end result was a three-way race in which the Republican candidate and a third-party candidate split the Republican vote. Hickenlooper won endorsements from the *Denver Post* and other newspapers as well as chambers of commerce around the state, including the Colorado Springs Chamber of Commerce. He was elected governor with about 51 percent of the vote, 14 percent ahead of third-party candidate Tom Tancredo, and 40 percent ahead of Republican candidate Dan Maes.

Hickenlooper won 95 percent of Democrats, 51 percent of unaffiliated voters, and even 12 percent of Republicans. He won a remarkable 74 percent in the City and County of Denver. He also won about 57 percent of the female vote. All of this was accomplished in an otherwise Republican "wave election" across the nation.

Hickenlooper's early pledges included promises to be probusiness, to help create jobs, to work closely with the military in the state, and "to make the state government more efficient while retaining our highest shared principles." He fully realized that Colorado faced serious deficiencies in properly financing K–12 education, higher education, upgrading highways and bridges, and much more. He also realized he would have to propose major spending cuts until the economy rebounded.

In both his inaugural remarks and in his first state-of-the-state address, Hickenlooper called on everyone to cooperate to create jobs, balance the budget, and eliminate waste and unnecessary business regulations. He said: "Our first task, our highest priority, is jobs." He pledged to "find the budget cuts that caused the least damage to the people of Colorado."[62]

Hickenlooper was proud of recruiting a diverse cabinet that included several Republicans and a good representation from Southern Colorado and the Western Slope.

A month into his governorship Hickenlooper proposed sweeping cuts in K–12 and higher education funding and called for closing or "repurposing" a few state parks in rural areas. Republicans generally applauded his budget-slashing initiatives. Democrats were generally dismayed but kept their grumbling to a minimum. Later that year, the legislature adopted Hickenlooper's proposed state budget with only minor adjustments.

Asked what he learned from his first legislative session, Hickenlooper joked: "Always watch your back." He implied that most of what he needed to know as governor he had learned at his Wynkoop Brewery restaurant: "We learned the lessons you learned in the restaurant business. When someone is upset, you listen very carefully and find out what they are really upset about. It's not often the first thing they are talking about."[63]

Hickenlooper began his second year with about a 60-percent public approval rating and strong support among state business leaders. He was well liked in both parties and won credit for helping to lure several businesses to the state. He also won praise for brokering a compromise between oil companies and environmentalists on the regulation of hydraulic fracturing, or "fracking." (Fracking refers to the process of injecting high-pressured fluids into deep underground rocks, inducing the release of fossil fuels. The concerns are that this impressive technology can produce toxic and radio-active wastewater that may contaminate drinking water.)

"I don't have the same style as most elected officials," said Hickenloop-er. "I try to spend more time listening and less time shouting."[64] He plainly enjoyed being governor just as he had enjoyed serving as mayor. He en-dorsed civil unions for same-sex couples and pledged again to make gov-ernment more efficient. But both he and legislative leaders knew all too well that critical budget and tax reform  challenges loomed, and that Colo-rado's own "fiscal cliff" was imminent.

### CONCLUSIONS

As discussed, Colorado has a modest governorship in terms of formal pow-ers. Part of the problem lies in the Colorado Constitution. It also is a matter of tradition. Over the years, the tendency has been to put many executive functions under the control of appointed boards and commissions rather than under the direct control of the governor. At the same time, some, and sometimes much, of the budgetary power has moved from the executive branch to the legislative branch, and then from the legislative branch to the voters because of the TABOR Amendment.

Yet effective governors learn to stretch or maximize the power of the governorship. They do this by personal leadership, executive orders, long-range planning, effective bargaining, negotiation, and persuasion. They pyramid their resources; form alliances with interest groups, lobbyists, and legislators; promote public-private partnerships; frame the agenda; and in-fuse vision into the enterprise of state government.

Most Colorado citizens, as discussed, are inherently skeptical of govern-ment. Governors have to demonstrate that government can work and that state government has affirmative responsibilities. This invariably involves explain-ing the need for shared sacrifices. This is no small challenge in Colorado.

The effectiveness of every governor depends on at least two enduring realities. One is the economic climate in the state. Second is the degree to which a governor can persuade citizens to support the few initiatives any governor is allowed to launch. Citizens in Colorado, like citizens in most states, are predisposed to resist sweeping measures of any kind that will increase the power of government and raise property, sales, and personal income taxes. As discussed earlier, a love of liberty, private property, and a free-market economy means that Coloradans are skeptical about political promises that might threaten their "Colorado dream," or at least what they think the Colorado dream should be.

Governors can be creative or effective leaders only to the extent citizens recruit and elect good ones in the first place, insist on their integrity in office, and vigorously support them when they make sound strategic decisions. It is the job of every Colorado governor to remind the people that the shared aspirations that unite Coloradans are stronger than those that divide them. And in the end, governors learn, as all leaders have to learn, that their job is to produce—not followers but large numbers of collegial civic and political leaders who will work together to achieve common shared goals.

# CHAPTER NINE

# Judges and Justice in Colorado

Many people have called the judiciary in American government the most removed from politics or the least political branch. Yet judges and courts at all levels of government play a vital role in determining who gets what, where, when, and how. Judges play a role in making public policy. Most of the law under which we live is the law of our states. State and municipal judges resolve many of the most important legal matters in our lives, including most criminal offenses, foreclosures, business contract disputes, child custody cases, marriage contracts, automobile accidents, settlement of estates, and much more.

If anything, state courts have become increasingly prominent in the political life of the nation in recent years. State judges apply the state bill of rights to more and more matters. And there have been significant developments in state law dealing with damages to compensate people for legal wrongs done to them. Many of these changes have opened state courts to more people to sue more often about more things.

As state courts have become more active, state judges have become embroiled in visible controversial issues and have antagonized various interests. And as the public has grown more sophisticated about the importance of judges as policy makers, judicial politics has become a significant feature of the political landscape.

This has been the case in Colorado, where people of varying political views are occasionally irritated with both state supreme court and lower court opinions. One such feud arose in 1991 when the Colorado Supreme Court declared the state's death penalty unconstitutional on grounds that legislative revisions to the law in 1988 made the death penalty too "automatic." More recently, critics charge that murderers have been let off because of technicalities.

Another state court ruling that upset some conservatives was a 2009 decision, *Mesa County Board of County Commissioners v. State of Colorado*. The decision kept property taxes from decreasing. The money that otherwise would have gone back to taxpayers was directed to be allocated to public schools. The state supreme court in this case overturned a lower court decision that said not giving the money back to taxpayers violated Colorado's TABOR restrictions.

In *Lobato vs. Colorado* (2011) a Denver district judge ruled on behalf of a group of parents and school districts that the Colorado state constitution's stipulation for a "thorough and uniform" system of free public education needs to be interpreted to require specific and more equitable funding across the state.

Conservatives as well as others faulted the judge for assuming the role that elected officials, especially legislators, should play. They also questioned the logic and rationality of the judge's understanding of the economic consequences of her judgment.[1]

Governor Hickenlooper and the attorney general immediately signaled they would appeal this decision to the Colorado Supreme Court. But the *Lobato* case, however it is ultimately decided, raises educational and political issues that Colorado will be wrestling with for years to come.

Such decisions prompt some Colorado citizens to complain about "policy-oriented" or overly lenient judges. Perhaps the loudest criticism of the state supreme court has come from staunch conservatives who claim too many liberals on the court have been reckless "black-robed attorneys" too often rewriting the law. Former state senate president John Andrews and former U.S. representative Tom Tancredo are among conservative leaders calling for term limits for justices and judges.

"These justices have gone too far," said Andrews, "in weakening property rights and Second Amendment freedoms, among many other things. . . . They are legislating judges."[2]

Attorneys sometimes complain about court delays or the uneven quality of the judges serving on the court bench in Colorado. Most attorneys express great respect, however, for the Colorado judiciary as a whole. They say it has improved steadily over the years and is far preferable to the courts in neighboring states.

The court system's own surveys of citizen users of the courts indicated satisfaction with the way the citizens are treated.[3] Our Colorado College statewide poll in 2010 found a two-to-one approval-to-disapproval rating for Colorado courts in general. Forty-nine percent of Coloradans said they approve of the way Colorado courts perform while 24 percent indicated disapproval.

Still, a certain amount of controversy will always surround the courts, especially as to how justices and judges should be appointed and held accountable.

In short, the judiciary in Colorado has its own politics. Although judges are generally removed from overt electioneering and day-to-day political pulling and tugging, they are important public figures and are shaped by and help shape the political life of the state.

### FRONTIER JUSTICE

Prior to the gold rush of 1858–59, law-and-order matters in the Rockies were essentially an "everyone for themselves" situation. Mountain trappers and prairie buffalo hunters, the first non-Native Americans to come to the region, relied on pistols and rifles to guarantee their safety and property. A rough sort of frontier order, and once in a while a trial or two, took place at the trappers' rendezvous or at the fur trading post. By and large, each person and every party out in the Colorado wilderness were "on their own."

After 1854 the territorial governments of Utah, New Mexico, Nebraska, and Kansas were supposedly maintaining order and dispensing justice in the Colorado region. These governments, however, were too far away to have effective legal and judicial control. Not until gold was discovered at Dry Creek and thousands of people migrated to Colorado did the early mining camps and valley towns begin organizing "miner's courts," "claim clubs," and "people's courts" to dispense something approaching orderly justice.

"In a virtually rootless society, jails and prison terms cost tax money to build and oversee, none of which the fifty-niners wanted to pay," writes Colorado historian Duane Smith.[4] So these early settlers devised pragmatic and expedient punishments. Any person guilty of willful murder, upon conviction, was hanged by the neck until dead. Banishment was a frequent remedy. One of the mining districts called for lashes on the bare back, from ten to one hundred, depending on the crime. Informal juries were called to decide which penalty applied to murder, robbery, horse thievery, or cattle thievery.

With Colorado's admission as a state in 1876, a judiciary largely patterned after that in other states was provided for in the newly adopted state constitution. The state was divided into four large judicial districts, each with a district court to hear and try major crimes. Lesser crimes were tried in separate county courts. Each of the then twenty-six counties covered a large land area, and it often was quite a trek to the county seat for a county court trial. It was usually even longer, of course, to get to one of the four district courts.

The first Colorado Supreme Court was elected in 1876 with three justices beginning service in Denver on October 3, 1876.

High mountains and vast rolling prairies were formidable barriers, isolating the dispersed communities that collectively constituted Colorado in the late 1870s. Plainly there was a need for local courts that could try criminals quickly and reasonably settle disputes. Thus justice of the peace courts were organized in each community to provide the desired local law enforcement and to settle minor civil matters.

From its earliest development, Colorado's judicial system was highly decentralized with local justices of the peace playing a leading role. The number of justice of the peace courts expanded rapidly as the state grew in population. There was little or no coordination between these local courts, however, and the elected justices of the peace often were local residents who had minimal or sometimes no legal training. Justices of the peace set up court the way they liked. Further, the quality of justice varied greatly from one local court to the next, as did the "j.p.'s" qualifications and, importantly, the extent to which decisions actually corresponded with state law.

### JUDICIAL REFORM

The rapid expansion in Colorado's population during and after World War II highlighted some of the inadequacies of the justice of the peace courts. In 1962, following a number of studies, the state legislature referred to the voters a constitutional amendment that provided for the first major reorganization of the court system since 1876.

The amendment was adopted overwhelmingly by a vote of 303,740 to 169,032. It abolished all justice of the peace courts, set higher qualifications for judges, and gave the state supreme court the responsibility of setting uniform standards and procedures for the various courts throughout Colorado. This court reorganization plan went into effect in 1965 and provided an integrated statewide rather than a localized focus for the state judicial system.

The judicial reform movement that swept through Colorado in the early 1960s next turned its attention to the way in which judges were selected. Colorado selected judges by means of partisan elections. To be a judge, a person had to be nominated by a political party and then elected, like any other candidate for office, in a partisan general election.

Party politics, whether a candidate was a "good Democrat" or a "good Republican," often was the chief factor in who was or was not elected to the bench. Thus loyal Democrats became judges in Pueblo and Denver while loyal Republicans won the elections in Colorado Springs and in many of the Denver suburbs and outlying agricultural regions.

Another problem was that the names of the various candidates for judges appeared at the bottom of the general election ballot. Judicial election campaigns received little attention or newspaper coverage, thus making it hard for voters to know the candidates and their qualifications.

Still another problem was the concern that judges, facing an upcoming reelection contest, might be tempted to shade or even shape decisions to curry votes rather than impartially administer justice. There was also the worry that judges would raise money from lawyers to fund their campaign.

Pressure was put on the legislature to change the judicial selection process in Colorado. When such efforts failed, several prominent lawyers and citizen groups, notably the League of Women Voters, began to collect signatures for an initiated constitutional amendment to be placed before the voters. Their proposal, long backed by the Colorado Bar Association, provided for judges to be appointed rather than elected. They successfully collected more than forty-seven thousand signatures and thus were able to place Amendment No. 3 on the 1966 election ballot.

Their amendment recommended a version of what in legal circles is known as the Missouri Plan, so called because the state of Missouri pioneered the idea in 1940. This plan gives the governor the power to appoint people to state courts when a vacancy occurs, but the prospective judges must come from lists of nominees provided by specially appointed judicial nominating commissions.

When a vacancy occurs in a district or county court, a judicial nominating commission already in place for that district or county submits two or three names of potential candidates to the governor's office. The plan assumes that the nominating commission will submit names of people who have the proper training and experience. The governor and the governor's staff conduct interview evaluations and telephone checks on the nominees.

Then the governor chooses from this short list. The governor's choice automatically becomes the judge until the next general election. At the next general election the voters are asked: "Shall judge X be retained in office?" If a majority agrees, the judge serves a new full term.

(A "full term" depends on what level of the court system a judge is serving. County judges serve only four years. District judges serve six years.

State court of appeals judges serve eight years, and state supreme court justices serve ten-year terms.)

If the judge fails to win a majority, the judicial nominating commission begins its search all over again.

Judges, according to this plan, do not run against an opponent but only against their own record. Also, judges running for retention in office are not identified with any political party on the ballot. Once on the court, district judges, for example, can serve as long as they are able to earn reelection every six years or until they reach the mandatory retirement age of seventy-two.

The mandatory retirement age of seventy-two was not in the original Colorado Constitution. It was put in the 1966 reform package that came along with the adoption of the Missouri Plan amendment. It was undoubtedly a concession to those who feared judges might stay on too long and be too removed from the politics of the day.

Back in 1966, one of the arguments for voting against Colorado's version of the Missouri Plan was that the retirement age of seventy-two was arbitrary and "has no relation to the ability of a judge to perform his [or her] duties. Some judges should probably retire earlier, while others are capable of excellent performance for many years beyond age 72."[5]

Who serves on these nonpaid volunteer judicial nominating commissions? Members are selected from the geographical area corresponding to a court's jurisdiction. Thus a commission nominating candidates to the Fourth District Court (El Paso and Teller Counties) will be selected from those counties. A commission nominating candidates to the state supreme court will be selected from the entire state.

A district nominating commission is composed of seven members. Three members must be lawyers and are appointed jointly by the governor, the state attorney general, and the chief justice of the state supreme court. The other four members must be nonlawyers and are appointed solely by the governor. No more than four of the members of the seven-member commission can belong to the same political party. Judicial nominating commission members serve a six-year term in office and cannot be reappointed.

When a vacancy opens on the Colorado Supreme Court or the Colorado Court of Appeals, a special supreme court nominating commission comes into play. This commission is composed of fifteen members, two from each of Colorado's seven congressional districts plus one at-large member. One member from each congressional district must be a lawyer, and one must be a nonlawyer. The lawyers are appointed jointly by the governor, the state attorney general, and the chief justice of the state supreme court. The governor appoints the nonlawyers.

A governor has fourteen days to appoint from the commission's short list. Governors always interview the finalists. If a governor fails to select someone, the chief justice makes the appointment. However, this has never happened. The fourteen days provides ample time for the governor to check out the nominees. It also provides adequate time for supporters and/ or detractors to lobby the governor about which nominee to appoint.

In August 2010, for example, such a commission met and nominated three candidates for an opening on the state supreme court. Shortly thereafter, Governor Ritter chose Colorado deputy attorney general Monica Marquez, a forty-one-year-old gay Latina with impressive legal experience. In October of 2011, Governor Hickenlooper selected state district judge Brian Boatright for the state supreme court. Boatright is a registered Republican with extensive juvenile and criminal case experience.

Commission members, lawyers and nonlawyers alike, are usually civic, professional, and party leaders. They come from the ranks of law firms, banks, small and large businesses, former party officials, college professors, and citizens' groups. The 1966 state constitutional amendment stipulated that no person serving as a member of a nominating commission could hold any elective office or any elective political party office.

How political are Colorado's judicial nominating commissions? Under Republican governors John Love and Bill Owens, the commissions were more conservative. Under Democratic governors Richard Lamm, Roy Romer, and Bill Ritter, the commissions reflected a more liberal or at least middle-of-the-road cast. Democratic governors did appoint some Republicans, yet they were more likely to appoint moderate or progressive Republicans to the nominating commissions.

Commission members from both parties typically seek out the best candidates, and the party affiliation of the nominees is often never even considered. Commission members say they have been impressed by the nonpartisan, professional character of these deliberations and the overall emphasis on competence of the prospective nominees.

The Missouri Plan attempts to create a more neutral appointment process and thereby remove judicial selection from narrow partisan politics. It also is an attempt to enlarge the list of those who would become judges. In one-party areas in the past, people from the minority parties, not to mention those who disliked campaigning and electioneering for office, were eliminated from being considered as judges.

Plainly, while it is possible to take the opposing candidate out of judicial elections, it is impossible to take politics entirely out of the judicial selection process. In the version of the Missouri Plan the reformers proposed for Colorado, the governor is given a decisive role in determining who becomes a judge.

The governor has a role in naming the lawyers on the commissions and has the sole say in the appointment of the nonlawyers. A determined governor clearly can have a major influence in shaping these commissions. In addition, it is the governor who makes the final appointment from the two or three names the nominating commission submits to the governor's office. In political terms, this plan strengthened the hand of governors and gave them a leading role in shaping the state's judiciary. Thus, over time, both these commissions and the judiciary reflect the politics of the governor.

### Evaluating Judicial Reform

In the 1966 election, Amendment No. 3, the Missouri Plan, was approved by state voters by 293,771 to 261,558. Nearly 53 percent of the voters voting on this measure approved it.

The Missouri Plan is widely accepted in Colorado as an improvement over the old days. It has widened the nominating pool. The nominating commissions have worked reasonably well, according to most reports.

Early in 1990 Joseph R. Quinn, chief justice of the Colorado Supreme Court at the time, gave the following evaluation of the judicial nominating process in Colorado: "I practiced law under the prior judicial selection system, which was partisan and political, and the difference between what Colorado had then [elections] and what Colorado has now [appointment] was like night and day. Now we truly have a merit system."

Chief Justice Quinn said that Colorado's recent governors, both Republicans and Democrats, have been very responsible in both appointments to judicial nominating commissions and in appointing judges to the bench. Above all, he argued, the judicial nominating commissions have functioned in such a way that they have nominated candidates for judge with no political considerations at all.[6]

Many others echoed Justice Quinn's positive view. Former supreme court justice Jean Dubofsky, the first woman to sit on that body, agreed that the Missouri Plan and its nominating commissions have worked well. "The quality of judges is definitely higher now than in the past, and judges and justices are clearly more insulated from politics and party and election pressures."

Yet there have been other subtle changes as well, said Dubofsky. On the positive side most judges make decisions on a case by case basis, not according to their campaign platforms or with their eye on their next election opponent. On the negative side, judges these days may not be quite as polite and cordial to those who appear in their courtrooms as in the past. When you do not have to campaign or worry about a serious political challenger at the next election, "judges are less responsive politically to the moods of the day and probably also less courteous to those who show up in their chambers."[7]

Retired Colorado Supreme Court justice Rebecca Love Kourlis believes good people are recruited to serve on the nominating commissions, and the commissions are almost entirely motivated to nominate people on the basis of legal merit. The commissions support people who have given back to their communities rather than favoring would-be judges on the basis of partisanship.

Justice Kourlis did recommend, however, a bit more transparency about the names nominated. She also favors more detailed examinations of the judicial performance of sitting judges, and she would make the results of these examinations public. But overall, she said the judicial appointment system works well.[8]

Colorado Supreme Court chief justice Mary Mullarkey hailed the Missouri Plan's success: "Looking back over the past four decades, we can see that the merit selection of judges has been the key to developing a fair and impartial state court system that is able to adapt to the changing times."[9]

It is not a perfect system, yet most Colorado court watchers are pleased at how well it has worked for more than forty-five years. "Access to fair and impartial justice under constitutions and laws of the United States and the state of Colorado is the most fundamental purpose of the legal profession and the judiciary. Thanks to the voters of Colorado, we have a judicial selection and tenure system that lends itself to this great work," writes Justice Greg Hobbs of the Colorado Supreme Court. Hobbs adds these additional achievements:

- Judges are not subject to currying favor with political party officials or financial contributors.

- One actually can consider being a judge in Colorado as the professional continuum of being a lawyer who has served clients well and now wishes to have the responsibility of being a decision maker.

- A judge appointed through merit selection does not have to consider what interest group might be offended or benefited when making a decision. The judge listens to the evidence, studies the law, and concentrates on rendering fair and impartial judgment in the case.[10]

Most attorneys and the Colorado Bar Association also share this satisfaction with the nearly five decades of experience with this reform.

There are always exceptions. A few years ago, several state legislators, led by former state senator Ralph A. Cole, a Republican from Littleton, introduced various measures either to go back to the old system or modify the new one in ways to weaken the power of the governor. Senator Cole, for example, introduced legislation that would have required a governor's nomination to the district and state courts to be confirmed by a majority vote of the state Senate. That is, after all, the practice of the U.S. government in approving members of the U.S. Supreme Court.

Senator Cole also introduced legislation returning to a system of electing judges and having judges run against other candidates, but to do so in nonpartisan elections. The legislation did not win approval.

Senator Cole said he thought Governor Lamm abused his appointive powers. Cole claimed Colorado merely substituted one form of politics in the selection of judges for another. "Moreover," he said, "it's more undercover these days, and these appointments are for life. You need political pull with the governor to win appointment, and you need to politick to get on the bench." Senator Cole also complained that too many liberals have been appointed in recent years.[11]

Gov. Richard Lamm became frustrated with some of his own appointees after they had been on the bench a while. He thought some of his nominees were or became insensitive to the public's concern about crime and the desire for tougher sentencing. "I made a mistake in being overly impressed by brains and legal talent," Lamm said. In the process, "I unbalanced the Court, which I never meant to do."[12]

After having been in office for a few years, Lamm began appointing more "hard line" judges who he hoped would rule somewhat differently on criminal issues than several of his earlier appointments. Aides and associates said Lamm began appointing people who almost exclusively had experience as prosecutors and district attorneys, presumably to get judges more sympathetic to the victims and the prosecutors.

It was said by his critics, a bit in derision perhaps: "Lamm wants to be governor of all of the people." The comment suggested Lamm now knew where the voters' sentiments were on criminal issues. Whether or not this change in his judicial nominating practices made a political difference is hard to determine, but it is worth noting that Lamm won a landslide reelection victory in 1982.

Gov. Roy Romer spent considerable time interviewing his prospective nominees for judges at all levels, including even county judges. He often traveled to a district or county and personally interviewed the finalists. He questioned the would-be judges about their experience and judicial philosophy. More recent governors similarly have made it a top priority to interview all the nominees at all levels of the judiciary.

An occasional complaint about the quality of judges comes from attorneys who practice before the district courts. They complain, not about the Missouri Plan, but about the uneven or sometimes poor quality of people applying for the bench. The workloads are heavy and the pay is low. As a result, Colorado may not get the best people to serve.

Former district judge John F. Gallagher was first elected to the bench in 1964 (before the Missouri Plan was approved in Colorado). He served with distinction for twenty-five years in the Fourth Judicial District (El Paso and Teller Counties). Judge Gallagher told us that the increased workload and low salary are a challenge to the quality of the court system in Colorado. "You just do not have time any more to think and read and reflect." Further, Gallagher said, it is difficult to say judges appointed in recent years are, as a group, better qualified by experience, intellect, and temperament than their elected predecessors.

Gallagher believed, however, the problems facing the Colorado courts had nothing to do with merit selection as opposed to election but rather with the fact that the staffing and resources allocated to the court system were too meager. In addition, he said, judicial salaries were not even close to competitive with what judges were paid in other states or in the federal system or with what lawyers earn in the private sector, at least in metropolitan areas.[13]

In recent years, district court judges have been paid about $130,000 a year, less than most law professors make and a lot less than their counterparts in urban law firms. On the other hand, this was a decent salary in most rural parts of the state.

Throughout the late 1990s, there was little improvement in the financing of the court system in Colorado. As the effects of the TABOR Amendment limited the growth in the size of the Colorado state budget, the state courts joined most of the other branches of state government in being underfinanced. The situation deteriorated even further when economic downturns in 2001 and 2008 further limited state spending on courts, judges, and other court personnel.

By 2012 Colorado had added a few dozen new judges for a total of about 350 statewide, yet the additions have not matched population growth or the even greater increase in court filings. Data from the Colorado Office of the Court Administrator indicate that Gov. Bill Ritter appointed 112 judges to various Colorado courts during his four-year term, including 73 men, 39 women, 69 in private practice, 48 who had been or were prosecutors, and 15 who had served as public defenders.

Gov. Bill Owens appointed 174 judges during his eight years in office. Thirty-five percent of Ritter's appointees were women compared with 30 percent of Owens's appointees.

## JUDICIAL DISCIPLINE

The Missouri Plan reform effort also provided for an additional improvement to the system. It created a Commission on Judicial Discipline. As amended in 1982, this provision allowed for the removal or the disciplining of a judge or justice "for willful misconduct in office, willful or persistent failure to perform his [or her] duties, intemperance or violation of any canon of the Colorado code of judicial conduct, or he may be retired for disability interfering with the performance of his duties which is, or likely to become, of a permanent character."

Until the adoption of this program, there was no practical way of getting rid of a "bad" judge except at a subsequent election (which sometimes did not work) or by impeachment (which is a cumbersome process).

A few critics complain that this Commission on Judicial Discipline has not really done much. But the commission has to work under restrictive confidentiality rules and thus most of its work is done quietly. Each year the commission receives about two hundred complaints against judges, but only twenty or so warrant serious investigation and follow-up. Complaints include inappropriate conduct, ineffective or inefficient docket management, questionable demeanor, or inadequate knowledge of certain aspects of the law.

Actions by the commission can include a letter of reprimand, private discussions with the judge, censure, and though rarely used, calling for a trial to assess the appropriateness or inappropriateness of a judge's behavior. Most lawyers and close observers believe the commission has achieved its purpose.[14] A few people, however, contend that the more serious instances of judicial discipline should be made public.

## JUDICIAL EVALUATION

When Colorado judges come up for reelection and run against their own record, the voting public receives little information on how the various judges have performed on the bench. Retention elections, moreover, usually generate little interest and low voter turnout. The Colorado legislature passed legislation in 1988 establishing judicial performance evaluation commissions for the state's courts. A commission consists of ten members. There are four lawyers and six nonlawyers. The governor appoints three members, the chief justice of the Colorado Supreme Court appoints three members, the president of the state Senate appoints two members, and the speaker of the state House of Representatives appoints two members.

The commission studies and evaluates the record of a judge coming up for reelection. They can interview or survey lawyers, jurors, and anyone else who has worked with various judges. Pollsters who do the surveys say those surveyed give almost all judges a positive evaluation. Judges are rated on such qualities as integrity, preparation, knowledge of law, handling of proceedings, and sentencing practices.

The goals of judicial performance evaluation are twofold. The first is to provide persons voting on the retention of justices and judges with fair, responsible, and constructive information about judicial performance. The second goal is to provide justices and judges with useful feedback on their own performance for the purposes of self-improvement.

The judicial performance evaluation commission can make one of three recommendations. It can vote FOR retention of the judge, AGAINST retention, or give NO OPINION. Although "no opinion" was not intended as a negative evaluation of a judge, early tests of the program indicated that voters were interpreting "no opinion" as a somewhat negative evaluation.

Prior to the formulation of a final narrative profile and recommendation, each commission on judicial performance supplies the judge under evaluation with a draft of their evaluation. The judge then has the opportunity to meet with the commission or at least to respond to its draft within a few days. If such a meeting takes place or a reasonable response is made, a commission may revise its evaluation and recommendation. It is not uncommon for judges who get negative performance evaluations to opt to retire rather than face voters with either a "negative" or "no opinion" evaluation.

Judicial performance evaluation commissions represented a serious attempt to have more realistic judicial retention elections. Beginning with the 1990 November elections, the public received more information about the various judges, and the information was provided by a diverse and professional group of commission members. Judicial performance evaluation commissions have become a useful addition to maintaining a quality judiciary in Colorado.

A few reformers urge that evaluation commissions should release to the public a more detailed narrative about their ratings and not just their general ratings. Attorney General John W. Suthers told us he believed the evaluation process in many instances should set the bar a bit higher. "There are still more judges," he said, "who should not earn the right to be retained."[15]

Judicial performance evaluations began in Colorado in 1990. By 2010 over a thousand judges had been up for retention election. Of these, only about sixteen received "do not retain" recommendations, about eleven had "no opinion" ratings, and only about ten judges were actually voted out of office.[16] One Pueblo County judge was reelected in 2010 despite a recommendation of "do not retain." A judge in Denver handily won despite a "no opinion" evaluation. Elsewhere in the state, however, two Larimer County district judges and one Baca County judge with "retain" recommendations were voted off the court.

## U.S. COURTS

Colorado is not the only government operating a court system in the state. The United States government has its own parallel court system for enforcing federal civil law and trying those persons accused of breaking federal criminal laws. Generally referred to as federal courts, these U.S. government courts also try cases involving controversies between states, cases in which the United States is a party, controversies between citizens of different states involving large amounts of money, and cases involving a federal question.

There are also certain U.S. government enclaves in Colorado such as national parks, national forests, and military bases (i.e., Fort Carson in Colorado Springs) where U.S. law rather than state law applies. There are also some hybrid areas such as the U.S. Air Force Academy, where both federal courts and Colorado courts may be involved.

Denver is an important federal court center. Each state has at least one U.S. District Court within its boundaries, and the U.S. District Court for Colorado sits in Denver. Also located in Denver is the Tenth Circuit U.S. Court of Appeals. Decisions can be appealed to this court from the U.S. District Court for Colorado and U.S. District Courts in the surrounding states that compose the Tenth Circuit.

At the top of the federal court system is the United States Supreme Court in Washington DC. This court, "the highest court in the land," hears appeals from the various U.S. appeals courts scattered throughout the nation. If a state court decision is alleged to violate the U.S. Constitution, the decision can be appealed from the Colorado Supreme Court to the U.S. Supreme Court.

For cases that originate in both the U.S. courts and the Colorado courts, the U.S. Supreme Court is "the court of last resort." Its decisions are final. There is no higher court to which its decisions can be appealed. Decisions by the U.S. Supreme Court concerning state powers and state laws have to be recognized and followed by all Colorado courts.

## COLORADO SUPREME COURT

The state supreme court has seven justices who serve ten-year terms. As of this writing, they each earn about $140,000 annually. Until a woman was appointed to the Colorado Supreme Court in 1979, this body was all male. More recently, several other women have served on the state's highest court, including Mary J. Mullarkey, who joined the Colorado Supreme Court in 1987 and served as chief justice from 1998 to 2010. As of this writing, three of the seven justices are women.

The state supreme court decides cases appealed to it from lower courts in the state. In addition, the Colorado Constitution allows the Colorado Supreme Court to give "advisory opinions" on important questions presented to it by the governor or by either house of the state legislature. The supreme court also has to approve state legislature redistricting plans every ten years.

The chief justice of the state supreme court is elected by his or her colleagues on the court and serves as long as they keep reelecting him or her. Elections are held only on an "as needed" basis and not yearly. This process differs significantly from the U.S. Supreme Court and from many states, where the president or the governor has the power to nominate and in effect select the chief justice. Long-term supreme court justice and former public defender Michael L. Bender was chosen by his colleagues in late 2010 to become the Colorado Supreme Court's forty-fourth chief justice.

This intracourt selection process leads to certain ongoing, if muted, politicking on the court. While not every member would want to serve as the chief justice (they get paid just a few thousand dollars more in salary), those who do get selected or retain their role must display an evenhanded approach, be skilled listeners, be willing to fashion necessary compromises, work to maintain harmony on the court, and oversee the administration of the judiciary system for the whole state.

On average, state judges tend to serve for about nine to ten years. Some leave if they are appointed to a higher court. Some leave for health reasons. Still others leave to make more money or because of the mandatory retirement age.[17]

Colorado Supreme Court justices are, as noted, subject to mandatory retirement at age seventy-two, unlike U.S. justices and judges who serve as
long as their health permits or until they wish to step down. In addition to
serving as presiding officer of the state supreme court, the chief justice, as
noted, also is the executive head of the entire Colorado court system. This
means that, in addition to working with colleagues rendering decisions on
cases appealed to the Colorado Supreme Court, the chief justice must administer the supreme court and the lower courts in the state court system.

One chief justice described his job and the job of his fellow justices on
the Colorado Supreme Court. He noted that as chief justice, he participates
in all Colorado Supreme Court decisions. In addition, he has administrative
responsibility for the entire state court system. "I spend about forty hours a
week researching cases, presiding over Supreme Court sessions, and writing opinions. I spend another twenty hours a week administering the state
court system." Fortunately, his colleagues on the state supreme court help
him with administrative duties by serving on public education committees,
grievance committees, long-term court planning committees, and so on.[18]

Similar to the U.S. Supreme Court, the Colorado Supreme Court justices are not always unanimous in their decisions, although the vast majority of decisions (more than 90 percent) are unanimous. When there is a
"split decision," the majority and minority opinions are written by different
justices.

Oral arguments before the state supreme court are open to the public.
But the real debate and clash of opinions often occur in the court's private
chamber. Chief Justice Luis D. Rovira described the scene: "It's only seven
of us. Nobody else is there. It's just a conference room, and there's barely
room for the seven of us there. And we don't wear our judicial robes."[19]

They use a rule of "juniority," making the most recently appointed justice speak first. One by one, the justices state how they stand on the case
before the court. The chief justice assigns one of the justices on the majority side to write the opinion. After the majority opinion is written and cir-
culated, an even more heated debate occasionally takes place. If someone
disagrees strongly with the majority opinion, that person prepares a dissent
and circulates it among the justices.

Occasionally a dissenting opinion is so persuasive it convinces some of
the justices to change sides, with the result that sometimes the dissent becomes the majority view.

According to Chief Justice Rovira: "Someone may say, if you can
change this, then I can join the opinion, but if you leave it this way to say
that, then I can't join you." Then the individual justice must think whether

he or she can change the wording as asked without destroying the integrity of the opinion, Rovira said. He thought there would be a lot more arm-twisting between the various members of the court, "but there really isn't."[20]

Below we list a few illustrative rulings of the Colorado Supreme Court in recent years.[21]

- In 2003 the court ruled 5 to 2, in *Salazar v. Davidson*, to reject a Republican redistricting effort favorable to the Republican Party. The court held that, until the U.S. Congress apportions seats to Colorado (for the U.S. House of Representatives) after the next U.S. census, the secretary of state is ordered to conduct congressional elections according to the plan already approved. The court declared such boundaries could only be redrawn every ten years, and that this had already been done by a Denver judge the previous year (2002). This case was appealed to the U.S. Supreme Court, which denied the appeal.

- On August 16, 2003, in an alleged rape case involving National Basketball Association star player Kobe Bryant, the Colorado Supreme Court refused to consider the prosecution's appeal of a lower court ruling that barred use of information about the accuser's previous sexual conduct. This criminal case was subsequently dismissed in a lower court, but a settlement was negotiated between the parties involved in a civil trial.

- On June 2, 2008, in a 6 to 1 ruling in *Town of Telluride v. San Miguel Valley Corporation*, the court rejected the contention that Telluride's power of eminent domain was limited to the purposes enumerated in the state constitution. In affirming a district court ruling, the court disagreed with the development company owners that Telluride was barred from condemning 572 acres of land for parks and open space purposes. Critics of this decision said the court wrongly expanded the use of eminent domain and diminished property rights.

- On March 16, 2009, in a 6 to 1 decision, the Colorado Supreme Court in *Mesa County Board of County Commissioners v. State of Colorado* reversed a district court ruling and held that the Colorado state legislature was acting within constitutional limits when it amended a school finance act so as to waive revenue limits. This allowed the public schools to retain funds that otherwise would have had to be returned to taxpayers.

• In December 2009 the Colorado Supreme Court ruled that a Weld County raid on tax records the previous year violated the Fourth Amendment to the U.S. Constitution which protects the right to privacy. The Weld County district attorney and sheriff had attempted to use tax returns to search out suspected illegal immigrants.

RALPH L. CARR JUDICIAL CENTER

The Colorado Supreme Court originally occupied a large courtroom in the north wing of the state capitol in Denver. From 1977 to mid-2010 it occupied a high-rise building at East Fourteenth Avenue and Broadway specifically constructed for the state courts.

This old Judicial Building was demolished in 2010 to make way for a new home for the Colorado Supreme Court and the Colorado Court of Appeals. The new skyscraper also housed the headquarters for the Colorado judicial branch as well as the attorney general's offices and a major detention center. This modern 615,000-square-foot building, dedicated in 2013, is named the Ralph L. Carr Judicial Center in honor of a popular and principled governor (1939–43). It is located on two city blocks between Lincoln and Broadway and East Thirteenth and East Fourteenth Avenues. The $368 million cost is being paid by a combination of tax-exempt bonds, to be paid off over the years by court fees, rent from state agencies, and gambling revenues.[22]

The Colorado Supreme Court hears oral argument usually for about three days every few weeks from September through June. Cases are typically heard for an hour with each side of the case allotted a half hour to make their case. As at the U.S. Supreme Court, justices can interrupt at any time and question the attorney making his or her case. Often a justice will ask for clarification or for a better example or explanation or citation of a precedent.

The justices sit together on a raised platform, and the contending attorneys argue their positions from behind a lectern about fifteen to twenty feet away. Each justice has at least two and sometimes three law clerks who assist them in their research and opinion writing. Law clerks typically serve for a year right after they have graduated from law school. They also double as bailiffs on oral argument days.

A "LIBERAL" STATE SUPREME COURT?

The U.S. Supreme Court has grown somewhat more conservative in the past generation. The Colorado Supreme Court, however, has occasionally engaged in a more expansive interpretation of certain provisions of the Colorado Constitution. In a number of cases, the court has taken a broader approach than the U.S. Supreme Court.

Chief Justice Rovira said it is not that the Colorado high court is more liberal but that "in a few areas, such as equal protection of the laws, due process of law, and double jeopardy, we have been somewhat more expansive in our reading of the Colorado constitution."[23]

For example, in *People v. Oates* (Colorado, 1985), the state supreme court held that the Colorado Constitution's prohibition of unreasonable searches and seizures protects a greater range of privacy interests than does the U.S. counterpart. Here the court departed from the U.S. Supreme Court's reasoning, finding that the presence of a beeper placed in a drum of acid used for the manufacture of methamphetamines infringed upon the defendant's constitutionally protected right against searches without a warrant.

In 1991, in yet another instance of a more expansive Colorado interpretation, *Bock v. Westminster Mall*, the state supreme court addressed the rights of an unincorporated political association to distribute political leaflets in the between-stores areas of a privately owned shopping center. Finding that there was government involvement in the mall and that the open spaces of the mall essentially operate as a public place, the Colorado Supreme Court held that the free speech provision of the Colorado Constitution prevented the shopping mall owner from excluding citizens engaged in nonviolent political "speech."

Colorado's justices ruled in effect that the state constitution provides greater protections of freedom of speech than does the First Amendment of the U.S. Constitution. These rulings and a number of similar ones illustrate how, especially in civil rights cases, the Colorado Supreme Court can base its decisions on the state constitution rather than the U.S. Constitution.

But the Colorado Supreme Court also enforces the U.S. Constitution when it chooses to do so. In *People v. Schaefer* (Colorado, 1997), the Colorado Supreme Court held that a person camping on unimproved and apparently unused land that is not fenced or posted against trespassing has a reasonable expectation of privacy in a tent used for shelter and personal effects. Police in Cortez, Colorado, conducted a search without a warrant of such a tent and used evidence obtained to help convict a man.

Supreme court justice Greg Hobbs wrote: "Taking notice of the long history of the use of tents for habitation in Colorado and the West, the Supreme Court determines, under the Fourth Amendment to the United States Constitution, that one's intent in a tent used for overnight or longer term stay is entitled to equivalent protection from unreasonable government intrusion as that afforded to homes and hotel rooms."[24]

## COLORADO COURT OF APPEALS

The workload for the Colorado Supreme Court became so great in the late 1960s that in 1970 the Colorado Court of Appeals was created to hear appeals from lower courts. The state court of appeals consists of twenty-two judges who serve eight-year terms.

This court was created to help ease the civil caseload on the crowded state supreme court schedule. It is not a trial court. Although the decisions of the court of appeals can be appealed to the state supreme court, such appeals are not made often. Only a small percent of the workload of the Colorado Supreme Court consists of hearing cases that have been appealed from the Colorado Court of Appeals.

The state court of appeals has its own courtroom, also located in the Ralph L. Carr Judicial Center. Court of appeals judges have law clerks and also are assisted by a small group of staff attorneys.[25]

## DISTRICT COURTS

Colorado is divided into twenty-two judicial districts. Each district must be a compact territory containing one or more counties, and judicial district lines must correspond to county lines. Five of Colorado's twenty-two judicial districts are composed of one county each (Boulder, Denver, Mesa, Pueblo, and Weld Counties). The other seventeen contain between two and seven counties each.

Each district court has one or more judges who serve a six-year term. Even if there is only one district court judge, the chief justice of the state supreme court will appoint a chief judge to administer the district. The chief judge of the district will supervise the district court as well as preside over his or her appropriate share of district court cases.

District courts in Colorado have original jurisdiction in criminal cases that are felonies (serious crimes for which a sentence of one year or more in the penitentiary may be imposed). Major civil cases must originate in district courts, as must cases involving mental health, divorce, child custody, adoption, juvenile delinquency, dependent and neglected children, and probate matters.

Many of the district courts have set up what are called "problem-solving" courts, such as a Drug Court or Driving under the Influence (DUI)

Court to handle specialized cases. The district court in El Paso and Teller Counties now has a Veterans' Court to deal with cases involving former members of the military.

The Colorado Constitution endeavors to protect the district courts from undue meddling by the legislature. A change in judicial district boundary lines requires a two-thirds vote in each house of the legislature. An increase or decrease in the number of judges assigned to each district also requires a two-thirds vote in each house.

### DISTRICT ATTORNEYS

In each judicial district there is a district attorney elected by the voters of the district. The district attorney has the responsibility of prosecuting all violators of state law. Unlike judges in Colorado, who are insulated from partisan politics by the complex judicial-nominating procedure, district attorneys run for office as Republicans or Democrats. Former governor Bill Ritter, for example, served for many years as Denver's district attorney. Earlier in his career, Colorado attorney general John Suthers served as the district attorney for El Paso and Teller Counties.

The justice system needs dedicated and fearless district attorneys and prosecutors who can competently review evidence, make principled decisions, and rigorously yet fairly press for conviction and just punishment.

This is no place for part-timers or dilettantes. "The sacrifices involved in a career in prosecution aren't just financial. I've lost some friends as a result of carrying out my obligations as a prosecutor," notes Suthers, who has served as a district attorney, U.S. attorney, and Colorado attorney general. "Even the social lives of my wife and children have been affected somewhat. On a number of occasions, I've had genuine concern about threats made to my personal safety. Phone calls in the middle of the night can become routine. But I, like most prosecutors, long ago concluded that the rewards of working as a prosecutor far exceeded the liabilities."[26]

In heavily populated judicial districts, the district attorney can appoint an appropriate number of assistant district attorneys, and these assistants are often (though not always) appointed on a partisan basis. The district attorneys are represented at the state capitol by their own lobbying organization, the Colorado District Attorneys' Council.

Some people wonder whether Colorado is doing the right thing by electing district attorneys in partisan elections. They fear that partisan district attorneys can become too political and start "throwing the book" at alleged criminals in an effort to boost their reelection chances. "We ought not to elect DA's," observed former justice Jean Dubofsky. "We ought to have an appointive process just as the U.S. government has for U.S. attorneys."[27]

On the other hand, some contend that appointed district attorneys could turn into faceless bureaucrats unresponsive to the public's concerns.

## COUNTY COURTS

Each of Colorado's counties has a county court with at least one judge. County courts try misdemeanors (minor crimes such as traffic offenses, loose dogs, and disturbing the peace) and handle minor civil suits. Prior to 1975, county courts mainly handled traffic cases, but this workload was substantially reduced when the legislature passed a law permitting all but the most serious traffic fines to be paid by mail.

Only ten Colorado counties have more than one county court judge (Adams, Arapahoe, Boulder, Denver, El Paso, Jefferson, Larimer, Mesa, Pueblo, and Weld Counties). The state legislature sets the number of county judges in each county except Denver. County court judges serve a four-year term.

In the larger counties in Colorado, the county court judges are required to be lawyers, yet in some of the smaller counties only a high school diploma is required. This is because a number of rural counties are so small in population that a lawyer from the county is not always available to serve as county court judge. County judges who are not lawyers are required to attend classes on the duties and functioning of the county court. The classes are conducted under the supervision of the state supreme court.

In Colorado's smaller rural counties, such as Baca or Hinsdale Counties, judges often serve on a part-time basis. This is in part because of the lower workload yet also because the state constitution mandates there shall be a county judge in each county.

County court decisions can be appealed to the district court and from there to the Colorado Court of Appeals and the Colorado Supreme Court.

## MUNICIPAL COURTS

Cities and towns in Colorado may create municipal courts to try cases involving municipal ordinances. Similar to county courts, municipal courts try traffic cases, although serious traffic offenses, such as drunk driving or hit and run, must be tried in county court.

Similar to judges in small rural counties, municipal court judges are not required by state law to be lawyers. In the larger cities, however, city laws mandate that municipal court judges have a law degree.

State law requires that municipal judges be paid a salary rather than a fee for each case handled. This is to prevent municipal court judges from being tempted to increase their pay by encouraging the police to arrest more citizens and thus bring more cases (and more fees for the judge) into court.

Municipal courts are the lowest courts. Decisions by municipal court judges can be appealed to county court and from there to district court, the state court of appeals, and the state supreme court.

## SPECIALIZED COURTS

There are a number of courts in Colorado that have been created for specialized purposes:

*Small Claims Court.* Each county court has a small claims court where trials involving small sums of money (less than $7,500) are held as inexpensively and rapidly as possible. There is no jury, and neither side in the dispute is represented by a lawyer. Evening and Saturday sessions are often held to make the small claims court as convenient and accessible to the public as possible. Parties to a dispute file all their own papers (with the assistance of court clerks) and present their own cases to the judge for decision.

*Water Courts.* Colorado has had water courts since 1969. The purpose of these courts is to simplify the process of establishing water rights and to keep more accurate water rights records. There are seven water courts in the state, one for each major river drainage basin. Each water court has a "water judge." He or she is appointed by the Colorado Supreme Court from among the district court judges in the particular area.

Well over a thousand water cases get considered every year.[28] And as many as ten are heard by the state supreme court each year.

*Denver Juvenile Court.* Because it is the largest city in the state, Denver has three specialized courts that carry out functions that district courts handle elsewhere in the state. One of the most important is the Denver Juvenile Court, which tries all cases in Denver involving juvenile delinquency, adoption, child neglect, and child support.

Denver was one of the first cities in the United States to experiment with a juvenile court. Judge Ben Lindsey, who became a legend throughout the country for his progressive values and innovations, instituted the Denver Juvenile Court in 1907 as a creative social experiment. He came up with ways of rehabilitating young offenders other than sending them off to regular jails. Such jails, Judge Lindsey knew, were schools for crime.

He set up separate jails for juveniles and spoke out against child labor practices. His ideas spread rapidly throughout Colorado and the United States.[29] Unfortunately, the Ku Klux Klan targeted him and he was defeated in the 1928 election.

*Denver Probate Court.* A second specialized court is the Denver Probate Court, which administers the settling of estates of deceased persons. The court decides on wills, appoints and supervises conservators of estates, and provides guardianship for funds inherited by minors. It also appoints guardians for incapacitated adults and minors and selects conservators who administer the finances of incapacitated adults and minors.

## PUBLIC DEFENDER

One of the most challenging problems in state court systems is the provision of lawyers to indigent persons accused of crime. An indigent person is someone who cannot provide for his or her own support and thus does not have funds available to hire and pay an attorney. Because the state and local governments pay prosecutors to prosecute criminal cases aggressively, it is not regarded as fair to send a person of limited means into court without a paid attorney who will be as aggressive as the prosecutor in providing a defense.

Moreover, the U.S. Supreme Court ruled in the 1962 case of *Gideon v. Wainwright* that virtually every indigent criminal defendant has a basic right to defense counsel.[30]

Prior to 1970, Colorado used court-appointed lawyers to represent defendants who were too poor to hire their own. Court-appointed lawyers received low payment for their services and thus young and inexperienced lawyers generally represented indigent defendants. Low pay also often prevented court-appointed lawyers from devoting sufficient time to individual cases to mount an effective defense.

Since 1970 Colorado has had an agency of the state judiciary known as the Office of the State Public Defender. Headquartered in Denver, the state public defender employs at least three hundred trial lawyers, thirty appellate attorneys, and various investigators and staff spread throughout the state. The operating budget exceeds $55 million. The state public defender handles well over 125,000 cases a year.

Public defenders are paid full-time though not generous salaries. This enables them to spend all their working hours representing indigent defendants. The state public defender is appointed by the state supreme court to a five-year term of office.

Public defenders are brought into criminal cases either at the request of the defendant or by order of the court. Customarily public defenders handle felony cases, yet they can represent people accused of misdemeanors and also indigent youths in juvenile court. The public defender determines whether a particular defendant is indigent and thus qualified for free representation, but the decision can be appealed to the courts.

Public defenders are viewed as doing a pretty good job on behalf of those without the means to hire their own attorneys. One result of this system is that nearly every criminal defendant who wants one gets an appeal, which is another reason why criminal cases take up so much of the judicial system's time. Budget restrictions have placed an enormous strain on this system.

In civil cases, the Colorado legal services program is a weak attempt to parallel the public defender program for criminal cases. The legal services program, however, is extremely limited in its representation of indigents in civil courts. There is no U.S. Supreme Court mandate that attorneys be provided for indigent persons in civil cases. Most indigent plaintiffs and defendants in civil and domestic cases try to represent themselves.

GENDER BIAS

In 1988 Chief Justice Quinn appointed a volunteer committee of twenty-six persons to study possible sexual discrimination in the state court system. The Colorado Task Force on Gender Bias in the Courts specifically addressed the question of whether women were treated differently from men in court in any of their contemporary roles.

The task force found that much of the information on gender bias in Colorado courts is "conversational" and "anecdotal." In those cases where the task force endeavored to "measure" the extent of gender bias, it was often difficult to verify that the differences in treatment of men and women were really the result of gender bias and not other factors.

The task force established that the most frequent complaints concerning gender bias in Colorado courts occurred in child custody cases. Ironically, in many instances, divorcing fathers and mothers had the same complaint. The fathers complained that courts tended to exclude men as fit parents for young children. The mothers complained that courts tended to give young children to the mother, thus saddling her with the demanding and time-consuming task of raising young children.

A task force cochair said: "The task force had to struggle with the difficult question of whether gender bias was producing custody decisions that put small children with the mother or whether the courts were simply reflecting the parenting values of the larger society."[31]

Another instance of apparent gender bias was the tendency of judges to give lighter sentences to women than those given to men who had committed the same crime. Lighter sentences were particularly given to women who were caring for small children. "When confronted with this fact of lighter sentences for women with children, however, judges defended the practice as the desirable thing to do under the circumstances."[32]

The task force found instances where concern for treating the sexes evenly still led to gender bias. Courts assumed that women in divorce cases would have equal earning power with men. In reality, however, the women often had lower earning power, mainly due to the fact that women more frequently stayed home with children and thus were absent from the workforce for a number of years.

Courts often gave the former wife and the former husband equal financial responsibility in a divorce case, but the financial burdens would fall more heavily on the former wife due to her lower earning power. This is changing in recent years, however. One report claims women are primary breadwinners in about 40 percent of U.S. households.[33]

The Task Force on Gender Bias in the Courts concluded its report by recommending that court personnel learn to recognize gender bias, both in themselves and in others, and to work to reduce it whenever possible.

"I was on that task force, and we have implemented most of those recommendations and have made a lot of progress over the past generation," said former Colorado Supreme Court associate justice Rebecca Love Kourlis. "More women have been appointed [as judges]. Yet to be representative, especially of today's bar, there have to be even more women on the bench."[34]

### JUDICIAL INNOVATION

Because of the rapid population growth in Colorado over the past sixty years, the state's court system struggles with a heavier caseload. This has resulted in overworked judges and delays in cases coming to trial. The legislature has increased appropriations for the judicial system and authorized the hiring of additional judges, yet the improvements always seem to run behind the increases in the caseload. "These are chronic problems that will always be there. The Colorado court system has no choice but to live with limited resources."[35]

In recent years, by order of the chief justice of the Colorado Supreme Court, criminal cases have been given top priority in the state court system. Domestic relations cases (divorce and child custody) are second priority, and general civil cases are treated as third priority. Under this system, state courts are keeping up with criminal caseloads yet are experiencing delays and "backup" in bringing civil cases and domestic relations cases to trial.

As a result of the heavy caseload pressure, the Colorado court system has been experimenting with a number of innovations, most of them seeking inventive and judicially sound systems for more rapidly and efficiently processing court cases.

### Arbitration and Mediation

People throughout history have tried to settle or negotiate their disputes without resorting to violence. Judicial systems merely provide a formal forum for dispute resolution. But as the judicial system's workload has grown and delays have greatly increased, political leaders have experimented, generally successfully, with what are now called "alternate dispute resolution" practices.

The most well known are mediation and arbitration procedures. Colorado legislative and judicial leaders have for decades advocated their use and provided legislation enabling citizens to turn to these less costly and usually speedier processes.

Most judicial districts in Colorado now have an office of dispute resolution that gives information about alternatives to litigation and provides mediators who can mediate disputes for reasonable fees. The University of Colorado at Boulder operates a Conflict Information Consortium providing background materials on a variety of dispute resolution procedures.

*Arbitration* is a dispute resolution process where contending parties present their case to a neutral third party or to a panel of arbitrators. The arbitrator, or arbitrators, examine the evidence and then provide a resolution decision for the disputants. This decision is usually binding.

Similar to a court procedure, arbitration is an adversarial process where each side is trying to prove it is right. But arbitration is generally not as formal as in regular court and the rules can be modified to some extent to meet the disputants' needs.

Arbitrations are usually settled in a few months, and the only prehearing discovery permitted is an exchange of documents. This cuts costs. Most decisions are not appealed, and in cases of binding arbitration cannot be appealed.

Arbitration is commonly used in labor management and consumer and commercial relations. Indeed, most collective-bargaining labor contracts require some form of arbitration.

There are several ways that voluntary arbitration is different from courtroom litigation. First, the parties involved have some control over who serves as the arbitrator. Instead of selecting a person with legal experience, such as a former judge or attorney, either or both parties may prefer an arbitrator with industry experience or technical knowledge bearing on the dispute.

Second, arbitrators do not have to follow technical courtroom rules of evidence and do not have to strictly apply federal, state, or local law in rendering their decisions.

Third, arbitrations are conducted in private. The news media and other members of the public can be excluded. This contrasts with courtroom trials, which are public events and subject to close press scrutiny.

But some judicial system watchers are concerned about the increase in arbitrations, both mandatory and voluntary. They worry that as corporate and general business interests shift away from the district courts, this segment of the general public will be less inclined to work on behalf of a quality public court system with the needed pay and personnel to do its job. Yet some of these concerns are offset by arbitration's effect on civil caseloads and reducing costs.

*Mediation* is an additional system for expediting court work and reducing delays. Indeed, many judicial districts in Colorado require that parties try to mediate their disputes before the case is heard. Under mediation, both parties voluntarily meet with a mediator and work to solve their differences as amicably, and cheaply, as possible. No testimony is taken, and rather than competing with each other, the parties to the dispute are encouraged to cooperate.

Mediation is most likely to be used in divorce cases as a noncombative way of settling alimony, child custody, and property settlement issues. Under mediation, the court abstains from arbitrarily dividing children and property between divorcing couples, encouraging the former husband and wife to work things out on their own.

Mediation customarily involves a neutral third party, often a former judge or a professional facilitator, who meets with the parties, with or without their lawyers, to attempt to find a mutually satisfactory nonbinding resolution to a dispute. A compromise of both parties' original positions is usually the end result.

An effective mediator guides disputants in identifying the central issues, ranking their needs and desires and determining the best means of resolution. Mediators do not tell people how to solve their dispute but generally assist them in generating their own optimal solutions. Mediation is voluntary, confidential, and seeks to be cooperative and creative. It is a highly useful problem-solving process when the parties can at least partially control the outcome and avoid having to "fight things out" in court.

Mediation is a process that helps lessen both the emotional and financial expense of protracted litigation. Mediation is especially useful in family disputes such as juvenile cases, probate (settling estates), or divorce and child custody matters. Most parties achieve full or partial settlements and in using this process save a lot in attorneys' fees and court costs.[36]

Arbitration and mediation are the best-known dispute-resolution procedures. There are a number of other processes, including family conferencing, pretrial discovery dispute resolution, criminal mediation, and traditional negotiating formats.

### E-Filing Case Initiations

Yet another innovation, championed by former chief justice Mary Mullarkey, was electronic filing. Parties can file their court pleadings and initiate cases online. Judges can review the pleadings online and send out judicial orders in a secure system operated by LexisNexis.

### PRISON OVERCROWDING

Like most other states, Colorado faces an overcrowding problem in its prisons. In 1985 the state legislature, reacting to a surge of citizens' concerns about increasing crime rates, passed laws providing for mandatory prison sentences and longer sentences for persons convicted of violent crimes. The result was more convicts going to prison and staying longer.

As would be expected, the prison system soon was overloaded and overcrowded with violent offenders. Colorado went from slightly over three thousand to nearly twenty-two thousand prisoners in state prisons from 1985 to 2012.

Colorado has a number of state prisons spread around the state in Sterling, Cañon City, Crowley County, Buena Vista, and elsewhere. There also are a handful of private prisons in the state, but some of these are being slowly retired. The U.S. government has four prisons in Florence and another three in the Denver suburb of Englewood. The state Department of Human Services operates a handful of separate facilities for juvenile prisoners.

The Colorado Board of Parole, attached to the Department of Corrections, may grant parole (a conditional release under various supervisory provisions) to state prisoners. The Parole Board supervises anywhere from seven thousand to eleven thousand parolees. There also are city and county jails.

Gov. Bill Ritter, as a cost-saving measure, initiated an early-release program for qualified state prisoners. His program had the backing of many state law enforcement officials, yet his program was attacked by partisan opponents as too risky and as being soft on criminals.

Governor Ritter's early-release program was scaled back after corrections officials found fewer prisoners than anticipated to be prudent release risks. Most of the expected savings thus never materialized.

One solution Colorado has tried to relieve prison overcrowding is more effective use of probation and probation officers. At the time of sentencing, judges can elect to place a convicted felon on probation rather than sending him or her to state prison. A prisoner on probation is required to check in periodically with a probation officer. In most cases a convict on probation also is required to refrain from destructive behavior, such as taking drugs or drinking too much alcohol.

In most states the probation program is administered by the governor. Colorado, however, is one of a small number of states that have placed criminal probation in the state court system.

One of the probation techniques used in the 1990s was *risk-needs assessment*. Under this program, probationers were extensively tested and interviewed by probation officers and then evaluated according to their "risk" to society, that is, the extent to which they were likely to commit a violent crime against the public in the future. Probationers are then classified into one of three risk categories. First is maximum risk, second is medium risk, and third is minimum risk.

This classification system enabled the probation office to assign extra time and attention to maximum-risk probationers, thereby reducing the likelihood that they would commit a serious crime while on probation. Judges, knowing that maximum-risk probationers would be supervised more closely, were more likely to give probation in place of a prison sentence.

At the same time probationers are evaluated in terms of risk, they are also analyzed in terms of their personal needs. Probationers with alcohol problems were placed into alcohol control programs. Probationers with drug problems were placed in drug control programs, such as methadone substitution programs for heroin addicts.

For several years Colorado's Department of Corrections experimented with a military-style prison boot camp. It began in the early 1990s and was shut down in 2010. Prisoners in the program were nonviolent offenders. They could study for their general equivalency diploma (GED) and had access to substance abuse counseling. If they completed the rigorous program they could gain early release.

It was a physically and emotionally challenging program located in Buena Vista. It was heavily populated by offenders with alcohol or drug abuse problems. It proved to be an expensive program. About one-third who entered the program dropped out or were booted out. It also had a recidivism rate of around 50 percent, not much better than the regular record for state inmates. These disappointing results, as well as growing state budget shortfalls, forced the state to shift funding from the boot camp experiment to high-security prisons.[37]

In recent years the Department of Corrections has intensified what it calls the "wraparound" services program. This is where judges, court officers, or probation counselors determine what services an offender needs to be rehabilitated. Some need GED programs. Many need substance abuse programs. A staggering 85 percent of Colorado's convicted offenders have drug and alcohol addictions. "We have increased all of these [addiction abatement] programs," said Department of Corrections spokesperson Katherine Sanguinetti, "because they have proven to work, and because we need to divert more and more people out of the prisons because of tight budget constraints."[38]

Colorado has long struggled with the problem of prison overcrowding. The situation was equally bad at both the county and the state level. Falling state revenues (adjusted for inflation) brought about inadequate staffing in state prisons.

In recent years several counties were having great difficulty just housing increased numbers of prisoners. In El Paso County (Colorado Springs), the county sheriff once put up a large tent next to the county jail in order to give at least some kind of shelter to the county's ever-increasing prison population.

Colorado officials are currently experimenting with a wide variety of alternatives to incarceration that include home detention, day reporting, ankle bracelets, and even GPS tracking systems.

### Violence in Prisons

State prison officials have been forced to deal with a major increase in violence in state prisons. The violence frequently forced corrections officers to lock down prisons and keep prisoners confined to their cells for long periods of time. One cause of the increase in violence was budget cuts that slashed programs designed to keep inmates busy and away from trouble.

There were 148 lockdowns in Colorado prisons in one recent year. That was 66 more lockdowns than the previous year, which was an 88 percent increase. There was a 19.5 percent increase in assaults by prison inmates on other inmates and an 11 percent increase in assaults by inmates on prison guards.

Corrections spokesperson Katherine Sanguinetti said the cause of the increased violence was budget problems that led to a decrease in the corrections budget of $56 million and the elimination of more than five hundred full-time state prison employees. "Along with [those employees]," Sanguinetti noted, "we lost a lot of education programs and treatment for inmates. One of the key principles of offender management is to keep them busy because they are less likely to be destructive."

Budget cuts eliminated a program designed to change prisoner behavior by having staff take photographs of prisoners and mail them to the inmates' families. Inmate morale was further reduced by a reduction in prisoner pay from a few dollars a day to only sixty cents a day. Money given to prisoners when they were released from prison has stayed frozen at $100 for more than thirty years, a period of substantial inflation in U.S. economic history.

Colorado prison officials have been forced to handle more prisoners with less budgeted money at exactly the time when more gang members were coming into the prisons. More than nine thousand of some twenty-two thousand inmates have been identified in recent years as gang members or affiliated with gangs.

### "MAKE MY DAY" LAW

In 1985 Colorado lawmakers attracted national publicity for a controversial innovation. They enacted legislation to provide additional protection to homeowners who might use force, even deadly physical force, against intruders into their homes who they believe are committing or intend to commit a crime.

This legislation was explicitly designed to protect homeowners from prosecution or civil suits when they used deadly force against strangers who intruded into their homes. In many ways this was merely an effort to strengthen existing laws. But prosecutors and the Colorado District Attorneys' Council lobbied against it. The National Rifle Association lobbied for it. Governor Lamm tried to get prosecutors and conservative legislators to fashion a compromise, which they eventually did.[39]

People nicknamed this home protection law the "Make My Day" law, giving it a notoriety it probably did not deserve. The expression "Make My Day" came from a scene in a popular Clint Eastwood film of the mid-1980s. The film's star, Eastwood, had his revolver pointed at the head of a criminal. The criminal appeared as though he might try to escape, so Eastwood said: "Go ahead. Make my day!" The implication was that it is acceptable to shoot lawbreakers who are threatening you or endeavoring to escape.

The "Make My Day" law polarized opinion in Colorado. Still, the legislation had very real substantive consequences as well as high symbolic value. The symbolism was clear. It was an effort by legislators to communicate to law-abiding homeowners that they, too, have rights, and that too much attention in the courts and elsewhere had been paid to the rights of criminals.

The legislation, which plainly had wide popular appeal, raised a number of issues. One of the issues had to do with a homeowner's right to use force against uninvited law enforcement officials. Another ambiguity of the law had to do with what kind of force could be used against unarmed, harmless, or fleeing intruders.

This Colorado law differed from laws elsewhere in that the law provided that property crimes, not just violent crimes, were grounds for use of force, perhaps recalling shades of the state's frontier heritage. Concerns about lawful use of force were often raised by prosecutors, and have led to suggestions for modifying the Colorado "Make My Day" law.[40]

But no modifications have been made, and the "Make My Day" law became a permanent part of the political and legal culture in Colorado.

### CONSERVATIVE BACKLASH

Nowadays former skeptics and most conservatives accept Colorado's Missouri Plan for nominating and retaining Colorado's judges and justices. But some conservatives remain upset at what they believe is an overly liberal-dominated Colorado Supreme Court.

In the 1990s there was a proposal, which failed, that would have allowed citizens to recall a judge or justice. In 2006 a libertarian-conservative Republican, John Andrews, helped put Amendment 40 on the November ballot. As an initiated state constitutional amendment, it would have in effect provided for a term limit of ten years for all judges and justices.

Preliminary surveys suggested Amendment 40 would be passed by the voters. But the Colorado Bar Association and its allies, supported by several recent governors (including then-incumbent governor Bill Owens), strongly opposed the Andrews term limits for judges proposal. It was defeated 57 percent to 43 percent in the November 2006 election.

John Andrews was a former president of the Colorado Senate. He ran unsuccessfully as the Republican candidate for governor of Colorado in 1990. He explained his support for Amendment 40 this way: "I'm okay with the Missouri Plan. I just think term limits can be made compatible with it. We need a better way to get rid of incompetent judges and, especially, recklessly legislating judges who are threatening our traditional values such as private property rights and so on."[41]

Andrews and his supporters say the performance evaluation process is inadequate. "What kind of screen are they if over 99 percent of judges standing for reelection keep getting reelected?"

Andrews is not alone. Other critics say that the performance reviews are too thin in providing analysis to the voters. In effect, they say, this so-called reform in Colorado is too much of a "rubber stamp" in practice, an exercise that benefits judges and justices far more than the voters.[42]

In 2009 a grassroots movement came into existence calling itself "Clear the Bench Colorado." The group shared John Andrews's views and had much in common with the Tea Party movement, an ultraconservative political group that sprang up at much the same time.

Clear the Bench Colorado set an explicit political goal to mount a campaign to vote out of office four Democrats serving on the Colorado Supreme Court who were scheduled to be up for retention election on the November 2010 general election ballot.

On its Internet website, Clear the Bench Colorado bluntly proclaimed that these Democrats sitting on the Colorado Supreme Court "have betrayed the trust of the people of Colorado, neglecting the proper judicial function of *upholding* the law in favor of *imposing* their partisan political will."

Such critics, of course, have every right to contest judicial retention elections. And they may enjoy some success. In fact, Clear the Bench Colorado's main target, Chief Justice Mary Mullarkey, decided not to run for retention in 2010. The sixty-six-year-old Mullarkey, who had long suffered from multiple sclerosis, denied she retired because of this populist protest group. But Matt Arnold, the founder and chief organizer of Clear the Bench Colorado, called Mullarkey's decision not to run a "partial victory" for the group's crusade.[43]

Clear the Bench Colorado failed in its 2010 effort to remove the three other state supreme court justices standing for retention, although the vote for their retention (averaging around 60 percent) was 13 percent or more lower than the favorable retention vote in recent years for supreme court justices. It was a decline that current justices and court watchers certainly noticed.

Still, most attorneys and political leaders in Colorado like the system pretty much as it is. They fear that term limits or too much volatility in judicial careers would deter people from wanting to serve on the bench. The current system of regular retention elections provides for voters to decide whether or not to keep a judge in office.

Those who like the existing system share the view of retired U.S. Supreme Court associate justice Sandra Day O'Connor, who wrote: "When you enter one of these [state] courtrooms, the last thing you want to worry about is whether the judge is more accountable to a campaign contributor or an ideological group than the law. In our system, the judiciary, unlike the legislative and executive branches, is supposed to answer only to the law and the constitution. Courts must be the one safe place where every citizen can receive a fair hearing."[44]

State courts, just like the U.S. courts, are never entirely removed from politics. Courts will always have an impact on policy and politics. Political developments and political culture invariably will continue to have an impact on the court and judicial decision making. U.S. associate justice Oliver Wendell Holmes once said of the U.S. Supreme Court that it is very quiet there, but it is like "the quiet in the eye of a storm."

CONCLUSIONS

Despite ongoing funding struggles, Colorado has an effective and progressive state judicial system. The statewide reorganization of the court system and the Missouri Plan for appointing judges, both adopted in the 1960s, have given Colorado a state judiciary that is widely admired.

Colorado continues to approach judicial problems in an imaginative fashion. Whether it was studying gender bias in the courtroom, working to make probation a more successful alternative to a prison sentence, or searching for new ways of measuring judicial fairness and performance, Colorado is viewed as having one of the more innovative state judicial systems. "We're pretty close to getting it right," said longtime *Denver Post* editor Bob Ewegen, "especially compared with other states."[45]

The judicial system and the quality of justice in Colorado are continually tested. The reforms of the past few generations do not make the Colorado judicial system perfect. Nothing will accomplish that lofty goal. Yet reforms have made the system work much better in recent decades.

# CHAPTER TEN

# Colorado in the Federal System

When Zebulon Montgomery Pike was exploring eastern Colorado in the early 1800s, he built a small fortification, a breastwork of logs, for defense against hostile Native Americans or Spaniards. He located this minor military project on the north bank of the Arkansas River at the site of the present-day city of Pueblo.

Pike's breastwork of logs in Pueblo represents an important aspect, perhaps the most important aspect, of Colorado governmental history. Modest though it doubtless was, the little log fortification represented the first United States government project undertaken and successfully completed in Colorado. It was a harbinger of projects to come. The U.S. government has played a major role, in many ways *the* major role, in the growth and development of the Centennial State.

There are several reasons for the important role of the U.S. government. Colorado was not one of the original thirteen colonies. It began as a territory in 1861 rather than as an independent state. The first official government in Colorado, the territorial government, was created by the U.S. Congress in Washington DC and not by the people of Colorado themselves. Colorado would win its statehood and its own state government later.

Another reason why the U.S. government is so important in Colorado is its enormous landownership. About 37 percent of the land in Colorado (and about two-thirds of all the land west of Denver) is owned by the U.S. government. Most of it is in national forests, or national parks, or owned by the U.S. Department of the Interior's Bureau of Land Management. Four percent is designated as wilderness area. As the principal landowner, the U.S. government has a major voice in what happens in Colorado.

An additional factor adding to the influence of the U.S. government is the harsh mountain and desert climate in Colorado. Large U.S. government public works projects, particularly water projects, have been undertaken to make the state more suitable for agricultural and urban development. Colorado lacked the resources to build large water diversion and electrical generation projects itself. The U.S. government provided much of the capital for Colorado's internal development, thereby helping the state to overcome its challenging semiarid climate.

Last, and anything but least, since the end of World War II, U.S. government civilian and military installations and related private industries have become a major component of the Colorado economy. Decisions made in Washington DC to locate major U.S. government facilities in Colorado have been indispensable to the development of the state. Lobbying the U.S. government to locate military installations and governmental offices in Colorado has been a regular part of the state's effort to better itself. Gov. John Hickenlooper emphasized this theme in late 2010 and again in his 2012 state of the state address when he said Colorado needs to do everything it can to work closely with the military, noting that the military is a key part of the state's economy.[1]

Thus, more than in most states, Colorado's relationship to the U.S. government has been a critical part of the state's history. Ironically, although Colorado is dependent on the U.S. government for much of its economic success, the state's citizens often have little good to say about the national government and its politicians and administrators.

## THE CIVIL WAR

Because Denver is approximately sixteen hundred miles from Washington DC, government officials back in Washington often do not see things the way people in Colorado see them. Colorado is a vastly different place from the nation's capital. Its dry climate and forbidding mountains create problems that are unfamiliar to people in Washington, most of whom are from states with large amounts of annual rainfall and much less challenging geography.

Colorado was designated a United States territory on February 28, 1861. Within a year the newly appointed territorial governor, William Gilpin, became embroiled in a strenuous argument with Washington over how the Civil War should be handled in Colorado.

Gilpin arrived in Denver in May of 1861. He found Denver and Colorado solidly in the Union camp, yet there were pockets of Confederate activity in the territory, particularly near Pueblo and Leadville. Denver's first mayor, John C. Moore, left the territory to join the Confederate army. Another Southern sympathizer, A. B. Miller, openly recruited volunteers to join him in going back to the South to fight for secession.[2]

The U.S. government did have a military presence in the region. The army had two garrison forts, Fort Garland in the San Luis Valley and Fort Wise (later renamed Fort Lyon) in eastern Colorado on the Arkansas River. Governor Gilpin worried, however, that the intensity of the Civil War in the East would cause the U.S. Army to ignore frontier areas such as Colorado. He was particularly concerned Confederate troops from Texas or Oklahoma might invade the territory in an attempt to capture Colorado's newly discovered gold mines and thereby help to finance the Southern war effort.

Gilpin decided to act. He appointed a military staff, began to raise a volunteer infantry regiment, and started collecting guns and rifles and other necessary instruments of warfare. To finance this essentially unilateral and in effect unauthorized territorial militia, he issued $375,000 in draft notes and guaranteed that the drafts would be paid by the U.S. Treasury. Colorado merchants and tradespeople honored the drafts, and soon the territory had a well-trained and well-equipped infantry regiment composed of ten companies of soldiers.

U.S. government officials in Washington did not share Governor Gilpin's fears of a Confederate invasion. They announced that the U.S. Treasury would not honor Gilpin's drafts. This made Governor Gilpin unpopular with the merchants and others who had put up money for his venture. Gilpin then had to do what governor after governor has done in more recent years. He went to Washington DC to explain the situation and plead the case for Colorado to unsympathetic federal officials.

In the meantime, Governor Gilpin's view of the military situation in the Mountain West turned out to be more accurate than the view prevailing in the national capital. A Confederate army moved across the southwestern desert from Texas up the Rio Grande into northern New Mexico. Led by West Point–educated General John Sibley, the Confederates captured Santa Fe and then marched north toward Colorado and its mineral riches.

## Glorieta Pass

Gilpin's regiment of infantry, known as the First Colorado Volunteers, headed south out of Denver in February of 1862. Word had come from the Union regulars in New Mexico that help was indeed needed. North met South, or Coloradans plus other Union regulars met Texans, in battle about sixteen miles east of Santa Fe at Glorieta Pass. Located at the southernmost tip of the Sangre de Cristo range, this pass has an altitude of at least seventy-five hundred feet and is marked by rugged piñon and other scrub pine trees and reddish soil.

The Battle of Glorieta Pass took place in late March 1862. Texans outnumbered Union forces and made initial advances. On March 27, however, Major John P. Chivington of the Colorado forces took a group of men and, with the help of local guides, marched in a twelve-mile sweep through unmarked trails around and behind the Texas forces.

This maneuver succeeded brilliantly. Once Chivington's men had wiped out a small rear guard of Confederates, they destroyed wagonloads of food, ammunition, and supplies. They killed a dozen or so mules and disabled a cannon or two as well. Too undermanned to attack the rebel forces from the rear, they slipped back through the forests around the fighting to rejoin the Union troops.[3]

General Sibley, the Confederate leader, soon was informed his supplies had been destroyed. He had no choice but to retreat. He led his troops back down the Rio Grande to Texas. The heroic Coloradans had helped to deal the Texas Confederates a fatal blow in this "Gettysburg of the West." The Civil War was over for Colorado.[4]

Governor Gilpin's decisive actions in preparing Colorado for war were vindicated. The Treasury Department eventually honored the $375,000 in drafts. Governor Gilpin had become so controversial, however, that President Abraham Lincoln had to remove him as territorial governor. In this first conflict between the "Colorado view" and the "Washington view," however, the "Colorado view" had proven to be the correct one.

## REMOVAL OF NATIVE AMERICANS

Prior to the discovery of gold in what is now Colorado, the U.S. government had negotiated a treaty with the Native Americans designating large stretches of land between the South Platte River and the Arkansas River as Native American hunting lands. As soon as gold was discovered, however, miners and tradesmen raced across eastern Colorado toward the gold fields, trespassing on Native American lands and demanding that the federal government extinguish the Native American claims and make the land available for settlement and ranching.

Federal agents tried to solve the problem by restricting the Native Americans, mainly Arapahos and Cheyennes, to a triangular-shaped reservation on the banks of Sand Creek, a tributary of the Arkansas River in southeastern Colorado. The U.S. government provided neither fences nor soldiers to mark the boundaries of the reservation, however, and the younger and more aggressive Indians began raiding ranches and settlements nearby. On June 11, 1864, Indian raiders savagely attacked a ranch about thirty miles southeast of Denver, killing a rancher, his wife, and two daughters. The victims' mutilated bodies were publicly displayed at the post office in Denver.[5]

Later that summer, Indians murdered several dozen travelers in eastern Colorado and western Kansas. Wagon trains were especially targeted.

Native Americans were considered a U.S. government problem, but the people of Colorado Territory demanded instant action. John P. Chivington, the Colorado hero of the Battle of Glorieta Pass during the Civil War, was now a colonel. He and a regiment of seven hundred volunteer soldiers, authorized by the War Department in Washington, set out to retaliate against the Native Americans camped at Sand Creek.

The Cheyenne and Arapaho residents in Sand Creek, it should be noted, had surrendered most of their weapons to a nearby army fort that fall. "They moved to Sand Creek at the request of the regional authorities in Colorado with a white flag of surrender and an American flag of protection to signify their willingness to cooperate," writes Lindsay Calhoun.[6]

As the sun rose on the morning of November 29, 1864, Colonel Chivington ordered his men to attack the unsuspecting Native Americans camped at Sand Creek. The troops, according to most accounts, went out of control, killing and mutilating men, women, and children, many of whom had indicated they were surrendering.

"Troopers raped and mutilated Indian women and shot children for sport," wrote Colorado historians. "The 'blood thirsters' brought back scalps to display in a Denver theater and to drape around mirrors in saloons."[7]

Later estimates of the number of Native Americans killed ranged from 160 to 200. Chivington himself boasted of killing at least twice that number. Native Americans who escaped the attack, many of them wounded, fled to the north.

The Sand Creek engagement is one of the most controversial events in Colorado history. Former Colorado U.S. senator Ben Nighthorse Campbell, a Native American, looked back at it as "one of the most disgraceful moments in American history—one of the darkest pages in Colorado history."[8] Others have called it genocide and a "war crime."

A small town close to the massacre site was named Chivington in honor of the commander of the Colorado forces at Sand Creek. Senator Campbell was infuriated that any community should be named for Chivington. Asked once what he would do to the town of Chivington if he became governor of Colorado, Campbell said he intended to "burn that sucker down."[9]

Supporters of the Native Americans, and there were many, pointed out that the Native Americans at Sand Creek were camped on a U.S. government–designated reservation and were sleeping peacefully at the time they were attacked. Supporters of Chivington contended that a number of settlers had lost their lives in Native American attacks and that fresh white scalps were found in the camp when the conflict was over.

Three separate investigations into this attack described Sand Creek as a disgrace and "a foul and dastardly massacre." In 2007 the massacre site became a National Historic Site staffed by the National Park Service.[10]

In the immediate aftermath of Sand Creek, the U.S. government continued to remove the Native Americans from Colorado. In 1879, following the massacre of Nathan Meeker and eleven other men in northwestern Colorado, the Utes, the last group of Native Americans to roam free in the state, were removed to large but remote reservations in the southwestern corner of Colorado.

In recent years, one of Colorado's major Native-American tribes, the Southern Utes, has prospered from the great mineral wealth on its reservation. By skillfully exploiting coal-bed methane and natural gas deposits on its land, the Southern Utes have become major players in the United States energy industry. Their tribal businesses extend to fourteen states and include prospecting for undersea oil deposits in the Gulf of Mexico and speculating in upscale San Diego real estate.

An elderly Southern Ute told a newspaper reporter that in 2009 his share of the proceeds from the energy and related investments of the tribe was $77,500. An article in the *High Country News* summed up this recent success of the Southern Ute tribe this way: "They've achieved cultural, environmental and economic self-determination through energy self-determination."[11]

### HOMESTEAD ACT

The U.S. government carried out the wishes of many Coloradans where removal of the Native Americans was concerned. In the case of the Homestead Act, however, the national government failed to comprehend the situation in Colorado completely. Passed by the U.S. Congress in 1862, the Homestead Act permitted the head of a family to gain title to 160 acres of government land by settling on the land and paying a small fee.

The members of Congress who voted for the Homestead Act assumed that the size of the average family farm in the United States should be 160 acres. A farm that size made perfect sense in the well-watered East and Midwest. In high and dry Colorado, however, 160 acres was much too small for a farm to be a viable economic operation. Low rainfall meant low crop yields, thus a successful farm in dryland areas needed to be considerably larger. The same logic applied to cattle ranching. In a state where a rancher needed fifty acres of land for each cow, a ranch of 160 acres, enough for only three cows, made a lot less sense.

Congress failed to respond to the cries from Colorado to permit larger homesteads in low-rainfall areas. Homesteading was such a popular concept, however, that farmers from the East and the Midwest continued to come and attempt to operate a dryland farm on only 160 acres. As might be expected, the result was frequent failure. The abandoned cabins and houses of these unfortunate homesteaders, who had the cards stacked against them before they ever began, still dot the Colorado countryside.

Early in the twentieth century Congress began to raise the acreage for homesteading, yet it never raised the acreage enough to make homesteading on the dry plains a successful venture. In 1909 the basic homestead size was raised from 160 to 320 acres, and in 1916 the size for homesteads used for raising cattle and sheep was raised from 320 to 640 acres. These actions were too little and too late, however. Only where irrigation was available, mainly in the Arkansas and South Platte River valleys, were the 160-acre farms mandated by the Homestead Act generally successful in Colorado.

In the 1870s Colorado cattle growers strongly lobbied Congress to preserve the "open range" style of raising cattle by creating three-thousand-acre homesteads for ranching in dry areas. Congress failed to act on this proposal, however, and the opportunity to preserve the giant cattle herds of Colorado's early frontier history was lost.

To be fair, the U.S. government did a few things right. As noted, water-scarce Colorado adopted the concept of "prior appropriation," the idea that water in a stream or river belonged to the first person who found and used it. Congress recognized the unique water situation in Colorado and the Rocky Mountain West when in 1866 it enacted legislation endorsing the doctrine of "prior appropriation" for scarce western water resources.

The U.S. government also joined Colorado in experimenting with and developing improved techniques for dryland farming. The U.S. Department of Agriculture, for example, opened a dryland experiment station at Akron, Colorado, in 1907, thus enhancing the efforts of the state dryland experiment station at Cheyenne Wells, which had been in operation since 1893.

## THE SILVER STRUGGLE

The greatest conflict between the U.S. government and the state of Colorado was over the issue of silver coinage in the 1890s.

The silver mines in Colorado were so productive that by 1874 the value of the silver being mined in the state exceeded the value of the gold being mined. By 1881 Colorado was the leading silver-producing state in the nation. As silver production increased, however, the price of silver fell. Silver was such a large part of the state economy that almost everyone in the state believed a way must be found to maintain a high price for silver.

As so often happens when the free market fails to produce results, Coloradans turned to the U.S. government to support the price of silver. The most popular suggestion was that Congress purchase silver for coinage at a fixed rate of sixteen ounces of silver for the same price as one ounce of gold. This 16 to 1 ratio, advocates contended, would increase the price paid for silver and at the same time enlarge the money supply and thereby inflate the national economy.

Throughout the 1880s the citizens of Colorado organized to build public support for the free and unlimited coinage of silver. A national Silver Convention was held in Denver in 1885. It created the Silver Alliance, which organized silver supporters throughout the state. In 1889 Colorado sent forty-three delegates to a second national Silver Convention, held in St. Louis. In 1892, when a third national Silver Convention was called in Washington DC, Colorado sent representatives from 220 silver clubs with more than forty thousand members. "The foundation had been laid; the silver banner raised," it proclaimed.[12]

Congress responded to the clamor for free silver with the Sherman Silver Purchase Act of 1890. This law doubled the amount of silver being purchased by the U.S. government to 4.5 million ounces a month. Instead of purchasing the silver at a ratio of 16 to 1 with gold, however, the new law provided for the national government to purchase the silver at the market price.

At first the Sherman Silver Purchase Act increased the market value of silver. As hoped, increased U.S. government purchases reduced the supply of silver. The effect on Colorado was entirely beneficial, because by 1890 Colorado was producing almost 60 percent of all the silver mined in the United States.

The high prices did not last, however, as production quickly increased to meet the government-stimulated demand. By 1892 the price of silver was falling again, and the economic health of the state of Colorado was falling with it.

In terms of national politics, neither the Republican nor the Democratic parties wanted to offend their eastern supporters, most of whom believed in a noninflationary currency based on gold. The result was disillusionment with both national political parties on the part of many Colorado voters.

The situation improved for Coloradans in 1892 when a third political party, the Populists, endorsed the free coinage of silver. The Populists believed that increasing the supply of silver coins would have an inflationary effect on the national economy and thereby make things easier financially for the common people.

In 1892 the Populists nominated James B. Weaver of Iowa as the party's candidate for president. Within Colorado, a full slate of Populist candidates was nominated for all major state offices and the state legislature.

Democrat Grover Cleveland won the national presidential election in 1892, but Colorado cast its electoral votes for Weaver. The free silver–Populist political revolution did not stop there, however. The Populists elected the governor, the state's two members of the U.S. House of Representatives, and gained a majority in the Colorado Senate. The silver crusade in Colorado did not win much of a response in Washington, yet it had an extensive, if temporary, impact on Centennial State politics.

The price of silver continued to fall, and Colorado went into an economic depression. Silver mines closed, businesses that supplied them went bankrupt, and Denver banks failed. Instead of coming to Colorado's rescue, however, the national government in Washington marched in the opposite direction. President Cleveland called for the repeal of the Sherman Silver Purchase Act, blaming it for the economic depression that was gripping the entire nation at the time.

Despite the heroic efforts of Colorado's senators and representatives in Congress to save it, the Sherman Silver Purchase Act was repealed, and almost all hope of the U.S. government supporting the price of silver was lost.

Silver made its last political stand in the presidential election of 1896. Although there were many Republican elected officials in Colorado in the late nineteenth century, the Republican national convention of 1896 refused to help Colorado in any way. William McKinley received the Republican nomination for president and vowed to run on a platform supporting a single monetary standard for the United States, which was gold. Colorado's best-known Republican, U.S. senator Henry Teller, walked out of the 1896 Republican national convention in protest.

At the Democratic national convention, however, the "silverites" were in control. William Jennings Bryan received the Democratic nomination for president. The party platform called for free and unlimited coinage of silver at the 16 to 1 ratio. In one of the most famous political speeches in U.S. history, Democrat Bryan pledged to save the nation from crucifixion upon "the cross of gold." The election of 1896 would be known as the "battle of the standards" because Republicans were completely committed to the gold standard and Democrats were completely committed to bimetallism, basing the currency on both gold and silver standards.

The election of 1896 thoroughly disrupted normal political party voting patterns in Colorado. U.S. senator Henry Teller and the "Silver Republicans" threw their support to Bryan and the Democratic candidate for governor, Alva Adams. Colorado Republicans who supported the national ticket ended up in the difficult position of arguing for both William McKinley and the free silver McKinley so vociferously opposed.

On Election Day in 1896, William Jennings Bryan and the Democratic ticket swept the state. Bryan defeated McKinley in Colorado by 161,269 votes to 26,279. Democrat Alva Adams was elected governor, and the Democratic–Silver Republican coalition swept all the major state offices.

For all the hue and cry, however, the great silver crusade failed to change national politics. Republican William McKinley won the 1896 presidential election, and in doing so he defeated once and for all the idea of free coinage of silver. His victory made it plain that the U.S. government was not going to subsidize the silver industry. The great boom days of the silver mines were now definitely over.

Gold mining in Colorado met the same fate. The U.S. government let the market determine the price of gold, and slowly that price fell so low it was no longer profitable to mine gold. Most of the gold camps gradually turned into near ghost towns.

Unlike silver, however, the gold mines shut down quietly, and there was no major political effort in the state to save them. The failure of the silver crusade of the 1890s probably convinced most Coloradans that efforts to save gold mining by means of U.S. government purchases and price supports would prove fruitless.

More than any other event in the state's history, the silver controversy illustrated the extent to which Colorado's fortunes were tied to national politics and policies. Although silver never came back, the U.S. government playing a leading role in what happens in Colorado certainly did.

## NATIONAL FORESTS

One of the most controversial federal policies in Colorado has been conservation. Many of the state's citizens strongly support the idea of the United States pursuing policies that preserve Colorado's mountain forests, prairie grasslands, and wild rivers and streams. Other Coloradans become anxious when the U.S. government implements conservationist policies, fearing that lumber companies will be prevented from cutting timber, cement companies will not be allowed to operate gravel quarries, scenic lands will not be available for real estate development and sale, and traditional energy companies will be unduly restricted in their efforts to explore and extract.

By the mid 1880s conservation-minded citizens had become concerned about the overcutting of forests in the state, particularly those forests that surrounded the headwaters of major rivers. If these areas were logged off and used for agriculture, the denuding of the mountainsides would greatly reduce stream flow in the rivers, disturbing the irrigation systems and city water supply systems located farther down the river valley. Because virtually all high-mountain forest areas were on public lands belonging to the U.S. government, Colorado's early conservationists began lobbying Congress to preserve and regulate the use of these critical forestlands.

In 1891 President Benjamin Harrison placed more than 1 million acres in northwestern Colorado in the White River Plateau forest reserve. It was the first forest reserve designated in Colorado, and the second one designated in the nation. By placing the White River Plateau in the forest reserve, President Harrison was in effect halting unregulated use of these lands by private citizens. Over the next two years, President Harrison designated four more forest reserves in Colorado, one of which included Pike's Peak and its surrounding foothills immediately west of Colorado Springs.

At first the forest reserves stirred little controversy in Colorado, mainly because the United States did not patrol them and enforce the forest laws. In 1897, however, the national government tightened its procedures for administering the forest reserves, putting an end to unregulated timber cutting and stock grazing. In some instances fences and corrals built by stock grazers were physically destroyed by U.S. government personnel. Immediate protests arose, and critics of the forest reserves charged that Colorado's "states' rights" were being callously overridden by the U.S. government.

Under President Theodore Roosevelt, whose "stewardship" concept called for active U.S. involvement in preserving the natural beauty of the nation, fourteen new forest reserves were created in Colorado between 1902 and 1907. By 1908 almost 16 million acres of Colorado fields and forests had been withdrawn from the public domain and placed in forest reserves.

In June 1907 a Public Lands Convention was held in Denver to oppose the expansion of the forest reserves. Speakers at the convention condemned both government interference in individual activity and the extension of national power into matters that they said should only be of state concern. These speakers were assuming, perhaps rightly, that Colorado would not be as aggressive as the U.S. government in adding large amounts of land to the forest reserves. The Public Lands Convention gave western opponents of the forest reserves an opportunity to express their antagonism toward national forest policies, yet the forest reserve program was not reversed.

There were some minor adjustments, however. Congress combined and consolidated the forest reserves into a system of "national forests." A greater emphasis was placed on wise use of national forestlands, with scientific timbering and private stock grazing permitted on a fee basis under watchful government regulation. Later on, portions of the national forests would be developed into major ski areas in Colorado. Hiking trails and camping facilities also were located on national forestlands. As the national forests came to serve agricultural and recreational uses as well as conservation goals, they became increasingly popular.

### NATIONAL PARKS

Throughout the 1880s and 1890s, professional and amateur archaeologists unearthed and carried away the Native American artifacts they found in the cliff dwellings and mesa-top pueblos at Mesa Verde. Hundreds of bowls, baskets, tools, and other items of archaeological value were removed, some of them ending up in museums as far away as Helsinki, Finland. In 1906 preservationist groups in Colorado convinced the U.S. government to create Mesa Verde National Park, both to prevent the "ruining of the ruins" and to make this ancient Native American dwelling place accessible to the public.

In 1911, southwest of Grand Junction, the national government created Colorado National Monument. This action preserved a valley filled with giant red and yellow rock formations, many of them carved by the elements into fascinating shapes.

In 1915 Colorado received its second national park. Rocky Mountain National Park consists of more than four hundred square miles of spectacular mountain scenery atop the Continental Divide northwest of Denver.

In 1932 Great Sand Dunes National Monument, now Great Sand Dunes National Park and Preserve, was created on the west slopes of the Sangre de Cristo Mountains northeast of Alamosa. In 1933, east of Montrose in western Colorado, a breathtakingly beautiful deep canyon lined with black rock was designated Black Canyon of the Gunnison National Monument.

Similar to national forests, national parks and national monuments had their critics. Once designated, these lands were removed from state and local tax rolls, thereby increasing the taxes that had to be paid by private landholders in the area. Unlike national forests, where timbering and stock grazing could be carried out on a fee basis, national parks and national monuments were closed to logging and animal raising.

With the rapid development of the automobile in the early twentieth century, the national parks and national monuments began to attract large numbers of automobile tourists to the Centennial State. The citizens of Colorado not only enjoyed the national parks and monuments themselves but also benefited from the considerable income generated by the large influx of out-of-state visitors.

Plainly, the major natural and scenic attractions in Colorado have been protected and developed by the national rather than by the state government. Colorado has a state park system and a small number of state forests, but they pale to insignificance when compared with the national parks, monuments, and forests. The pattern is so firmly established in Colorado that those wishing to preserve natural and scenic areas in the state almost automatically turn to the U.S. government for action and financing rather than to the state government.

There are two reasons for this. First, the U.S. government has greater financial resources. Second, most of the lands that now comprise Colorado's national parks, monuments, and forests were the property of the U.S. government to begin with. Thus, the U.S. government did not have to raise large sums of money to "buy" them. The United States could create national parks, monuments, and forests simply by implementing such uses on public lands it already owned.

### TRANSMOUNTAIN DIVERSION

Even before Colorado became a state in 1876, Coloradans were looking to the United States for aid in building water projects. James Belford, Colorado Territory's nonvoting member of the U.S. House of Representatives, beseeched Congress for $50,000 in aid to build dams, reservoirs, and canals in order to irrigate lands along the Arkansas, South Platte, and Cache La Poudre Rivers. Although Belford's pleas went unheeded, the precedent was set for Colorado to look to the national government for help in planning and financing major water diversion projects.

By the early twentieth century it had become obvious that large water projects in the arid West could only be financed by the U.S. government. This was particularly true of projects that involved large dams and expensive tunnels carrying water from one river valley to another. Private investors would not fund such projects because of the long waiting period before original capital was paid back. State governments lacked both the financial resources and the political will to plan and complete such gigantic public ventures.

In 1902 Congress passed the Newlands Act, the first major legislation providing for the surveying, construction, and maintenance of large water projects in sixteen western states. The new law created a reclamation fund to be financed by the sale of public lands. Once water projects were constructed and operating, water users would pay user fees that would replenish the reclamation fund and thereby provide new capital for additional projects.

Coloradans moved quickly to make use of the Newlands Act and the U.S. government agency it created, the Bureau of Reclamation. The Uncompahgre River valley in western Colorado was bordered by good agricultural land, but the river had little water. Nearby, the Gunnison River had plenty of water but surrounding lands were unfit for agricultural development. In 1904 the U.S. Bureau of Reclamation undertook the first U.S.-sponsored reclamation project in Colorado. It built a dam and reservoir on the Gunnison River, dug a six-mile-long tunnel over to the Uncompahgre River, and thereby diverted water for irrigation from the Gunnison valley to the Uncompahgre valley.

Colorado's second major U.S. reclamation project was built on the Colorado River near Grand Junction. By 1917, when the project was completed, the Bureau of Reclamation had constructed a dam and major canal stretching sixty-two miles down the Colorado River valley.

The most spectacular water projects were those that diverted water from the western slope of the Continental Divide to the eastern slope. Such projects consisted of building dams on western slope rivers, collecting the rain and melted snow in reservoirs, and then digging water tunnels from west to east under the Continental Divide so the water could be piped into eastern slope rivers. Once on the eastern slope, the water could be used to irrigate farmlands in eastern Colorado and western Kansas and Nebraska. Some of the water also could be used to add to the municipal water supplies of fast-growing cities on the Front Range.

During the national depression of the 1930s, the U.S. government took the lead in financing transmountain water diversion projects in Colorado. The most spectacular of all the U.S. government water projects was the Colorado River–Big Thompson River Water Diversion Project.[13] This ambitious plan, enacted by Congress in 1937, provided for the construction of two dams high in the Rocky Mountains near the headwaters of the Colorado River. The reservoirs created, Lake Granby and Shadow Mountain, became two of the most scenic and most popular recreational bodies of water in the state.

Water from these two reservoirs, along with water from already existing Grand Lake, flows through a tunnel under the Continental Divide in Rocky Mountain National Park. At Estes Park the falling water is used to generate electric power before flowing into the Big Thompson River on the eastern slope. The Big Thompson carries the diverted water to the South Platte River, where it is used to irrigate more than six hundred thousand acres of farmland.

Like other big U.S. government projects, the Colorado–Big Thompson Project had its critics. A nation with food surpluses should not spend millions of dollars for irrigation projects that will increase food production, said the critics. Construction of a long water tunnel and a major electrical generating plant should not be permitted in the pristine natural beauty of Rocky Mountain National Park, they complained. Initially western Colorado interests opposed diversion of western slope waters over to the eastern slope, but Congress shrewdly gained their support by including water for western Colorado irrigation projects in the total Colorado–Big Thompson package.

U.S. government planning and financing of water projects has become a permanent part of Colorado politics. In the 1960s and 1970s the Bureau of Reclamation undertook the Upper Colorado River Project and the Frying Pan–Arkansas project. The Upper Colorado River Project resulted in the construction of a series of dams, reservoirs, and power plants in the Colorado River valley in western Colorado. The largest reservoir created, Blue Mesa, immediately became a popular boating and camping destination for tourists and state residents alike.

The Frying Pan–Arkansas project diverted western slope water from the Frying Pan River to the Arkansas River in southeastern Colorado. Pueblo Reservoir, located on the Arkansas River just west of Pueblo, stored the diverted water. The reservoir, later named Lake Pueblo, was close enough to Denver and Colorado Springs that it rapidly became Colorado's most popular recreational lake. In addition to irrigating farmland in eastern Colorado and western Kansas, the "Fry-Ark" project provides substantial amounts of water for the Colorado Springs municipal water supply system.

### THE DEPRESSION AND THE NEW DEAL

The 1929 Wall Street stock market crash inaugurated a period of extended economic depression in the United States. Although not as hard hit as the more industrialized states, Colorado had its share of economic problems during the depression decade of the 1930s.

One reason Colorado was somewhat less affected by the Great Depression was that the state's principal industry, gold and silver mining, had become depressed long before the stock market crash. As previously noted, the refusal of the U.S. government to fix the prices paid for silver and gold had, by the early 1920s, reduced those two Colorado industries to mere shadows of their former selves.

Mother Nature decided to add to the distress of Colorado during the depression years. The early 1930s were years of extended drought, resulting in the great dust storms of the period. Particularly on the dry plains of eastern Colorado, winds picked up the topsoil from failed attempts at dryland farming and blew it for miles in swirling clouds of stifling dirt. The "dust bowl" was the final result of lands that might better have remained stock-grazing lands with their natural plant cover intact.

What industry there was in Colorado felt the effects of the Great Depression. In 1933 the Colorado Fuel and Iron Company, owner and operator of the large steel mills in Pueblo, went into receivership. Colorado's home-town railroad, the Denver and Rio Grande Western, went bankrupt in 1935. As industry failed, so did the banks that financed it. More than one-third of the banks in Colorado went out of business as the depression spread.

Franklin Delano Roosevelt, a Democrat, was elected president of the United States in 1932 and immediately inaugurated a series of U.S. government programs to end the Great Depression. Known collectively as the New Deal, President Roosevelt's programs pumped millions of U.S. dollars into state and local welfare and construction programs.

At the time the depression began, Colorado had neither a state sales tax nor an income tax. Anxious to avoid raising state taxes, the Colorado legislature said county and city governments should operate welfare and relief programs and get whatever additional help they needed from U.S. aid programs. The state legislature was saying, in effect, that it wanted no part of helping to pay the bills for mitigating the effects of the depression in Colorado.

Federal authorities made it clear, however, that the U.S. government would not continue to fund welfare programs in Colorado without a state contribution. Word came from Washington that if the legislature would not raise some revenue and make a contribution to local welfare programs, U.S. government funds would be "cut off."

With many a grumble about unfair pressure from the national government, the Colorado legislature met in special session in August 1933 and enacted a tax on motor vehicles, with the revenues earmarked for relief. When this law was declared unconstitutional by the Colorado Supreme

Court, the legislature held another special session in December 1933 and imposed a tax on gasoline, with a portion of the revenues set aside for public relief. It was not much of a contribution, but it was enough to keep the U.S. government welfare monies coming into Colorado.

Despite the obvious and overt lack of cooperation from the state legislature, Colorado benefited greatly from New Deal programs. The Civil Conservation Corps (CCC) had been organized to give young men jobs building roads and bridges and other facilities on U.S. government property. With its two national parks and many national forests, Colorado became the scene of much CCC activity. The CCC did not just create outdoor "leaf-raking" jobs. By building roads, bridges, hiking trails, and picnic grounds, the CCC made the national parks and forests more accessible to Colorado citizens and out-of-state tourists.

Another important U.S. government program during the Great Depression was the Works Projects Administration (WPA). With U.S. government help, a large number of public improvement projects were undertaken throughout Colorado. They included building mountain highways, erecting dams and embankments for flood control, and constructing playgrounds. The biggest WPA-style endeavor, of course, was the Colorado–Big Thompson water diversion project.

The state of Colorado benefited greatly from the New Deal. Yet Coloradans continued to express mixed feelings about the U.S. government, and as we discuss in chapter 2, Coloradans are still suspicious if not hostile toward the "feds." Colorado ranked tenth of the forty-eight states in terms of the U.S. government's per capita expenditures in the state from New Deal programs. As in most states, Colorado voted heavily Democratic during the depression and New Deal periods.

However, the two men who won the governorship during the 1930s for the Democratic Party, Alva B. Adams and Ed Johnson, positioned themselves as anti-Roosevelt and anti–New Deal. They criticized Roosevelt's policies, repeatedly warning that U.S. government aid meant U.S. government control of state and local matters. In 1940, when Democratic president Franklin D. Roosevelt ran for a third term in the White House, Colorado Democrats Adams and Johnson opposed him and threw their support to the Republican candidate, Wendell Willkie. Republican Willkie won Colorado, but Democrat Roosevelt was reelected president of the United States.

From a liberal and progressive point of view, the New Deal period represented a lost opportunity for progressive reform at the state level in Colorado. With large Democratic majorities in both houses of the state legislature, and a reform- and progress-oriented Democratic administration in power in Washington, pro–New Deal Democratic governors probably could have initiated and passed into law notable reform programs for the state. As it was, however, the two Democratic governors during the New Deal period were conservative and anti-Roosevelt, and they opposed liberal reform in Colorado.

Yet liberal and progressive voices were heard in Colorado during the New Deal period. U.S. senator Edward P. Costigan, a former Teddy Roosevelt Republican and progressive, served as a pro-FDR and pro–New Deal Democrat from 1931 to 1937.[14]

### JAPANESE AMERICANS

In 1938 a Republican, Ralph Carr, won the governorship. When the U.S. government removed Americans of Japanese ancestry from California and other West Coast states during World War II, a large group of them were interned a mile west of the small town of Granada in the Arkansas Valley in southeastern Colorado. Governor Carr supported fair treatment for the displaced Japanese Americans and worked to make their stay in Colorado as comfortable as possible under difficult conditions, yet anti–Japanese American sentiment was quite prevalent around the state.

In fact the Japanese American resettlement camp, named Camp Amache, was practically in Kansas, because Granada is only fourteen miles west of the Colorado-Kansas border. At one point, more than seven thousand internees (mostly from southern California) were detained behind fences and guarded by military police in six high watchtowers. The camp opened in 1942 and was fully operational until World War II ended in 1945.[15] Estimates suggest that more than ten thousand internees passed through this camp.

Camp Amache was one of ten Japanese internment camps that the U.S. government used to house Japanese forcefully displaced from their homes on the West Coast. These Japanese, two-thirds of whom were American citizens, were moved inland because they were thought to be security risks during the World War II conflict with Japan. The internees lived in barracks hastily constructed by the U.S. Army Corps of Engineers.

It was by all accounts a peaceful camp. Hundreds of its occupants volunteered to go into the U.S. military. Thirty-one of its former residents died while in military service to the nation that had forcibly relocated them and their families. Many were in the highly decorated 442nd Army Regiment that saw heavy combat in Italy and France.

Camp Amache was as quickly demolished in 1945 and 1946 as it had been hastily built. A small museum and an Amache Preservation Society are located in the nearby small town of Granada. The museum helps to remind the United States of this much-debated byproduct of World War II.[16]

Governor Carr worked to have Colorado treat with kindness this group of Japanese Americans who were being roughly treated by the U.S. government. His actions were in the best tradition of fairness and social justice.

Carr's defense of the civil liberties of those detained at Camp Amache doubtless hurt him when he ran for the U.S. Senate against Democrat Ed Johnson in 1942. Carr's sympathetic treatment of Japanese Americans was an issue in the election campaign. In one of the closer elections in Colorado history, Ed Johnson edged out Ralph Carr in the U.S. Senate race.[17]

Governor Carr's voice on behalf of Japanese Americans interned in Colorado was a lonely yet stalwart voice on behalf of tolerance.

### HIGHWAYS AND AIRPORTS

Transportation has always been a critical problem in Colorado. The great mountain barrier that runs through the state from north to south is a splendid scenic asset. It is also a mammoth challenge when it comes to building roads and highways. As automobiles became more widely used in the early twentieth century, it became more important for Colorado to find the money to build smooth and safe highways through its mountain and desert wilderness.

Although most of the state's population lives on the Front Range, the remainder is widely dispersed. The net result is that Colorado needs to build and maintain many miles of rural roads and has to raise the revenues needed to finance them.

In the 1920s the U.S. government began matching state expenditures for highway construction with federal funds. As a result, the U.S. highways in Colorado, principally US 40, US 50, US 85, and US 87, rapidly became the principal tourist routes into the state.

In 1929 the U.S. government constructed Trail Ridge Road through Rocky Mountain National Park. The highest continuous highway in the United States, more than five miles of Trail Ridge Road is above twelve thousand feet in altitude. From the moment it opened, Trail Ridge Road has been one of the major automobile tourist attractions in Colorado.

Trail Ridge Road illustrates, however, both the positive and the negative side of such U.S. government projects. The National Park Service closes Trail Ridge Road in the late fall, winter, and early spring because of the heavy snowfall at such high elevations. The first heavy snows in October or November mark the closing of the road until the spring thaw. It could be argued that Trail Ridge Road should be kept open all year. There are many sunny winter days in the high Rockies when a drive down such a spectacular mountain highway would be a once-in-a-lifetime experience. In addition, the Colorado State Highway Department is able, through regular plowing and sanding, to keep nearby state highways at high elevations open during the winter months.

Trail Ridge Road is an invaluable asset to the state tourism industry, yet it is an asset that belongs to the U.S. government, and thus Colorado cannot use it exactly as some Coloradans might please.

The inauguration of the U.S. interstate highway program in the 1950s made a tremendous contribution to highway construction in Colorado. It meant that 90 percent of the cost of building interstate highways through the mountains, deserts, foothills, and high plains of the state would be paid by the U.S. government.

Interstate 25, the major interstate highway running north to south through Colorado, provides a high-speed automobile connection between the major cities of the Front Range.

Interstate 70 runs east to west through the state. The eastern portion of the expressway links Denver to Kansas City and St. Louis. Originally the U.S. government did not plan to build Interstate 70 west of Denver. Once again it appeared wiser to go around Colorado's mountain barrier rather than face the engineering challenge and financial expense of building an expressway through it. Heavy lobbying by Colorado's senators and representatives, however, convinced Congress to authorize building I-70 west from Denver to Glenwood Springs, Grand Junction, and on into central Utah.

This decision has had a major impact on the development of tourism and snow skiing in Colorado. As construction progressed on I-70 into the Rocky Mountains, major ski resorts were constructed along its route. Not only could Denver area skiers access the newly developed ski areas via I-70, but out-of-state skiers could fly into Denver's airport and either take a shuttle or rent a car to take I-70 to their chosen destination. During the summertime I-70 gave Denver area residents and out-of-state tourists easier automobile access to Colorado's hiking trails and scenic mountain vistas.

In 1973 the Eisenhower Tunnel, two highway lanes wide, was completed as part of I-70. Later on a second tunnel bore widened the tunnel to four highway lanes wide. More than a mile long, the tunnel carries interstate motorists under the Continental Divide, eliminating a tortuous and dangerous drive over a high mountain pass, Loveland Pass, and shortening the driving time between Denver and many major Rocky Mountain ski resorts by up to an hour.

At the same time the U.S. government was subsidizing expensive highway and expressway building, U.S. dollars also were provided to help with airport construction and air traffic control. The rising popularity of air travel provided a splendid opportunity for Colorado. Unlike the wagon, the railroad, and the automobile, the airplane was not stopped or slowed down by the high Rocky Mountains. Commercial airliners could fly over the mountains almost as cheaply and easily as they could fly over plains and prairies.

The rise of air travel, one of the most heavily subsidized industries in the United States, greatly benefited Colorado. Travelers now could get to Denver and Colorado Springs almost as easily as to any other city in the United States. Further, because of its closeness to the geographical center of the forty-eight contiguous states, Denver began to develop as a major regional "hub" airport where transcontinental travelers could conveniently change from one airplane to another.

Many Coloradans, and a majority of Denver residents, wanted to enhance Denver's role as a major transcontinental air travel hub. In the 1980s, with some financial help from the state, Denver began the process of planning a major new airport to replace Stapleton Airport. The first step, successfully accomplished in 1989, was to get a major appropriation from the U.S. government to help with the planning and design. As would be expected, the financing package called for the U.S. government to pay a major share of the construction costs. And that is indeed what happened. Denver International Airport, known by the initials DIA, opened for business in the early 1990s.

## THE MILITARY

We have already noted how Colorado was changed by World War II. The U.S. Government located so many facilities in the state during the war and the post–World War II period that Colorado's economy and character were changed forever. Because the vast majority of these U.S. government projects were military installations, the U.S. military budget and related contracts became a major boost to the economic well-being of Colorado.

## OIL SHALE

Colorado contains a lot of the nation's usable oil shale. Most of it is on federally owned land. In the aftermath of the national energy crisis of the mid-1970s, the oil in the oil shale became a natural resource that appeared to be in great demand.

The U.S. government, in partnership with Exxon and a number of smaller entrepreneurs, launched a major effort to begin extracting oil from oil shale. It built large processing plants and brought large numbers of people into western Colorado communities in and around Rifle and Grand Junction.

Eventually the oil shale boom busted. On "Black Sunday," May 2, 1982, Exxon and other producers stopped trying to get oil from oil shale and left the state. The result was severe hardship in terms of lost jobs and people moving away from the central Western Slope.

The strains between Coloradans and federal officials were great before, during, and even after the mid-1970s oil shale boom. Congress had created the Synthetic Fuels Corporation (which lessened environmental regulations) to encourage oil shale development. Government and corporate economists and others assumed technological breakthroughs could occur that would make oil shale a major part of the nation's energy self-sufficiency campaign. But they erred. The price of oil came down and the oil shale boom never arrived. Yet the dislocations and human costs of this "boomlet" were substantial.[18]

In recent years there is once again a boom in finding ways to extract the oil and natural gas from oil shale all over Colorado. A number of voices, however, are warning Coloradans not to repeat the overspeculation that produced the great oil shale bust of 1982. "We've seen this movie before," said former Colorado governor Dick Lamm, who was in office during the first oil shale boom. "Lamm recommended that local governments in the oil-shale regions receive help from either the oil companies or the U.S. government with the costs of serving the large populations that full-scale oil-shale development would bring to certain parts of Colorado.[19]

RELATIONS WITH OTHER STATES

Colorado also must deal with the other forty-nine states. In particular, Colorado must coexist with its immediate neighbors, most of which have the same semiarid climate or are more arid. As might be expected, most of Colorado's relations with other states have to do with water.

In 1907, in the landmark case of *Kansas v. Colorado*, the United States Supreme Court ruled that it had the authority to determine the equitable appropriation of river water among the various states located along a river. In the particular case, the court ruled that Colorado would have to allow a portion of the water in the Arkansas River to flow into western Kansas.

The significance of the Supreme Court's decision was that Colorado would not be allowed to keep all the water that arose in its major rivers for its own use. Although the major source of the water was rain and snow that fell in the high Rocky Mountains of Colorado, the water would have to be shared with states downstream.

Rather than allow the United States Supreme Court to make all the decisions concerning the allocation of river water between states, Colorado began negotiating interstate compacts dividing up water supplies in interstate rivers with its neighboring states. A Colorado River compact was negotiated in 1922 with the six other states bordering that river. Shortly thereafter, Colorado and New Mexico negotiated an agreement on water flowing in the La Plata River, and Colorado and Nebraska negotiated an agreement for the South Platte River. In 1948 the division of Colorado River waters was further clarified with the negotiation and adoption of the Upper Colorado River Compact.

The interstate water compacts had an effect on water use within Colorado. The compacts required that states either use their allocations of river water or else give them to other states needing the water. This "use it or lose it" philosophy put pressure on Colorado to divert its allocation of Colorado River water from the western slope, where it was not needed, to the eastern slope, where it could be used for farming and city water supply.

### MEDICAID

Similar to other states, Colorado has faced the problem of the U.S. government providing funds for specific programs but mandating that U.S. funds be matched with state funds. An example of such a program is Medicaid, which finances health care for low-income persons and families. Medicaid is required by the U.S. government and has become the major driver in increases in the health and human services budget in Colorado.

A major study of Colorado state finances revealed that in 1970–71, the health and human services program received about $55 million. That was 13.3 percent of the total state budget. Thirty years later, however, in 2011–12, health and human services expenditures skyrocketed to $2.3 billion. That figure was 32 percent of total state expenditures.

Looked at a different way, in 1970–71 health and human services were the fourth largest recipient of state funds. By 2011–12, however, health and human services were the second largest recipient of state funds. Only kindergarten through twelfth-grade education (K–12) was getting more state money than health and human services.[20]

The long-term effect of programs like Medicaid, therefore, is to have the U.S. Congress, rather than the Colorado state legislature, determine much of what happens in the formation of the Colorado state budget. The problem is a long-term one. Because of Medicaid going up in cost every year, health and human services have become the fastest-growing component of the Colorado state budget and are slowly but surely "stealing" funds from a variety of other state services.[21]

As a result of these trends, the Colorado state legislature and governor have progressively lost some of their ability to govern the state. A big part of that loss stems from Medicaid being mandated, and thus shaped, by the U.S. government. Longer-term battles over how to comply with the Affordable Care Act of 2010 will ensure these issues will continue.

### CONCLUSIONS

A constant theme in the history of federal-state relations in Colorado has been the unending struggle by Colorado politicians and promoters to involve the U.S. government in financing the development of the state. Particularly in terms of national parks, national forests, water diversion projects, and military installations, the U.S. government has responded favorably to calls for help and is very much a presence in Colorado.

When preserving Colorado's natural beauty with national parks, national monuments, and national forests, the U.S. government has played the role of often curtailing individual interests in order to further the public good. The same moralistic and communitarian influence can be found in the many water diversion projects, and highways and airports, that were largely planned and financed by the U.S. government in Colorado. These projects represent organized community action to build public facilities that add to the commonwealth and well-being of the overall society.

By and large the critics of U.S. government involvement and control over Colorado affairs have spoken from the perspective of an individualistic and libertarian political culture. They object to government control over vast amounts of public land, which in their opinion would be better used if placed in private hands and private control. When calling for more state control and less national control, critics of the U.S. government usually are asserting states' rights because they believe the state will be more responsive to individual needs and ambitions than the U.S. government often is.[22]

Colorado has a love-hate relationship with the U.S. government. Coloradans love to have U.S. government projects, yet they hate the controls, requirements for state matching funds, and limits on individual ambitions that so often come with the U.S. dollars. Typically, however, the conflict has been resolved in favor of having the U.S. government play as active a role in Colorado as possible, coupled with grudging acceptance of the resulting controls and restrictions.

Colorado politicians ritualistically criticize the U.S. government when campaigning for office. Once elected to office, however, they spend much, if not most, of their time lobbying for more U.S. government projects (like the relatively new regional U.S. Patent Office) and protecting existing operations such as Fort Carson, the U.S. Space Command, National Renewable Energy Laboratory, and many related technology, space, and aerospace contracts, even as they seek to minimize various U.S. government restrictions and regulations.

# CHAPTER ELEVEN

# The Important Role of Local Government

State government and state politics get the lion's share of attention in state newspapers as well as in this book. Yet there are almost two thousand other governments in Colorado, and the number grows. In addition to the state government, and of course the large presence of the U.S. government, there are sixty-four counties, more than 250 cities and towns, and about fifteen hundred or more special districts for libraries, schools, fire departments, and other services. There are some Native American tribal governments as well.

Does Colorado have too many local governments? Many people believe it does. Yet local and county governments enjoy staunch loyalty from constituents. For the most part, they are here to stay, even though they are constitutionally dependent on the state government.

New local governments, particularly cities and special districts, are being formed in Colorado all the time. Two small cities, Castle Pines and Centennial, were recently incorporated in the southern portion of the Denver metropolitan area.[1]

The history of governmental life in Colorado has been a history of strong, tenacious local governments. They generally perform the same services in this state as are performed elsewhere, yet somehow the political clout of local officials (mayors, city council members, sheriffs, district attorneys, and county commissioners) is stronger in Colorado. These officials and their lobbyists in the statehouse are often viewed as some of the most influential voices in state lawmaking.

Further, in recent years, program cuts and tax cuts at both the state and federal levels greatly increased the responsibilities and tax burdens of local levels of government. Such cuts often resulted in severe reductions in local government services.

## FRONTIER GOVERNMENT

Colorado was made a territory early in 1861. A territorial legislature was elected, and during its first legislative session it divided Colorado into seventeen counties. Legal local government was underway in Colorado. When the territory became a state in 1876, provisions for local government, both counties and cities, were included in the state constitution.

Local government plays a large role in Colorado. With the U.S. government playing such a prominent role in the state, and with local government as powerful as it is, state government plays a lesser role in Colorado than in most other states. As one state government official in Colorado expressed this idea:

"In one sense, there really is no such thing as a State of Colorado. It is more a collection of powerful local governments. One additional reason for this is that Colorado is a large and geographically difficult state. State legislators mainly come to the capitol in Denver to represent their local governments [city councils, county commissioners, local school boards, etc.] rather than to strongly pursue statewide concerns."[2]

## URBAN REFORM

In 1904 conditions in Denver were producing public outrage. Gambling houses and saloons flourished. In local elections, a corrupt political machine allegedly was buying the votes that kept its supporters in office.

A major cause of the trouble, reformers believed, was that the governor and state legislators continued to directly control the bureaus and governing boards of the municipality. City reform leaders devised a series of proposals to separate Denver's government from state government and make the new city government simple and streamlined.

The first step was a constitutional amendment giving Denver the right to establish a "home rule" city government. This meant that instead of having their city structured and run by the state legislature, the voters of Denver could write and adopt a city charter creating their own unique form of city government. The constitutional amendment gave Denver a wide range of local powers, enough so that the people of Denver would look to their city government, rather than state government, to solve problems and provide a large number of basic services.

The second step was to make Denver a single city and county. Originally Denver had been located in Arapahoe County. Some local government functions were carried out by the city and some by the county. The reformers decided to reduce confusion and eliminate overlapping governmental jurisdictions by creating one body politic, the City and County of Denver. Arapahoe County continued to exist, but as a suburban and rural county outside Denver that no longer included the city.

In a stunning victory for progressive local government, these two reforms were adopted at the 1904 general election. The principle of "home rule" for local government, although limited to Denver at first, became firmly established in the Colorado Constitution. Denver would no longer be directly under the thumb of state government. A subsequent constitutional amendment extended strong home-rule powers to Colorado cities other than Denver. Over the following years, all the major cities in the state adopted their own city charters and became "home rule cities."

The adoption of the constitutional amendment granting home-rule powers to Denver in 1904 probably was the most significant event in the history of local government in Colorado. It firmly established municipal home rule as the norm rather than the exception. This broad grant of power, later extended to almost every city in the state, put Colorado cities in a position to be major policy makers and service providers.

## AN URBANIZED STATE

The vast majority of Coloradans live in densely populated cities and suburbs, mainly in the Denver-Boulder and Colorado Springs metropolitan areas.

The Denver-Boulder metropolitan area consists of seven counties. They are Adams, Arapahoe, Boulder, Broomfield, Douglas, Jefferson, and the City and County of Denver.

## THE CITY AND COUNTY OF DENVER

Similar to large cities in many states, Denver has had unique status in Colorado local government. For many years it was the only *major* combined city and county government in the state. Broomfield, a small suburban city near Denver, became a combined city and county on November 15, 2001.

As a combined city and county, Denver is similar to Philadelphia and San Francisco, which are also simultaneously cities and counties. Instead of having city officials and county officials, Denver has just one set of officials and administrators, although they carry out both city and county duties.

Although technically, local government is created and controlled by state government, Denver's unique status is provided for in the Colorado Constitution. As a result, Denver's basic structure and home-rule powers cannot be easily changed by the legislature. In fact, more than five pages of the Colorado Constitution are devoted to setting up the structure and home-rule governing powers of the City and County of Denver.

Because they are now a city and a county government combined, Denver and Broomfield have more authority and power than other municipal governments in the state. Unlike other cities in Colorado, they do not have to deal with, or compete with, a separate county government. Denver and Broomfield, each one a combined city and county, are the *only* cities in Colorado that have most major local government functions (except for schools) under their direct control.

The Denver city charter provides for a mayor-council form of city government. That means Denver has a strong mayor who is separately elected by the voters and not selected from among city council members, as in many city governments. The legislative power in Denver is vested in a thirteen-member city council. Eleven of the council members are elected from single-member districts and two are elected by the entire city. As of 2012, Denver paid its mayor $145,601 and its council members $78,173. The Denver city council president earned $87,539.

The mayor of Denver is elected by the entire city to a four-year term of office. The mayor is the undisputed head of the city's executive branch. The mayor has veto power over the city budget. It is these strong executive and budget powers that lead most observers to characterize Denver as having a "strong mayor" form of city government.

City elections are nonpartisan in Denver, so there are no party primaries. Republicans and Democrats alike run against each other in the primary, and the top two finishers, regardless of party affiliation, run against each other in the general election. If one candidate gets a majority of the vote in the primary, he or she is elected and a "runoff" is not held.

The mayor of Denver is almost always a Democrat, and Democrats customarily enjoy a large majority on the city council. Only rarely does a strong Republican candidate come along and make a serious challenge to the Democratic Party for control of the mayor's office or a seat on the city council.

Because almost 60 percent of state residents live in the Denver metropolitan area, the mayor of Denver can become a highly visible and influential figure in Colorado politics. For over a hundred years, however, no Denver mayor was elected governor of the state. Denver mayor John Hickenlooper turned the trick in 2010. On January 11, 2011, he walked across Civic Center Park in Denver from the mayor's office in the City and County Building up to the state capitol, where he was inaugurated governor on the west-facing capitol steps.

Denver for years was the largest and most densely populated city in Colorado. Not surprisingly, it is usually the first local government in the state to encounter "urban problems." It is also usually the first to propose solutions to them. As one member of the city council expressed it:

"Denver is on the cutting edge of city problems in Colorado. For instance, Denver was the first city in the state to identify an air pollution problem from people burning wood in home fireplaces. Our law controlling wood burning in home fireplaces was the first one in Colorado and was soon copied by many other cities and counties in the state."[3]

Although Denver gets the big city problems in Colorado first, and usually tries to solve them first, other cities have similar problems. Typical are deteriorating roads and bridges, high crime rates in downtown neighborhoods, and hot debates over whether to provide city subsidies in order to attract new industry.

Due to its historical role as a powerful local government in Colorado, Denver traditionally has taken the initiative in providing various public facilities that serve all the state rather than just Denver. The Denver Convention Center, Sports Authority Field at Mile High (where professional football is played), the Pepsi Center (where professional basketball and professional hockey are played and rock concerts are performed), Coors Field (where professional baseball is played), and Denver International Airport (the "hub" airport for the entire Rocky Mountain West) are all examples of projects initiated by the City and County of Denver that benefit all of Colorado.

The best example of Denver's leadership role in the growth and development of Colorado is Denver International Airport. By the mid-1980s the city's old Stapleton Airport was one of the busiest regional airports in the United States. Unable to expand because of the adjacent Rocky Mountain Arsenal, a U.S. government facility, Stapleton was becoming overcrowded and a source of airline delays, particularly on bad weather days.

Denver officials took the lead in developing the new airport for the region. Located twenty miles northeast of Stapleton Airport on vacant land in Adams County, which Denver annexed, this new airport has sufficient space to accommodate anticipated air traffic growth in the Denver area during the early years of the twenty-first century.

Although both the U.S. government and the State of Colorado contributed funds to begin the construction of the new airport, and Colorado governor Roy Romer supported it strongly from his "bully pulpit," the major planning, financing, and promoting of the project, the largest public works project in Colorado history up to that time, were all undertaken by the City and County of Denver.

### THE "CITY-STATE" OF DENVER

With almost 60 percent of the population of Colorado living in the Denver metropolitan area, and Denver providing such strong governmental leadership in the metropolitan area, it could be argued that Colorado is not really a state but is actually the "city-state" of Denver. This viewpoint holds that the state government does not provide leadership, but Denver decides what will and will not be happening of significance in Colorado.

A few years ago, the *Denver Post* waxed ecstatic over the leadership provided to Colorado by the citizens of metropolitan Denver. The newspaper noted that the following projects, most of which would benefit the entire state, were approved by voters and elected officials in the Denver area:

- Planning and building one of the world's largest airports (Denver International).

- Constructing one of the finest convention facilities in America.

- Financing major improvements in the city's main library and its branches.

- Providing tax funds to support museums, the city zoo, community theaters, musical groups, and other artistic organizations throughout the metropolitan area.

- Authorizing a major bond issue to finance better roads and public facilities.

- Agreeing to pay a metropolitan-wide sales tax to build a major league baseball stadium for Denver's new National League team, the Colorado Rockies.

- Attracting the nation's best retailers into a massive new regional mall.

- Working hard to clean up the air, which previously had been known as some of the most polluted in the United States.

- Investing nearly $200 million in the Denver core city school system.

With the boosterism expected of a hometown newspaper, the *Denver Post* concluded: "No other city [and its suburbs] in the nation has so dramatic a record of believing in itself."[4]

Three of the glamorous and commodious major projects initiated by the city, the Denver Convention Center, the Pepsi Center, and Sports Authority Field at Mile High, had an unanticipated political payoff for Denver. They played a key role in Denver being able to attract the 2008 Democratic National Convention to the city. The headquarters for the convention was at the Denver Convention Center. The actual convention itself met in the Pepsi Center. The acceptance speech by the Democratic presidential nominee, Barack Obama, was held before a giant cheering crowd, mostly Coloradans, at Sports Authority Field at Mile High.

### CITIES AND TOWNS OTHER THAN DENVER

Denver and Broomfield are the only cities specifically provided for *by name* in the Colorado Constitution. All the other cities and towns are provided for by general legislation passed by the legislature, or by a general grant of home-rule power to cities and towns contained in the state constitution.

Cities and towns that organize under laws passed by the state legislature are called "statutory" cities and towns. If *less* than two thousand citizens in a community in Colorado want to incorporate, they are required by state law to form a "town." If *more* than two thousand citizens want to incorporate, they are required to form a "city." These "statutory" towns and cities have a government structure and an array of city government powers that have been predetermined for them by the state legislature in Denver.

Instead of becoming statutory cities, however, most major cities in Colorado have chosen instead to become *home rule* cities. Under the home-rule provisions of the state constitution, a charter commission is elected to write a city charter that structures a city's own particular form of government. The proposed charter is then adopted by a majority vote of the citizens of the city.

### Towns

There are about 180 statutory towns in Colorado. By state law, they are governed by a six-member town council and a mayor. The mayor presides at council meetings but has none of the executive powers associated with a strong mayor form of government. The council hires the executive officials needed to run the government, such as the town clerk and the town marshal.

Theoretically the town council could hire a professional *town manager* to administer the town government, yet there is no specific provision for

Table 12. Colorado's Twenty Most-Populous Cities in 2010

| Rank | City | Population |
|---|---|---|
| 1 | Denver | 600,158 |
| 2 | Colorado Springs | 416,427 |
| 3 | Aurora | 325,078 |
| 4 | Fort Collins | 143,986 |
| 5 | Lakewood | 142,980 |
| 6 | Thornton | 118,772 |
| 7 | Pueblo | 106,595 |
| 8 | Arvada | 106,433 |
| 9 | Westminster | 106,114 |
| 10 | Centennial | 100,377 |
| 11 | Boulder | 97,385 |
| 12 | Greeley | 92,889 |
| 13 | Longmont | 86,270 |
| 14 | Loveland | 66,859 |
| 15 | Grand Junction | 58,566 |
| 16 | Broomfield | 55,889 |
| 17 | Castle Rock | 48,231 |
| 18 | Commerce City | 45,913 |
| 19 | Parker | 45,297 |
| 20 | Littleton | 41,737 |

*Source*: U.S. Census, 2010.

this in state law. Although there is a provision in the state constitution for *home rule* towns, virtually all the towns in Colorado have chosen to remain statutory towns.

### Cities

Only about fifteen of Colorado's some 260 cities are statutory cities. All the other 245 or so cities have opted for home rule, adopting their own particular structure of city government. Most of the principal cities in Colorado other than Denver, such as Aurora, Boulder, Fort Collins, Grand Junction, Greeley, Lakewood, and Pueblo, have all adopted a variation of the *council manager* form of city government.

In 2010 Colorado Springs citizens voted to shift from the council manager form to the strong mayor form used in Denver. Unlike Denver, however, Colorado Springs did not merge with El Paso County and become a unified city and county. The major support for converting to strong mayor in Colorado Springs came from a major housing developer who contributed more than $700,000 of his own money to the election campaign for approval.[5]

Under the council manager form, legislative power is held by a small city council, usually composed of seven or nine council members. In some cases council members are elected from single-member districts. In other instances they are elected at large by the city's voting citizens.

The responsibility for running the city government is given to a city manager, a trained professional who hires all other employees required to provide city services. The city manager is hired by the city council and can be fired by the city council. The council enacts the city's laws and sets general city policies. It is the city manager's job to enforce the laws and implement the council's policies.

In most home-rule cities in Colorado, a mayor is elected to preside over city council meetings. In some cases the mayor is elected by the voters. In other instances the city council elects one of its own members to be mayor. Under the council manager form of municipal government, however, the mayor has no executive or administrative powers. The day-to-day responsibility of running the city government belongs to the city manager, not to the mayor.

The mayor's power and visibility can be significant, however. Often the mayor in a council manager city will take the lead in building support for important programs, such as reducing crime, undertaking major public improvements (performance halls and sports stadiums), luring new industry and jobs to the city, and so on.

Perhaps the most important characteristic of home-rule cities in Colorado is the broad grant of governing power that is given to them by the state constitution. They are given all powers over "municipal affairs." In effect, this means that Colorado home-rule cities rarely need to go to the state legislature to obtain a grant of power to solve a new problem or undertake a new program of action.

Equally important, the broad grant of power to home-rule cities contained in the Colorado Constitution limits the ability of the state legislature to interfere in city matters. The Colorado courts decide when an action is "municipal" in character or is of "statewide concern" and can be regulated by the state legislature. By and large, Colorado courts have interpreted the term "municipal affairs" broadly, encouraging home-rule cities to govern themselves and reducing attempts by the state legislature to make policy for home-rule cities.

In practice, home-rule cities are an important element in Colorado government. With their broad grant of power firmly anchored in the state constitution, they have the ability to solve a wide range of problems at the city level. As a result, the average city dweller in Colorado is more likely to turn to city government rather than state government to solve local problems.

An argument can be made that municipal government is the most important form of state and local government in Colorado.

## ANNEXATION

In 1965 the state legislature enacted a law giving strong annexation powers to Colorado cities. The law gave a city the power to annex any adjacent parcel of land (not located in another city or town) if one-sixth of the boundary line of the parcel was contiguous to the city boundary line. In the case of large parcels of land that failed to meet the one-sixth contiguity requirement, these parcels could be broken up into smaller parcels that did have one-sixth contiguity and then could be annexed parcel by parcel.

Because Colorado is a semiarid state, land cannot be developed for homes, stores, office buildings, and factories unless water is available. In Colorado, domestic water systems mainly are owned and controlled by the cities. Landowners who want to develop their land thus are most anxious to have it annexed into a city, thereby guaranteeing them access to city water supplies and sewer services.

The liberal annexation law in Colorado coupled with the desire of landowners to get city water and sewer service resulted in a wave of urban annexations from the late 1960s to around 2005. Except for Denver, Colorado's major cities rapidly annexed surrounding vacant land. Landowners, after getting the land annexed, developed it for housing, shopping centers, and office parks.

Unfortunately for the City and County of Denver, it is surrounded by suburban incorporated municipalities and thus has few opportunities to annex vacant land into Denver. The ability to annex land into Denver was further limited by the 1974 Poundstone Amendment to the state constitution, which required a vote of the people being annexed before their area could be taken into Denver.

Because of this ability to annex their surrounding suburbs (when property owners want to be annexed), most Colorado cities do not have the urban problems associated with Denver and many other large cities in the United States. Through the annexation process, they have been able to increase their property tax income and sales tax income by absorbing the housing projects and commercial establishments developing on their periphery.

The result of liberal city annexation laws was that by 2005, Colorado's cities (other than Denver) contained within their city limits most of the people living in the metropolitan area. Instead of being surrounded by uncooperative suburbs, these cities had long since annexed these communities. This meant that many cities outside the Denver metropolitan area could take a "metropolitan" approach to solving problems because most of the people living in the metropolitan area also lived inside the city boundary line.

## COUNTIES

Colorado has sixty-four counties. It has more counties than two states that are much larger in population, California and New York. Perhaps the major characteristic of Colorado counties is their diversity. San Juan and Hinsdale Counties in southwestern Colorado both have less than 850 permanent residents. Denver and El Paso Counties along Interstate Highway 25, however, each have well over six hundred thousand residents. Now that is diversity!

Colorado has about ten counties with less than four thousand residents each. At the other end of the spectrum, about eleven counties have more than one hundred thousand residents each.

In Colorado as in many other states, counties were intended to be administrative units of the state and were organized according to laws passed by the legislature. Except for Denver and Broomfield, which are combined city-counties and possess extensive home-rule powers, counties enforce and administer state laws and do not enact legislation in their own right.

As in many other states, however, counties in Colorado have evolved into something more than "administrative units of the state." For the large number of rural Coloradans who do not reside in a city or a town, their county government is viewed as "local government" rather than a branch of state government.

The state legislature has given Colorado's sixty-four counties plenty of work to do. They finance and operate the district courts, providing courtroom and jail facilities. The district attorney's office, which supplies the prosecutors for district courts, is also financed by counties. County governments also conduct state elections, title automobiles and sell license plates, build and maintain county roads, and administer state welfare programs.

Most counties are typically administered by a three-person board of county commissioners elected in partisan elections. Both political parties successfully elect commissioners. In Denver and Broomfield, now combined city-county governments, the city council members function as county commissioners.

Table 13. Colorado's Twenty Most-Populous Counties in 2010

| Rank | County | County seat | County population |
|------|--------|-------------|-------------------|
| 1 | El Paso | Colorado Springs | 622,263 |
| 2 | Denver | Denver | 600,158 |
| 3 | Arapahoe | Littleton | 572,003 |
| 4 | Jefferson | Golden | 534,543 |
| 5 | Adams | Brighton | 441,604 |
| 6 | Larimer | Fort Collins | 299,630 |
| 7 | Boulder | Boulder | 294,567 |
| 8 | Douglas | Castle Rock | 285,465 |
| 9 | Weld | Greeley | 252,825 |
| 10 | Pueblo | Pueblo | 159,063 |
| 11 | Mesa | Grand Junction | 146,723 |
| 12 | Garfield | Glenwood Springs | 56,389 |
| 13 | Broomfield | Broomfield | 55,889 |
| 14 | Eagle | Eagle | 52,197 |
| 15 | La Plata | Durango | 51,334 |
| 16 | Fremont | Cañon City | 46,824 |
| 17 | Montrose | Montrose | 41,276 |
| 18 | Delta | Delta | 30,952 |
| 19 | Morgan | Fort Morgan | 28,159 |
| 20 | Summit | Breckenridge | 27,994 |

*Source*: U.S. Census, 2010.

Counties with more than seventy thousand residents can expand the board of county commissioners to five members. El Paso County, which contains the city of Colorado Springs, was one of the first counties to do so.

The state constitution requires each county to have a number of elected officials. These include the county clerk, sheriff, treasurer, surveyor, assessor, and coroner. The county attorney may be elected or appointed. If it wishes, a county may elect a superintendent of schools to supervise public education in the county, although the schools will be directly administered by elected local school boards.

A limited form of county home rule is available in Colorado. An elected charter commission draws up a proposed county charter, which is then approved or disapproved by county voters.

County home rule in Colorado, however, only allows for county citizens to determine the *structure* of county government. It does not increase the *power and authority* of county government or give home-rule counties the power to pass county laws. Very few of the sixty-four counties have voted to become home-rule counties and structure their own form of county government.[6]

One of the major problems with county government in Colorado is that the state legislature passes the same laws for counties with more than one hundred thousand residents as it does for counties with fewer than four thousand residents. This is particularly difficult when the lightly populated counties are rural and the heavily populated counties are suburban and located on the Front Range.

County governments are represented in Denver by Colorado Counties, Inc. This lobbying organization has to serve both the large and the small counties at the same time, but it generally takes a position in favor of urging the state legislature to modernize county government.

According to one Colorado Counties, Inc., official, "county government is the most archaic form of local government in Colorado. When it comes to reforming and modernizing county government, the Colorado state legislature needs to be dragged kicking and screaming into the twentieth century."[7]

## CITY-COUNTY RELATIONSHIPS

It is impossible to fully comprehend local government in Colorado without looking at the way city and county governments relate to each other.

One reason the state legislature has not modernized county government is that there is a tacit assumption that as urban populations develop within Colorado counties, those urban populations will be incorporated into new cities or will be annexed into existing cities. In other words, county governments do not need to be given the power to solve urban problems because, under Colorado's strong municipal incorporation and annexation laws, all significant urban populations in the state will eventually be living in cities.

There is no question that city and town annexations are a key element in city-county relations in Colorado. In most instances, county governments register no complaints about the annexation of urbanizing portions of a county into a city.

There are times, however, when county and city interests conflict over annexation. Some cities carry out "flagpole" annexations that reach far away from the city line to take in a new shopping center or other large taxpaying facility. The county government is left to plan and solve urban problems in the large land area "skipped over" by the flagpole annexation.[8]

In some cases county governments face the problem of cities racing each other to see which city can annex the most land. Instead of growing in a logical and well-timed fashion, cities begin annexing large amounts of raw land for no other purpose than to make certain that a competing city does not annex it. Under such conditions, it is difficult for a county government to competently plan for future population growth in the county.

The biggest problem with city-county relationships in Colorado is that many of the urbanizing areas are not being annexed by cities. These thickly populated areas have to receive urban services from archaic county governments. In some cases, real estate developers want to develop county land that is not adjacent to an existing city. The developers go ahead and build on the land, adhering only to county planning and zoning rules, which tend to be less strict than city rules.

Another problem was created by Poundstone II, a constitutional amendment that required a vote of the people to be annexed when a city wanted to annex adjoining communities. Developed areas remained under county services if their citizens refused to vote them into an adjoining city.

Many counties in Colorado, particularly those on the Front Range and near resort communities in the Rocky Mountains, are beginning to experience a phenomenon known as *low-density urban sprawl.*

People are building homes on large lots, five acres and larger, and then are living urban lives in what appear to be rural environments. In some cases real estate developers are building and selling large subdivisions composed of homes on five-acre lots. Far from any city that might annex them, these "urban" developments have to be served by county government.

On the Eastern Plains adjacent to the Front Range, such developments could be called "ranchurbia." In the foothills and mountains near Colorado's major ski areas, they are referred to as "resort sprawl."

The people moving into these low-density communities want a rural lifestyle but also demand high-quality urban services, such as roads cleared of snow in the winter, fire and police protection, and more. If the county commissioners are not already providing such urban services in these urban-style developments, they soon find themselves under political pressure to provide them.

Colorado counties, particularly those on the Front Range and in the ski resort areas in the mountains, will continue to experience urban development that is not incorporated or annexed into cities. This means that these counties, designed mainly to govern rural agricultural areas, will increasingly engage in the provision of urban services to large urban populations. In order to permit urbanizing Colorado counties to adequately provide such services, the state legislature should, many people believe, modernize county government.

## SCHOOL DISTRICTS

Public schools in Colorado are governed by elected school boards that are completely separate from city and county government. Local school boards not only set school policies but also are in charge of raising the required revenues to support the local school system. School boards thus determine the school portion of local property-tax rates and, with the approval of local voters, float bond issues for the construction of new schools and school facilities. TABOR restrictions apply to school districts, so taxes to support schools cannot be raised without a vote of the registered voters in the school district.

School board members are elected in nonpartisan elections to a four-year term of office. They are considered citizen volunteers and serve without pay. A president of the school board is elected from among its own membership, but the president's only responsibility is to preside at school board meetings. The board hires a salaried administrator to take charge of the day-to-day operation of the school system.

As has been the case in most other states, there has been a movement in recent years to reduce the number of school districts in Colorado. In many counties, school districts have been combined into larger districts. At the same time, schools have been consolidated into a smaller number of larger schools.

In some instances there is only one school district for an entire county. Colorado has more than 170 school districts spread over its sixty-four counties.

Colorado has been a progressive state when it comes to experimenting with reform of public schools. In 1994 the state legislature passed "one of the country's first open-enrollment laws, allowing parents to cross [school] district lines to find a better fit for their children—if there are openings. . . . And in the early 1990s, Colorado became one of the first states to embrace charter schools."[9]

## SPECIAL DISTRICTS

Under state law, Coloradans can organize to provide themselves specific government services by creating "special districts." These districts provide such services as water supply, sewage treatment, agricultural irrigation, fire protection, library services, road building, and regional mass transit.

Citizens who wish to form a special district begin by circulating a petition that describes the boundaries of the district and the services it will provide. If a sufficient number of citizens sign the petition, a special election is held in which the proposed district must be approved by a majority of the voters living within it. If created, the special district is governed by a five-member elected board of directors.

Special districts are often used to provide water systems for rural housing developments, particularly in resort areas in the Colorado mountains. Housing developers organize the water districts and then, after the homes are built and sold, the residents of the housing development take over the management of the special district and tax themselves to pay off the bonds. Note that this use of the special district puts the burden of paying for providing water to the new housing development on the future owners rather than the housing developer.

The number of new special districts in Colorado has rapidly increased in recent decades. As more and more people, old residents and newcomers alike, opt for a rural lifestyle in areas not served by established municipal water and sewer systems, housing developers have turned to special districts to provide these essential services.

In some instances sales lag in the housing development and the developer pulls out. When this happens, the special district providing water either goes bankrupt or the limited number of people who have moved into the development pay excessively high water charges.

### METROPOLITAN GOVERNANCE

Cities and counties in Colorado have attempted to solve problems on a metropolitan-wide basis, particularly in the Denver metropolitan area. Denver and its surrounding suburbs have undertaken a number of joint efforts to provide needed services and cultural amenities throughout the entire Denver region.

### *Regional Sewer Service and Flood Control*

One example of metropolitan government in Denver is the Metropolitan Denver Sewage Disposal District No. 1, which handles sewage treatment and disposal throughout the Denver area. There also is the Urban Drainage and Flood Control District, which works to reduce and control flooding on the South Platte River as it flows through the Denver region.

### *The Denver Regional Transportation District*

The best example of metropolitan government in Denver is the Regional Transportation District (RTD), a special district that operates the bus system. Originally known and promoted as "The Ride," the RTD mainly provides bus service between downtown Denver and its surrounding suburban communities. The RTD has the authority to collect taxes throughout the participating portion of the metropolitan area to finance and operate its bus services. All tax increases to support service expansions, however, must be approved by the voters.

Legislation setting up the Denver RTD was passed by the Colorado legislature in 1969. Shortly thereafter, in 1974, the RTD purchased existing Denver bus lines from the City and County of Denver and expanded them into a regional system that included the development of "park-n-ride" parking lots for downtown-bound bus commuters.

### Denver's Light Rail

In 1994 the RTD inaugurated *light rail* passenger train service across downtown Denver and then out to the southern suburbs of Englewood and Littleton. The "light rail," as everyone called it, was an instant success, with the number of riders exceeding early estimates and passenger traffic growing from year to year. The light rail vehicles were nimble enough to navigate city streets in downtown Denver but then go fifty miles per hour on a private right of way when they rolled out into the suburbs.

At the same time the T-REX highway project expanded traffic lanes in the southern approach of Interstate 25 into Denver, the light rail was extended in a parallel right of way out to the Denver Tech Center and beyond.

By the time this project was completed in 2006, the light rail had become so popular that voters in the Denver metropolitan area voted to finance the construction of rail transit out of Denver in all four directions of the compass. Light rail lines and commuter railroads (so-called heavy rail) were planned to go west to the city of Golden, northeast to Denver International Airport, and to a number of other suburban destinations. This ambitious program, known as FasTracks, was to be completed sometime around 2020.

The light rail commuter train service in Denver once again illustrated the dependence of Colorado on financing from the U.S. government. Much of the cost of building and equipping the light rail system was paid for by the Urban Mass Transit Administration in Washington DC.

RTD was designing the light rail system to be a metropolitan planning tool as well as an urban transportation system. The various stops on the light rail lines, and future stops on the heavy rail commuter lines, were designed to be high-density community centers with apartment residences, office buildings, and commercial areas clustered around the transit station and its parking lot.

This "transit-oriented development," or TOD, would help to revive declining inner suburbs as well as provide for well-planned newer suburbs developing farther out the line. Many designers referred to these pedestrian-friendly TOD communities, with their close mixture of office, residential, and commercial uses, as the "New Urbanism."[10]

Lauren Martens, executive director of Transit Alliance, a coalition of transit-oriented Denver-area business and resident groups, described RTD's light rail and heavy rail plans as "part of a smart-growth effort for dealing with a million more people in the [Denver] metro area in 20 years."[11]

### Denver's Union Station

An additional achievement of metropolitan government in Denver was the RTD project for turning Denver's historic Union Station into a rail and bus transportation hub with easy transfer from one mode of travel to another (intermodal connectivity).

Union Station was a large and commodious relic from the great days of intercity passenger train service in the United States. Its Romanesque arches, beautiful glass-paned windows, and stately rooftop clocks were a wonderful reminder of an age when most intercity travel was by passenger train. It was an age when big architect-designed passenger stations reflected the monetary success of the railroad industry.

By 2000, however, Union Station in Denver was down to just two Amtrak passenger trains a day. The eastbound California Zephyr, running between Oakland, California, and Chicago, Illinois, stopped in Denver in the early evening. Its westbound counterpart picked up and left off passengers in Denver in the morning.

Operating through the Denver Union Station Project Authority, the RTD built a new light rail station, an underground bus terminal, and a commuter rail (heavy rail) station on twenty acres of ground surrounding the old Union Station. In addition, the Sixteenth Street Mall bus line was extended to the project so that commuters coming into Denver by bus, light rail, and heavy rail could catch the free mall bus shuttle and ride into the heart of Denver's commercial downtown. Amtrak intercity passenger trains continued to stop near the old Union Station.

The old Union Station building was rehabilitated but for much more than only two passenger trains a day. Space for retailers and other commercial uses were designed into the interior of the building without disturbing its historic external appearance.[12] A plan was being developed and implemented to turn part of the original building into a new downtown hotel.[13]

## Special Districts for Metropolitan Goals

By the first decade of the twenty-first century it was clear that the Denver region was mainly using special districts to achieve metropolitan-wide goals. A new baseball stadium, a new football stadium, the arts and culture program, a bus and commuter rail system, and an intermodal downtown transit center and hotel at Union Station had all been achieved through the governmental technique of creating a special district. It was reasonable to expect that the Denver area would continue to use special districts well into the future in order to solve metropolitan problems.

The success of special districts for achieving metropolitan-wide solutions to problems in Denver was mainly due to the willingness of citizens throughout the metro area to vote to tax themselves to support the various special districts financially. It is important to note that suburban residents of the Denver metropolitan area appeared quite willing to tax themselves to build facilities that were located in and centered around downtown Denver, even though these facilities were not located in their own suburban city or county and they would have to transport themselves downtown to use them.

## Front Range Transit

Coloradans have wondered whether a special district could eventually be created in Colorado to provide express bus or commuter rail service throughout the entire Front Range rather than only in the Denver Metropolitan Area. They speculate whether it will be possible someday to ride quality public transit from Fort Collins to Denver or Greeley to Pueblo. Such a program would be governmentally possible if not politically possible through a special district.[14]

Another area where a special district could be used to provide higher-speed bus or passenger train service would be from Denver International Airport through downtown Denver and out the Interstate 70 corridor to major ski areas such as Breckinridge and Vail. Of course the state government could organize and operate such services if the state legislature voted to do so. However, there is reason to think that with its current successful use in the Denver metropolitan area, the special district will end up being the way to go. One of the greatest merits of the special district over a statewide program is that only the taxpayers in the limited area receiving the service have to pay for it.

## REDEVELOPMENT IN OTHER CITIES

Denver was not the only city in the state working hard to redevelop its community with modern facilities. In the city of Pueblo, 110 miles south of Denver on the Front Range, a number of projects were undertaken under the leadership of Allan Blomquist, a regional planner.

Brought into being were a fine arts and conference center, redevelopment of the business section of downtown Pueblo, a biker-hiker trail running through the community along Fountain Creek and the Arkansas River, and development of city and state parks in connection with the construction of Pueblo Reservoir, the largest recreational body of water in Colorado.[15]

Pueblo also redeveloped its central downtown area by constructing a "river walk," a long artificial canal lined with smart shops and various forms of public entertainment. In the summer, visitors could ride tour boats up and down the canal. The project was inspired by the famous downtown river walk in San Antonio, Texas.

In Colorado Springs, a declining industrial and residential area southwest of downtown was cleared out and replaced with an inner-city park. The formally landscaped lawns had beautiful views of Pike's Peak to the west. The park also serves as a central meeting point for the city's expanding bike trail system.

The park is located close to the confluence of Monument and Fountain Creeks, the only two streams in the area that run with water all year long. The park was named America the Beautiful Park in honor of the popular national song "America the Beautiful," which was composed in Colorado Springs following a trip to the top of Pike's Peak by its author, Katharine Lee Bates.

Colorado Springs followed the lead of Denver and created a special district, a regional transportation authority, to take over road building and road maintenance in the Colorado Springs metropolitan area. The Pike's Peak Rural Transportation Authority, approved by the voters and financially supported by a dedicated one-cent sales tax, soon had its own fleet of dump trucks and other road building and maintenance equipment out repairing area roads and highways.[16]

## THE DISAPPEARING COUNTY COURTHOUSE

As county governments along the Front Range grew in size along with their expanding populations, the old and venerable county courthouse proved increasingly inadequate to house the many new employees and functions of county government.

El Paso County solved the problem by abandoning its historic 1904 courthouse altogether and giving it to the city of Colorado Springs for its local city museum, called the Pioneers' Museum. County functions and employees moved into a brand new judicial building, a multipurpose building for the county clerk that included a public assembly hall, and into a variety of rented offices in downtown Colorado Springs.

In 2011, however, much to the chagrin of downtown business interests, the county began locating some of its county offices far from downtown in a former high-tech factory building located in an industrial park in northern Colorado Springs. It took heavy lobbying and dramatic appeals by downtown interests "to keep [at least part of] the county seat downtown."[17]

In Denver, the courts and the mayor's office remained in the well-known City and County Building across Civic Center Park facing the state capitol. Many city-county offices, however, were moved to a new municipal building named for former Denver mayor Wellington Webb.

Adams County, the suburban county located northeast of the City and County of Denver, decided to build a completely new county government center and use it as the economic base for a $1 billion development project named Adams Crossing. The $103 million Adams County Government Center was designed to house five hundred employees and be the cornerstone of a future community in which twenty-two thousand people will live and work by 2020.

Back in the county seat of Brighton, Colorado, the existing County Administration Building, built in 1976, was turned over to the city of Brighton for its employees, who previously had been crowded into an old city hall.

The linking of the new, built-from-scratch Adams County Government Center to a major private development project could possibly serve as a model for other counties in Colorado with rapidly expanding populations. When completely built, Adams Crossing was expected to have "2 million square feet of commercial space, 1 million square feet of retail space, 2,500 multi-family homes, 750 single-family homes, and 100 acres of open space and trails."[18]

## THE IMPACT OF TABOR

The initiated constitutional amendment known as the Taxpayers' Bill of Rights (TABOR) applied its stringent financial limitations to local governments in Colorado as well as the state government. That means that cities, counties, and school boards cannot raise taxes without a vote of the people. It also means these governments must operate within strict rules that limit annual budget increases to the previous year's budget plus adjustments for population growth and inflation.

The impact of TABOR on local government in Colorado is hotly debated. Some argue the requirement for a vote on all tax increases has made city councils and boards of county commissioners hesitant to send to the voters the tax increases needed to maintain a decent level of public services in the community. Others cite the considerable number of tax increases that have been approved in various cities and counties throughout the state as proof that TABOR is working exactly as the voters who passed it intended.

In many instances, city, county, and school district voters have taken advantage of an important provision in the TABOR constitutional amendment. By a vote of the people, local governments can escape the required limits on revenues and keep funds that otherwise would have to be returned to the taxpayers. When such a vote is successful, a local government entity is said to have "de-Bruced." The name comes from Douglas Bruce, author and chief supporter of TABOR from Colorado Springs.

Also hotly debated is the relationship of TABOR to the sharp economic downturn that hit Colorado and the United States in 2008. Opponents of TABOR argue that its limitations on taxes and spending, which have been in effect since TABOR was adopted by the voters in 1992, put cities, counties, and school districts in poor financial shape when the Great Recession hit in 2008. The result was that local governments, faced with rapidly declining sales tax revenues due to the recession, joined the state in the need to severely cut back services. TABOR had robbed them, so the argument goes, of the financial reserves that might have helped them through the economic difficulties of the economic recession of 2008.

TABOR supporters argue back, however, that TABOR helped local governments weather the economic downturn that began in 2008. TABOR put the brakes on cities, counties, and school districts raising taxes and greatly expanding services. Thus there were fewer local government programs that needed to be cut back when the Great Recession hit.

Particularly hard hit by the combination of TABOR and the Great Recession was the city of Colorado Springs. In 1991, in an effort to build support for his statewide TABOR adoption campaign in 1992, Douglas Bruce persuaded the voters of Colorado Springs to put a local form of TABOR in the Colorado Springs city charter. Colorado Springs thus was the only local government in Colorado to have its finances limited by both a statewide and a local version of TABOR.

By the year 2010, the City of Colorado Springs was making an undesirable reputation for itself because of the considerable number of public services, many considered basic necessities, that were pruned out of the city budget. Most notable was when the streetlights went out. The city turned off and marked with a bright orange marker one-third of the streetlights, even those on major arterial streets. This event was covered in detail by national news media such as ABC News and the *Wall Street Journal*.

Other cuts in Colorado Springs were just as noteworthy. Trash cans were removed from city parks because there was no money to pay workers to empty them. Most of the city's swimming pools were closed during the summer of 2010, depriving children of their neighborhood swim center. In March of 2010, the city stopped repairing potholes and cracks in city streets. Colorado Springs's beautiful landscaped medians on its major downtown streets went unwatered and the grass unmowed.

Stung by the bad national publicity, the Colorado Springs City Council at least began to turn the streetlights back on and resumed maintaining the landscaped street medians in 2011. On the last day of 2010, the *Denver Post* noted that the lights going out in Colorado Springs was the second-most clicked-on story on its website. More than 315,425 people throughout cyberspace read about the city's financial woes and Draconian service cuts.[19]

The combination of TABOR tax and revenue limits during the 1990s and the 2000 and 2008 economic recessions left Colorado local governments in woeful financial shape. The City and County of Denver was facing a $100 million cut in its annual budget from 2011 to 2012. Temporary fixes for the city budget had mainly been used up by the effects of TABOR. "Those are all temporary fixes," said Ed Scholz, Denver's budget chief. "We are running out of options. Every year there are less and less triggers to pull."[20]

In El Paso County (Colorado Springs), the Health Department budget was cut in half from 2001 to 2010. As a result of the severe reduction in health funds, restaurant inspections were curtailed and swimming pool inspections were suspended. The *Colorado Springs Gazette* reported: "Programs that include sexually transmitted disease surveillance, meth-lab cleanups, teen suicide prevention and air and water quality monitoring have been axed or truncated."[21]

In Colorado's third largest city, the Denver suburb of Aurora, fiscal problems created by the combination of TABOR and the economic downturn forced the closure of four of the city's seven libraries.[22]

## LOCAL GOVERNMENT AND LAND USE

Colorado is regarded by everyone as a beautiful place. The state is filled with high mountains, rolling prairies, pine-forested foothills, scenic river valleys, mesa tops, and rocky canyons. As the population increases, how-

ever, housing developments and shopping centers continually encroach on
and invade many of the most beautiful parts of the state.

Because of this, "land use" planning is one of the most important, and
controversial, political and governmental issues in Colorado.

Land use is the process whereby governments determine how land will
be used. Through the twin processes of planning and zoning, governments
adopt general plans for how land will be used and then zone specific parcels of land for specific purposes.

The three most important zones are residential, which provides for constructing houses or apartments on the land; commercial, which permits
shopping centers and retail stores; and industrial, which provides for manufacturing plants, office buildings, and the like.

At the same time land is zoned for houses, stores, or factories, governments usually will also designate which lands will be used for public purposes, such as parks, schools, government buildings, and so on.

In Colorado, most of the responsibility for determining land use has
been given to local government. Cities and towns make the major decisions
for land use within their boundaries. County governments determine land
use in those portions of the county that are not included in a city or town.

Almost without exception, each city, town, and county in Colorado has
a planning department, which has the job of proposing general land use
plans for the area and recommending specific zones for specific parcels of
land. The city council or the county commissioners will make the final decision as to what plans are adopted and what zones are placed on each specific piece of ground.

Given the rapid population increase in Colorado in recent decades, and
given the particular concern on the part of many citizens of the state to
preserving its natural beauty, land use has become a major political issue.
Local citizens sensitive to conservation values strenuously oppose zone
changes that will result in construction in scenic areas.

Before any form of construction occurs, citizen groups often press city
councils and county commissioners to purchase areas of local beauty for
parkland or open space. Even when development is permitted, environmentally oriented citizens will call for lowering population densities and designating scenic areas, such as wooded stream valleys or pine-forested ridge
tops, as private open space.

A number of cities have adopted innovative land use programs. In the
late 1960s Boulder adopted and implemented an extensive plan for buying
a green belt of open land around the city. Jefferson County, the large suburban county to the west of Denver, adopted a program for buying natural open
space and constructing a county-wide system of recreational bicycle trails.

Colorado Springs expanded a beautiful red rocks park, the Garden of the Gods, and then purchased a similar scenic area known as Red Rocks Park.

A major influence on preserving open space and developing parks and trails at the local government level has been the Colorado lottery. Profits from the state-run lottery, distributed through Great Outdoors Colorado (GOCO), have funded a large number of local government open space and parks purchases. This rich supply of state moneys, guaranteed by a financial mandate sealed into the state constitution by voter initiative, has somewhat reduced the pressure to use planning and zoning to preserve scenic areas. City and county governments simply buy such beautiful areas and preserve them as public property.

The state government has tended to stay removed from land use issues, leaving it to the city and county governments to decide how the significant natural beauty of Colorado will be integrated with the desire of private-property owners to develop and build buildings on their property.

CONCLUSIONS

Local government is of central importance in Colorado. Because home-rule cities, including Denver, have such strong powers, cities often take the lead in terms of initiating major governmental projects. Denver, through such projects as the convention center, airport, baseball stadium, basketball arena, and so on, has been particularly aggressive in undertaking projects that benefit most Coloradans.

Because of their strong home-rule powers, and because at least three out of every four Coloradans live in a city, city governments have generally been able to fend off attempts by the state legislature to interfere in city affairs. County governments, because they do not enjoy the broad grant of home-rule powers that cities possess, are more subject to control by the legislature than are the cities.

Strong city annexation laws are another important characteristic of local government in Colorado. As long as Colorado cities are able to annex most of the urban growth in their general area, they will continue to have strong financial resources and will be able to provide effective local government. The inability of Denver to undertake significant annexations is one of the major drawbacks to local government in Colorado's capital city.

In their zeal for building parks, performing arts centers, airports, museums, zoos, and convention centers, the larger home-rule cities are illustrative of the moralistic political tradition in Colorado and provide the amenities or services that enrich the common wealth (or *commonwealth*).

# CHAPTER TWELVE

# Colorado's Assets and Liabilities

Colorado citizens and elected officials face an unending stream of planning, budgeting, tax, and policy choices. Colorado's needs, many observers agree, are much greater than its current or projected revenue sources.

Unlike the nation, Colorado essentially has no debt. But a variety of laws and state constitutional amendments almost guarantee a decline in Colorado's ability to meet its higher education, transportation, and related economic development and environmental needs.

It is easier to outline Colorado's looming policy challenges than it is to suggest solutions or remedies. But we will tackle policy concerns and policy opportunities as well as offer some suggestions about the policy process in Colorado.

Before we examine Colorado's challenges, it is useful to remind ourselves of Colorado's notable advantages.

## IMPRESSIVE ASSETS

Coloradans, for a whole range of reasons, love living in Colorado. Forgive us for sounding like the state chamber of commerce or the Metro Denver Economic Development Corporation, but Colorado has a large number of assets worth celebrating.

- Colorado's relatively mild climate, majestic beauty, incomparable recreational opportunities, and rich natural resources set it apart from almost all its sister states. Colorado is regularly ranked among the most desirable places to live by the Pew Research Center. Coloradans are regularly ranked as happier than those living in other states. Coloradans have the lowest obesity rate and are among the most active and fit participants in outdoor sports.

- The U.S. Census Bureau ranks Colorado as the second most highly educated state, and similar surveys rank Colorado near the top in high-scoring SAT test takers. Colorado ranks third in tech-worker concentration and eighth in the United States for scientists and engineers as a percentage of the state workforce.

- Denver has been hailed as one of the nation's "most sustainable metro areas." *Lonely Planet* calls it "a Paris in the West." And most experts agree that the Denver Performing Arts Complex, with its nearly eleven thousand seats in ten theaters or performance stages under one roof, is one of the most impressive such centers west of New York City. A top panel of convention planners put together by Canada's largest newspaper, the *Toronto Globe and Mail*, designated Denver as the best city in the world in which to hold a convention. And convention business has been good.

- The U.S. Department of Energy's National Renewable Energy Laboratory in Golden, Colorado, is the nation's premier laboratory for renewable energy research. Colorado has won national praise for "green energy" initiatives, such as shutting down some of its dirtiest coal-fired electric plants and retrofitting others to burn clean natural gas. And Colorado has become a center for the development of "clean technology."

- Colorado ranks fourth in the United States for renewable energy and energy research employment. It ranks sixth for highest total solar energy capacity. It recently ranked number three in installed photovoltaic capacity. Denver ranked fourth in the nation for Energy Star (energy efficient) buildings and seventh as the "greenest city." Loveland is becoming home to the Aerospace Clean Energy Manufacturing and Innovation Park. And General Electric is building a major solar manufacturing company here.

- Colorado has become a national leader in the booming aerospace industry. The state's Lockheed Martin Space Systems Company builds NASA's Multi-Purpose Crew Vehicle. Colorado is home to several important national companies, such as Liberty Media, Dish Network, Newmont Mining, Western Union, DaVita, Chipotle, Arrow Electronics, the Ball Corporation, and Molycorp (the owner of the world's largest non-Chinese rare-earth mineral deposits).

- The national business magazine *Forbes* has several times ranked Colorado among the top five states for business, especially crediting Colorado for its favorable labor supply and overall business climate.

- CNBC, the cable news network, ranks Colorado as one of the top three states for businesses, crediting its access to capital and overall business friendliness. *MarketWatch* ranked Denver the third-best metropolitan region in the nation for business. And Denver International Airport is the fifth busiest U.S. airport and the tenth busiest in the world and is regularly saluted by *Business Traveller* magazine as the best in the nation.[1]

- The national magazine *Chief Executive* surveys about 650 corporate chief executive officers each year. These business leaders draw on their direct experiences to rate each state in three general categories. First was taxation and regulation. Second was quality of workforce. Third was living environment. *Chief Executive* rated Colorado the eighth-best state for business overall in 2010. The state won especially favorable rankings for living environment and workforce quality. Colorado was judged lower for taxation and regulation. Texas and North Carolina won the highest rankings for tax and regulatory policies.[2]

- Colorado's economy, particularly when compared to its not too distant past, is reasonably diverse. Tourism has become a growth industry and generally serves as an economic cushion for the state, even in hard economic times. Colorado's workforce is better educated and younger than the national average. Racial and ethnic tensions have been low.

- Colorado's recent oil and gas boom has probably just started. The commercial oil reserves in the Niobrara formation north, east, and southeast of Denver stretch from El Paso County into southern Wyoming. Optimistic forecasts say there could be the equivalent of 1.5 to 2 billion barrels of new oil in Colorado.

- No other state has twenty-six major ski destinations and fifty-four striking mountain peaks towering over fourteen thousand feet high. Few states have so many major river headwaters or as many hot springs (forty). Not many states can boast 4 million acres of designated wilderness and 15 million acres of national forest lands. And the Arkansas River as it flows through Colorado is the most rafted river in the United States.

- Colorado sometimes gets called the "Napa Valley of Beer" in recognition of its 150 or more microbreweries. Colorado has ranked second in the nation for total number of breweries and sixth in the number of craft breweries per capita.

♦ Colorado is ranked forty-sixth lowest out of the fifty states for the amount of state taxes, although few Coloradans appreciate this is the case.

♦ The U.S. Patent and Trademark Office listed Colorado as among the top dozen states in terms of having patents issued to state residents. Coloradans earned 1,848 patents in 2010. And, in 2013, the U.S. Commerce Department established a new federal satellite U.S. Patent Office in the Denver area.

♦ Moody's www.economy.com developed a "business vitality index" a few years ago, and three Colorado metropolitan areas were listed as among the top fifty (out of 379 metropolitan areas measured). Fort Collins was sixteenth, Denver was twenty-fourth, and Colorado Springs was forty-seventh. The index measured labor availability, regional cost structure, employment, and economic risk stability, among other things.

♦ Yet other rankings peg Colorado as ninth in the nation for investments in venture-backed companies and as fourth in the number of new companies per capita and small business grants. Leading the list in these rankings were California, Massachusetts, Texas, New York, and Washington state.

♦ Colorado in recent decades has not had political machines or political bosses. The state's politics are basically transparent and honest when compared to most other states. Political scandals in Colorado are the exception rather than the rule. Only one Colorado governor ever went to jail. That was Clarence Morley, a Republican who served from 1925 to 1927. However, he was living in Indiana, years after he left Colorado, when he was convicted of a felony there.

### CHARACTERISTICS OF COLORADANS

Coloradans, as discussed, are on the whole moderately conservative, especially on fiscal matters. Yet they are also pragmatic and more centrist when it comes to civil rights, civil liberties, quality of life, and conservation policy issues. "Coloradans show a deep streak of independence and libertarianism in their voting habits," wrote *Denver Post* political columnist Fred Brown, "but they aren't anarchists."

Coloradans generally believe, Brown added, "that it's not a good idea to have one [political] party running everything."[3]

In sum, Colorado is very much politically a purple state, perhaps a match for Katharine Lee Bates's famous description in *America the Beautiful* of "purple mountain majesties."

Most of the public officials we have interviewed say Colorado is an unpredictable combination of pragmatism and conservatism, but the state's voters can be progressive on social or human issues. Overall, however, Coloradans are usually conservative on fiscal policies and express a clear preference for lean and limited government.

Colorado is still a small enough state that the people in and around public life either know one another or can get to know one another. And while Colorado, like the nation, has experienced an increase of political polarization, there is a genuine legacy of bipartisan collaboration and good government. This phenomenon is personified by a series of hardworking, dedicated, and accessible Colorado governors. The list includes Steve McNichols, John Love, John Vanderhoof, Richard Lamm, Roy Romer, Bill Owens, Bill Ritter, and John Hickenlooper.

This cooperative atmosphere is reflected in the state's leading newspaper, the *Denver Post*, which has a generally bipartisan outlook and has conservative as well as progressive columnists writing for its op-ed page. Also working cooperatively for good government in Colorado are advocacy groups such as Colorado Concern, the Colorado Forum, the Denver Metro Chamber of Commerce, the Colorado Bar Association, the Colorado Water Congress, and the Bell Policy Center, among others.

Finally, Coloradans have a healthy skepticism about governments at all levels but especially at the national and state levels. They believe in liberty, decentralization, limited government, and a system of robust checks and balances.

## COLORADO'S LIABILITIES

Colorado's enviable assets and attractive characteristics need to be weighed against several less-attractive trends or realities that, at least in the near term, present formidable challenges to the portrait of Colorado as a happy, healthy, optimistic, and economically competitive state.

First, we share a relatively brief list of harsher facts that Coloradans and our public relations firms understandably deemphasize. Then we will discuss in detail several of Colorado's more daunting public policy challenges.

Here is a brief list of Colorado's major liabilities:

- The Great Recession of 2008–10 left Colorado's budget in fragile straits, forcing billions of dollars of cuts in services and infrastructure investments. Home foreclosures soared to the point where Colorado was one of the top ten states for foreclosed homes. Colorado's unemployment rate rose to over 9 percent, higher than in most states. At least eight banks failed, including the $2 billion United Western Bank in the Denver area, New Frontier Bank in Greeley, and Southern Colorado National Bank in Pueblo. Banks in Castle Rock and Louisville also failed.

- Colorado's economy, measured on an inflation-adjusted per capita basis, grew under 4 percent over the past decade, about 3 percent lower than the nation as a whole.

- Colorado is among the top ten states with high percentages of their population homeless.

- Colorado's nearly one thousand suicides per year make it one of the top states in that lamentable ranking.

- Colorado's teens top the nation in depression, and they drink, smoke, and use drugs more than their counterparts in most other states. Child and adolescent health ratings are low.

- More than 25 percent of Colorado teenagers entering ninth grade will drop out of high school. As a result, Colorado ranks twenty-ninth in the nation in terms of high school graduation rates. Of those who complete high school and go on to college, nearly 30 percent will need to take remedial classes at the beginning of their college career.

- Colorado's investment in public higher education has been on a steep slide and is one of the lowest in the nation. At times it has ranked as low as forty-eighth in terms of state funding per resident student.

- Recent years have witnessed an increasing inequality between rich and poor families, between non-Latino and Latino families, and between what might be called "Whole Foods" counties (wealthy) and "Food Stamp" counties (economically challenged). Census data indicate the number of Colorado neighborhoods with a significant number of residents living in poverty doubled from 2000 to 2010.

- Colorado also has had in recent years one of the fastest-growing child-poverty rates in the nation. More than 200,000 children in the state are living in poverty.

◆ A number of well-known corporate headquarters have moved out of Colorado: Celestial Seasonings, Coors Brewing Company, First Data, Qwest (now CenturyLink), Prologis, and StorageTek.

◆ Civil engineers rate an alarming number of the state's bridges and highways in "poor" condition.

◆ Many experts fear the state has done inadequate planning to deal with providing adequate water supplies, constructing sufficient wastewater treatment facilities, and dealing with all the anticipated side effects of expanding oil, natural gas, and oil shale development. Concerns especially persist about water-supply safety of hydraulic fracturing used in the booming natural gas exploration in Colorado.

◆ While overall crime rates have dropped, as they have in the nation, there are major public safety issues. There are nearly eighty gangs of youths in Denver, and Colorado Springs ranks as the eleventh worst in the United States, out of four hundred cities, for rapes. Colorado Springs in 2011 had an alarming thirty-two murders.

◆ Enrollment in Colorado's Medicaid program (government medical care for the poor) grew from under 300,000 to 615,000 in just over a decade (2000–2012). Some analysts project Medicaid in Colorado may well double again in the next several years. Colorado's share of Medicaid (the U.S. government pays 50 percent of the cost) is the fastest-growing part of the state budget.

◆ Women in Colorado earn 78 percent of what men in Colorado earn in comparable jobs. That figure is lower than the national percentage and lower than in Arizona, California, Florida, North Carolina, Nevada, and Texas.

◆ Colorado, as noted, boasts one of the lowest rates of state taxation per capita. It rates forty-sixth in the nation. But this has consequences. It helps explain why Colorado also ranks low in state expenditures per capita, at forty-fifth in the nation. It ranks forty-eighth in spending on highways, forty-eighth in outlays for higher education, forty-ninth in financial support for Medicaid, and thirty-second in state investment in kindergarten through twelfth grade (K–12) education.

◆ Both Colorado and the nation have set as a goal the narrowing of the educational achievement gap between lower-income and middle-class students and between racial and ethnic groups. Sadly, in Colorado the educational gaps between these groups are growing.

◆ Each year Colorado loses at least thirty thousand acres of agricultural lands to residential and commercial development. More than three hundred thousand acres devoted to or reserved for farming disappeared in this manner from 2000 to 2010. Hundreds of thousands of acres more are forecast to be lost to houses, shopping centers, office buildings, and water rights transfers in the next two decades.

◆ Colorado has also lost millions of pine trees to bark beetle infestations, a scourge that turns beautiful mountainsides of green to a depressing brown. The beetles have moved from lodgepole pine trees to Colorado's beautiful ponderosa pine forests. These infestations of bark beetles are part of natural cycles, yet warmer temperatures and drought worsen this challenge to the beauty of the Colorado landscape.

◆ Colorado state parks officials say they will close some state parks and probably open up others to limited oil and gas extraction in order to gain needed financial support for the state park system. And a few state parks, mainly in remote areas, are now closed due to budget problems.

◆ There are enormous new challenges facing K–12 school districts around the state. Take, for example, the Aurora public school system that serves about forty thousand students in suburban Denver. Students there come from an amazing 120 countries and speak about 95 different languages. Seventy percent are entitled, because of low-income backgrounds, to federally paid lunches. Fifty percent are Latino, nearly a quarter are African American, and non-Latino whites make up just 20 percent or so. Estimated dropout rates range from 51 to 59 percent depending on what is taken into account. The changing demographics and dynamics make educating these young Coloradans a challenge.

◆ Finally, Colorado is losing significant sales tax revenue because it does not tax sales on the Internet, an increasingly popular form of shopping. Similarly, gas tax revenues are declining as vehicles get better mileage from each gallon of fuel.

### BUDGET POLITICS

Central to understanding Colorado's politics and public policies is first understanding its uncommonly complicated taxing and budgeting policies.

All this needs to be understood in the context of Colorado's political culture. Colorado is divided on a number of issues, but on taxing and funding matters there are at least three groups.

The first group is composed of staunch, principled conservatives, who insist on low taxes and minimal regulations. They deride "liberals" as people who like to generously spend other people's money.

A second group is made up of the people these conservatives attack so strenuously. These are committed and principled liberals with a communitarian philosophy who generally favor progressive taxation to finance public investments in education, health care, and parks, and to lessen economic inequality.

The third group is pragmatic centrists. They strive to find a middle way. On the one hand they favor limited government and relying on the free market economic system. On the other hand, they realize that good schools, well-run hospitals, adequate roads and highways, effective public colleges and universities, and furthering economic opportunity are indispensable to a competitive economic climate.

Citizens hold governors and, to a certain extent, state legislators responsible for the overall economic health of the state. This is especially true for economic growth, employment, taxes, and budget shortfalls.

But a variety of constitutional amendments, statutory referenda, and external developments have increasingly made it hard for Colorado elected officials to shape and steer Colorado's economy.

Colorado State University political scientist John A. Straayer laments the handful of relatively new fiscal initiatives that in some cases constrain tax increases and in other cases force increased spending. These constitutional mandates, he contends, have largely stripped state and local elected officials of much of their fiscal authority. Taxes in most instances can be reduced or eliminated by these public officials, but those same taxes can only be raised by a vote of the people.

Straayer explained: "Spending priorities are largely pre-set by constitutional provisions, federal requirements, corrections policy [jails and prisons], and specific-use dedication of gambling taxes. . . . [Spending priorities also are] partially driven by the ebb and flow of the economy and tax revenue."

State officials are less and less in control of both revenues and expenditures, Straayer emphasized. "Effectively, representative government [in Colorado] is a thing of the past."[4]

Here, in brief, are some of the contending requirements that have reshaped planning and budgeting in Colorado:

- U.S. government Medicaid requirements that force states to pay increasing large sums as their share. From 2000 to 2010, Colorado's Medicaid enrollment increased by over 120 percent.

- The Taxpayer's Bill of Rights (TABOR), the citizen initiative in 1992 that amended the state constitution. It requires a public vote in any jurisdiction in the state that wants to raise an existing tax or create a new one. TABOR also sets limits on the revenues governments in Colorado can keep. For the state, for example, the limit each year is the revenue from the highest previous year plus a modest increase for inflation and population growth.

- Amendment 23, approved by voters in 2000, fixed the required level of K–12 per pupil spending in public schools at the amount spent the previous year plus increases to account for inflation and student population growth. In 2010, for example, forty thousand new students were added to Colorado's K–12 public schools. This should have increased state funding. But during the last few years the state legislature has modified the spending formula in ways that have cut funding. This action by the legislature has been challenged in the courts.

- A major portion of profits earned from the state lottery in Colorado are required by constitutional amendment to be spent on parks, conservation, open space, and outdoors recreation projects. This money is distributed, as we have noted, by an independent group named Great Outdoors Colorado (GOCO). Such funds have done some wonderful things in Colorado, yet it should be noted that neither the governor nor the state legislature have a say in the allocation of these funds.

- The Gallagher Amendment to the Colorado Constitution was referred by the state legislature and adopted by the voters in 1982. It set in motion an explicit ratio between the property taxes businesses pay (high) and the property taxes that residential homeowners pay (low). It has the effect of increasing property taxes on business to the point where some businesses have moved out of the state. The Gallagher Amendment has also had the effect of shifting the costs of operating the K–12 public schools from local school boards to the state government.

## Effects of Financial Restrictions

The major effect of these and other restrictions on state spending in Colorado is to leave elected officials with much reduced control over state finances. It also means that in hard economic times, such as the 2008–10 recession, the state and local governments in Colorado have to dramatically reduce state and local public services.

Gov. John Hickenlooper proposed for his second year in office, 2012–13, a budget of nearly $20 billion. This included the state's general fund, federal assistance, and income from various user fees. But it involved painful choices because, as Hickenlooper said, Colorado was still in rough water. "If you account for inflation," Hickenlooper said, "the state's general revenue is $1 billion less than it was five years ago when the state had fewer people and was economically stronger—$1 billion—and demand for government services has surged."[5] During the same time, for example, public higher education enrollment increased by 20 percent, K–12 enrollment increased by 7 percent, annual state park visits increased by over 6 percent, and Medicaid enrollment increased by a staggering 72 percent.

Both Governors Bill Ritter and Hickenlooper tried to minimize the budget-cutting pain and spread the sacrifice widely throughout state government. Few options remained, however, without making cuts in core state services such as higher education and K–12 education. State workers had an effective pay cut extended for several years in a row.

Two things were especially striking about fiscal year 2011–12 general fund expenditures:

First, 95 percent of the general fund budget went to just five public policy areas: 39 percent to K–12 education; 22 percent to health care and Medicaid financing; 15 percent to public safety, jails, and the courts; 10 percent to human services (safety nets and welfare); and less than 9 percent to higher education (colleges and universities). All other functions of state government, including the judicial system and state parks, received less than 5 percent.

Second, the general fund portion of the proposed fiscal year 2012–13 budget, which is the part the state legislature has to approve and the governor has to sign, constituted just slightly more than one-third of state expenditures. For 2012–13 the proposed breakdown of the budget looked like this:

- $7.4 billion general fund. This is the fund into which general tax revenues, such as state income and sales taxes, are deposited. The general fund is used to pay, in whole or in part, many of the state programs that benefit citizens, such as education, corrections, and transportation.

- $6.0 billion cash funds. These are user fees, such as fishing and hunting licenses, severance taxes, gas taxes, and college tuition.

**General Fund Revenues**

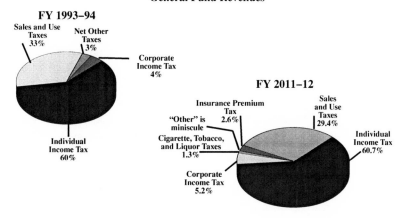

FY 1993–94

Sales and Use Taxes 33%
Net Other Taxes 3%
Corporate Income Tax 4%
Individual Income Tax 60%

FY 2011–12

Insurance Premium Tax 2.6%
"Other" is miniscule
Cigarette, Tobacco, and Liquor Taxes 1.3%
Corporate Income Tax 5.2%
Sales and Use Taxes 29.4%
Individual Income Tax 60.7%

**General Fund Expenditures**

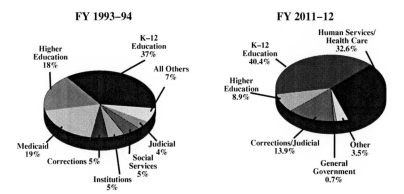

FY 1993–94

Higher Education 18%
K–12 Education 37%
All Others 7%
Medicaid 19%
Corrections 5%
Institutions 5%
Social Services 5%
Judicial 4%

FY 2011–12

Human Services/Health Care 32.6%
K–12 Education 40.4%
Higher Education 8.9%
Corrections/Judicial 13.9%
Other 3.5%
General Government 0.7%

Figure 13. Comparing Colorado State General Fund Budgets,
Fiscal Years 1993–94 and 2011–12

*Source*: Governor's Office and Colorado Legislature's Joint Budget Committee.

- ♦ $5.2 billion U.S. government (federal) funds. These are moneys provided by the United States to pay the federal share of programs such as Medicaid, public welfare, and airport subsidies.

- ♦ $1.47 billion reappropriated funds. Beginning in 2009, Colorado began accounting for moneys that were appropriated a second or third time to a different use in the same fiscal year as reappropriated funds. For example, funds appropriated to one executive department of state government and then transferred to another department in the same fiscal year are reappropriated funds.

Notice that elected state officials—the state legislature and the governor—have less and less control of the overall state budget. That is because they get to "formally" approve less than 40 percent of the state budget. And, as we have discussed, the general fund, the 40 percent part about which elected officials have some say, is in fact tightly constricted by the constitutional requirements listed above.

This is good news for people such as TABOR author Douglas Bruce. They want limited state government. It poses a major challenge, however, for those who believe Colorado needs to invest in its highways, higher education, and other programs that will make Colorado competitive for business, innovation, tourism, and overall quality of life.

How long can Colorado afford to starve its higher education system? How long can it continue to ignore its deteriorating public works? As a *Denver Post* editorial put it: "The state typically runs on a pretty lean budget, and by and large we as Coloradans like it that way."[6]

But people who take a longer view generally agree that a state such as Colorado needs a reliable income stream to maintain its bridges and highways and to upgrade, not starve, its higher education system.

Companies, their site-selection consultants, and investors who look closely at Colorado's business and political climate regularly ask tough questions about the quality of Colorado schools, universities, hospitals and medical centers, infrastructure, public safety, and the stability or volatility of public policy processes.[7]

Key businesses have moved operations and/or headquarters out of Colorado for a variety of reasons. Business executives are pragmatic. Colorado's great distance from both Europe and Asia hurts the state with companies that do a lot of international business. Colorado's antibusiness ballot measures and complicated tax and budgeting policies raise worries for businesspeople as well.

The state government's Colorado Office of Economic Development and International Trade does some excellent work recruiting employers to locate in Colorado, but that office's small staff and low budget limit it.

The privately run Metro Denver Economic Development Corporation, an affiliate of the Denver Metro Chamber of Commerce, was established in 2003 to market the state and encourage job creation. Its leaders know that Colorado cannot rely alone on its mountains, ski resorts, and beneficial climate to drive its economic growth. They know as well that the state needs a sustainable long-term economic development plan pursued by appropriate leaders who can skillfully communicate Colorado's strengths as a good place to locate a new business, factory, or branch office.

But many of the decisions facing Colorado will require hard choices about finding new or alternative revenue streams to fund long-delayed public needs. Since a constitutional convention to make budgeting more rational is unlikely, that leaves the state sales tax and income tax as the primary sources for Colorado state revenues.

Increases in user fees and license fees, so-called indirect taxation, offer some new sources of income, but these fees and other charges for state services are increasingly unpopular with the citizenry. Many Coloradans realize that backdoor solutions such as these do not offer long-range solutions to the state's daunting fiscal problems.

In sum, Colorado government is already lean and, in most instances, run efficiently and effectively. But Colorado lives in a very competitive world. Forty-nine other states compete vigorously for employers, for U.S. government installations, for tourists, and for bright students to come to their state colleges and universities.[8]

### Higher Education

Most everyone appreciates the importance of a highly educated population as a contributing factor to economic development, innovation, and a healthy economic climate. It is equally important for the social, cultural, and intellectual vitality of a state.

Colorado benefits from a huge in-migration of people who have earned college and advanced degrees in other states or other nations. Colorado boasts several nationally ranked colleges such as the U.S. Air Force Academy, the independent liberal arts college Colorado College, and the fast-growing University of Denver. But the vast majority of the students attending those institutions come from out of state and leave after they graduate.

As of 2013, Colorado's investment in public higher education was extremely low compared to that of other states. Colorado ranked forty-eighth of the fifty states in state funding per resident student.

According to *Kiplinger's Personal Finance* magazine's rankings of best values in public universities, the University of Colorado at Boulder ranked eighty-fifth and Colorado State University at Fort Collins ranked ninetieth. The two Colorado schools trailed a large number of other universities, including lesser-known institutions of higher learning in such states as Alabama, Arkansas, Louisiana, Missouri, Oklahoma, and Vermont.[9] The University of Colorado at Boulder did win two regretable rankings in 2011, as *Playboy* magazine's number-one party school and the "druggiest" college in America according to *Newsweek*.

A recent strategic plan for higher education in Colorado laments that "Colorado's financial support for higher education has been declining and is now dramatically off-track."[10] This report to the governor and state legislature documents that between 1990 and 2010, state support for higher education in Colorado decreased from over 20 percent to less than 9 percent of the state's general fund. Relative to other state services, the higher education share of state investment has been reduced by over 55 percent. This decline is expected to continue over the next several years.

The total amount Colorado residents pay for tuition has doubled in the last decade, and there is an unmistakable and probably irreversible shifting of higher education costs to students and their families. An economic report on Southern Colorado found that between 2000 and 2010, state support for students at the University of Colorado at Colorado Springs went down about 70 percent while the costs to students and their families increased by roughly 120 percent.[11]

Colorado's public institutions of higher education accept a large number of out-of-state students in order to get the higher tuition these nonresident students pay. That out-of-state tuition is three times higher than what Colorado residents pay, but those extra moneys do not come near to solving the overall fiscal crisis in Colorado higher education.

Business leaders join state educators in saying Colorado's future depends on having a well-educated population and vital intellectual infrastructure. It is well documented that many of the most successful centers for business innovation and entrepreneurial vitality are in regions with a variety of outstanding higher education and "brainpower" research institutions. The Boston area in Massachusetts, the Research Triangle in North Carolina, the Austin area in Texas, and the California Bay Area's Silicon Valley are notable examples.

Colorado's public universities and colleges have done cost cutting and terminated programs. University of Colorado president Bruce Benson noted: "We cut $29 million from our budget last year and are in the midst of another $21 million in budget-balancing measures this year through a combination of efficiencies, revenue generation and strategic cuts."[12] A year later, further cuts were announced.

One fear, shared by many public policy leaders in the state, is that the dramatic erosion of higher education funding in Colorado might, at some time in the future, influence existing and prospective businesses to choose to locate in other states. They will be seeking a better-educated workforce and greater opportunities for their employees to take additional courses.

They will also be looking for their employees to engage in research collaboration with nearby university faculty.[13]

What is not openly admitted in Colorado is that the state government has been able to starve its public higher education system because the state naturally attracts so many well-educated people to move to it. To its credit, Colorado's public higher education system has done a laudable job with the meager resources it has been given.

But a combination of forces, as previously discussed, have created a dire fiscal situation for higher education in Colorado. These forces are the TABOR restrictions on state taxation and expenditures, Amendment 23 that mandates steady increases in K–12 funding, the huge increase in costs in the state's share of Medicaid, and the 2008 recession. The end result is far less money than is needed to support higher education.

Colorado's public community colleges get some modest help as a result of a 2008 constitutional initiative. A portion of funds generated from expanded legalized gambling in several historic mountain mining towns has been dedicated exclusively to community colleges, no matter how large the total amount of those funds might become.

Yet Colorado's community colleges have also endured major fiscal strain. They have had tuition increases of around 9 percent per year, soaring enrollments, and declining fiscal help from the state. They have had to cut programs, and they pay their full-time faculty poorly. "Full-time faculty on average make about $46,000 a year, $10,000 less than the national average."[14] Community colleges have had to rely on more part-time adjunct teachers and online instruction to lower their costs. Dwindling state funding, public community college officials now understand, is the new normal.

A high-profile task force that evaluated public higher education in Colorado concluded in 2010 that "Colorado must increase its investment and ensure the affordability of higher education. We must value higher education at the same level we value jobs, quality of life, and economic vitality." The task force concluded: "We cannot afford to be among the last in the nation."[15]

This blue-ribbon commission examined a range of ways to increase revenues for higher education. Among the suggestions were raising the state income tax rate to 5 percent, increasing the state sales tax rate to 3 percent, and imposing a 1 percent surcharge on extraction of minerals.

Note that each of these is a new or increased tax. As we have discussed at length earlier in this book, TABOR would require a favorable vote from the electorate of the state for each one.

Coloradans would like to have a well-funded, affordable, accessible, and highly acclaimed public higher education system, but most Coloradans and their elected representatives have in recent years been unwilling to tax themselves to achieve this aspiration.

Asked about his recommendations for raising revenues for higher education in Colorado, Gov. John Hickenlooper responds that he sees no appetite among Coloradans "at this time" to move forward by adopting such new taxes by a referendum vote. His "at this time" might of course change if the state's economy gets much better or a vibrant coalition of civic, business, and educational leaders rallies around this priority. Hickenlooper also repeatedly says the state must show Coloradans it is operating as efficiently as possible before they can be asked for increased taxes. But that may be awhile.

At some point, however, some state elected officials will have to take the lead in finding a new secure revenue stream for Colorado's higher education system. Under TABOR, only those functions that have a revenue source clearly defined in the state constitution have remained adequately funded. If such elected leadership does not emerge in the near future, Colorado will end up with a de facto privatized higher education system that receives virtually no funds from the state government. Tuitions will rise and a number of programs will be cut. It will be especially hard on the already-strapped local colleges.

### Transportation Backlog

Experts say Colorado is facing an annual backlog of at least $1.5 billion in public works, or infrastructure. This means the state has been neglecting to repair state highways, state bridges, state parks, state buildings, and other essential structures. This situation exists as perhaps 3 million or so new residents are expected to move to Colorado in the next thirty to forty years.

One estimate from state and national engineers claimed that 52 percent of Colorado's highways and bridges were officially rated in "poor" condition.

One problem with financing a major rebuild of highways and bridges is that much of funding for these projects in the past came from U.S. government and state gasoline tax revenues. But gas tax revenues are declining in an era when automobiles and trucks are getting much better miles per gallon. With the wider adoption of hybrid and electric automobiles, these gasoline-based revenue sources will diminish further.

Gov. Bill Ritter proposed and convinced the state legislature to adopt the FASTER initiative. FASTER was an acronym for "Funding Advancement for Surface Transportation and Economic Recovery." This new law raised vehicle registration fees by $40 per vehicle and increased state fees on rental cars. FASTER funds were designated specifically for work on state highways and bridges. Although these additional moneys helped a lot, they were only enough to help at the margins, so great was the need for highway and bridge funds.

FASTER was expected to generate about $250 million per year to help deal with Colorado's scores of structurally deficient and functionally obsolete highway bridges. It also was to help with repair and maintenance on the state's nearly ten thousand miles of state highways. Tony Milo, head of the Colorado Contractors Association, warns that FASTER fees address only about one-sixth of Colorado's real infrastructure backlog.

Milo also explained that keeping up with road and bridge maintenance was, in the long run, a money saver. "Once a road deteriorates to the point where we must reconstruct it, taxpayers pay literally seven times more than they otherwise would had we completed the necessary prevention and deferred maintenance in a timely manner."[16]

Colorado's state gasoline tax, 22 cents per gallon, was last raised in 1991. It is considerably less than the national average. Some states, such as California, Illinois, New York, Hawaii, and Connecticut, average around 44 cents per gallon.

Elected officials, some believe, are probably less inclined to invest in needed repair and maintenance programs than to spend money on brand-new roads and bridges. There is more "glory," and immediate electoral dividends, in new projects. Meanwhile, the "quiet crisis" in infrastructure decline gets worse every year.

Prudent economic development and job creation as well as quality of life are directly related to having safe highways and bridges. The same holds true for public school buildings and other vital state structures.

At some point this neglect of public works in Colorado may translate into lives lost, tourists lost, and businesses that will either not come to the state or will move elsewhere. One day the citizens of Colorado may suddenly wake up and wonder: "What were the state's elected leaders thinking? Who was asleep at the switch when Colorado's infrastructure began really falling apart?"

## CRIME AND CORRECTIONS

Chambers of commerce rarely talk about crime, but crime, gangs, and drug problems are also part of Colorado and its policy challenges.

One report not long ago claimed Denver was home to nearly eighty gangs and almost nine thousand gang members. A national ranking by *Congressional Quarterly Press* (*CQ Press*) placed Aurora, Denver, Colorado Springs, Lakewood, and Pueblo above average in crimes committed among the nation's four hundred most-populous cities. Colorado Springs was ranked a dismal eleventh worst in the nation for rapes per one hundred thousand residents and also had an unacceptably high (much higher than the national average) rate of burglaries per person.[17]

Colorado's state prisons, as in most states, are full of inmates with drug and alcohol addictions. The state has had to cut back on programs that might address these problems. And also, as in similar states, recidivism rates exceed 50 percent.

Both the state and localities have cut back, sometimes drastically, on their public safety programs. The small town of San Luis in Southern Colorado even abolished the police department. San Luis went from having three police officers to having zero police officers. Emergencies in this town of over one thousand people are now called into the Costilla County sheriff's office.[18] Police services in Rio Blanco County have also been cut back.

Cities such as Colorado Springs no longer send police out to answer neighborhood requests unless there is a serious crime of violence occurring. The Colorado Springs Police Department sold off its two helicopters because the city budget could no longer afford to operate them. Such budgetary cutbacks throughout the state have made police forces leaner and leaner, partly as a result of TABOR restrictions and also due to economic downturns that greatly diminished revenues in many communities in Colorado.

Colorado's prison and statewide public safety costs will keep climbing because population increases alone will guarantee it. The state's challenging inequality divide, driven by homelessness and poverty, also contributes to the high cost to the public of crime. Drug addiction and alcoholism, neither of them diminishing, are a big part of the problem as well.

Governor Hickenlooper proposed the shutdown of the Fort Lyon Correctional Facility in Las Animas (Bent County). The prison employs two hundred people and, it turns out, is the second largest employer in that county. The facility holds about five hundred inmates. Closing it saves $6.3 million. But such closings, or even proposed closings, stir heated political opposition. One prison facility officer got choked up as he complained: "You talk about closing a facility . . . You're talking about closing my home . . . It's not a facility. It's a family . . . This is our way of life. You can't take it away. We're not going to let you take it away." His lament brought a robust standing ovation at a Las Animas town meeting.[19]

Even if the current prison population remains steady, corrections and public safety costs are still likely to climb due to the labor-intensive aspect of the work.

### WATER, ENERGY, AND THE ENVIRONMENT

Water in Colorado has always been a strategic source of life and prosperity. Along with the air the state's citizens breath and the remarkable land they inhabit, water ranks high as an indispensable precious resource. Governor Hickenlooper emphasized this imperative at the start of his administration when he declared: "But the natural resource that may, in the end, have the greatest impact on Colorado's economic growth is water."[20]

Population forecasts along with projected decreases in the amount of water available in the Colorado River Basin will make water in Colorado even more precious. There is also the problem that aquifers, a source of well water in several areas of the state, are getting low and may eventually dry up.

Water specialists warn that competition for limited water supplies will continue to intensify: "Population growth, drought, recreation needs, water quality, and federal mandates for endangered species continue to create pressure on Colorado's limited water resources. Current sources and projects are insufficient to meet anticipated demands, and present legal frameworks are straining under the pressure of Colorado's growth."[21]

Cities on the Front Range like Aurora and Colorado Springs are constantly buying up water rights in the more rural counties of Colorado and are building high-priced water diversion systems to bring the water to their citizens. Forecasters predict hundreds of acres of irrigated farmlands will be lost over the next generation to urban water uses. These once-productive agricultural lands will revert to dry desert or low-grade livestock grazing lands. In some cases, agricultural water will be purchased and devoted to energy development.

All of this raises complex policy questions. "Are we trading rural agricultural lands under cultivation for urban water uses that have higher market value? Can such farms thrive through equitable water transfers and the development of more efficient irrigation techniques?" asked several specialists.[22]

And what about economic vitality and cultural heritage in the already poor and struggling rural counties that are being deprived of water? Without water, they lose their main economic base, which is irrigated agriculture.

Alarmists (or are they prophetic realists?) warn: "No farms. No food." Yet Colorado still has thirty-six thousand farms and ranches. Colorado may lose about one hundred farms a year, according to some reports, but there is some consolidation going on. According to U.S. Department of Agriculture statistics, 31 million acres in Colorado are in farms, with the average size of farms about 865 acres.

On the other hand, respected Western Slope farmer and former Colorado agriculture commissioner Tom Kourlis says: "The prediction that we are going to become a net importer of food is becoming a reality because we keep taking productive land out of farming."[23]

Another controversy surrounding Colorado's water is the expansive oil and natural gas exploration that diverts water from both agricultural and urban uses. Two environmental activists warned: "Based on the average estimates for water use, the oil industry might need more water per year than is used by metro Denver each year."[24]

Colorado faces major planning and financing challenges in how it builds the water delivery and wastewater treatment systems needed to meet future population growth. "Hundreds of miles of our pipes are more than 100 years old," says Denver Water's chief executive officer Jim Lochhead. "We have treatment plants, pumps, reservoirs and other facilities that need upgrading or replacing."[25]

Overall, current water practices in the state are unsustainable. Colorado leaders will need to devise a variety of creative conservation and development initiatives to correct the current path the state is on. Several cities such as Denver and Colorado Springs continue to secure more and more water with a minimum of overall state planning and direction. Few people are looking at the big picture, particularly the future big picture.

It is not comforting that scarce and diminishing water resources are an issue in every western state, many of which are downstream from Colorado and would like to legally obtain more of Colorado's abundant water resources for their own use. Colorado regularly has to go into U.S. courts to defend its water supplies from encroachment by other states.

We asked the executive director of the Colorado Department of Natural Resources to identify the two biggest challenges facing Colorado in the next decade or two. He quickly responded that the first was planning for water sustainability. The second was how to keep up with [and presumably prudently regulate] the various energy booms going on in Colorado. He noted that both his staff and his budget had been cut. Such cuts make the job of managing Colorado's water resources all the more complicated.

Leaders in the oil and natural gas industry in Colorado complain that they are overregulated by the state. The Colorado Oil and Gas Association and the Western Energy Alliance, among others, lobby the state and the U.S. government to open up more public lands for coal mining and oil and natural gas extraction. They complain that slow permitting and a variety of other bureaucratic regulations "kill jobs" and impede efforts to provide the nation with reliable and less-expensive energy.

Meanwhile, conservation groups such as the Colorado Wildlife Federation, Colorado Backcountry Hunters and Anglers, Colorado Trout Unlimited, and their allies call on the state to preserve and protect as much of Colorado's precious wilderness and recreational areas as possible.

The fate of the celebrated Roan Plateau has been one of a number of highly visible political battles between conservationists and community groups on the one hand and the energy industry on the other. Both state and U.S. officials invariably get drawn into these policy controversies. The mineral-rich Roan is also a prime location for fishing, hunting, and other recreational uses. It is also noted for its biodiversity and its wildlife.

Colorado is blessed with enormous oil and natural gas supplies. Colorado may have as much natural gas underground as any other state. Gov. John Hickenlooper was at one time a geologist for energy companies. He is more sympathetic than his predecessor to expediting not just "green energy" but also the old reliables such as natural gas and oil. Hickenlooper sees his job, when possible, as getting government out of the way of job creation. "If a company is drilling for fractured shale gas—if we can cut the time for permitting that—that's better than creating additional government jobs."[26]

Energy and conservation issues are destined always to be hotly contested. Once again, Coloradans say they want it both ways. They want new jobs, a growing economy, and plentiful and cheap water and energy. Yet they simultaneously want to be able to hunt, fish, ski, backpack, and recreate in the state's incomparable wilderness areas. They hate the toxic side effects of careless energy developments, but they want the energy.

Low-cost natural gas from deep underground shale formations has become a boon to Colorado's economy. But it has also become a challenge for state and federal regulators. "The natural gas industry has spent many millions of dollars over the years establishing its product as a clean fuel, and not without reason," write Tim Wirth and Alice Madden. "Natural gas burns much cleaner than coal in power plants or oil in transportation. But all that advertising will go up in smoke if the industry resists regulation and lets its worst performers define the fuel."

What should be done? The natural gas industry has to be "encouraged" to disclose the chemicals it uses when it "fracks." Independent monitors are needed to ensure the industry is doing what it says it is doing.

Wirth and Madden sensibly argue that natural gas producers should take positive proactive steps: "The industry's best practices are protective of the water, land and air. Instead of trying to suggest that the public's concerns are not real, or are trivial and can be ignored, industry leaders should come together around a recommended code of conduct . . . and then work closely with regulatory authorities to make sure everyone follows the code. It's the bad actors that will get penalized, and that's in the interest of the industry as well as the public.[27]

The challenge, of course, is how to balance contending desires and how to manage and finance appropriate public policies and public-private partnerships that will allow Colorado to prosper but remain environmentally sound. That is a tall order.

## ECONOMIC DEVELOPMENT

The mountains and the environment will always be Colorado's greatest assets. Quality of life issues are really important in the Centennial State.

Yet people need jobs if they are going to live in Colorado. The state's business and political leaders are always trying to lure new employers to Colorado, encourage startup companies in the state, and help existing companies expand their factories and/or offices. There is also a constant emphasis on boosting tourism in Colorado.

Enormous efforts were made in the past to successfully lure to Colorado several major league sports teams, an Apple computer plant, the DaVita corporation, and dozens of other firms and projects. The city of Colorado Springs spent lavishly to retain the U.S. Olympic Training Committee headquarters. The state and its business leaders also work hard to retain and expand the military bases and related defense facilities and several national laboratories in Colorado.

Many people contend the best way to aid the state's economy is to help local companies expand their operations. They encourage state leaders to visit such companies and help identify job-creation opportunities. Easing burdensome government regulations that may be obstacles to company expansion is a big part of this process. "Any state government action, by legislation or regulation, that increases the cost of doing business for employers will hamper their efforts to create and retain jobs," says the Colorado Association of Commerce and Industry. "Don't try," they urge, "to balance the state's budget on the backs of employers by increasing taxes."[28]

A number of state and local committees and chambers of commerce engage in economic development work. Prominent among them is Colorado Concern, an alliance of senior executives that includes some of Colorado's wealthiest "movers and shakers." They promote "an environment that maximizes business profitability and sustainability opportunity, and shapes public policy."

The leaders of Colorado Concern have easy access to the governor, members of the governor's cabinet, and key state legislators. Although they do not always agree on specific policies, the chief executives in Colorado Concern look hard to find ways to enhance economic growth and encourage public investments in transportation and higher education, both of which they believe are key to twenty-first-century Colorado job creation. They also understandably favor stability and predictability when it comes to taxes and oppose tax increases or regulations that they think impede economic development.

Other groups that regularly advocate or lobby on behalf of economic development and a favorable "economic climate" include the Colorado Association of Commerce and Industry and the Denver Metro Economic Development Corporation, which works to gain new industry of behalf of the Metro Denver Chamber of Commerce. Club 20, a coalition of twenty-two western Colorado counties, works for economic development in that part of the state. Also active are the Colorado Springs Chamber of Commerce, the Boulder Chamber of Commerce, and economic development councils around the state.

These groups recognize the need to work with state officials to help create the ideal conditions for a prosperous state. These groups are not antigovernment or "reflexively anti-tax," writes *Denver Post* political pundit Fred Brown. "The Denver chamber and most of its counterparts around the state are on the same page. They want a pragmatic government, not an impotent one."[29]

These groups are nominally nonpartisan and eagerly work with governors and legislators regardless of party affiliation. Most are on record favoring lawmaking by elected officials rather than through the constitutional initiative process.[30]

Many of these groups are especially opposed to measures such as the Gallagher Amendment (referred to the electorate by the state legislature) that places a greater share of the property tax on businesses rather than on private residences.

A Denver Metro Chamber of Commerce pamphlet outlined the kinds of legislation the group lobbies for and against:

For:

- Infrastructure investment to address critical state needs and create jobs that put Colorado's citizens back to work.

- Maintaining the current balance between organized labor and management through the preservation of the Colorado Labor Peace Act.

- A predictable worker's compensation and unemployment insurance system.

- Streamline the regulatory and tax compliance process and support fair and equitable tax policies.

- Consider the statewide impact of growing industry clusters, such as conventional and renewable energy, that could bring additional jobs to Colorado.

- Encourage sustainable economic growth with consideration of impacts on the environment and natural resources.

Against:

- Mandates of any kind that lead to cost shifts for businesses and their employees.

- Measures that enhance opportunities for frivolous lawsuits.

- Public sector efforts to interfere with private contracts.

- Growth limitations that hinder economic activity, devalue land, and place undue burdens on local governments.

While the Denver Metro Chamber of Commerce strives to be nonpartisan, it does provide an end-of-the-year "Wrap-up and Scorecard" of how individual legislators voted on measures before the state legislature. The 2010 scorecard showed that Democrats voted with the Denver Chamber about 30 percent of the time, while Republicans voted about 80 percent of the time for chamber-supported issues.[31]

Colorado Conservation Voters similarly scores legislators' votes on environmental and conservation issues. Not surprisingly, Democrats win "high marks" for pro-conservation initiatives whereas Republicans average around the 30 percent level of support.

## TOURISM

Another economic development opportunity is promoting tourism. Colorado has a state Colorado Tourism Office, but most of tourism promotion has been decentralized to individual localities and even individual resorts and attractions. But here again, private-public partnerships could be critically important.

Colorado's state and local governments as well as its tourism industries try to be creative in convincing tourists to make Colorado a destination place for vacations. Year-round tourism is vital to Colorado's economic future.

Most experts agree that it is not just how much money is spent to promote tourism, it is how it is spent. Colorado needs to think strategically about its tourism opportunities.

The citizens of Colorado voted to eliminate tourist promotion supported by public taxation. The tourist interests in the state have struggled to find nongovernmental ways to promote travel to and within the state. It is a tribute to the great natural beauty of Colorado, and the state's enduring reputation for that beauty, that the number of tourists coming to Colorado continues to grow despite the lack of significant public financing of tourist promotion.

If Colorado is to compete in the intensive tourist-luring competition with other states and nations, it has to:

- Improve highway signs in rural areas of the state, pointing out mountain ranges and providing better indication of distances between locations.

- Provide more markers of historic and scenic points of interest at or near major points of interest.

- Promote the mountain climbing and cycling virtues of Colorado as well as its ski resorts and golf courses.

- Encourage more and better hiking, biking, and horseback riding trails throughout the state. So-called ecotouring, where visitors are encouraged to spend more of their time in the great outdoors of Colorado, has become increasingly popular and profitable.

- Encourage more arts districts and centers for all the creative arts, including filmmaking, photography, sculpture, and so on.

- Help publicize tourist attractions in the less-visible regions of the state, such as the Shrine of Sangre de Cristo in San Luis, the Guadalupe Church in Conejos, Camp Amache in Granada, Great Sand Dunes National Park north of Alamosa, and the Creede Repertory Theater in Creede. Governor Hickenlooper helped, with the *Denver Post*, to create a "Pedal the Plains" bicycle tour to the farm regions on the Eastern Plains. Among the benefits of this, he says, is seeing where our food comes from.

◆ Promote iconic Colorado restaurants and cafes such as Pine Creek Cookhouse in Ashcroft, Adams Mountain Café in Manitou Springs, Lucille's Café and the Flagstaff House in Boulder, Gaspacho's in Durango, Jay's in Fort Collins, Piñons in Aspen, the Well-Knit Café in Crestone, Kate's Place in Ridgway, the Red Barn in Montrose, and the historic Meeker Hotel and Café in Rio Blanco County.

These are merely illustrative of a range of opportunities both the public and private sectors must exploit to ensure Colorado's role as a tourist attraction.

### Encouraging Innovation

Economic development involves promoting innovation. The Colorado Office of Economic Development and International Trade provides some help in this regard, but most of the promotion of innovation is done by local economic development councils. The City of Boulder and Boulder County have been especially active and productive. Startups in the Boulder area have received more than 40 percent of the venture capital invested in Colorado. Nearly ten thousand businesses with fewer than twenty employees call the city of Boulder or nearby Broomfield home.[32]

Boulder is now known as a supportive community for startup and innovative companies. Mentoring and seed money are there to help young entrepreneurs. "Boulder is an amazing place to find the peers and financing you need to build a great company," says businessman Kimbal Musk. "I think Boulder is what Silicon Valley wishes it could be in many ways. The entrepreneurial spirit in Boulder is raw and honest, and the community is rooting for you. I love Silicon Valley and am involved in many companies there, but my first choice to start a company would be Boulder every time."[33]

Colorado officials very much want Colorado to be a center for innovation in clean technology, alternative energy, natural foods, sports equipment and clothing, aerospace technology, and related computer and communications technologies.

One advantage Colorado has is a variety of national research and space centers, including the U.S. Space Command headquarters in Colorado Springs. The National Renewable Energy Laboratory is in Golden. Boulder County hosts a number of such national research centers: the National Wind Technology Center, the National Center for Atmospheric Research, the National Center of Standards and Technology, and the National Oceanic and Atmospheric Administration (NOAA). A national seed laboratory is located in Fort Collins. In addition to all of the above, the National Aeronautics and Space Administration (NASA) has several alliances with major Colorado firms and the University of Colorado.

Still, it is a challenge for Colorado to compete with California's Silicon Valley, Boston's legendary Route 28, and North Carolina's Research Triangle. There are many competing cities and states for new businesses and government facilities, including Huntsville, Alabama, in aerospace. Texas is regularly one of Colorado's chief competitors. It has a lot of money and is willing to spend it to get startups and established companies to move there.

Here are a few things Colorado's public- and private-sector leaders can do to promote more innovation in the state:

- Place even greater emphasis on math and advanced sciences in Colorado secondary schools and colleges.

- Publicly celebrate inventions, patents, and successful companies that create jobs.

- Provide selective tax credits or exemptions for venture investments and for fledgling startup ventures. Review and consider for elimination those regulatory policies that unnecessarily handicap startups.

- Closely study how Singapore, Israel, Finland, and South Korea have made technological, biological, and design innovation a national priority and have experienced considerable success. Note that some of these countries have about the same population as Colorado.[34]

- Restructure Colorado universities to partner with private sector and foundation groups to invest more in basic research and to collaborate even more entrepreneurially with the multiple national laboratories already located in Colorado. This will require taking the long view in light of the grim fiscal realities facing Colorado public higher education in the early twenty-first century.[35]

- A newly established state Innovation Council and chief innovation officer are a step forward and need to work with Colorado foundations, Colorado educators, and state and private-sector leadership on ways to leverage resources to encourage the education of creative people, encourage the state's "creative capital," and promote intellectual infrastructure throughout the state. Colorado's success with startup companies has been largely geographically confined to a narrow belt running north from Jefferson County through Boulder County and into the Fort Collins area. But this includes only three

or four counties and largely leaves behind Colorado's sixty other
counties.

- ◆ Encourage even more private-sector mentoring and venture capital
  financial seed money for worthy ideas in Colorado's already-existing
  clusters of strength: aerospace, clean energy technology, mining, oil
  and gas, telecommunications, sports, agricultural seed research, and
  medical technologies.

- ◆ Finally, state leaders and the public need to support the Hickenlooper initiative to engage entrepreneurs from all walks of life to
  help discover and implement solutions to many of the major challenges facing Colorado, challenges such as the I-70 traffic mess,
  the possible side-effects of fracking, and how to fund public higher
  education.

### INEQUALITY IN COLORADO

Colorado's median annual household income of around $60,000 is higher
than the national average and the ninth highest among the fifty states. But
Colorado ranked below average in one recent study that compared pretax
incomes of the top as opposed to the bottom fifth of families. Its low-income families averaged slightly more than $20,000 in family income com-
pared to the top fifth's average of $182,000.[36]

Yet this ranking fails to reflect several growing disparities between
wealth and poverty in Colorado. The state has a number of superwealthy
communities such as Aspen, Vail, Cherry Hills Village (south of Denver),
the Broadmoor area (in Colorado Springs), Broomfield, Boulder, and many
others. Huge estates and private "trophy ranches" are found in or near the
destination ski resorts scattered about the Western Slope. Actor Tom Cruise
has a spread near Telluride. Fashion designer Ralph Lauren has a huge
ranch near Ridgway. Billionaire hedge fund manager Louis Bacon owns a
172,000-acre ranch in Costilla County, one of Colorado's poorest counties.
Actor Kevin Costner owns a pricey acreage outside Aspen with his own
*Field of Dreams* softball field.

The Denver metropolitan area has a number of high-income enclaves,
many of them in the foothills of Jefferson County west of Denver or in
Arapahoe and Douglas Counties south of Denver.

But for every one of these "Whole Foods" neighborhoods, there are just
as many "Food Stamp" neighborhoods.

Most of the poorest counties are in Southern Colorado or close by in southeastern Colorado. Joining them in their poverty is rural, sparsely populated Jackson County in north-central Colorado along the Wyoming border. See Map 6.

The dozen wealthiest counties in Colorado often have three times as much median annual household income as the poorest counties. These counties are found mainly in the Denver suburbs or are counties that contain the destination ski resorts. The true wealth in the destination ski counties is understated because thousands of people who own property and play there make their official residences in other states. Their personal wealth is usually measured in the other states, not in Colorado.

The sharpest contrast is between the Denver suburb of Douglas County, with a nearly $100,000 median annual household income, and Costilla County, which sits in Southern Colorado adjacent to the New Mexico border, with a median annual household income of $23,000. Boulder has at least three upscale Whole Foods stores. There are none in the state south of Colorado Springs.

In El Paso County, which contains Colorado Springs and has surpassed Denver to be Colorado's most-populous county, there are a number of "gated communities" that are home to affluent families. But in recent years, El Paso County also had nearly 12 percent of its population, about seventy thousand residents, living below the poverty level. More than twenty-five thousand families were on "food assistance."[37] Unemployment and foreclosures ran high in recent years despite the fact that 40 percent of the Colorado Springs economy was U.S. Department of Defense related.

Colorado, like elsewhere around the nation, has considerable poverty in its most-populous cities. But also similar to elsewhere, the Denver suburbs are seeing large increases in the number of poor people, many of them minorities. Thus the Denver-suburban cities of Aurora and Arvada are having a rise in low-income, high-need residents. Jefferson County, one of the more prosperous counties adjacent to Denver, has noted a dramatic increase in its public school system of students from single-parent, low-income homes as well as children from virtually homeless backgrounds.

Colorado has one of the fastest-growing child-poverty rates in the nation. This dubious distinction is attributed to a huge increase of low-income people in Denver's nearby suburbs and also to a widening gap between Latino and non-Latino incomes.

"The state's non-Latinos are actually higher-income than the national average, but Latinos in Colorado are among the poorest in the nation," wrote *Denver Post* reporter Allison Sherry. "In other words, Colorado's

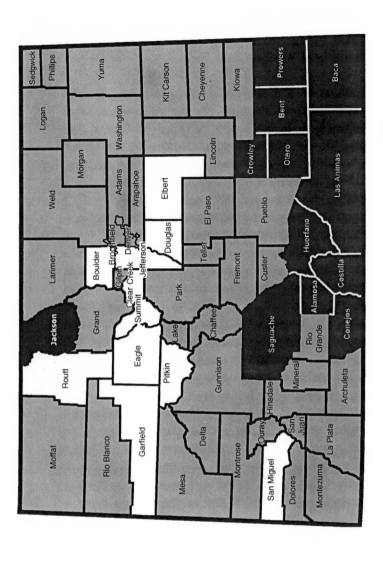

Richest

Poorest

Map 6. Income Inequality: Colorado's Twelve Richest and Twelve Poorest Counties

*Source:* Adapted from U.S. census data for Colorado through 2009.

large income gap between Latinos and non-Latinos is creating what advocates say is a 'Tale of Two Colorados.'"[38]

The Latino population is growing, especially as a proportion of Colorado's children and teenagers. But the Latino school dropout rate is high, and Latino representation in the state's four-year colleges and research universities lags well behind the non-Latino, non–African American representation.

Hispanics were the first Europeans to settle Colorado, and the state's name is a Spanish word. It is true that a number of Hispanics have been elected to Colorado's highest political offices, including U.S. senator, U.S. representative, Colorado attorney general, Colorado lieutenant governor, Denver mayor, and Colorado Springs mayor. Despite these important examples of personal success, many Hispanics in Colorado have struggled economically.

Researchers find the highest child poverty exists in Denver and in Southern Colorado, but the biggest increase in child poverty is in the counties surrounding Denver, which saw an increase of more than thirty-five thousand children living in poverty from 2000 to 2010.

Colorado's business and political leaders are aware of the growing inequalities in their state, yet they seldom talk about it. Little has been done to reverse these trends. The economic recession that began in 2008 made economic inequality worse in Colorado. As in most states, Colorado effectively cut school aid, Medicaid, transportation, state employee salaries, and social services, usually to the financial detriment of the state's most vulnerable citizens. These included the poor, the laid-off, the disabled, and students.

There are always competing conceptions of what the role of government should be when it comes to issues of liberty and equality. National studies indicate that large majorities of U.S. citizens understand that there is less economic equality in the country than used to be the case. Large numbers of U.S. citizens, even though they are philosophically conservative, would like to see less inequality of wealth and income than currently exists.

At the same time, as Ben Page and Larry Jacobs assert: "Nearly all Americans believe deeply in the American Dream. They want themselves and their children to have a chance to study, work hard, and achieve great economic success. They believe in material incentives and economic rewards. They do not want to level all incomes or confiscate the gains of the rich. They accept substantial levels of economic inequality in order to create the possibility of spectacular success and to sharpen motivations to work and achieve."[39]

More than one in ten Coloradans are poor. Many of them are children living with a single parent. These people, especially the children, face many obstacles in trying to pursue the American dream.

Most Americans favor programs to ensure no one is without food, clothing, or shelter. And most U.S. citizens believe that quality schooling can be the great equalizer. But all such programs come with a price tag. Major donors at election time, and those who fund the best-paid lobbyists, with a few exceptions, want to keep state taxes at current levels or lower. Not surprisingly, elected officials pay considerable attention to campaign donors and established economic interests and far less to poor people. Many Colorado politicians fear the wrath of the Douglas Bruce type of antitax advocates, Tea Party supporters, and others who label even political centrists as socialists.

Political scientists Page and Jacobs worry that there are damaging side effects that arise when inequality increases. It can, they write, sap "the moral foundation of our economic and social system—the notion of equal opportunity and the promise that rewards will flow to those who educate themselves and work hard." They add: "Attainment of the American Dream can still be found in the success of certain remarkable Americans. But these are exceptions to a general pattern of dwindling opportunity."[40]

This is an apt warning. U.S. citizens have always defined Jefferson's "all men are created equal" in terms of equality before the law, equal access to voting, and especially equality of opportunity. These are central to what it means to be a citizen of the United States and a Coloradan. But what are the preconditions and ground rules that have to exist for meaningful equality of opportunity? This will have to be answered by those who aspire to lead Colorado over the next generation.

Inequality is, to be sure, a national problem in the United States. The richest 1 percent of U.S. households has a higher net worth than the bottom 90 percent. And the annual household income of the richest twelve thousand families is greater than that of the poorest 24 million households.

People are obviously not all equal in ability. There are always some people with greater drive, initiative, and entrepreneurial skills who thrive and prosper in the free-market portion of the national economy. "Income inequality is the inevitable consequence of the unequal distribution of skill, intelligence, ambition, dedication, parental involvement, market evaluation, risk-taking and just plain luck, to name only a few variables," writes conservative Denver talk radio host Mike Rosen. This isn't a reason, he adds, to justify state and national redistribution programs. No, says Rosen, articulating his principled individualistic, or even libertarian, position.

"Government intrusion inevitably reduces aggregate income and wealth creation in a society."[41]

However, many others believe that inequality of the scope now present in Colorado and in the United States in general is divisive and corrosive. "These inequities seem profoundly unhealthy, for us and for our nation's soul," wrote Nicholas Kristof.[42] They weaken community trust and the social glue that is indispensable to making healthy communities function successfully. And the problem of inequality in Colorado is likely to get worse.

Yes, in principle, every Coloradan has an equal say in the state's political processes. And, yes, Colorado is a one-person, one-vote state. In practice, however, exceptionally wealthy individuals such as Phil Anschutz, Tim Gill, Larry Mizel, Pat Stryker, John Malone, and some of their friends in Colorado's 527 coalitions can funnel strategic investments to candidate campaigns, fund think tanks, hire lobbyists, and enjoy a much larger voice than ordinary Coloradans. This is a major challenge for the American ideal of equality of opportunity.

In the end, the fundamental character of a state is judged by how it treats and provides for its least advantaged. Every state, and Colorado can be no exception, has to behave as if its most precious resources are its citizens—all its citizens. A society should be committed to encouraging equal opportunities and ensuring that its young people develop their abilities as far as is possible. When young people can't climb up the ladder, it's bad for the economy and bad for Colorado.

Such a society has to provide the necessary investments in human capital to make equality of opportunity a reality. Colorado has a way to go to achieve such a goal.

## PLANNING STRATEGICALLY

Colorado needs to periodically assess all its assets and liabilities and think strategically and comprehensively about its competitive advantages compared to other states. Every state competes for business, tourists, military installations, research scientists, sports teams, nonprofit headquarters, and ski and snowboard championships (if they have the snow). Thus strategic planning is essential for Colorado to gain a systematic edge over its competitors.

Colorado citizens need to have the best possible brainpower, in both the private as well as the public sector, devising plans that can help the state position, or reposition, itself competitively in national and international markets.

State budget planners and political leaders are asked to think comprehensively about Colorado's future. But they are understaffed and subject to frequent turnover, partly due to term limits on the governor and the state legislature. There are a variety of groups, such as the Colorado Forum, the Colorado Roundtable, and Colorado Concern that bring people together to think boldly about the state's challenges and opportunities. But most of these groups have limited staff support or other needed planning resources. Many of them unfortunately have had to spend a lot of their time and money defeating citizen initiatives that would have further eroded the state's ability to govern wisely.

Part of the problem surrounding the planning capacity of state government, or the lack of such capacity, arises because not everyone in Colorado believes in planning. And many who do believe in planning think it should be done either by private interests or mainly at the county and city level. After all, as many people say, the needs of Denver citizens are very different from the needs of people in small towns such as Creede, Dove Creek, Fowler, Holyoke, Kit Carson, Ridgway, or Meeker.

Coloradans of an individualistic or libertarian political leaning suspect, sometimes correctly, that "planners" are of a reformist, progressive political orientation. Moreover, they suspect planners try to discern a desirable and more just future for all Coloradans and then try to steer the state from the here-and-now toward their idea of that desirable future.

Wary "individualists" are never certain that the planner's conception of a desirable future will be the same as theirs. Even if it is, individualists are understandably concerned about the cost of moving from the present to that desirable future, and the possible loss of freedom that might come as part of the process.

But despite this type of debate, there are documents that constitute much of Colorado's plans for the future. The first document is Colorado's state constitution. The second is the state budget. The third is the aggregate tax policies of the state, county, and city and town governments of Colorado.

It turns out that these documents send competing messages and often create a patchwork of limits, restrictions, and mandates, all of which make it hard to plan comprehensively. In the end, several challenges face Colorado leaders and citizens. Briefly put, they are as follows:

- Too many groups now know that major changes in Colorado public policy can almost as easily be made through the citizen-initiative process as through conventional representative government (the governor and state legislature).

- Term limits have weakened the state legislature and enhanced the influence of lobbyists, staffs, and the governor.

- What to do about TABOR tax and expenditure limitations has become the "elephant in the room" in Colorado. Few people in elected office want to speak about changing TABOR for fear of being labeled an "irresponsible spender and tax increaser." Yet many elected and private-sector leaders believe TABOR has put a stranglehold on public investment for both economic development and social justice.[43]

- Colorado's tax policies are in need of revision, yet there is little appetite and leadership in Colorado to change them.

- Colorado's efforts at reforming campaign finance have failed. One result is that the costs of running for office have skyrocketed, and the money flowing into both Democratic and Republican political campaigns from unregulated independent spending groups have mainly been used to increase divisive negative campaign advertising (mainly on television and in mailed brochures). The proliferation of attack ads has soured voters in Colorado and, in some cases, driven potential candidates from seeking public office. The U.S. Supreme Court's ruling in *Citizens United v. Federal Election Commission* in 2010, which allows corporations and labor unions to spend freely in election campaigns, offers little hope on this front.

All the above issues need to be addressed. Here are a few suggestions on these and related matters:

- We support making it harder for citizens to amend the state constitution. One way to accomplish that would be to raise the percentage of signatures required to 10 percent of the total vote in the most recent election for governor. Another way is to require that constitutional amendments win 60 percent of the vote, rather than just 50 percent plus one, to be adopted.

- We support abolishing term limits for members of the state legislature. A distant second choice would be raising the current eight-year term limits to twelve-year term limits.

- We support strengthening the governor's appointment powers. Colorado governors should be able to appoint most agency heads and division directors, either from within or without state government.

- We support raising the salaries of state officials. Governors might be paid $200,000 per year, not the $90,000 currently being paid. The attorney general, lieutenant governor, treasurer, and secretary of state should be paid $150,000 per year, not the current $80,000 for the attorney general and $68,500 for the other three. None of these state officers should have to moonlight or earn honorariums for speaking to elite groups.

+ We recommend state legislators be paid $75,000 per year, not the present $30,000 per year. Why should lobbyists earn five to ten times as much as the people's representatives? These proposed salaries are hardly exorbitant and just make common sense. And these jobs are nearly full-time commitments, much more so than was once the case.

+ When there is a year or more left to serve, we support filling legislative vacancies by holding special primaries and then a special general election. The present system of filling vacancies by party-dominated vacancy committees leaves the electorate completely out of the decision.

+ We support the state providing more authority and encouragement to county-county and county-city mergers. A recent example was the creation of the City and County of Broomfield from the old city of Broomfield and parts of four counties. Prime candidates for a city-county combination are Colorado Springs and El Paso County. More than two-thirds of the population of El Paso County lives in Colorado Springs. The new government, perhaps named the "City and County of Colorado Springs," would join Denver and Broomfield as consolidated city-county governments.

+ We support the proposal to identify a reliable revenue stream for public higher education. The lack of adequate state funding for the state's public colleges and universities has become an embarrassment.

+ We similarly believe Colorado will need to identify alternative revenue streams for maintaining and repairing the state's infrastructure and public works. Highways and bridges can only be ignored so long before their deterioration becomes a crisis. And the 1-70 problem needs to be addressed. This will require new revenue.

+ We support imaginative efforts at promoting equal opportunity and for diminishing the increased inequality in the state. An "invisible Colorado" or "other Colorado" has inadvertently been allowed to grow in this otherwise prosperous and much-blessed state. This, as well as the above two recommendations, will require leadership partnerships that call for shared sacrifice. Coloradans, we believe, would be responsive to shared sacrifice if (1) it was really shared, and (2) if the programs funded were run effectively and efficiently and clearly served the public interest.

- We support the idea that the governor and state legislature appoint, every five years, a blue-ribbon bipartisan commission modeled on the 2010 Erskine Bowles–Alan Simpson cochaired National Commission on Fiscal Responsibility and Reform to review Colorado state taxing, spending, and general governmental operations. The goal would be to examine for efficiency, effectiveness, fairness, and fiscal responsibility, and to evaluate state services according to metrics such as program outcomes, public satisfaction, cost per capita, and similar measures.

- We are sufficiently realistic to understand that the central feature of TABOR, the right for citizens to vote on all new tax increases, will likely remain in the Colorado Constitution for the foreseeable future. A lawsuit filed against it in 2011 in the U.S. courts is not likely to succeed. But we support those who want to modify TABOR by including a formula that takes into account economic growth rather than having spending limits tied only to population growth and economic inflation increases.

- We support raising the age justices and judges can serve to seventy-seven years from the mandatory seventy-two that was established back in 1966 when life expectancy was five or six years less than it is today.

- Finally, we support even more creative efforts to support both innovation and creativity in Colorado. The state has already enjoyed some success in these two areas. The Denver-Boulder area has become a vibrant "creative capital" location. Colorado can also be proud of incubating hundreds of new companies. The potential payoff is huge if the state can continue to become a hotbed of invention and innovation. The state should also be a place that proudly celebrates its artists, poets, and writers and rigorously cultivates the creative and performing arts.

## BEWARE REFORMERS BEARING SIMPLE SOLUTIONS

Former *Denver Post* columnist Bob Ewegen made the following comment about reform in Colorado: "Reformers here in Colorado are always calling for more 'sunshine' or 'transparency.' Whether it is liberals or conservatives or Tea Party activists, they always seem dissatisfied. The truth is that Colorado government in recent decades has been pretty much clean, honest, and effective."[44]

Sometimes the tinkering of reformers does no good. Sometimes it undermines healthy politics. Term limits is a prime example. Research by John Straayer finds that legislative term limits of eight years have mostly had negative consequences for the way the state legislature works. He found there has been less civility, less institutional memory, more "crappy little bills," fewer champions of strategic policies, and more committee and leadership turnover. Straayer further argues there probably has been a shift of political power away from the legislature and toward the executive branch, the lobbyists, and, in some cases, the staff. Straayer concluded: "Legislators are less knowledgeable about statewide issues and legislative procedures and are less collegial."[45] Several former legislators and current lobbyists interviewed for this book share Straayer's views.

Straayer adds: "Term limits have added to the inability of the institution [the Colorado state legislature] to focus on long-term goals and policy."[46] The institution's leadership capacity has been greatly weakened, much more so than was the case in the pre-term-limits era.

Others agree. Former governor Bill Owens, who championed term limits when he was a state legislator, now says it was not the right thing for the legislature and for Colorado. Former state senator Josh Penry told us that although he still favors term limits for the state legislature, he now believes the limits should be for twelve years, not eight.

One reform adopted by constitutional initiative in Colorado severely restricted the amounts of money lobbyists can spend buying meals or cocktails for state legislators. This noble-sounding reform had the unintended effect of lessening the opportunities for state legislators to get out and socialize across political party lines and develop bipartisan relationships.

We would ordinarily add the TABOR reform to this list, but Douglas Bruce made it clear that TABOR was designed to require a vote of the people on every tax rate increase. What he did not make clear, in fact he never even mentioned it, was the part of that state constitutional amendment that so severely limited state and local government revenues.

The overused and too-easy-to-use citizens' initiative to amend the state constitution, though obviously introduced with the best of populist intentions, has in recent decades had unfortunate policy consequences. What might be considered a "counterreform" panel put it this way back in 2005:

"Central to the problem is the practice of making fiscal policy by public referendum through amendments to the Colorado constitution. "Ballot-box budgeting" is a haphazard approach where citizens are asked to make major fiscal decisions in isolation based on one-sided facts provided by proponents and, in some cases, opponents. Making fiscal policy by referendum is a process where oversimplification and under analysis are the established norms; where conflicting policies and unintended consequences are the logical outcome."[47]

This panel and other analysts emphasize that Colorado's citizen-initiative signature threshold for constitutional initiatives, 5 percent of the votes for Colorado secretary of state in the most recent election, is the lowest in the nation when measured as a percentage of state population.

Once language is in the state constitution, the legislature is not allowed to amend it, no matter how badly the new amendment might affect the state once the amendment is put into practice.

Voters may not want to do this, but it makes sense to make it harder to amend the state constitution and instead to strengthen the state legislature and the governor. With these added powers, the state legislature and the governor should be better able to provide more responsible, accountable, and comprehensive fiscal policies for Colorado.[48]

It is too often the case that initiated reforms, such as trying to equalize campaign financing and limit the influence of lobbyists over state legislators by limiting entertainment expenditures, complicate and exacerbate the election process rather than improve it.

In sum: Beware reformers bearing simple solutions. Reforms can often have totally unanticipated results. They also can contain hidden agendas that the majority of voters underestimate or do not realize are there.

### CONCLUSIONS

Colorado is an uncommonly rich state, blessed with breathless beauty, wondrous natural resources, unmatched recreational opportunities, and talented people.

The state's business and political leaders have great aspirations for the state. They want its economy to grow steadily, they want high employment, they want a better public higher education system, they want prudent water storage, they want sound environmental planning, they want the state to become ever more attractive to tourists and corporate headquarters, and they want to attract intellectual, cultural, and economic capital. They want to capitalize on the state's traditional as well as nonrenewable energy sources.

The institutions of government in Colorado are mostly responsive to the electorate and function in a reasonably efficient manner. The state's elected officials are honest and work hard to make Colorado an attractive, responsible, and caring place. Elected and unelected leaders alike try to find a balance between economic growth and preserving the glorious natural beauty that has long made Colorado such an attractive and special place.

Yet policy disputes over taxes, education, water, the environment, transportation, business regulations, and reducing economic and social inequality will continue to exist as they have always existed in Colorado politics. A continuing tug of war is likely among long-standing contending factions. The political battle will rage on between libertarian conservatives and communitarian progressives, between dedicated antitax advocates and those who want to use government to promote equality of opportunity, between Democrats and Republicans, between conservationists and developers, between creationists and evolutionists, between those who are pro-life on the abortion issue and those who are pro-choice, between those who favor and those who oppose civil unions, between governors and state legislators, between rural and urban counties, between the Front Range and the Western Slope, and between Colorado and the "Feds." These natural political and government factions will be with Colorado for the long term.

Perhaps the crucial political leadership battle over the next decade will be the struggle between those who would free the state from some of the constitutional limits on government taxation and expenditures and those committed in the name of personal freedom and liberty to preserve such limits. The question is not whether TABOR and related financial restrictions will be modified. It is when and how. What form will these modifications take and who will lead the counterreformation?

An impressive coalition of business leaders, policy analysts, and a few elected leaders share modifying TABOR as a goal.[49] But they are opposed by a less-sympathetic general public and by politicians who fear for their political careers if they so much as mention changing TABOR.

The state's assets outweigh its liabilities. Colorado's public policy problems are solvable, even though actually solving them will prove politically difficult and take time. Improvements in the governmental and political system are needed. Political will, vision, leadership, and shared sacrifice will be needed. To paraphrase former president Dwight Eisenhower, who loved to play golf in Colorado: The nature of public leadership necessarily involves persuasion, conciliation, education, and patience: "It's long, slow, tough work."

Part of the challenge is devising a vision that emphasizes shared values and common ground. Leadership requires an ongoing engagement of leaders and citizens. The "ship" in leadership can never be forgotten. The "ship" in this case is Coloradans, especially those among the "attentive public," who can be educated about policy choices, policy tradeoffs, and the interconnectedness of public investments and private sacrifices that need to be made to help leverage a vital economy and preserve Colorado's incomparable quality of life assets.

Colorado leaders alone cannot solve much. Leaders and led have to collaborate, and so a myriad of public-private partnerships will be key to unlocking the talents and energies of Coloradans. Politics, as always, is about creating human communities and about trying to solve public problems and helping communities become healthier, more productive, and inclusive. It is all undertaken in an effort to help people achieve shared aspirations.

The good news is that most Coloradans, at least 50 to 60 percent, are not on the extreme left or right. Some politicians may be sharply polarized, but most Coloradans are relatively pragmatic and moderate. Independents play a big role in Colorado elections. Coloradans agree on more policy matters than not. Coloradans want a better Colorado and want problem-solving leaders.

Politics and partisanship are inevitable, necessary, and mostly desirable. People here as elsewhere have different views about the relative importance of liberty, equality, and social justice. Politics exists because societies have to make choices about how best to solve common problems. There are always disagreements.

Most of Colorado's political leaders can and will amicably debate Colorado's policy challenges without becoming mean-spirited. They understand, as all of us should, that politics is the art of the possible, and debate, compromise, and problem-solving are the artistry of constitutional democracies.[50]

# Notes

I. THE CHARACTER AND SPIRIT OF COLORADO

1. Population forecasts are by Colorado state demographer Elizabeth Garner, interview by T. Cronin, May 25, 2010. See also Jerd Smith, "Colorado's Ranks Still Swelling," *Rocky Mountain News* (Denver), December 23, 2008, 8.

2. Walt Hecox, interview by T. Cronin and R. Loevy, January 2011.

3. John Gunther, *Inside U.S.A.* (New York: Harper and Brothers, 1947), 213.

4. Hecox interview. Also see Jeffrey Leib, "Experts Turn on 'Tunnel Vision'; CDOT Convenes Workshop to Ease I-70 Congestion," *Denver Post*, February 22, 2011, 1A.

5. See Patricia Nelson Limerick, *The Legacy of Conquest* (New York: Norton, 1987), for useful revision of the cowboy and mountain men legends.

6. P. Andrew Jones and Tom Cech, *Colorado Water Law for Non-Lawyers* (Boulder: University Press of Colorado, 2009).

7. Dan Frosch, "White-Water Rift," *New York Times*, April 17, 2010, A9; Jerd Smith, "Fighting for the Right," *Headwaters*, Fall 2010, 10–17.

8. Edward Abbey, quoted in Miriam Horn, "The New Old West," *Rocky Mountain News Sunday Magazine*, July 15, 1990, 13M.

9. Colorado Association of Commerce and Industry Educational Foundation, *Blueprint for Colorado: A Look at the 90s*, June 1990, 15.

10. John Fielder, *Best of Colorado* (Boulder CO: Westcliffe Publishers, 2010), 17.

11. Richard D. Lamm and Michael McCarthy, *The Angry West: A Vulnerable Land and Its Future* (Boston: Houghton Mifflin, 1982), 277.

12. Thomas H. Simmons, "Colorado," in *The Political Life of the American States*, ed. Alan Rosenthal and Maureen Moakley (New York: Praeger, 1984), 64. See also Daniel J. Elazar, *Cities of the Prairie: The Metropolitan Frontier and American Politics* (New York: Basic Books, 1970), 348–51.

13. Richard Stacy, "Colorado's Water Future: A Cup Half-Full," *Denver Post*, December 21, 2008, 2D.

14. Duane Vandenbusche and Duane Smith, *A Land Alone: Colorado's Western Slope* (Boulder: Pruett Publishing, 1981).

15. Gunther, *Inside U.S.A.*, 213. See also Neal R. Pierce, *The Mountain States of America* (New York: Norton, 1972), chap. 2.

16. Paul Talmey, interview by T. Cronin, June 7, 1990, Boulder CO.

17. Bob Ewegen, interview by T. Cronin, July 1990, Denver.

18. Robert D. Loevy, updated from "More Subtle Shades of Red and Blue" (paper presented at the 2008 annual conference of the Western Political Science Association, San Diego, March 2008).

19. Limerick, *Legacy of Conquest*.

20. Walt Klein, interview by T. Cronin, June 14, 1990.

21. Kevin Simpson, "Call for Help," *Denver Post*, May 3, 2010, 8A.

22. R. Todd Laugen, *The Gospel of Progressivism, 1900–1930* (Boulder: University Press of Colorado, 2010).

23. Author notes from attending this debate at Sheraton Hotel South, Colorado Springs CO, June 20, 1990.

24. James A. Michener, *Centennial* (New York: Random House, 1974), 926.

25. James Edward Wright, *The Politics of Populism: Dissent in Colorado* (New Haven: Yale University Press, 1974), 191.

26. Caleb Crain, "There Was Blood," *New Yorker*, January 19, 2009, 76–81; Thomas G. Andrews, *Killing for Coal* (Cambridge: Harvard University Press, 2008).

27. Lynn Bartels, "Era of Klan-Destine Bigotry," *Rocky Mountain News*, January 3, 2009, 13.

28. See Robert Alan Goldberg, *Hooded Empire: The Ku Klux Klan in Colorado* (Urbana: University of Illinois, 1981).

29. Dirk Johnson, "Colorado Klansman Refines Message for the '90s," *New York Times* (national edition), February 23, 1992, 16.

30. Richard D. Lamm and Duane A. Smith, *Pioneers and Politicians: Ten Colorado Governors in Profile* (Boulder: Pruett Publishing, 1984), 132.

31. Richard D. Lamm, interview by T. Cronin, August 7, 1990.

32. See Elazar, *Cities of the Prairie*, chap. 6; Daniel J. Elazar, *American Federalism: A View from the States*, 2nd ed. (New York: Thomas Y. Crowell, 1972), 84–126. See also John Kincaid, ed., *Political Culture, Public Policy, and the American States* (Philadelphia: ISHI Press, 1982) and a special issue of *Publius: The Journal of Federalism* (Spring 1991).

33. Talmey interview.

34. Ronald J. Hrebenar and Clive S. Thomas, *Interest Group Politics in the American West* (Salt Lake City: University of Utah Press, 1987).

## 2. COLORADANS AND THEIR POLITICAL BELIEFS

1. See Burt Hubbard, "Graying Colorado," *Denver Post*, May 30, 2010, 1, 20A.

2. Harold L. Hodgkinson, *Colorado: The State and Its Educational System* (Washington DC: Institute for Educational Leadership, 1990), 1.

3. See Colorado Higher Education Planning Commission, "The Degree Dividend: Colorado's Strategic Plan for Higher Education," a report of the Colorado Department of Higher Education, 2010, www.highered.colorado.gov.

4. Crawford citizen, interview by T. Cronin, August 9, 1990.

5. Dan Haley, "All Trust Is Local," *Denver Post*, April 25, 2010, 30.

6. See "The 2010 Congressional Battleground Polls" of twelve hundred likely voters, conducted by Greenburg Quinland Rossner Research for National Public Radio, June 14, 2010.

7. Matt Bai, "In the New Populism, Add the Government to the List of Fat Cats," *New York Times*, June 17, 2010, A17.

8. County leader, interview by T. Cronin, July 24, 2010, Creede CO.

9. Tim Wirth, "Diary of a Dropout," *New York Times Magazine*, August 9, 1992, 34.

10. Paul Talmey, quoted in *Talmey-Drake Report* 1, no. 5 (September 1992): 1.

11. Dan Balz and Jon Cohen, "Where Do You Fit In—The American Political Spectrum?" *Denver Post*, May 5, 2011, 1A.

12. Report from Colorado Legislative Council Staff, State Capitol, Denver, January 28, 2009, 1.

13. These views are documented in a 2007 statewide survey of Colorado registered voters commissioned by the Denver Metro Chamber of Commerce. *Colorado Statewide Voter Opinion Poll*, Hill Research Consultants (August 2007).

14. See Bruce E. Keith, David B. Magleby, Candice J. Nelson, Elizabeth Orr, Mark C. Westlye, and Raymond E. Wolfinger, *The Myth of the Independent Voter* (Berkeley: University of California Press, 1992).

15. Adapted from Susan Page and Naomi Jagoda, "What Is the Tea Party? A Growing State of Mind," *USA Today*, July 2, 2010, 1A, 6A. Data from a May/June 2010 national *USA Today*/Gallup Poll ($N = 697$).

16. Mike Rosen, "The Libertarian Dilemma," *Denver Post*, June 3, 2010, 11B.

17. These and the related findings in the next few paragraphs come from "Conservation in the West," a short summary report dated January 2011, prepared by Lori Weigel of Public Opinion Strategies and David Metz of FM3 in collaboration with Colorado College's "State of the Rockies" report. See also Walter Hecox and Mark Barna, "Western Values," *Denver Post*, April 17, 2011, 1D.

18. Carl Miller, former editor, *Denver Post*, interview by T. Cronin, June 26, 1990.

19. Vincent Carroll, then-editor, *Rocky Mountain News*, interview by T. Cronin, August 11, 1990.

20. See Robert D. Putnam and David E. Campbell, *American Grace* (New York: Simon and Schuster, 2010), 27.

21. Erica Meltzer, "Pot Advocates Look to 2012 Ballot for Full Legalization," *Denver Post*, June 13, 2010, 3B. Updated Rasmussen polls, 2012.

22. Talmey-Drake poll, June 2000, $N = 600$.

23. These responses were shared with us from a survey conducted by Talmey-Drake Research and Strategy in 2006. Random sample of Colorado adults ($N =$ over 600).

24. Eric Sondermann, Denver political consultant, interview by T. Cronin, September 29, 2010, Colorado Springs.

25. David Brooks, *The Social Animal* (New York: Random House, 2011), 302–3.

### 3. A BRIEF SOCIOPOLITICAL HISTORY OF COLORADO

1. See Carl Abbott, Stephen J. Leonard, and Thomas J. Noel, *Colorado: A History of the Centennial State*, 4th ed. (Boulder: University Press of Colorado, 2005), chap. 2.

2. Carl Ubbelohde, Maxine Benson, and Duane A. Smith, eds., *A Colorado History*, 5th ed. (Boulder CO: Pruett Publishing, 1982), 60.

3. Vandenbusche and Smith, *A Land Alone*, 77. See also Duane A. Smith, *The Trail of Gold and Silver: Mining in Colorado, 1859–2000* (Boulder: University Press of Colorado, 2009), chaps. 3, 4.

4. Emma F. Langdon, *The Cripple Creek Strike* (Denver: Great Western Publishing, 1904), 16.

5. Robert G. Athearn, *Rebel of the Rockies: A History of the Denver and Rio Grande Western Railroad* (New Haven: Yale University Press, 1962), 101. Also see George L. Anderson, *General William J. Palmer: A Decade of Colorado Railroad Building, 1870–1880* (Colorado Springs: Colorado College, 1936).

6. See Marshall Sprague, *Money Mountain: The Story of Cripple Creek Gold* (Boston: Little, Brown, 1953).

7. See George S. McGovern and Leonard F. Guttridge, *The Great Coalfield War* (Boston: Houghton Mifflin, 1972). See also Thomas G. Andrews, *Killing for Coal* and David Mason's epic poem about this historical period and location entitled *Ludlow: A Verse Novel* (Pasadena CA: Red Hen Press, 2007).

8. Vandenbusche and Smith, *A Land Alone*, 124. See also Elinor McGinn, *A Wide-Awake Woman: Josephine Roche in the Era of Reform* (Denver: Colorado Historical Society, 2002).

9. Ubbelohde, Benson, and Smith, *Colorado History*, 174.

10. Ubbelohde, Benson, and Smith, *Colorado History*, 331. See also Vandenbusche and Smith, *A Land Alone*, 209–62.

11. John Parr, letter to T. Cronin and R. Loevy, February 9, 1991.

12. For a range of views, see Lamm and McCarthy, *The Angry West*, and the novels of Edward Abbey.

### 4. THE COLORADO CONSTITUTION AND ITS POLITICS

1. Table 5.2, "State Constitution Characteristics," in Christopher Simon, Brent S. Steel, and Nicholas P. Lovrich, *State and Local Government: Sustainability in the Twenty-First Century* (New York: Oxford University Press, 2010), 109.

2. Table 5.2 in Simon, Steel, and Lovrich, *State and Local Government*, 109.

3. A good analysis of the bill of rights of the proposed Colorado constitution of 1875–76 appears in Mort Stern and Albert F. Frantz, "Making the Colorado Constitution Good for Another 100 Years: Taking a New Look at the Colorado Constitution," *Denver Post*, October 10, 1976, reprinted in *The Colorado Constitution: Is It Adequate for the Next Century?*, Report of the Citizens' Assembly on the State Constitution, Boulder CO, August 27–29, 1976, 44–46.

4. Sharon Eubanks, deputy director, Office of Legislative Legal Services, Colorado General Assembly, "Memorandum on the Colorado Constitution" to T. Cronin and R. Loevy, February 7, 2011, 2.

5. See Zeke Sher, "When Women Won Colorado," *Denver Post Empire Magazine*, March 4, 1979.

6. The expression "Supreme Ruler of the Universe" probably is a paraphrase of the reference in the U.S. Declaration of Independence to the "Supreme Judge of the World."

7. Curtis W. Martin and Rudolph Gomez, *Colorado Government and Politics* (Boulder CO: Pruett Press, 1972), 29.

8. As originally adopted in 1910, the Colorado initiative required signatures equal to 8 percent of the number of voters for Colorado secretary of state. The signers were not required to be registered voters, however, which made authentication of the signatures more difficult. A 1980 constitutional amendment, referred by the state legislature, stipulated that signers be registered voters, but in an effort to compensate for this tougher requirement, it reduced the number of signatures required from 8 percent of the number of voters for Colorado secretary of state to 5 percent.

9. John F. Shafroth, quoted in *Rocky Mountain News*, February 12, 1910.

10. Editorial, *Denver Republican*, October 4, 1910.

11. Amendment No. 3, 1974, general election.

12. See Amendment No. 4, in Legislative Council of the Colorado General Assembly, *An Analysis of 1988 Ballot Proposals*, Research Publication No. 326 (Denver: Legislative Council of the Colorado General Assembly, 1988), 7.

13. Legislative Council of the Colorado General Assembly, *2010 State Ballot Information Booklet*, Research Publication No. 599-94 (Denver: Legislative Council of the Colorado General Assembly, 2010), 53–54.

14. Amendment No. 3, 1972, general election.

15. Amendment No. 6, 1976, general election.

16. See Amendment No. 1, in Legislative Council, *Analysis of 1988 Ballot Proposals*, 1–3.

17. Legislative Council, *Analysis of 1988 Ballot Proposals*, 2–3.

18. Colorado Secretary of State, *1988 Colorado Campaign Reform Act Summary: Contributions and Expenditures* (Denver: Colorado Secretary of State), 53.

19. Amendment No. 7, in Legislative Council, *Analysis of 1988 Ballot Proposals*, 16–19.

20. Colorado Secretary of State, *1988 Colorado Campaign Reform Act Summary*, 56.

21. Legislative Council, *2010 State Ballot Information Booklet*, 26–29.

22. Amendment No. 10, 1976 general election. The quotes describing the proponents of the amendment are from R. D. Sloan Jr., *Proposed Amendments, Referred and Initiated, to the Colorado Constitution, 1946–1976* (Boulder: Bureau of Governmental Research and Service, University of Colorado, 1981), 43–44.

23. R. D. Sloan Jr., *Proposed Amendments, Referred and Initiated, to the Colorado Constitution in 1978 and 1980* (Boulder: Bureau of Governmental Research and Service, University of Colorado, 1981), 4. This short update article can be found in a pocket at the back of later printings of Sloan, *Proposed Amendments, Referred and Initiated, to the Colorado Constitution, 1946–1976*.

24. Amendment No. 6, in Legislative Council, *Analysis of 1988 Ballot Proposals*, 11–16; Colorado Secretary of State, *1988 Colorado Campaign Reform Act Summary*, 54–56.

25. *Colorado Springs Gazette Telegraph*, November 8, 1990, A3.

26. Eubanks, "Memorandum on the Colorado Constitution," 3.

27. "Municipal Election Results," news releases, Colorado Municipal League, November 2, 2011, 1.

28. Colorado Department of Treasury, quoted in "Amendment 23," *Denver Post*, January 16, 2011, 6D.

29. Eubanks, "Memorandum on the Colorado Constitution," 4. For the effects of the Gallagher Amendment on Colorado municipal government, see Tommy M. Brown, "Colorado Tax and Expenditure Limitation in Colorado: The Impact on Municipal Governments" (PhD diss., University of Colorado at Denver, 1999), 29, 211.

30. Tim Hoover, "Bruce Relates Role in Anti-Tax Efforts," *Denver Post*, October 14, 2010, 3B. Also see "Better Tools to Track Initiatives," *Denver Post*, October 21, 2010, 10B.

31. Legislative Council, *2010 State Ballot Information Booklet*, 12, 23, 44. See also "No Small Measures: Big Changes at Stake," *Colorado Springs Gazette*, October 10, 2010, A1.

32. "Election 2010: The Numbers," *Denver Post*, November 7, 2010, 26A.

33. Sarah Kurz and Janice Sinden, "Moving Beyond Colorado's Ballot Issue Battles," *Denver Post*, November 8, 2010, 19A.

34. Richard Lamm and Bob Tointon, "Resolved to End Ballot Imbecility," *Denver Post*, February 18, 2011, 11B.

35. Eubanks, "Memorandum on the Colorado Constitution," 4.

36. For both sides of the issue, see Kirk Johnson, "Colorado Lawsuit Challenges Wisdom of the Ballot Box," *New York Times*, January 31, 2012, A12.

37. *2008 Fact Book*, Great Outdoors Colorado, 1600 Broadway, Suite 1650, Denver CO, 80202, 3.

38. Bruce Finley, "GOCO Puts Cash in Preserves," *Denver Post*, December 9, 2010, 1A.

39. Carrie Johnson, "U.S. Eases Stance on Medical Marijuana," *Washington Post*, October 20, 2009, A1.

40. Susan Greene, "Greene: Romer to Colleagues: Quit Pot Huffing, Get Puffing," *Denver Post*, January 14, 2010.

41. John Ingold, "More than 2,000 Apply for Various Pot Licenses," *Denver Post*, August 3, 2010.

42. John Morse, majority leader (Democratic) of the Colorado Senate, interview by T. Cronin and R. Loevy, December 7, 2010, Colorado Springs.

43. John W. Suthers, attorney general of Colorado, interview by T. Cronin and R. Loevy, February 19, 2011.

44. Tim Hoover, "8 Pot Initiatives Vie for '12 Ballot," *Denver Post*, May 20, 2011.

45. For a history of these direct democracy devices and the interests that have used them, see Thomas E. Cronin, *Direct Democracy* (Cambridge: Harvard University Press, 1989).

46. Lyle Kyle, president, Colorado Expenditure Council, and former director, Legislative Council of the Colorado General Assembly, interview by authors, June 30, 1989, Denver.

47. Grant v. Meyer, 486 U.S. 414 (1988).

48. Donetta Davidson, elections officer, Office of the Colorado Secretary of State, interview by authors, June 30, 1989, Denver.

49. "Raising the Bar on Amending Colorado's Constitution," *Denver Post*, April 14, 2010. See also "A Less Malleable Colorado Charter," *Denver Post*, February 27, 2011, 3D; Fred Brown, "A Higher Vote Threshold Would Have Changed Colorado History," *Denver Post*, March 7, 2011, 17A.

50. "Building a Better Colorado through Civic Engagement," Colorado's Future, www.coloradosfuture.org, April 15, 2010, 4.

51. Dan Ritchie, interview by T. Cronin, December 9, 2010; Reeves Brown, interview by T. Cronin, December 14, 2010.

52. The same mixed sentiments exist in most other states too. See the useful overview essay by John Kincaid, "State Constitutions in the Federal System," *Annals of the American Academy of Political and Social Science* 496, no. 1. (March 1988), 12–22.

## 5. POLITICAL PARTIES AND ELECTIONS IN COLORADO

1. See the useful appendixes in Richard D. Lamm and Duane A. Smith, *Pioneers and Politicians: Colorado Governors in Profile*, 2nd ed. (Golden CO: Fulcrum, 2008), 200–203.

2. Fred Brown, "Evenly Divided Voters Mean Tricky Governing," *Denver Post*, May 23, 2009, 11B.

3. Technically speaking, when the county convention is nominating candidates for state and local offices, it is known as the county *assembly*. When it is nominating delegates to go to the state convention and vote on delegates to the party national convention, it is known as the county *convention*.

4. The same nomenclature applies to the state convention that applies to the county convention. When nominating candidates for state offices, the state convention is technically known as the state *assembly*. When electing delegates to the party national convention (at which the party candidate for president of the United States is nominated), the state convention is officially the state *convention*.

5. "David Nolan, 66, Is Dead; Started Libertarian Party," *New York Times*, November 23, 2010, A25.

## 6. ELECTING COLORADO LEGISLATORS

1. John Sanko, "Campaign Trail Is No Primrose Path," *Rocky Mountain News*, August 5, 1990, 28.

2. Robert S. Lorch, *Colorado's Government*, 3rd ed. (Boulder: Colorado Associated University Press, 1983), 180.

3. Because state senate terms are staggered, with one-half of the senators elected every two years, the Colorado Reapportionment Commission has the additional task of designating which senate districts are scheduled for election in which election years. This job is more important than it might first appear. Incumbent state senators originally elected to a four-year term of office could have to run for reelection after only two years if the reapportionment commission designates their senate district to be elected at the next election.

4. For a full review of the 2011 Colorado Reapportionment Commission, see Rob-

ert Loevy, "Confessions of a Reapportionment Commissioner," Special Collections, Tutt Library, Colorado College. For a different way of looking at redistricting, see Seth E. Masket, Jonathan Winburn, and Gerald C. Wright, "The Gerrymanderers Are Coming! Legislative Redistricting Won't Affect Competition or Polarization Much, No Matter Who Does It," *ps: Political Science and Politics*, January 2012, 39–43.

5. Speech by Chuck Berry, Colorado House of Representatives, April 29, 1997, quoted in John Straayer, *The Colorado General Assembly*, 2nd ed. (Boulder: University Press of Colorado, 2000), 22.

6. One of the authors, R. Loevy, was a Republican member of the 2011 Colorado Reapportionment Commission.

7. Gene Nichol, "Legislative Reapportionment Panel Should Also Set Congressional District Lines," *Denver Post*, February 8, 1992, 7B.

8. For additional ideas on U.S. House of Representatives redistricting in Colorado, see Dottie Lamm, "Redrawing District Lines," *Denver Post*, November 10, 2010, 4D.

9. According to a study by Colorado Common Cause, eighteen of the incumbent Colorado legislators who ran for reelection in 1986 had no opposition. Eleven of these legislators with "super safe" seats were Republicans and seven were Democrats. See *"PACed" Houses II: Common Cause Reports on Campaign Financing in Colorado* (Denver: Colorado Common Cause, January 1988), 21.

10. John Britz, director, House Democratic Majority Fund, interview by R. Loevy, December 21, 1989, Denver.

11. "The Post's Picks for State House," *Denver Post*, October 15, 2010, 10B.

12. "The Post's Picks for State House."

13. The following list of reasons that the Democrats gained control of both houses of the Colorado legislature was summarized by Robert D. Loevy in Courtney Daum, Robert J. Duffy, and John A. Straayer, eds., *State of Change: Colorado Politics in the 21st Century* (Boulder: University Press of Colorado, 2011).

14. Sondermann interview, September 29, 2010.

15. The *Denver Post* summarized these financial techniques on the part of the Democratic Party in a major retrospective. See Adam Schrager and Rob Witwer, "How the Dems Won Colorado," *Denver Post*, April 11, 2010, D1.

16. Steve Durham, business lobbyist at the state legislature and former state senator, interview by T. Cronin and R. Loevy, January 2011.

17. Lynn Bartels, "State GOP Counsel Joins Race for Chair," *Denver Post*, February 9, 2011, 4B.

18. For a detailed description of how "the gang of four" did it, see Schrager and Witwer, "How the Dems Won Colorado."

19. Vincent Carroll, "Nuclear Attack Ad," *Denver Post*, September 26, 2010, 3D.

20. Carroll, "Nuclear Attack Ad."

21. Tom Roeder, "GOP Candidate Asks D.A. for a Ruling on Claim," *Colorado Springs Gazette*, October 6, 2010.

22. Sondermann interview, September 29, 2010.

23. Adam Schrager and Rob Witwer, *The Blueprint: How the Democrats Won Colorado (and Why Republicans Everywhere Should Care)* (Golden CO: Speaker's Corner Books, 2010), 63–65.

### 7. LEGISLATIVE POLITICS AND PROCESSES

1. John A. Straayer, *The Colorado General Assembly* (Boulder: University Press of Colorado, 1990), 12.

2. Chuck Berry, Speaker of the House, Colorado House of Representatives, notes by R. Loevy on speech to Taft Institute, Colorado Springs, June 27, 1991.

3. Lynn Bartels, "Women in 41% of Seats," *Denver Post*, February 9, 2011, 2B.

4. Lynn Bartels, "Female GOP Lawmaker Numbers Rebounding," *Denver Post*, January 5, 2011, 3B.

5. Lynn Bartels, "Three Latinas Moment Bittersweet," *Denver Post*, January 2, 2011, 4B.

6. Morse interview, December 7, 2010.

7. John A. Straayer, *The Colorado General Assembly*, 2nd ed. (Boulder: University Press of Colorado, 2000), 88.

8. Straayer, *Colorado General Assembly*, 2nd ed., 76.

9. David Hite, deputy director, Colorado Legislative Council staff, interview by R. Loevy, June 28, 1989, Denver.

10. Wayne Knox, Democratic state representative, District 3 (south-central Denver), interview by R. Loevy, December 21, 1989, Denver.

11. Tim Hoover, "A Crossover on Tuition Bill," *Denver Post*, February 3, 2011, 1A.

12. Tim Hoover, "House Chief Planning to Speak with Softened Tone," *Denver Post*, January 2, 2011, 1B.

13. Straayer, *Colorado General Assembly*, 2nd ed., 91.

14. Morse interview, December 7, 2010.

15. Straayer, *Colorado General Assembly*, 2nd ed., 57.

16. "Lawmaking Process to Undergo Reforms," *Denver Post*, November 9, 1988, 3AA.

17. Straayer, *Colorado General Assembly*, 2nd ed., 267.

18. Alan Rosenthal, director, Eagleton Institute, Rutgers University, quoted in "Lawmakers' Control of State Budget Limits Influence of Colorado Governor," *Denver Post*, January 29, 1989, 1B.

19. Colorado senator Mike Bird (Republican, Colorado Springs), conversation with R. Loevy during a tour of the Joint Budget Committee office suite, c. 1992. In

2011 Sarietha Ormsby of the JBC staff confirmed that the photograph of the men with the axes was still hanging on the wall of a JBC hearing room.

20. Shoemaker was so enthusiastic about the JBC that he wrote a book about it. See Joe Shoemaker, *Budgeting Is the Answer: A Story of a Unique Committee—The Joint Budget Committee of Colorado* (New York: World Press, 1977).

21. Alan Rosenthal, *Governors and Legislatures: Contending Powers* (Washington DC: Congressional Quarterly Press, 1990), 139.

22. Morse interview, December 7, 2010.

23. Durham interview, January 2011.

24. Morse interview, December 7, 2010.

25. Tim Hoover, "Power to the Budget Panel," *Denver Post*, February 8, 2009, 2B.

26. John Straayer, letter to T. Cronin and R. Loevy, May 2011.

27. Durham interview, January 2011. The authors benefited from several conversations with lobbyists, including Ken Smith and Ed Bowditch, among others. In earlier years we also interviewed Roger Walton, Stan Dempsey, Pat Ratliff, and Briggs Gamblin.

28. All quotes from Wade Buchanan, interview by T. Cronin and R. Loevy, February 4, 2011, Colorado Springs.

29. Roger Alan Walton, *Colorado: A Practical Guide to Its Government and Politics* (Fort Collins CO: Publisher's Consultants, 1983), 85.

30. William T. Bagley, *California's Golden Years: When Government Worked and Why* (Berkeley CA: Institute Of Governmental Studies, 2010).

31. Alan Rosenthal, *Engines of Democracy: Politics and Policymaking in State Legislatures* (Washington DC: CQ Press, 2009), 208. Also see John A. Straayer, "Colorado's Legislative Term Limits" (unpublished paper, Joint Project on Term Limits, Colorado State University, Fort Collins, August 2004).

32. Josh Penry, former state senator (Republican, Grand Junction), speaking at El Pomar Center in Colorado Springs, May 19, 2010.

33. Brandon Shaffer, interview in the *Colorado Statesman*, January 20, 2012, 4–5.

## 8. THE COLORADO GOVERNORSHIP

1. This state employee number is hard to verify. The state legislature's Joint Budget Committee's count for full-time-equivalent employees is about fifty-five thousand, yet this apparently does not count a lot of people who work for state colleges and universities. People in the state Department of Personnel are often confused by the question and say: "It's very complicated." They allow that state employment, counting everyone from adjunct professors to state parks summer employees, might run as high as ninety thousand.

2. William Porter, "Guv Box Crammed with a Lot of Duties," *Denver Post*, January 11, 2011, 4A.

3. The "Colorado Promise" was Gov. Bill Ritter's set of plans for Colorado espoused during his 2006 election campaign. Most of the Colorado Promise was watered down or abandoned because of the severe economic and budget difficulties in the state following the onset of the recession in 2008.

4. Josh Penry, interview by T. Cronin and R. Loevy, May 2010, Penrose House, Colorado Springs. Also see Josh Penry, "Legislative Leader's Outline . . . ," *Denver Post*, January 4, 2009, 1D, and Josh Penry, "Strapped State Budget . . . ," *Rocky Mountain News*, January 3, 2009, 26.

5. Love quoted in Lamm and Smith, *Pioneers and Politicians*, 4.

6. For background profiles of these and other contenders, see Lamm and Smith, *Pioneers and Politicians*. Also see Helen Williams, ed., *Roy Romer Is Alive and Well and Living in California* (Walden CO: Walden Press, 2004). Also see Adam Schrager, *The Principled Politician: Governor Ralph Carr and the Fight against Japanese American Internment* (Golden CO: Fulcrum, 2009).

7. Tim Hoover, "Recent Guvs Rue Move," *Denver Post*, December 10, 2010, 1.

8. "Introduced Bills Statistics, 2000–2010," provided by the Office of Legislative Legal Services, Colorado General Assembly, October 20, 2010.

9. "Introduced Bills Statistics, 2000–2010."

10. Tim Hoover and Lynn Bartels, "Hick Ready for Work," *Denver Post*, January 14, 2011, 12A.

11. Thad Beyle, "2010 Gubernatorial Institutional Power Index," private communication to T. Cronin and R. Loevy, August 2010. Data from Council of State Governments, *The Book of the States*, vol. 42 (Lexington KY: Council of State Governments, 2010).

12. Porter, "Guv Box Crammed With a Lot of Duties."

13. Dick Lamm, comments at Colorado College forum "Governing Colorado," March 31, 2010, Colorado Springs. Video available at Special Collections, Tutt Library, Colorado College.

14. Bill Owens, remarks at Fillmore Theater, Denver, January 13, 2011, from notes by T. Cronin.

15. Roy Romer, comments at Colorado College forum "Governing Colorado," March 31, 2010. Also see Leslie Jorgensen, "Colorado Governors Share Memories and Thoughts," *Colorado Statesman*, April 9, 2010, 15.

16. Mark P. Couch, "Ritter May Face 'Learning Curve' as Governor," *Denver Post*, November 21, 2006, 4B.

17. Porter, "Guv Box Crammed With a Lot of Duties."

18. See Dorothy F. Olshfski and Robert B. Cunningham, *Agendas and Decisions: How State Government Executives and Middle Managers Make and Administer Policy* (Albany NY: State University of New York Press, 2008), 3.

19. See, for example, Thad L. Beyle and Lynn R. Muchmore, eds., *Being Governor: The View from the Office* (Durham NC: Duke University Press, 1983).

20. B. J. Thornberry, deputy chief of staff to Colorado governor Roy Romer, interview by R. Loevy, January 22, 1990.

21. Eugene Petrone, former executive director, Colorado Office of State Planning and Budget, interview by R. Loevy, January 19, 1990.

22. Larry Kallenberger, director, Colorado Department of Local Affairs, interview by R. Loevy, January 26, 1990.

23. "Lawmakers' Control of State Budget Limits Influence of Colorado Governor," *Denver Post*, January 29, 1989, 1B.

24. Lynn Bartels, "Final Chapter Not Written," *Rocky Mountain News*, December 16, 2006, 30A.

25. Governor Ritter did not lose completely on oil and natural gas issues. He succeeded in reconfiguring the state commission that regulates oil and gas natural gas producers in Colorado, and he obtained new rules regulating drilling for oil and natural gas.

26. "Lawmakers' Control of State Budget Limits Influence of Colorado Governor," *Denver Post*, January 29, 1989, 1B.

27. Petrone interview, January 19, 1990.

28. Kallenberger interview, January 26, 1990.

29. Eugene Petrone, interview by T. Cronin, August 1, 1990.

30. Stewart Bliss, interview by T. Cronin, August 1, 1990.

31. Lamm interview, August 7, 1990.

32. John Andrews, interview by T. Cronin, February 5, 2010.

33. Lamm interview, August 7, 1990.

34. Kallenberger interview, January 26, 1990.

35. The Lamm and Smith views come from discussions with the authors in 2010. The Lorch and Null quote is from Robert S. Lorch and James A. Null, *Colorado's Government: Structure, Politics, Administration, and Policy*, 8th ed. (Colorado Springs CO: Center for the Study of Government and the Individual, 2005), 245.

36. Suthers interview, February 19, 2011. Also see John W. Suthers and Terri Connell, *The People's Lawyer: A History of the Colorado Attorney General's Office* (Kearney NE: Morris Publishing, 2007), chap. 7.

37. Ubbelohde, Benson, and Smith, *Colorado History*, 369.

38. *Newsweek*, September 17, 1979.

39. Lamm's remarks paraphrased from his comments at Colorado College forum "Governing Colorado," March 31, 2010.

40. Lamm and Smith, *Pioneers and Politicians*, 4.

41. Ed Quillen, interview by T. Cronin, July 23, 2010, Salida CO.

42. Lamm's remarks paraphrased from his comments at Colorado College forum "Governing Colorado," March 31, 2010.

43. Lamm, Colorado College forum, March 31, 2010.

44. Romer's remarks paraphrased from his comments at Colorado College forum "Governing Colorado," March 31, 2010.

45. Gov. Roy Romer, comments to Taft Institute Seminar in Room 0112, State Capitol, June 27, 1988.

46. Salazar served as legal counsel and later as executive director of the Department of Natural Resources for Romer. Quoted in Williams, *Roy Romer Is Alive and Well*, 117.

47. Romer's remarks paraphrased from his comments at Colorado College forum "Governing Colorado," March 31, 2010.

48. Thomas Frank, "Bill Owens Begins Race for Governor," *Denver Post*, January 7, 1998, 1B.

49. John Aloysius Farrell, "Owens Tenure Coming to an End," www.denverpost. com, December 10, 2006.

50. Owens's remarks paraphrased from his comments at Colorado College forum "Governing Colorado," March 31, 2010.

51. Owens, Colorado College forum, March 31, 2010.

52. Farrell, "Owens Tenure Coming to an End."

53. Owens, Colorado College forum, March 31, 2010.

54. Owens, Colorado College forum, March 31, 2010.

55. Miles Moffit, "Former DA Follows Own Path," *Denver Post*, July 30, 2006, 1A.

56. Todd Hartman, "Getting in Tune with Ritter," *Rocky Mountain News*, 2006, 25A.

57. Ryan Lizza, "The Code of the West: What Barack Obama Can Learn from Bill Ritter," *New Yorker*, www.newyorker.com, September 1, 2008.

58. Greg Griffin, "State Defends Green Push . . . ," *Denver Post*, July 25, 2010, 4K.

59. Floyd Ciruli, "Colorado Governor Struggles at Halfway Point in First Term," Ciruli Associates Poll, www.ciruli.com/polls/ritterrisk-808.htm, July 22, 2008, 2.

60. Eric Sondermann, interview by T. Cronin, September 29, 2010.

61. Bill Ritter, discussion with T. Cronin in governor's office, October 14, 2010.

62. John Hickenlooper, inaugural address, January 11, 2011, notes by T. Cronin. Also see Tim Hoover, "On Hick's First Day, a Nod to Business," *Denver Post*, January 12, 2011, 1A; Hoover and Bartels, "Hick Ready for Work"; Frank Bruni, "The Hickenlooper Exception," *New York Times Magazine*, January 9, 2011, 25.

63. Lynn Bartels, "A Look in Rearview Mirror as Session Fades," *Denver Post*, May 15, 2011, 4B. See also Tim Hoover, "The Governor's First 100 Days," *Denver Post*, April 21, 2011, 1B.

64. Tim Hoover, "Smooth Sailing, But . . . ," *Denver Post*, December 3, 2011, 1. See also Vincent Carroll, "Hick's Surprising Centrism," *Denver Post*, June 20, 2012, 25A.

### 9. JUDGES AND JUSTICE IN COLORADO

1. See Mike Rosen, "Lobato Case Defies Logic," *Denver Post*, January 5, 2012, 11B; and Mark Hillman, "Rationality Eludes Judge in School Financing Case," *Colorado Statesman*, January 6, 2012, 14, 31.

2. John Andrews, interview by T. Cronin, February 5, 2010. Andrews has expressed similar views in his op-ed columns in the *Denver Post*.

3. See Mary J. Mullarkey, chief justice, Colorado Supreme Court, "State of the Judiciary," Address to the General Assembly, January 9, 2009, 3.

4. Smith, *Trail of Gold and Silver*, 39. See also David L. Erickson, *Early Justice and the Formation of the Colorado Bar* (Denver: Colorado Bar Association, 2008), chap. 2.

5. As summarized in the evaluation provided by the Legislative Council of the Colorado state legislature: *An Analysis of the 1966 Ballot Proposals*, Research Publication No. 110 (Denver: Colorado Legislative Council, 1966), 150.

6. Joseph R. Quinn, chief justice, Colorado Supreme Court, interview by R. Loevy, February 9, 1990. For a similar view, see Charles Roos, "Colorado System among the Best for Selecting Qualified Judges," *Rocky Mountain News*, August 4, 1990, 90.

7. Jean E. Dubofsky, former associate justice, Colorado Supreme Court, interview by T. Cronin, June 7, 1990.

8. Rebecca Love Kourlis, former associate justice, Colorado Supreme Court, interview by T. Cronin, April 6, 2010.

9. Mullarkey quoted in *Colorado Justice*, a pamphlet "celebrating 40 years of fair and impartial courts through merit selection." The pamphlet was issued by the Colorado Judiciary Branch in 2006. See also Bob Ewegen, "Colorado's 'Gold Standard' for Impartial Courts," *Colorado Statesman*, May 6, 2011.

10. Greg Hobbs, "Colorado Judicial Merit Selection—A Well-Deserved 40th Anniversary Celebration," 35 *Colorado Lawyer* 13 (April 2006): 14.

11. Senator Ralph A. Cole, interview by T. Cronin, July 10, 1990. Former state senator Steve Durham shared similar views with the authors during an interview in January 2011.

12. Lamm quote in John Sanko, "State High Court Shifts Back to Center," *Rocky Mountain News*, August 4, 1991, 8.

13. Judge John E. Gallagher, interview by T. Cronin, August 21, 1990.

14. Information provided by Bill Campbell, executive director, Commission on Judicial Discipline, interview with T. Cronin, July 10, 2010. Additional information provided by a retired district court judge.

15. Suthers interview, February 19, 2011.

16. Data from Public Information Office, Colorado State Supreme Court, 2010.

17. Data provided by public information coordinators of the Colorado State Court Administrator's Office, January 2010.

18. Quinn interview, February 9, 1990.

19. John Sanko, "The Place Where Justice Is Done," *Rocky Mountain News*, August 4, 1991, 34.

20. Sanko, "Place Where Justice Is Done," 34.

21. Rulings from 1981 to 1991 are from the *Rocky Mountain News*, August 4, 1994, 34. Others from the *Rocky Mountain News*, *Denver Post*, or court documents.

22. For a popular biography of Gov. Ralph L. Carr, see Schrager, *The Principled Politician*.

23. Chief Justice Luis D. Rovira, interview by T. Cronin, February 27, 1992.

24. Greg Hobbs, *In Praise of Fair Colorado: The Practice of Poetry, History, and Judging* (Denver: Bradford Publishing, 2004), 369.

25. An informative history of the Colorado Court of Appeals is provided in Jeannie Towle Mellinger and Molly Wingate, *The Colorado Court of Appeals* (Denver: Colorado Bar Association, 2008).

26. John W. Suthers, *No Higher Calling, No Greater Responsibility: A Prosecutor Makes His Case* (Golden CO: Fulcrum, 2008), 162.

27. Dubofsky interview, June 7, 1990.

28. For an understanding of Colorado's water law, see Jones and Cech, *Colorado Water Law for Non-Lawyers*. See also several of the chapters in Hobbs, *In Praise of Fair Colorado*. Also useful are *Headwaters*, a magazine put out by the Colorado Foundation for Water Education, and *Colorado Water*, put out by the Water Center of Colorado State University.

29. Charles Larsen, *The Good Fight: The Life and Times of Ben B. Lindsey* (Chicago: Quadrangle Books, 1972), and see also Lindsey's own story in *The Beast* (New York: Doubleday, 1910).

30. See the splendid study by Anthony Lewis, *Gideon's Trumpet* (New York: Vintage, 1964).

31. David L. Wood, cochair, Colorado [Supreme Court] Task Force on Gender Bias in the Courts, interview by R. Loevy, February 20, 1990. Wood is an attorney in Fort Collins CO. See also Rebecca Virtue Smith, "The Colorado Supreme Court Task Force Examines Gender Bias," *Colorado Lawyer* 19, no. 9 (July 1990): 1291–96. The task force's report is available from the Office of the State Court Administrator, Denver.

32. Katherine Tamblyn, cochair, Colorado [Supreme Court] Task Force on Gender Bias in the Courts, interview by R. Loevy, February 22, 1990.

33. American Association Of Retired Persons (AARP), *AARP Bulletin*, January/February 2010, 47.

34. Kourlis interview, April 6, 2010.

35. Quinn interview, February 9, 1990. This is a view echoed again and again in more recent conversations with judges and justices.

36. For more on mediation, see Joseph Folger and Tricia Jones, eds., *New Directions in Mediation* (Thousand Oaks CA: Sage, 1994).

37. See Kirk Mitchell, "State Walks Away from Jail Boot Camp," *Denver Post*, May 28, 2010, 1A. See also "Costs Shut Down Prison Boot Camp," *Colorado Springs Gazette*, May 29, 2010, A8.

38. Katherine Sanguinetti, Colorado Department of Corrections, interview by T. Cronin, July 19, 2010.

39. See William Wilbanks, *The Make My Day Law: Colorado's Experiment in Home Protection* (Lanham MD: University Press of America, 1990).

40. Wilbanks, *Make My Day Law*, chap. 10.

41. Andrews interview, February 5, 2010.

42. See William Banta, "Evaluating the Performance of Justices," *Denver Post*, February 13, 2010, 11B. See also John Andrews, "Can 'Em or Keep 'Em," *Denver Post*, April 5, 2009, 5D.

43. Marianne Goodland, "Colorado Supreme Court Justice Mullarkey to Step Down from the Bench," *Colorado Statesman*, July 2, 2010, 32. See also Monte Whaley, "Colorado Groups Work to Kick Out Judges," *Denver Post*, July 18, 2010, 4B.

44. Retired U.S. Supreme Court associate justice Sandra Day O'Connor, "Take Justice Off the Ballot," *New York Times Week in Review*, May 23, 2010, 9.

45. Bob Ewegen, former columnist and editor of the *Denver Post*, interview by T. Cronin, July 19, 2010. This same view was shared with us by Justice Greg Hobbs, interview by T. Cronin, January 27, 2011, and by other respected state and U.S. judges as well as by Attorney General John W. Suthers.

## 10. COLORADO IN THE FEDERAL SYSTEM

1. John Shroyer, "Hick: Troops Key to Success," *Colorado Springs Gazette*, November 20, 2010, A3. Also, John Hickenlooper, state of the state address, State Capitol, Denver, January 12, 2012.

2. Duane A. Smith, *The Birth of Colorado: A Civil War Perspective* (Norman: University of Oklahoma Press, 1989), 20.

3. The state historical marker at Glorieta Pass these days simply reads: "The decisive battle of the Civil War fought in New Mexico was fought at the summit of Glorieta Pass on March 28, 1862. Union troops won the battle when a party of Colorado Volunteers burned the Confederate supply wagons, thus destroying Southern hopes for taking over New Mexico." The marker is about a mile off of present-day I-25. See, for background, Smith, *The Birth of Colorado*, and Marc Simmons, *New Mexico: An Interpretative History* (New York: Norton, 1977). We also consulted a memoir of Benjamin Franklin Ferris, who fought in the Colorado Volunteers, on file at the Civil War Museum at Glorieta Pass NM.

4. Alvin M. Josephy Jr., *The Civil War in the American West* (New York: Alfred A. Knopf, 1991), 76–86. Josephy entitled his chapter on the Battle of Glorieta Pass "Gettysburg of the West."

5. Smith, *The Birth of Colorado*, 210.

6. Lindsay Regan Calhoun, "Remembering Sand Creek: Nation, Identity, and

Collective Memory in Narrative and Performance" (PhD diss., University of Utah, 2007), 3.

7. Abbott, Leonard, and Noel, *Colorado: A History of the Centennial State*, 70–71. For a different interpretation of what happened at Sand Creek, see Irving Howbert, *Indians of the Pike's Peak Region* (Glorieta NM: Rio Grande Press, 1914).

8. Campbell quoted in James Brooke, "Efforts Grow to Unearth Killing Fields of Old West," *New York Times*, August 30, 1998, 16.

9. Herman J. Viola, *Ben Nighthorse Campbell: An American Warrior* (Boulder CO: Johnson Books, 2002), 334.

10. For further interpretations of what happened at Sand Creek, see Stan Hoig, *The Sand Creek Massacre* (Norman: University of Oklahoma Press, 1961); Reginald S. Craig, *The Fighting Parson: The Biography of Colonel John M. Chivington* (Los Angeles: Western Lore, 1959); and Norma V. Asadorian, "The Sand Creek Massacre: Genocide on the Colorado Plains" (MA thesis, Southern Illinois University at Edwardsville), 2000.

11. Jonathan Thompson, "Practical Sovereignty," *Denver Post*, September 12, 2010, 1D. See also *High Country News*, July 19, 2010.

12. Ubbelohde, Benson, and Smith, *Colorado History*, 223.

13. Oliver Knight, "Correcting Nature's Error: The Colorado–Big Thompson Project," *Agricultural History*, October 1956, 157–69.

14. See Fred Greenbaum, *Fighting Progressive: A Bibliography of Edward P. Costigan* (Washington DC: Public Affairs Press, 1971).

15. See the useful history by Robert Harvey, *Amache: The Story of Japanese Internment in Colorado during World War II* (Dallas: Taylor Trade Publishing, 2004).

16. Harvey, *Amache*.

17. Schrager, *The Principled Politician*. See also "Forgotten Hero: Ralph Carr," chap. 10 in Richard D. Lamm and Duane A. Smith, *Pioneers and Politicians: Colorado Governors in Profile* (Golden CO: Fulcrum, 2008), 135–43.

18. See Andrew Gulliford, *Boomtown Blues: Colorado's Oil Shale, 1885–1985* (Boulder: University Press of Colorado, 1989).

19. Jim Spehar, "Remembering Colorado's Oil-Shale 'Boom,'" *Denver Post*, November 28, 2010, 1D.

20. Brian D. Burnett, "Reduction in Public Funding for Post-Secondary Education in Colorado from 1970 to 2010" (PhD diss., University of Colorado at Colorado Springs, 2010), 132. We have updated some of these figures.

21. See figure 4.2, "Share of the Colorado state general fund appropriations by program, 1970–2010," in Burnett, "Reduction in Public Funding," 133.

22. Lamm and McCarthy's *The Angry West* represents a populist resentment of outsider control, whether it be by absentee landlord corporations or the U.S. government. Theirs is both an individualistic and moralistic lament.

11. THE IMPORTANT ROLE OF LOCAL GOVERNMENT

1. Debbie Kelley, "Residents May Again Vote on Becoming a City," *Colorado Springs Gazette*, February 1, 2011, A1.

2. Douglas G. Brown, director, Office of Legislative Legal Services, Colorado General Assembly, interview by T. Cronin and R. Loevy, July 18, 1989.

3. Cathy Reynolds, at-large member, Denver City Council, interview by R. Loevy, December 6, 1989.

4. "Credit Belongs to the People for Exerting Can-Do Spirit," *Denver Post*, August 19, 1990, 2H.

5. Daniel J. Chacon, "Developers Put $778,000 into Strong-Mayor Push," *Colorado Springs Gazette*, December 3, 2010, A1.

6. The three home-rule counties are Pitkin County, which contains the city of Aspen; Summit County, which contains the well-known ski resorts of Breckenridge and Keystone; and Weld County, which contains the city of Greeley.

7. Larry Bowes, chief executive officer, Colorado Counties, Inc., interview by R. Loevy, November 21, 1989.

8. The term "flagpole annexation" comes from how the annexation appears on a map. The "flagpole" is a thin strip of annexed land reaching out from the current city boundary line. The "flag" is the large piece of ground at the end of the "flagpole," some distance from the city boundary line, that is the main area being annexed. Flagpole annexations must be designed in such a way that they meet the one-sixth contiguity requirements of Colorado's municipal annexation law.

9. Dan Haley, "The Plight of Jailed Mom," *Denver Post*, January 30, 2011, 3D.

10. For a detailed description of the planning and development of the Denver-area RTD and its light rail and heavy rail services, see Walton W. Loevy, *Passenger Rail: The Transportation Alternative* (Baltimore: Publish America, 2005), chap. 12, 182–96.

11. Jeffrey Leib, "RTD to Seek Sales Tax Hike for Rail," *Denver Post*, March 2, 2001, 1A.

12. Jeffrey Lieb, "Full Speed Ahead," *Denver Post*, December 30, 2010, 1A.

13. "Denver Union Station," *Denver Post*, January 1, 2012, 3K.

14. Loevy, *Passenger Rail*, chap. 12, 218–21.

15. Allan Blomquist, interview by R. Loevy, February 12, 1992.

16. Debbie Kelley, "Voters Might Be Asked to Step Up; Extension of Tax Hike Could Be Sought Again," *Colorado Springs Gazette*, January 24, 2011, A1.

17. Debbie Kelley, "Building Will Be Fixed Up; Scaled Back Renovation of Centennial Hall Planned," *Colorado Springs Gazette*, January 7, 2011, A1.

18. Joey Kirchmer, "New Adams County Building in New Year," *Denver Post*, December 27, 2010, 13A.

19. "315,425 Clicks: Colorado Springs Cuts into Services Considered Basic by Many," *Denver Post*, December 31, 2010, 1B.
20. Jeremy P. Meyer, "Budget Woes' Bottom Line," *Denver Post*, January 20, 2011, 1B.
21. Barbara Cotter, "Cutting to the Bone on Health," *Colorado Springs Gazette*, November 8, 2010, A1.
22. Susan Thornton, "Aurorans Are Losing Library Access Again," *Denver Post*, January 2, 2011, 2D.

## 12. COLORADO'S ASSETS AND LIABILITIES

1. Federal Aviation Administration (FAA), 2010.
2. *www.chiefexecutive.net*, December 7, 2010.
3. Fred Brown, "Independence, Not Anarchy," *Denver Post*, November 7, 2010, 3D.
4. John A. Straayer, "Just One Thing After Another: Layers of Policy and Colorado's Fiscal Train Wreck," paper delivered at the Southwest Social Science Association meeting, Denver, April 2009, 19.
5. John Hickenlooper, second state of the state address, quoted in Tim Hoover and Lynn Bartels, "Tip of the Hat to State Spirit," *Denver Post*, January 13, 2012, 1.
6. "Colorado Budget Still Tied in Knots," *Denver Post*, November 7, 2010, 3D.
7. Tom Clark, "Is Metro Area Attractive to Outside Business?" *Denver Post*, September 13, 2010, 21A; Fred Brown, "State's Ballot Process Alienates Business Community," *Denver Post*, May 23, 2010, 2D; Tom Clark, interview by T. Cronin, January 19, 2011.
8. Andy Vuong, "Homework to Do," *Denver Post*, July 25, 2010, 1A.
9. *Kiplinger's Personal Finance*, February 2011, 63–64.
10. Colorado Higher Education Planning Commission, "The Degree Dividend," www.highered.colorado.gov, 13.
11. *Southern Colorado Economic Forum* (Colorado Springs: University of Colorado at Colorado Springs, October 1, 2010), 28.
12. Bruce D. Benson, "Multifaceted Legislation Effort Offers Hope for More Stability in Higher Education," *Colorado Statesman*, January 8, 2010, 5.
13. For a general discussion of these problems, see Tom McGhee, "Higher Ed Panel Suggests Tax Hike," *Denver Post*, November 5, 2010, B1.
14. Tom McGhee, "Community Colleges Feel Fiscal Strain," *Denver Post*, November 26, 2010, 3B.
15. Colorado Higher Education Planning Commission, "The Degree Dividend," 21. See also Burnett, "Reduction in Public Funding."
16. Tony Milo, "Thankfully, Some Chose to Lead," Colorado Contractors Association handout, November 2010, 2.

17. Carlos Illescas, "Pueblo Tops in State Crime," *Denver Post*, November 24, 2010, 1B.

18. San Luis city clerk, interview by T. Cronin, December 6, 2010.

19. Tina Griego, "Bent County Residents Fight Fiscal Lockdown," *Denver Post*, February 20, 2011, 2B.

20. Hickenlooper, state of the state address, January 13, 2011.

21. Jones and Cech, *Colorado Water Law for Non-Lawyers*, 48–49.

22. Tyler McMahon and Matthew Reuer, "Water Sustainability in the Rockies," in *State of the Rockies Report Card* (Colorado Springs: Colorado College, 2007), 40.

23. Jerd Smith, "Kourlises: Citizens of the West," *Headwaters*, Winter 2010, 12.

24. Suzanne O'Neill and Ken Neubecker, "Oil Shale's Thirst Is a Threat to the West," *Denver Post*, December 17, 2010, 11B.

25. Jim Lochhead, "Priorities for Denver Water," *Denver Post*, January 14, 2011, 11B.

26. Marle Samuelson, "Headed for the State House," *Denver Post*, January 2, 2011, 1R.

27. Timothy E. Wirth and Alice Madden, "Natural Gas Industry Should Welcome Oversight," *Denver Post*, March 28, 2011.

28. Colorado Association of Commerce and Industry advertisement, *Colorado Statesman*, January 7, 2011, 40.

29. Fred Brown, "State's Ballot Process Alienates Business Community," *Denver Post*, May 23, 2010, 2D.

30. "Shaping the Economic Future of Colorado," Colorado Economic Futures Panel, University of Denver, 2005.

31. Denver Metro Chamber of Commerce, "Scorecard Report," www.denverchamber.org/scorecardreport.

32. Greg Griffin, "Boulder: Where Innovation Is Hip," *Denver Post*, July 25, 2010, K1.

33. Cheryl Myers, "Is Boulder the Silicon Valley of the Rockies?" *5280 Magazine*, January 2011, 47.

34. John Kao, *Innovative Nation* (New York: Free Press, 2007), and Steven Johnson, *Where Good Ideas Come From* (New York: Riverhead Books, 2010).

35. Holden Thorp and Buck Goldstein, *Engines of Innovation: The Entrepreneurial University in the Twenty-First Century* (Chapel Hill: University of North Carolina, 2010).

36. Jared Bernstein, Elizabeth McNichol, and Andrew Nicholas, *Pulling Apart: A State-by-State Analysis of Income Trends* (Washington DC: Center on Budget and Policy Priorities, 2008), 29.

37. Maria St. Louis Sanchez, "El Paso County Poverty Rate," *Colorado Springs Gazette*, www.gazette.com, September 28, 2009.

38. Allison Sherry, "Child Poverty Skyrockets in Colorado," *Denver Post*, www. denverpost.com, April 4, 2010; Rich Jones et al., *Opportunities Lost: 2010 Update* (Denver: Bell Policy Center, 2010).

39. Benjamin I. Page and Lawrence R. Jacobs, *Class War? What Americans Really Think about Economic Inequality* (Chicago: University of Chicago Press, 2009), 97.

40. Page and Jacobs, *Class War?*, 46.

41. Mike Rosen, "Income Inequality is Inevitable," *Denver Post*, December 15, 2011, 9B.

42. Nicholas D. Kristoff, "Equality, a True Soul Food," *New York Times*, January 2, 2011, 10. See also Joseph Stiglitz, *The Price of Inequality* (New York, W. W. Norton, 2012).

43. For examples of those who want to reform or bypass TABOR restrictions, see Carol Hedges, "Raising Taxes Must Be on the Table in November," *Denver Post*, February 27, 2011, 1D. See also Tim Hoover, "Lawsuit Targets TABOR," *Denver Post*, May 23, 2011, 1A.

44. Ewegen interview, July 19, 2010.

45. John A. Straayer, paper delivered at El Pomar Center in Colorado Springs, June 28, 2006, and other conversations with T. Cronin in 2009 and 2010.

46. Straayer, "Just One Thing After Another."

47. "Shaping the Economic Future of Colorado," 3.

48. Some people argue that such a change would be elitist. See, for example, Vincent Carroll, "Olympic Hurdle for Initiatives," *Denver Post*, February 23, 2011, 11B. For a different perspective, see Bradley J. Young, *TABOR and Direct Democracy* (Golden CO: Fulcrum, 2006).

49. See, for example, the *Denver Post* editorial, "It's Time To Talk Taxes, Colorado," September 4, 2011, 3D. Also see a report for the state legislature on the state's budget problems prepared in late 2011 by the Center for Colorado's Economic Future at the University of Denver.

50. See, for elaboration, Amy Gutman and Dennis Thompson, *The Spirit of Compromise: Why Governing Demands It and Campaigning Undermines It* (Princeton NJ: Princeton University Press, 2012).

# Suggestions for Further Research

Colorado has a number of libraries that contain a rich lode of source material on the state's history and politics. The University of Colorado at Boulder has an excellent collection in Nolin Library, as does the University of Denver. See also the Colorado Room in the Tutt Library at Colorado College in Colorado Springs. This special collection of books, photographs, and other memorabilia about Colorado in general and Colorado Springs in particular is both helpful and accessible.

Useful materials are also available at the Colorado Historical Society, which has its own building and museum near the state capitol in Denver. The original copy of the state constitution is kept at the historical society, but it is not on display to the general public. A useful reference library is also found in the Ralph Carr Judicial Center, one block southwest of the state capitol.

Considerable polling is done in Colorado, and many of the pollsters allow scholars to study the results of previous polls. Talmey-Drake Research and Strategy in Boulder and Ciruli and Associates in Denver are two of the more prominent polling firms in Colorado. The *Denver Post* has an archive of poll results. The Denver Metro Chamber of Commerce also regularly conducts polls on policy and economic climate issues.

Official election results for Colorado statewide and national elections are available from the office of the Colorado secretary of state, which is located one block northwest of the state capitol in Denver. Political party registration data are also available from the same source, as are annual lists of registered lobbyists.

Colorado still is small enough that most high-ranking state officials, as well as political consultants, are willing to give interviews to scholars, researchers, and students.

The staff of the Legislative Council (located in the basement of the capitol) is generally helpful to scholars, has a great deal of information about Colorado immediately at hand, and usually knows which particular division of state government is responsible for which governmental and political functions. The Office of Legislative Legal Services serves in effect as the state legislature's law firm. It too can be helpful to researchers. The state geographer has a wealth of information about Colorado's physical features. The state demographer, in the Department of Local Affairs, can provide population- and census-related data and projections. A state climatologist works at Colorado State University at Fort Collins.

Researchers will find it useful to interview current and retired journalists who have covered Colorado politics and government for the Associated Press, the *Denver Post*, the *Colorado Springs Gazette,* and related media.

There are a dozen or so experts on the history and politics of Colorado who teach at the state's colleges and universities. Among the especially well informed are historians Duane Smith at Fort Lewis College in Durango and historian Tom Noel at the University of Colorado at Denver. Among the state's leading political scientists on state and local government issues are John Straayer at Colorado State University at Fort Collins and Seth E. Masket at the University of Denver.

Nor should one overlook former governors, retired judges, and former state legislators, particularly former legislative leaders. Although their expertise is concentrated in particular time periods, these former participants in the political process often can provide invaluable perspectives.

The careful student of Colorado politics and government will want to examine the standard writings. We provide, in "Selected Bibliography" on the following pages, a list of the many works we consulted for our research. We have not included everything available, yet we have tried to include the most important bibliographic materials.

# Selected Bibliography

Abbott, Carl, Stephen J. Leonard, and Thomas J. Noel. *Colorado: A History of the Centennial State*, 4th ed. Boulder: University Press of Colorado, 2005.

Andrews, Thomas G. *Killing for Coal*. Cambridge: Harvard University Press, 2008.

Athearn, Robert G. *The Coloradans*. Albuquerque: University of New Mexico Press, 1976.

————. *Rebel of the Rockies: A History of the Denver and Rio Grande Western Railroad*. New Haven: Yale University Press, 1962.

Atwood, Wallace W. *The Rocky Mountains*. New York: Vanguard Press, 1945.

Baker, James H., and LeRoy R. Hafen, eds. *History of Colorado*, vols. 1–5. Denver: State Historical Society of Colorado, 1927.

Beauprez, Bob. *A Return to Values: A Conservative Looks at His Party*. Golden CO: Fulcrum, 2009.

Blakey, Roy G. *The United States Beet-Sugar Industry and the Tariff*. New York: Longmans, Green, 1912.

Brown, Fred. *The Persistence of Vision*. Golden CO: Fulcrum, 2011.

Cassels, E. Steve. *The Archeology of Colorado*. Boulder CO: Johnson Books, 1983.

Chalmers, David M. *Hooded Americanism: The First Century of the Ku Klux Klan, 1865–1965*. New York: Doubleday, 1965.

Colton, Ray C. *The Civil War in the Western Territories: Arizona, Colorado, New Mexico, and Utah*. Norman: University of Oklahoma Press, 1959.

Cronin, Thomas E. *Direct Democracy: The Politics of Initiative, Referendum, and Recall*. Cambridge: Harvard University Press, 1989.

Daum, Courtney W., Robert J. Duffy, and John A. Straayer, eds. *State of Change: Colorado Politics in the Twenty-First Century*. Boulder: University Press of Colorado, 2011.

Donnelly, Thomas C., ed. *Rocky Mountain Politics*. Albuquerque: University of New Mexico Press, 1940.

Egan, Timothy. *The Worst Hard Time: The Untold Story of Those Who Survived the Great American Dust Bowl*. New York: Houghton Mifflin, 2006.

Ehrenhalt, Alan. *The United States of Ambition: Politicians, Power, and the Pursuit of Office*. New York: Random House, 1991.

Elazar, Daniel J. *American Federalism: A View from the States*. New York: Thomas Y. Crowell, 1972.

———. *Cities of the Prairie: The Metropolitan Frontier and American Politics*. New York: Basic Books, 1970.

———. *Cities of the Prairie Revisited: The Closing of the Metropolitan Frontier*. Lincoln: University of Nebraska Press, 1986.

Ellis, Elmer. *Henry Moore Teller: Defender of the West*. Caldwell ID: Caxton Printers, 1941.

Ellis, Richard N., and Duane A. Smith. *Colorado: A History in Photographs*. Boulder: University Press of Colorado, 1991.

Everett, Derek R. *The Colorado State Capitol: History, Politics, Preservation*. Boulder: University Press of Colorado, 2005.

Fielder, John. *Best of Colorado*. Boulder CO: Westcliffe Publishers, 2010.

Garnsey, Morris E. *America's New Frontier: The Mountain West*. New York: Alfred A. Knopf, 1950.

Goldberg, Robert A. *Hooded Empire: The Ku Klux Klan in Colorado*. Urbana: University of Illinois Press, 1981.

Gonzales, Rudolfo. *I Am Joaquin*. New York: Bantam Books, 1972.

Greenbaum, Fred. *Fighting Progressive: A Biography of Edward P Costigan*. Washington DC: Public Affairs Press, 1971.

Gulliford, Andrew. *Boomtown Blues: Colorado Oil Shale, 1885–1985*. Boulder: University Press of Colorado, 1989.

Hafen, LeRoy R. *Colorado: The Story of a Western Commonwealth*. Denver: Peerless Publishing, 1933.

Harvey, Lashley G., and Frank C. Spencer. *Colorado: Its Government and History*. Denver: Herrick Book and Stationery Co., 1934.

Harvey, Robert. *Amache: The Story of Japanese Internment in Colorado during World War II*. Dallas: Taylor Trade Publishing, 2004.

Hobbs, Greg. *In Praise of Fair Colorado: The Practice of Poetry, History, and Judging*. Denver: Bradford Publishing, 2004.

Hogan, Richard. *Class and Community in Frontier Colorado*. Lawrence: University Press of Kansas, 1990.

Hoig, Stan. *The Sand Creek Massacre*. Norman: University of Oklahoma Press, 1961.

———. *Tribal Wars of the Southwest Plains*. Norman: University of Oklahoma Press, 1993.

Hollister, Ovando J. *Boldly They Rode: A History of the First Regiment of Colorado Volunteers*. Lakewood CO: Golden Press, 1949.

Hollon, W. Eugene. *The Lost Pathfinder: Zebulon Montgomery Pike*. Norman: University of Oklahoma Press, 1949.

Hosokawa, Bill. *Thunder in the Rockies: The Incredible Denver Post*. New York: William Morrow, 1976.

Hrebenar, Ronald J., and Clive S. Thomas, eds. *Interest Group Politics in the American West*. Salt Lake City: University of Utah Press, 1987.

Hundley, Norris Jr. *Water and the West: The Colorado River Compact and the Politics of Water in the American West*. Berkeley: University of California Press, 1975.

Jackson, Donald. *Thomas Jefferson and the Stony Mountains: Exploring the West from Monticello*. Urbana: University of Illinois Press, 1981.

Jackson, Helen Hunt. *A Century of Dishonor*. New York: Harper and Row, 1965.

Jones, P. Andrew, and Tom Cech. *Colorado Water Law for Non-Lawyers*. Boulder: University Press of Colorado, 2009.

Johnson, Frank T. *Autobiography of a Centenarian*. Denver: Big Mountain Press, 1961.

Josephy, Alvin M. Jr. *The Civil War in the American West*. New York: Alfred A. Knopf, 1991.

Kelly, George V. *The Old Gray Mayors of Denver*. Boulder CO: Pruett Publishing, 1974.

King, Clyde L. *The History of the Government of Denver with Special References to Its Relations with Public Service Corporations*. Denver: Fisher Book, 1911.

Lamm, Richard D. *The Lamm Administration: A Retrospective Summary*. Denver: Office of the Governor, 1986.

Lamm, Richard D., and Michael McCarthy. *The Angry West: A Vulnerable Land and Its Future*. Boston: Houghton Mifflin, 1982.

Lamm, Richard D., and Duane A. Smith. *Pioneers and Politicians: Colorado Governors in Profile*. Golden CO: Fulcrum, 2008.

Langdon, Emma F. *The Cripple Creek Strike*. Denver: Great Western Publishing, 1904.

Larson, Charles. *The Good Fight: The Life and Times of Ben B. Lindsey*. Chicago: Quadrangle Books, 1972.

Larson, Robert W. *Populism in the Mountain West*. Albuquerque: University of New Mexico Press, 1986.

Laugen, R. Todd. *The Gospel of Progressivism: Moral Reform and Labor War in Colorado, 1900–1930*. Boulder: University Press of Colorado, 2010.

Lavender, David. *Bent's Fort*. Garden City NY: Doubleday, 1954.

Leonard, Stephen J., and Tom Noel. *Denver: Mining Camp to Metropolis*. Boulder: University Press of Colorado, 1990.

Limerick, Patricia Nelson. *The Legacy of Conquest*. New York: W. W. Norton, 1987.

Lindsey, Ben B., and Harvey Jerrold O'Higgins. *The Beast*. New York: Doubleday, 1910.

Loevy, Robert. *The Flawed Path to the Governorship*. Lanham MD: University Press of America, 1996.

Lorch, Robert S., and James A. Null. *Colorado's Government: Structure, Politics, Administration, and Policy*, 8th ed. Colorado Springs CO: Center for the Study of Government and the Individual, 2005.

McGovern, George S., and Leonard F. Guttridge. *The Great Coalfield War*. Boston: Houghton Mifflin, 1972.

Marin, Christine. *A Spokesman of the Mexican American Movement: Rodolofo "Corky" Gonzales and the Fight for Chicano Liberation, 1966–1972*. San Francisco: R and E Research Associates, 1977.

Martin, Curtis W., and Rudolph Gomez. *Colorado Government and Politics*, 3rd ed. Boulder CO: Pruett Press, 1972.

Mason, David. *Ludlow: A Verse Novel*. Pasadena CA: Red Hen Press, 2007.

Mellinger, Jeannie Towle, and Molly Wingate. *The Colorado Court of Appeals: History of Colorado's Intermediate Court*. Denver: Colorado Bar Association, 2008.

Michener, James A. *Centennial*. New York: Random House, 1974.

Monnett, John H., and Michael McCarthy. *Colorado Profiles: Men and Women Who Shaped the Centennial State*. Boulder: University Press of Colorado, 1996.

Morris, John R., and Davis H. Waite: *The Ideology of a Western Populist*. Washington DC: University Press of America, 1982.

Munsell, F. Darrell. *From Redstone to Ludlow: John Cleveland Osgood's Struggle against the United Mine Workers of America*. Boulder: University Press of Colorado, 2009.

Noel, Thomas J., and Duane A. Smith. *Colorado: The Highest State*. Boulder: University Press of Colorado, 1995.

Noel, Thomas J., Paul F. Mahoney, and Richard E. Stevens. *Historical Atlas of Colorado*. Norman: University of Oklahoma Press, 1994.

Olson, Robert C. *Speck: The Life and Times of Spencer Penrose*. Salt Lake City: Western Reflections Publishing, 2008.

Pepper, Henry C. *County Government in Colorado*. Fort Collins: Colorado Agricultural College, 1934.

Peirce, Neal R. *The Mountain States of America*. New York: W. W. Norton, 1972.

Pfaelzer, Jean. *Driven Out: The Forgotten War against Chinese Americans*. New York: Random House, 2007.

*Proceedings of the Constitutional Convention . . . to Frame a Constitution for the State of Colorado*. Denver: Smith-Brooks Press, State Printers, 1907.

Powell, John Wesley. *Report on the Lands of the Arid Region of the United States*. Washington DC: U.S. Government Printing Office, 1878.

Reisner, Marc. *Cadillac Desert: The American West and Its Disappearing Water*. New York: Penguin Books, 1987.

Reisner, Marc, and Sarah Bates. *Overtapped Oasis: Reform or Revolution for Western Water*. Washington DC: Island Press, 1990.

Rohrbough, Malcolm J. *Aspen: The History of a Silver Mining Town, 1879–1893*. New York: Oxford University Press, 1986.

Rinehart, Frederick, ed. *Chronicles of Colorado*. Boulder CO: Roberts Rinehart, 1984.

Rosenthal, Alan. *Engines of Democracy: Politics and Policymaking in State Legislatures*. Washington DC: Congressional Quarterly Press, 2009.

Rosenthal, Alan, and Maureen Moakley, eds. *The Political Life of the American States*. New York: Praeger, 1984.

Schrager, Adam. *The Principled Politician: Governor Ralph Carr and the Fight against Japanese American Internment*. Golden CO: Fulcrum, 2009.

Schrager, Adam, and Rob Witwer. *The Blueprint: How the Democrats Won Colorado (and Why Republicans Everywhere Should Care)*. Golden CO: Speaker's Corner Books, 2010.

Shockley, John S. *The Initiative Process in Colorado Politics: An Assessment*. Boulder CO: Bureau of Governmental Research and Service, University of Colorado at Boulder, 1980.

Shoemaker, Joe. *Budgeting Is the Answer: A Story of a Unique Committee, the JBC of Colorado*. Denver: World Press, 1977.

Simmons, Virginia McConnell. *The San Luis Valley*, 2nd ed. Boulder: University Press of Colorado, 1999.

Smith, Duane A. *The Birth of Colorado: A Civil War Perspective*. Norman: University of Oklahoma Press, 1989.

———. *Horace Tabor: His Life and Legend*. Boulder: Colorado Associated University Press, 1973.

———. *The Trail of Gold and Silver: Mining in Colorado, 1859–2009*. Boulder: University Press of Colorado, 2009.

Sprague, Marshall. *Colorado: A History*. New York: W. W. Norton, 1984.

———. *Massacre: The Tragedy at White River*. Boston: Little, Brown, 1957.

———. *Money Mountain: The Story of Cripple Creek Gold*. New York: Little, Brown, 1953.

Stegner, Wallace. *Beyond the Hundredth Meridian: John Wesley Powell and the*

*Second Opening of the West*. Introduction by Bernard DeVoto. Boston: Houghton, Mifflin, 1954.

Stone, William Fiske, ed. *History of Colorado*. Chicago: Clark Publishing, 1918.

Straayer, John A. *The Colorado General Assembly*, 2nd ed. Boulder: University Press of Colorado, 2000.

Suggs, George C. Jr. *Colorado's War on Military Unionism: James H. Peabody and the Western Federation of Miners*. Detroit: Wayne State University Press, 1972. Reissued with a new preface. Norman: University of Oklahoma Press, 1991.

Summer, Helen L. *Equal Suffrage: The Results of an Investigation in Colorado Made for the Collegiate Equal Suffrage League of New York State*. New York: Harper and Brothers, 1909.

Suthers, John W. *No Higher Calling, No Greater Responsibility: A Prosecutor Making His Case*. Golden CO: Fulcrum, 2008.

Suthers, John W., and Terri Connell. *The People's Lawyer: The History of the Colorado Attorney General's Office*. Kearney NE: Morris Publishing, 2007.

Suthers, John W., and Melba Deuprey. *That Justice Shall Be Done: The History of the U.S. Attorney's Office in Colorado*. Kearney NE: Morris Publishing, 2004.

Ubbelohde, Carl, Maxine Benson, and Duane Smith, eds. *A Colorado History*. 8th ed. Boulder CO: Pruett Publishing, 2001.

————, eds. *A Colorado Reader*, rev. ed. Boulder CO: Pruett Publishing, 1964.

Vandenbusche, Duane, and Duane A. Smith. *A Land Alone: Colorado's Western Slope*. Boulder CO: Pruett Publishing, 1981.

Viola, Herman J. *Ben Nighthorse Campbell: An American Warrior*, rev. ed. Boulder CO: Johnson Books, 2002.

Walton, Roger Alan. *Colorado: A Practical Guide to Its Government and Politics*. Fort Collins CO: Publisher's Consultants, 1983.

Waters, Frank. *The Colorado*. Athens OH: Swallow Press, 1984. First published in 1946.

Webb, Wellington, with Cindy Browsky. *Wellington Webb: The Man, the Mayor, and the Making of Modern Denver*. Golden CO: Fulcrum, 2007.

Whitford, William Clarke. *Colorado Volunteers in the Civil War*. Glorieta NM: Rio Grande, 1974.

Wilbanks, William. *The Make My Day Law: Colorado's Experiment in Home Protection*. Lanham MD: University Press of America, 1990.

Wilkinson, Charles F. *Crossing the Next Meridian: Land, Water, and the Future of the West*. Washington DC: Island Press, 1992.

Williams, Helen, ed. *Roy Romer Is Alive and Well and Living in California*. Walden CO: Walden Press, 2004.

Woodbury, David O. *The Colorado Conquest*. New York: Dodd, Mead, 1941.

Woodword, Phyllis. *The Adventure in the State House.* Denver: Colorado Department of Education, 1980.

Wright, James Edward. *The Politics of Populism: Dissent in Colorado.* New Haven: Yale University Press, 1974.

Young, Bradley J. *TABOR and Direct Democracy: An Essay on the End of the Republic.* Golden CO: Fulcrum, 2006.

# Index

## In the Politics and Governments of the American States series

*Alabama Government and Politics*
By James D. Thomas and William H. Stewart

*Alaska Politics and Government*
By Gerald A. McBeath and Thomas A. Morehouse

*Arizona Politics and Government: The Quest for Autonomy,*
*Democracy, and Development*
By David R. Berman

*Arkansas Politics and Government*, second edition
By Diane D. Blair and Jay Barth

*Colorado Politics and Government: Governing the Centennial State*
By Thomas E. Cronin and Robert D. Loevy

*Colorado Politics and Policy: Governing a Purple State*
By Thomas E. Cronin and Robert D. Loevy

*Delaware Politics and Government*
By William W. Boyer and Edward C. Ratledge

*Hawai'i Politics and Government: An American State in a Pacific World*
By Richard C. Pratt with Zachary Smith

*Illinois Politics and Government: The Expanding Metropolitan Frontier*
By Samuel K. Gove and James D. Nowlan

*Kansas Politics and Government: The Clash of Political Cultures*
By H. Edward Flentje and Joseph A. Aistrup

*Kentucky Politics and Government: Do We Stand United?*
By Penny M. Miller

*Maine Politics and Government*, second edition
By Kenneth T. Palmer, G. Thomas Taylor, Marcus A. LiBrizzi, and Jean E. Lavigne

*Maryland Politics and Government: Democratic Dominance*
By Herbert C. Smith and John T. Willis

*Michigan Politics and Government: Facing Change in a Complex State*
By William P. Browne and Kenneth VerBurg

*Minnesota Politics and Government*
By Daniel J. Elazar, Virginia Gray, and Wyman Spano

To order or obtain more information on these or other University of Nebraska Press
titles, visit www.nebraskapress.unl.edu.

# About the Authors

Thomas E. Cronin (Stanford University, PhD) is the McHugh Professor of American Government and Leadership at Colorado College. He has received awards for teaching, research, and advising, and has authored, coauthored, or edited more than a dozen books, including best-selling books on American government and the American presidency. His latest book is *Leadership Matters*, coauthored with Michael A. Genovese. He is president emeritus of Whitman College and a past president of the Western Political Science Association and of the Presidency Research Group. He has been involved in politics at all levels, from local precinct chair to member of the White House staff.

Robert D. Loevy (Johns Hopkins University, PhD) is a political scientist at Colorado College, focusing on political parties, American elections, Congress, and state and local government. The author or coauthor of ten books on American government, he has won many awards for his teaching and service. He has worked on the staff of a U.S. senator and has held a wide range of civic positions in Colorado, including serving on the Colorado Springs Planning Commission and the Colorado State Reapportionment Commission. His latest book is *Confessions of a Reapportionment Commissioner*, available online.

CPSIA information can be obtained at www.ICGtesting.com
Printed in the USA
BVOW020429011012

301696BV00004B/2/P